Beyond Displacement

Critical Human Rights

Series Editors

Steve J. Stern ❦ Scott Straus

Books in the series **Critical Human Rights** emphasize research that opens new ways to think about and understand human rights. The series values in particular empirically grounded and intellectually open research that eschews simplified accounts of human rights events and processes.

The atrocities in El Salvador drove tens of thousands into refugee camps in Honduras and drew enormous attention worldwide. In *Beyond Displacement*, Molly Todd enables us to see beyond the spectacle of displacement that fascinates and catalyzes the international community. Todd turns the classic image of displaced refugees—victims stripped of rights, capacity to act, and effective connection to homeland—on its head. Peasant survivors from El Salvador extended and adapted the understandings of community organizing and flight they had built in an earlier phase of political struggle and repression. As a result, they shaped the refugee camp experience, built a voice as exiled citizens, and intervened in transnational peacemaking. In this subtle grassroots history, Todd offers a fresh vision of peasants and community action during the Central American wars of the 1980s.

Beyond Displacement

Campesinos, Refugees, and Collective

Action in the Salvadoran Civil War

Molly Todd

The University of Wisconsin Press

Publication of this volume has been made possible, in part, through support from the ANONYMOUS FUND OF THE COLLEGE OF LETTERS AND SCIENCE at the University of Wisconsin–Madison, and from the EVJUE FOUNDATION, INC., the charitable arm of *The Capital Times*.

The University of Wisconsin Press
1930 Monroe Street, 3rd Floor
Madison, Wisconsin 53711-2059
uwpress.wisc.edu

3 Henrietta Street
London WC2E 8LU, England
eurospanbookstore.com

5   4   3   2   1

Printed in the United States of America

Library of Congress Cataloging-in-Publication Data
Todd, Molly.
Beyond displacement: campesinos, refugees, and collective action
    in the Salvadoran civil war / Molly Todd.
        p.   cm. — (Critical human rights)
        ISBN 978-0-299-25004-1 (pbk.: alk. paper)
        ISBN 978-0-299-25003-4 (e-book)
1. El Salvador—History—1979–1992.   2. Refugees—El Salvador
    I. Title.   II. Series: Critical human rights.
F1488.3.T63   2010
972.8405′3—dc22
2010011578

For
Marge and Tom

Organization brings unity and strength to be able to accomplish whatever one desires. . . . Day after day you gain one, two, and so the organization grows. It is most important to be organized to be able to bring about social change.

José S., Chalatenango, El Salvador

Contents

Illustrations

Figures

Charts

Maps

List of Illustrations

Acknowledgments

Without a doubt, I have collected innumerable personal and professional debts along the decadelong path of this project. I would be remiss if I did not begin by recognizing the many individuals in Central America who have contributed to this project in one form or another. Foremost among them are those campesinos from northern El Salvador who shared with me their homes and histories. I would like to list each and every one of them by name; it seems such a small and easy step toward providing credit where credit is due. I have chosen not to, however. While these Salvadorans have taught me much about their history, I have also learned of and lived in El Salvador— and life there is far from easy. Many of the campesinos with whom I worked continue today as activists at the local, regional, and national levels. Although they deserve tribute for their efforts (past and present), such tribute often prompts harassment and attack. I do not wish for them to suffer because they collaborated with me in writing their histories; withholding their names is intended to stay possible direct retaliation. Yet without each and every one of them this book would not have been possible. So, *mil gracias, compañeros*. You know who you are.

In addition to the Salvadoran campesinos, there were many others in El Salvador who contributed to this project in one way or another. Yvonne López Esquivel, Georgina Hernández Rivas, and Carlos Henríquez Consalvi of the Museo de la Palabra y la Imagen offered documentation not available elsewhere. I found additional materials with the assistance of Eugenia López Velásquez at the Archivo Nacional de la Nación; Olinda Estela Gómez, Aydee de Martínez, and the staff at the Biblioteca "Doctor José Gustavo Guerrero" of the Ministerio de Relaciones Exteriores; and Gladis Aguirre and her colleagues at the Centro de Documentación e Investigación Histórica (CEPAZ). Erin Conrad, Walter Navarrette, Adán Estrada, and many others at Comité

Cristiano Pro Desplazados de El Salvador (CRIPDES), Comité de Reconstrucción y Desarrollo Económico-Social de las Comunidades de Suchitoto, Cuscatlán (CRCC), Fundación Salvadoreña para la Reconstrucción y el Desarrollo (REDES), and San Vicente Productivo shared meals, homes, stories, and contacts. I am especially indebted to Ariane de Bremond, Sarah Loose, and David Holiday for resources, insights, contacts, and amazing document caches. And Nidia Cueva was my home away from home.

In Honduras the following individuals and organizations made research not only possible but also enjoyable: Leo Valladares Lanza; Mario Argueta; Colonel Abrahám García Turcios; the staff at the Biblioteca Nacional de Honduras; Víctor Meza and his colleagues at the Centro de Documentación de Honduras; everyone at the Comisión Cristiana de Desarrollo; Bishop Luis Santos; Albert Depienne; Centro de Investigación y Promoción de los Derechos Humanos (CIPRODEH); Alma Mateo; and the people of Santa Rosa de Copán and San Marcos de Ocotepeque, especially Father M., Marta, Mario, and Rosalinda.

In Costa Rica I received crucial assistance from the staff at the Biblioteca Conjunta of the Inter-American Court of Human Rights and the Inter-American Institute of Human Rights, the Fundación Arias para la Paz y El Progreso Humano, Mark Manly and Juan Carlos Murillo at the United Nations High Commissioner for Refugees (UNHCR), Juan Carlos Gutiérrez at the Center for Justice and International Law (CEJIL), and Yamilette Solano and her colleagues at the Biblioteca Nacional de Costa Rica.

In Switzerland Patricia Fluckiger and Montserrat Canela Garayoa opened to me the Central American files of the UNHCR and Thomas Todd helped ensure that I made it through the stacks of folders.

In the United States Barbara Alvarado, Marc Rosenthal, Ian Davies, and others of the U.S.–El Salvador Sister Cities network accompanied me during the first parts of this journey and introduced me to many of the *comunidades organizadas* of northern El Salvador. And Beth Cagan and Steve Cagan shared their home, their stories, and their phenomenal personal archive.

This book would not have been possible without financial assistance from a variety of sources. A Fulbright fellowship funded the bulk of my initial field research in Central America. Many departments and programs at the University of Wisconsin–Madison provided financial support at the various stages of this project: the History Department; the Latin American, Caribbean and Iberian Studies Program; the Global Studies Program; and the Graduate Student Council. A Presidential Research Fellowship and New Faculty Research Funds from Augustana College were crucial in helping me finalize the project, as were

Acknowledgments

funds from the college's Research Foundation, Faculty Research Committee, Alumni Foundation, and Office of the Dean.

Julie Roy, Pamela Larson, Eric Ellefsen, and Thomas Todd provided important research and technical assistance at various stages of the project.

I have benefited from the comments and critiques of many readers along the way. Abigail Markwyn, Michelle Morgan, Gary Marquardt, Libbie Freed, Leo Garófalo, and Marc Hertzman carefully reviewed the earliest drafts. Aldo Lauria-Santiago, Jeffrey Gould, Jane Simonsen, Mariano Magalhães, and Steve Warren commented on parts of the project. Colleagues at various meetings of the Congreso Centroamericano de Historia, the North Central Council of Latin Americanists, the American Historical Association, and the Augustana Faculty Research Forum helped me hone specific chapters' arguments. Neil Kodesh, Leigh Payne, and Francisco Scarano offered advice for transforming the text from dissertation to book. Special *agradecimientos* go to Steve Stern and Florencia Mallon. Steve initially set me on the path that led to the comunidades organizadas of northern El Salvador, and Florencia made it clear that she believed in my sense of direction even when I could not see where I was going. Their influence is visible in both the breadth and depth of my work in these pages.

At the University of Wisconsin Press, I have been fortunate to work with Gwen Walker, whose interest in the project and attention to detail have eased the process of letting go. Two reviewers, Aldo Lauria-Santiago and Jeffrey Gould, prompted a last round of revisions, which made the end result far stronger. Terry Emmrich, Adam Mehring, Sheila Moermond, Jan Opdyke, Lauren Vedal, and countless others at the press have made this whole process quite enjoyable. Thank you all.

Finally, this book never would have come to fruition without the support and encouragement of close friends and family. Nidia Cueva's companionship and sense of humor kept me going when I considered stopping. Eric Ellefsen kept me grounded with great patience and grace. And to Susan and Thomas Bailey, Matt and Lisa Richey Todd, and Marjorie and Thomas Todd: words cannot even begin to convey my love and gratitude.

Abbreviations

ACNUR	Alto Comisionado de las Naciones Unidas para los Refugiados (UN High Commissioner for Refugees) (see also UNHCR)
ACUS	Acción Católica Universitaria de El Salvador (University Catholic Action of El Salvador)
ADES	Asociación de Desarrollo Económico y Social (Economic and Social Development Association)
AFL-CIO	American Federation of Labor and Congress of Industrial Organizations
AGN	Archivo General de la Nación (National Archive of El Salvador)
AIFLD	American Institute for Free Labor Development
ANDES	Asociación Nacional de Educadores Salvadoreños 21 de junio (National Association of Salvadoran Educators 21 of June)
ARENA	Alianza Republicana Nacional (National Republican Alliance)
AW	Americas Watch
BIRI	Batallón de Infantería de Reacción Inmediata (Rapid Deployment Infantry Brigade)
BPR	Bloque Popular Revolucionario (Popular Revolutionary Bloc)
CDA	Center for Democracy in the Americas
CEDOH	Centro de Documentación de Honduras (Documentation Center of Honduras)
CEB	Comunidad Eclesial de Base (Christian Base Community)

CEDEN	Comité Evangélico de Emergencia Nacional, subsequently Comité Evangélico de Desarrollo Nacional ([Honduran] Evangelical National Emergency Committee, then Evangelical National Development Committee)
CELAM	Conferencia Episcopal Latinoamericana (Conference of Latin American Bishops)
CEPAZ	Centro de Documentación e Investigación Histórica (Documentation and Historical Investigation Center)
CIA	Central Intelligence Agency
CIREFCA	Conferencia Internacional sobre los Refugiados de Centro América (International Conference on Central American Refugees)
CISPES	Committee in Solidarity with the People of El Salvador
CNR	Coordinadora Nacional de Repoblación (National Coordinator for Repopulation)
CONADES	Comisión Nacional para los Desplazados ([Salvadoran] National Commission for the Displaced)
CONARE	Comisión Nacional de Refugiados ([Honduran] National Commission on Refugees)
CPR	Comunidad de Población en Resistencia ([Guatemalan] Community of Population in Resistance)
CRCC	Comité de Reconstrucción y Desarrollo Económico-Social de las Comunidades de Suchitoto, Cuscatlán (Committee for Reconstruction and Socioeconomic Development in the Communities of Suchitoto, Cuscatlán)
CREM	Centro Regional de Entrenamiento Militar (Regional Military Training Center)
CRIPDES	Comité Cristiano Pro Desplazados de El Salvador (Christian Committee of Displaced Persons of El Salvador)
DIN	Directorio de Investigación Nacional ([Honduran] National Directorate of Investigations)
ERP	Ejército Revolucionario Popular (Popular Revolutionary Army)
FECCAS	Federación Cristiana de Campesinos Salvadoreños (Christian Federation of Salvadoran Campesinos)
FMLN	Frente Farabundo Martí para Liberación Nacional (Farabundo Martí National Liberation Front)
FPL	Fuerzas Populares de Liberación (Popular Liberation Forces)

FTC	Federación de Trabajadores del Campo (Rural Workers Federation)
INSAFOCOOP	Instituto Salvadoreño para el Fomento de Cooperativas (Salvadoran Institute of Cooperative Development)
IEPALA	Instituto de Estudios Políticos para América Latina y Africa (Institute of Political Studies for Latin America and Africa)
ICVA	International Council of Voluntary Agencies
IIDH	Instituto Inter-Americano de Derechos Humanos (Inter-American Institute of Human Rights)
ISTA	Instituto Salvadoreño de Transformación Agraria (Salvadoran Agrarian Transformation Institute)
LCIHR	Lawyers Committee for International Human Rights
MNR	Movimiento Nacional Revolucionario (National Revolutionary Movement)
MSF	Médecins Sans Frontières (Doctors without Borders)
NGO	nongovernmental organization
NSA	National Security Archive
ORDEN	Organización Democrática Nacionalista (Nationalist Democratic Organization)
PADECOES	Patronato para el Desarrollo Comunal en El Salvador (Association for Communal Development in El Salvador)
PADECOMSM	Patronato de Desarrollo de las Comunidades de Morazán y San Miguel (Community Development Council of Morazán and San Miguel)
PCN	Partido de Conciliación Nacional (National Conciliation Party)
PCS	Partido Comunista de El Salvador (Salvadoran Communist Party)
PDC	Partido Demócrata Cristiano (Christian Democrat Party)
PPL	Poder Popular Local (Local Popular Power)
PRTC	Partido Revolucionario de los Trabajadores (Workers Revolutionary Party)
REDES	Fundación Salvadoreña para la Reconstrucción y el Desarrollo (Salvadoran Foundation for Reconstruction and Development)
RN	Resistencia Nacional (National Resistance)
SJDPA	Servicio Jesuita para el Desarrollo "Pedro Arrupe" (Jesuit Development Service)

UCA	Universidad Centroamericana "José Simeón Cañas" (Central American University, El Salvador)
UCS	Unión Comunal Salvadoreña (Salvadoran Communal Union)
UDN	Unión Democrática Nacionalista (Nationalist Democratic Union)
UN	United Nations
UNAH	Universidad Nacional Autónoma de Honduras (National Autonomous University of Honduras)
UNHCR	United Nations High Commissioner for Refugees (see also ACNUR)
UNO	Unión Nacional Opositora (National Opposition Union)
UNOC	Unidad Nacional Obrero Campesina (National Union of Rural Workers)
UTC	Unión de Trabajadores del Campo (Rural Workers Union)
WSHS	Wisconsin State Historical Society

Beyond Displacement

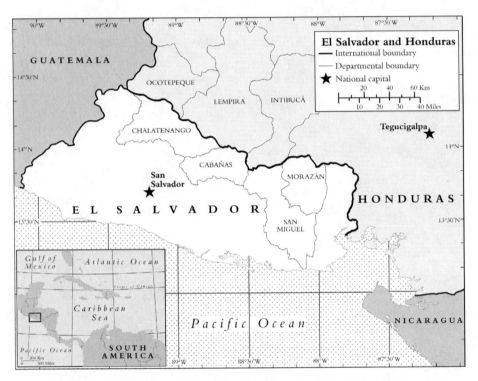

Map 1. General area of study. (Map by Pamela Larson, Augustana College)

Introduction

A People without History

In February 1982 a leading Honduran newspaper published an editorial cartoon depicting a Salvadoran refugee camp. In the center of the drawing, a male "refugee" kicks back in the shade of a palm tree. He sports a scruffy beard, a contented smile, and hefty boots. On the sand next to him rest a pistol, a rifle, and a bomb. A line of tents frames the sketch on one side; the flaps of one tent open slightly to reveal boxes of war matériel.[1]

When this cartoon appeared, Honduras hosted approximately 21,250 Salvadoran refugees in five official camps. An additional 12,750 Salvadorans lived in semiclandestinity, as unofficial refugees in many small villages tucked into the mountainous southern regions of Honduras.[2] The vast majority of these Salvadorans hailed from similar rural towns just a few kilometers away on the other side of the international border. There they had been campesinos, rural dwellers who survived primarily by combining subsistence agriculture, petty animal husbandry and seasonal wage labor.[3] They had begun fleeing El Salvador in the late 1970s as political violence became widespread and the country descended into civil war. When these Salvadorans crossed the border into Honduras, they became refugees under international law; they remained so until their return to El Salvador in the late 1980s and early 1990s.

By early 1981 the United Nations High Commissioner for Refugees (UNHCR), along with dozens of other national and international organizations, had arrived in Honduras to lend assistance to the new refugees. Although the Honduran government collaborated with UNHCR personnel throughout the decade and allowed the Salvadorans to remain in Honduras "on purely humanitarian grounds," Honduran officials never held their Salvadoran visitors in high esteem. As implied by the editorial cartoon described earlier, officials considered them not as true refugees but, rather, as soldiers and collaborators of the Salvadoran insurgent forces, the Frente Farabundo Martí para Liberación Nacional (Farabundo Martí National Liberation Front, FMLN). The refugee camps, from this perspective, were hotbeds of guerrilla activity.

Humanitarian aid personnel painted an entirely different picture of the Salvadoran refugees. To them Salvadorans were humble, even ignorant, peasants unwittingly tossed about in an unstable political climate. Nongovernmental groups often focused on the horrific events that prompted or accompanied departure from El Salvador: harassment and disappearances by extralegal vigilantes and death squads, the razing of villages during the military's scorched earth campaigns, and massacres. The UNHCR magazine *Refugees* presented similarly wrenching images of the Salvadoran refugees: caravans of barefoot women and children wending unpaved roads, solemnly trudging the dust toward an elusive safety; two young brothers peering through a chain-link fence, their small fingers gripping the metal as if to life itself; flatbed Fords, swarms of empty hands outstretched, waiting for the weight of a sack of maize, a family's ration for a week. Blunt pronouncements further distilled such images; in the words of one UNHCR representative, "The refugees are victims."[4]

At first glance, the humanitarian and government representations appear to exist on opposite ends of a spectrum. Upon closer examination, however, they reveal much in common. The humanitarian point of view presented Salvadorans who fled their war-torn homeland as all the same; they were refugees, ragged and poor, mute and dependent on the goodwill of others. Honduran and Salvadoran officials also presented the refugees as one undifferentiated mass, but where aid personnel saw passive victims, government representatives perceived rebel threats. In short, both essentialized the refugee populations, bypassed their roles as historical agents, and failed to place their experiences into historical context. As a result, millions of individuals and their communities remained suspended in time, disconnected from the larger national and international stories.

Popular and scholarly representations follow similar trends. Many case studies within the field of refugee studies, for example, adopt a state-centric perspective. This perspective assumes a "national order of things"—a natural association between people and place along with an ordered relation between nations.[5] Within this sedentarist order, movement often takes on negative connotations. This is particularly so in situations of conflict involving cross-border migration; those who move become "displaced" and "uprooted." Without a territorial connection to the nation, they are no longer considered citizens; they are "stateless." The refugee aid regime, moreover, operates with a supposedly "apolitical" mandate, which serves to further detach people from local and global historical and political contexts.[6] In short, as individuals *become* refugees, they *unbecome* everything else. They are marked by absence and loss. They are homeless, stateless, a people without history.

To date, studies of the Salvadoran civil war also have been largely state-centric. In explaining both the causes of conflict and its resolution, researchers have adopted a near exclusive focus on the national government and military, the FMLN opposition forces, and international influences such as the U.S. government and the United Nations. Rural dwellers, when included in the picture, lack control over their own actions; they are instead manipulated by external forces: radical priests, communists, international organizations. More often than not, however, the rural population simply does not appear. This is particularly true in discussions about El Salvador's transition to peace in the 1990s.[7]

Displaced populations have been further displaced from this historical record. Even studies that chronicle the repopulation of once-abandoned rural villages continue the same narrative of nonagency; they presume that the tools necessary for rebuilding society were not innate to rural folk. Instead, such studies suggest, campesinos acquired them while living as displaced persons either in Church-sponsored refuges in El Salvador's urban centers or in refugee camps abroad. In this sense, many texts glorify the experiences of displacement, likening life in the camps to a sort of rebirth into a new, more "modern" identity. In the words of one study, "They began as refugees, frightened and helpless, and they ended as citizens of a new land."[8]

Perhaps such an assessment is not entirely surprising in light of the fact that "El Salvador is Latin America's least researched nation-state."[9] Yet, even when one takes into account this nascent stage of research, the extent to which the displaced have been ignored is disturbing. Consider the numbers: between the late 1970s and the early 1990s, at least one-fifth of El Salvador's population was displaced. To put this into a comparative context, imagine how different contemporary U.S. history might look if the entire population of the states of California, New York, and Minnesota suddenly picked up and moved somewhere else. One would be hard-pressed to imagine a history that did not seriously consider such mass human movement. Yet that is precisely what has occurred in the case of El Salvador.

This study offers a corrective. It introduces the displaced into the historical narrative not as rebels, victims, or refugees per se but, rather, as campesinos possessing a history of community organizing, citizen action, and willing negotiation with state and nonstate actors. Reconceptualizing the role of Salvadorans in this way challenges current understandings of campesino involvement in the Salvadoran conflict as well as the concept of "refugeeness."

This challenge comes first and foremost through an examination of events from the vantage point of those who bore the brunt of the war's violence: poor rural inhabitants. More specifically it focuses on people from El Salvador's northern *tierra olvidada* (forgotten land) who abandoned home and village for a life on the move. They joined together to form mobile communities; while some eked out a precarious existence in the mountainous borderlands between El Salvador and Honduras, others established refuge points beyond the Salvadoran nation. An interweaving of oral history interviews and archival documentation offers a rich and complex picture of who these people were, what they did, and why. This history "from the ground up" reveals that war flight does not convert people into "bare life" or pure victims; rather, they continue to be informed and competent individuals striving to maintain as much control as possible over their own life paths.

Adopting a ground-level perspective allows the re-placing of displaced populations into a broader historical trajectory. In spite of the tendency of refugee studies to objectify, dehistoricize, and depoliticize, displaced persons' own narratives reveal their relation to and involvement in events past, present, and future. In other words, displacement does not cause them to stop being social and political beings. On the contrary, it can deepen collective sensibilities and heighten political mobilization.

In tracing the history of collective organization and mobilization among northern Salvadoran campesinos, this study draws from and contributes to current debates about peasant mobilization and protest, nation-state formation, and democratization in postauthoritarian societies. In the past couple of decades, historians of Mexico and Peru have revealed that peasants and other subaltern groups have been more active than previously understood in negotiating the contours of nation-state systems. Of particular interest here is the work by authors such as Florencia Mallon, Jeffrey Rubin, and Mark Thurner, among others, who reveal the interplay between local-level mobilizations, on the one hand, and regional and national processes on the other. These authors show that within these micro-macro interplays multiple formulations of identity, citizenship, and nationalism coexist.[10]

A number of scholars have explored similar themes for the Central American and Caribbean regions as well. Jeffrey Gould and Cindy Forster, for example, examine peasant agency and its limitations in Nicaragua and

Guatemala, respectively. Several other studies on Guatemala further expand our understanding of multiple nationalisms and identities by highlighting race and ethnicity as fluid categories that have shifted over time. Greg Grandin and Kay Warren, for example, explore how nineteenth- and twentieth-century Maya developed highly self-conscious ethnic identities; by the 1980s, they had created a "transcendent identity" that emphasized an ethnoracial identity above gender, class, religious, or community identity. Such essentialism was a strategic decision on behalf of the Maya elite; their intention was to construct an identity as a tool for political change.[11]

The Salvadoran case presented here explores a similar evolution of self-conscious identities among Salvadoran campesinos. It moves beyond interpretations of identity and nationalism as delimited by national geographical borders, however, by documenting how Salvadoran campesinos defined and asserted themselves not only in local and national terms but in international terms as well. As El Salvador's politico-military conflict intensified throughout the 1960s and 1970s, many rural townships purposefully forged a sense of community in order to moderate heightened internal fears, anxieties, and differences of opinion. While living in Honduran refugee camps during the 1980s, individuals employed both these community sensibilities and a new, adopted identity of "refugee" as strategies of negotiation on two interrelated levels. First, campesinos invoked community identities on a personal and emotive level to unify and empower a diverse and traumatized population. Second, they wielded both community and refugee identities for utilitarian and practical (and, some might say, Arcadian) purposes: to secure spaces of representation before national and international authorities, to claim and justify immediate and long-term needs and benefits, and to challenge the highly militarized and authoritarian Salvadoran regime.

The cross-border, international angle of my research expands on existing scholarship, moreover, in that rather than focusing on peasants espousing solely an oppositional culture in their struggle against external forces I examine collective actions also in terms of their adoption of an inclusionary ethos and rhetoric of community, nation, and international human rights in order to prompt internal democratic conciliation. Campesino refugees emphasized, for example, how their self-governance structures not only modeled the liberal ideals on which the Salvadoran nation originally had been founded (which stood in stark contrast to the Salvadoran government at the time) but also integrated newer developments in international law. In other words, they did not necessarily advocate the overthrow of the Salvadoran state system and its replacement with socialism or communism, as has been assumed; rather, they promoted reform and improvement of the existing system.

Given that one of my intentions in this book is to place refugee experiences into their broader historical contexts, I would be remiss if I did not acknowledge the broader contexts of this study. Research processes are multilayered, a sometimes strange mix of skill, tenacity, and chance. This project has been no exception. I began with the intention of focusing on archival materials; documents are, after all, the historian's gold. The realities of the field, however, quickly altered my plans. In many ways, documents proved hard to find. Many had been destroyed during the war—both accidentally and intentionally. Some caches were not yet available to the public. And access to other collections depended on a variety of "gatekeepers"—and politics, personalities, and moods.

Salvadoran officials, for instance, claimed that no records exist related to Salvadoran refugees in Honduras, internally displaced campesinos, or the mass repatriations and repopulations. An army commander argued that even if documentation along these lines did exist it would relate to an ongoing border dispute between El Salvador and Honduras; because such material was, at the time, in the hands of the members of the International Court of Justice at the Hague, I would have to await a ruling from them before continuing with my research.

If I had no luck with Salvadoran government documents, I had slightly more with Honduran government documents. The latter, I must say, was due in large part to the willingness of Dr. Leo Valladares Lanza to share his personal papers. A lawyer by training, Valladares advised the Honduran foreign minister on refugee-related issues during the 1980s, and he was subsequently appointed the country's first national commissioner for the protection of human rights. I first met Don Leo in Washington, D.C., in 1998 when he was putting the finishing touches on his book *In Search of Hidden Truths*.[12] The book reported on his efforts as commissioner to gain access to declassified documents from the U.S. government in order to assist his ongoing investigations into human rights abuses committed in Honduras during the 1980s. Throughout the declassification process, he collaborated closely with the National Security Archive (NSA), a nongovernmental research institute and library that collects and publicizes declassified documents acquired through the Freedom of Information Act. At the time of Valladares's 1998 visit, I was a research analyst in the Latin American section at the NSA. Valladares and his coauthor, Susan Peacock, a seasoned analyst at the archive, enlisted my assistance with a number of last-minute tasks. During this time, Susan, Don Leo, and I spoke of many things, among them my own ideas for a research project. Don Leo was, simply put, inspiring; he even offered his assistance if my research took me to Honduras.

Years later I appeared unannounced—and more than a little nervous—in the lobby of the Human Rights Commissioner's Office in Tegucigalpa, Honduras. Following a brief telephone page from his secretary, a slightly older but ever energetic Don Leo burst through a heavy wooden door to welcome me with a big bear hug. Laughing and greatly relieved, I admitted to him that I had been concerned that he might not remember who I was. "Aaah," he growled, "¿Cómo no? ¡Siempre la peliroja!" (How could I forget you? Always the redhead!).

In the months that followed, I spent many hours with Don Leo and his colleagues and family: interviews, meetings, introductions, meals, more meetings, and a lot of coffee. Shortly before my departure from Honduras, he announced to me, "Ya llegó la hora." I thought that this declaration of "the time has come" referred to my imminent return to the United States, but before I could respond he stripped off his suit jacket, loosened his tie, and dropped to the floor. On his hands and knees, he crawled to a small door underneath the stairwell. I heard the tinkle of keys and the release of a lock, and then Don Leo carefully backed out of the crawl space, padlock in hand. "I have a bad back," he said, "so the rest is up to you."

Following his directions, I extracted several huge cardboard boxes from the tiny closet under the stairs. Don Leo removed a ratty lid from one box and handed me the first of many file folders bearing the label *refugiados* (refugees). My eyes widened, and my jaw dropped as I realized what I was looking at: Honduran government documents pertaining to the refugee crisis of the 1980s. Throughout his years at the Ministry of Foreign Relations, Don Leo and his assistants had carefully filed away copies of important papers; when he left his position at the ministry to assume the role of human rights commissioner, he took his records with him. As I pawed through one file, then another and another, a decade of dirt and dust rose up to greet me. Don Leo, clearly enjoying the scene before him, said to me in low whisper, "*Fíjese*, Molly. Think about it. Your eyes are the first to see these documents in over ten years." I had figured as much; the dust spoke for itself.

This reminiscence illustrates an important point about the research process: many of my successes (and, I suppose, failures) derived largely from a mix of personal relationships and chance. Had Don Leo and I not shared a connection through the NSA, he might never have revealed to me the contents of that crawl space beneath the stairs. Likewise, had documentation been easy to find, I might not have relied so heavily on oral history interviews.

In light of the vagaries of acquiring documentation, however, interviews steadily gained in importance as this project progressed. This was a blessing in some ways. Firsthand accounts certainly revealed details that no amount of "official" documentation ever could have touched. Indeed, this project simply would not have been possible without the people who spent countless hours speaking with me about their life experiences, in particular, the Salvadoran campesinos who invited me into their homes and lives. The longer I slept in their hammocks, ate their tortillas and beans, read English texts with their children, and attended community events with them, the more they revealed to me. On treks along mountain paths, they uncovered for me the hidden landscape of the northern borderland: places where villages once stood, bomb craters, secret peasant meeting sites, the most popular trees used by death squads for hanging suspected subversives, the underground hideaways known as *tatús*. They also shared documents, memoirs scratched into notebooks, and even wartime photos and videos. Through these exchanges Salvadorans disclosed many secrets, insights into the lives of campesinos and refugees that cannot be found in existing books, including how people made the decision to seek refuge in Honduras, the internal control mechanisms adopted by leaders in the refugee camps, and tensions that emerged among peasants once they returned to El Salvador.

Despite their luster, however, the interviews presented a number of challenges, not least of which was finding people willing and able to share their stories. Many Salvadorans, for example, resisted speaking with me about the war, a fact that I attribute to several intertwined factors. First, it might be said that the prolonged period of violence in El Salvador led to a sort of psychological closing down of individuals and communities in their relations with outsiders. In some rural areas of the north, a long history of community solidarity combined with a distrust of outsiders to make it difficult for me to break into the midst of many towns on my own. I relied, therefore, on friends and colleagues with well-established ties to the towns; their companionship and introductions facilitated many interviews that otherwise might have been impossible. But even in the communities that welcomed me easily many simply refused to discuss anything beyond the evening's menu at the community *comedor* (cafeteria), the upcoming town fair or market, or the weather.

Some of this reticence may be attributed—even if partially—to a sense of lassitude toward history and historical issues in general.[13] This apparent disinterest in the past is clearly linked to the weight of the present; indeed, a favorite motto among many of today's popular organizations, including campesino groups, is *la lucha sigue* (the struggle continues). In other words, many Salvadorans believe that, despite the advances that have been made in El Salvador since the Peace Accords went into effect in 1992, the basic conditions of poverty and injustice that initially sparked the civil war continue to affect the country today. Many people who had been involved in the struggles of earlier decades continued to be active in current affairs through different civil society organizations. Issues such as the privatization of the Salvadoran hospital system and the promulgation of the Central American Free Trade Agreement prompted regular and repeated actions and protests of varying levels of intensity. Combine this with people's everyday commitments and it is no surprise that some had neither the energy nor the desire to rehash the past with me.

In a similar vein, many others resisted speaking about their wartime experiences because, simply put, they feared for their safety. Salvadorans of all stripes likened the situation of the early 2000s to that of the 1970s just prior to the outbreak of the most violent and bloody period of the civil war. This was particularly prominent during campaign and election periods. During those times, the national news media were replete with accounts of brutality: death threats; bombings; and the disbanding of protesters with tear gas, water cannons, and rubber bullets. In response to daily reports of human body parts being found in public spaces throughout the country, many believed that the wealthiest candidates for political office were hiring much feared street gangs such as the Mara Salvatrucha to disappear their opponents' supporters. With the resurgence of intimidation tactics such as these, many people felt uneasy, as if they were being watched; to speak out about the Salvadoran leadership—past or present—in such an environment, they believed, would only invite retribution.

While factors internal to El Salvador certainly influenced my research, so too did my own position as an outsider. Not surprisingly, having a preestablished relationship with a person often influenced how open they were in interviews. By the time I began my research, I had already established contacts in several communities in El Salvador through the U.S.–El Salvador Sister Cities network. As an interpreter with this organization, I had visited the area multiple times over the course of a few years with various international delegations of college students, elections observers, and medical personnel. Each time I visited, I fostered new contacts and reestablished connections with old hosts. This network of contacts led to heightened access to communities as a whole when I returned to the area specifically for research. In other words, with time the communities that knew me were willing to reveal more details.

At the same time, however, my previous contacts with those communities led them to label me *una internacional*, an "international" closely associated with solidarity organizations. This label influenced their framing of stories. Although they may have revealed more details to me, it is safe to assume that they revealed only certain kinds of details and that they framed those details in particular ways because of my associations with organizations considered to be in solidarity with their communities.

In communities where I had no preestablished contacts, Salvadorans often immediately distrusted me for being an outsider, especially so because of my status as a U.S. citizen. Many individuals asked where my money came from, whether or not I worked for the government, or how much I knew about the U.S. Central Intelligence Agency (CIA). And peoples' distrust of me only increased after the George W. Bush administration's invasion of Iraq. Perhaps it is needless to say that interviewees from such communities were much more reserved and revealed few details.

If Salvadorans often framed their interactions with me based on their understanding of who I was and where I came from, so too did I frame myself for them. With rural Salvadorans I frequently highlighted my links to solidarity organizations. I made use of key terms and concepts (e.g., *compañero*, *solidaridad*, and liberation theology) and exhibited knowledge of figures of great importance to many progressive campesino communities (e.g., Archbishop Oscar Romero, Father Rutilio Grande, and Jesús Rojas). Sometimes, I shared childhood memories of accompanying my mother on peace marches and protests against then U.S. President Ronald Reagan's actions in Central America and elsewhere. These practices sometimes helped to lighten conversations and loosen tongues. In contrast, with government and military officials I intentionally emphasized my academic credentials and government associations. My status as a Fulbright scholar, for example, helped me gain entrance into tight circles on more than one occasion. There were limits to this framing, of course; even official letters and shiny golden seals from the U.S. Embassy could not prompt access to Salvadoran military records.

These research contexts are important, for they recognize that multiple forces are involved in the creation of historical narratives. Thus, as I uncover a few layers of history in this case study, the texture of each of those layers is woven with threads from past and present, as well as the multiple colors of race, gender, age, economics, and politics.

In an effort to spite the complexities of the research process—and of history itself—these chapters follow a roughly chronological order as they synthesize and interweave oral history interviews and documents. The first chapter, which sets the scene of the preflight period, argues that to date observers have misconstrued the significance of the northern border region to the Salvadoran nation and, moreover, underestimated the role of the region's rural inhabitants as agents of historical change. Chalatenango, Cabañas, and Morazán—departments typically portrayed as tierra olvidada—emerged into the national spotlight during the 1980s civil war period. According to most observers, this transformation was due to the machinations of external forces—most specifically members of the FMLN. Chapter 1 offers an alternative approach by focusing instead on the actions of local campesino residents. The chapter begins by examining how processes of uneven development relegated the northern sector to a position of secondary importance to the nation. A reevaluation of Salvadoran census and agricultural data, however, reveals that this location "on the fringe" of the nation offered local residents unique opportunities that, in turn, stimulated and influenced the development of a strong campesino rights movement. Interviews and archival materials trace the expansion of campesino collective organizing from primarily local and informal levels to more formal campaigns on both regional and national scales by the 1960s. Likewise, campesinos shifted over time from subtle forms of resistance to more contentious and "radical" actions. Through their organizations and actions, campesinos willingly engaged with state and nonstate actors and institutions and in so doing inserted themselves—consciously and as a group—onto the national sociopolitical and economic scenes. As a result, chapter 1 reveals, northern campesinos began remapping the nation well before the civil war.

Whereas chapter 1 examines the preflight experiences of Salvadoran campesinos, the next five chapters focus on their experiences away from home as "mobile communities" between the mid-1970s and the late 1980s. Taken together, these chapters illustrate that campesinos continued to engage the Salvadoran nation even when displaced within and beyond the country's borders. More specifically, chapters 2 and 3 follow Salvadoran campesinos as they left their hometowns in northern El Salvador and sought refuge in other locations. It examines the decision to abandon one's home as a conscious strategy, a natural extension of the community defense systems established in the 1970s. Placing flight within the context of community security demonstrates that, contrary to both the images broadcast at the time and more recent scholarly depictions, flight was not always unanticipated, nor was it all chaos and desperation. Even the mass border crossings into Honduras occurred with at least some measure of organization and preparation, as chapter 3 illustrates.

Chapter 4 examines life in the refugee zones of Honduras. Although Salvadorans carried with them into exile many of the organizational patterns and sensibilities that they had developed and experienced at home during previous decades, the unique contexts and circumstances of life in Honduras prompted them to diversify their goals and devise fresh strategies to reach them. An important theme throughout the chapter is the refugees' strategic maneuvering of the international aid network, which, in effect, expanded their organizing from a national to an international level. As a whole, this chapter demonstrates that Salvadoran campesinos in exile succeeded in maintaining a great deal of control over themselves and the spaces of the refugee camps.

If chapter 4 examines how campesinos in exile presented themselves to others, then chapters 5 and 6 shift attention to their internal maneuvering. Chapter 5 examines the refugees' interpretations of contemporary Salvadoran reality and their own roles in that reality. The chapter explores the refugees' assessments of the overall state of their *patria* (homeland, fatherland, nation) and their evaluations of the central players on the ground (the Salvadoran government and the FMLN insurgent forces) and examines how refugees perceived themselves in relation to their homeland in general. It argues that, despite physical separation, campesinos considered themselves to be citizens of El Salvador and, as such, entitled to many thus far unrecognized rights and freedoms. As citizens they also had duties and obligations to their country and therefore defended it even while outside its borders.

Whereas chapter 5 focuses on the refugees' interpretations of contemporary El Salvador, chapter 6 examines how refugees wrote the history of El Salvador from their vantage point of exile. From their sites of exile, they re-remembered and literally rewrote such important events of Salvadoran history as the 1932 campesino uprising and massacre and the 1969 war with Honduras. By revising history—and highlighting the long-standing tradition of rural resistance therein—the refugees countered "official" historical narratives that both symbolically and literally marginalized the Salvadoran campesino and unequivocally inserted themselves and their forebears onto the national and international scenes as protagonists of history.

The final chapter continues in the same vein as previous chapters in terms of exploring how Salvadorans struggled to maintain control over their own lives and destinies. This chapter focuses on how, in response to continued marginalization, Salvadoran campesinos generated their own grassroots repopulation movement, which resulted in the rebirth of dozens of northern communities in El Salvador between 1986 and the early 1990s. For Salvadoran campesinos, this movement came to represent major victory on several levels; not only did it force officials (and Salvadoran authorities in particular) to recognize and respond to Salvadoran campesinos as agents, civilians, and citizens of the nation but it also impelled the national peace process.

As a whole, the Salvadoran case allows us to understand refugees as more than simple victims of war. In this history, told from the bottom up, Salvadoran campesino refugees are complex individuals with personal and community histories, hopes and dreams. They are human beings facing the challenges of life with all the strength that they can muster and with every tool at their disposal. They are informed and competent members of a larger body politic who consciously struggle to be agents of positive change.

1

Remapping the *Tierra Olvidada*

Lost Peoples, Forgotten Lands

El Salvador is an agrarian society. Generations of inhabitants of the region, as well as outside observers, have been able to agree on this. What has proven more difficult to define is the role of the campesino in that society. For the most part, characterizations of Salvadoran rural folk—both indigenous and ladino—have long been coarse. In step with his compatriots throughout Latin America and the Caribbean, the Spanish Crown representative to San Salvador in 1814 reported that the natives of the region had "no culture nor religious or social knowledge."[1] Salvadoran government and commercial publications continued to draw similar conclusions throughout the first century of independence. According to an 1854 *Diario Oficial* entry, "They remain as always, rude and superstitious. . . . Without social needs, without a wish to improve their condition . . . they do not pursue progress nor do they seem to consider the wellbeing of their descendants." Twenty-five years later, the same journal critiqued "the majority of the inhabitants of our villages" for being "content to grow crops of maize and beans that will never raise this miserable people above their sorry position."[2] More than fifty years later, in 1932, a Salvadoran Coffee Association bulletin claimed that the nation's rural population was "infinitely low and remote . . . that is, they have no civilization."[3] And as late as 1973, Ignacio Martín-Baró, a scholar and priest at San Salvador's Universidad Centroamericana (Central American University, El Salvador, UCA), concluded that campesinos assumed a passive, fatalist stance before the world: "They feel yoked to their destiny." As a result of this fatalism, Martín-Baró continued, campesinos perceived themselves "not as subjects capable of directing and modifying at the very least their own personal history" but rather as an object or, even worse, "a social plague."[4] In short, both colonial and contemporary elites often have characterized rural inhabitants as poor, passive, backward, and ignorant.

A similar tendency is visible in representations of El Salvador's geography. Most studies simply have dismissed the northern sector of the country—largely comprised of the departments of Chalatenango, Cabañas, and Morazán—as isolated and backward. Data compiled by the Salvadoran government confirm that throughout the twentieth century the northern departments had limited infrastructural development in comparison with other departments. Relying on such data, it became easy for analysts to dismiss the north and its population as superfluous. A 1965 Salvadoran daily, for example, characterized the region as the *tierra olvidada* (forgotten land).[5] The World Bank subsequently assessed it as follows: "The land is marginal, the terrain is difficult, farming is by and large subsistence with relatively small acreages put out to permanent crops; uncontrolled land-use has led to serious soil exhaustion and erosion problems."[6]

Scholarship on El Salvador has only further substantiated the north's peripheral position. Many studies have focused on the development of systems and structures, for example, centralization of the state, the formation of an export-oriented economy, and the organization of national security forces. Others sought understanding of the civil war period through a similar macro-level approach, highlighting explicitly political actors, in particular, the Salvadoran government and armed forces, opposition political parties, the FMLN, and the United States. Scholars have also paid significant attention to the 1932 uprising of indigenous and ladino agriculturists in western El Salvador and the government's violent quashing of the rebellion, known as *La Matanza* (the slaughter). Until recently this subgenre, too, found explanations in the country's socioeconomic and political systems and the actions of the government, the armed forces, and the Partido Comunista de El Salvador (Salvadoran Communist Party, PCS).[7] David Browning, for example, in his now classic text *El Salvador: Landscape and Society*, concluded, "Little affected by the sweeping agricultural change across the centre and south of the country, . . . this northern third of the country, with its thin soils de-forested, misused, exhausted and eroded, its primitive agriculture unassisted by capital investment or modern supervision, and its social cohesion weakened by economic decline, dispersal of settlement and migration, gradually became the country's poor, backward, and neglected *tierra olvidada* of the present century."[8] Other authors preceded brief notes about the north with phrases such as "only in zones that were backward and on the periphery."[9]

Just as rural inhabitants "remained as always," so too was the north's insignificance "natural." Yet, this "periphery" existed only in relation to El Salvador's "center." In other words, the tierra olvidada was socially constructed over time.

Legislation played a crucial role in this process. In the century after independence, Salvadoran statesmen passed a series of decrees regarding landownership and use; these mandates confidently linked national progress to international markets. Political leaders offered awards and prizes to encourage landowners to introduce new, high-demand products: a gold medal for the country's first harvest of silk (1838); a cash award for the first thousand grapevines with fruit ready for harvest (1855); a variety of dispensations for those who produced coffee (1840s and after), including exemptions from national and municipal taxes, reduction of export duties, tariff protections, and exemption of laborers from required military service; and, for cotton producers (1940s and after), access to low-interest loans, improved seeds and fertilizers, and crop-spraying services.[10]

With both legislation and bonuses, Salvadoran statesmen acted on the conviction that "agriculture is the Nation's chief source of life and prosperity."[11] Yet they commended not just any kind of agriculture but specifically export agriculture. In the early and mid-twentieth century, this meant coffee, cotton, and sugar in particular. Given this, infrastructural development efforts focused almost exclusively on regions with the highest yields of these crops.[12] Communication and transportation lines first appeared in the lower third of the country, connecting the coffee, sugar, and cotton districts with major ports and the capital city of San Salvador. By 1972 the departments showcasing commercial agriculture for export held over 70 percent of the country's paved roads. These same departments also had the best rural access to public water and electricity, as well as education and medical services. The northern departments, in contrast, consistently ranked lowest in development indicators. In 1950, Cabañas, Morazán, and Chalatenango ranked first, second, and third, respectively, as departments with the highest rates of illiteracy in the country. In a similar vein, only 2 percent of inhabitants of Morazán and Cabañas had access to public water or electricity in the early 1970s, and only about 7 percent of the roads in these departments were paved. In sum, export-producing regions received high levels of state attention whereas the northern sector, which could not support wide production of export crops like coffee or cotton, virtually fell off the map.

By 1980, however, the map changed; the north and its inhabitants had emerged into both the national and international spotlights. The apparent swiftness of this shift was remarkable; whereas virtually no local or world news reporting addressed the northern departments during the mid-twentieth century, beginning in 1980 hundreds of articles appeared each year. What accounted for this change?

At the time, many observers attributed the transformation of the north to "outside forces," in particular priests promoting liberation theology and the guerrilla forces of the Frente Farabundo Martí para Liberación Nacional (FMLN). According to Salvadoran government officials, these two groups— both with presumed connections to international "terrorists" from "the Communist world"—were responsible for agitating the rural populace.[13] Campesino demands for civil rights became the work of "foreign Communist priests" while protests against human rights violations became the work of "FMLN front organizations" and their international supporters who "take a group of campesinos [and] force them to carry signs and banners with subversive slogans and they take them like cattle to the city."[14] From this perspective, the north was a subversive haven; even if campesinos there were not guerrilla combatants themselves, they were guilty by association. According to a common refrain of the period, they were, in essence, "the sea in which the guerrilla fish swam."

Although both insurgents and progressive Christians influenced campesinos in important ways during the 1970s and 1980s, it is unfair to assume that these groups caused rural Salvadorans to awake from a lengthy stupor. Such a narrow approach seriously underestimates the role that campesinos have played in Salvadoran history.

Since the 1990s, scholars of the process of nation-state formation in Mexico and Peru have been especially spirited in demonstrating the agency of rural dwellers previously assumed to be passive. Works by Florencia Mallon, Jennie Purnell, Jeffrey Rubin, and Mark Thurner, for example, reveal how localized popular movements and discourses influenced regional and national affairs. Rather than focusing on the state as an entity, these authors conceptualize it as a process, an ongoing negotiation among different—sometimes conflicting and sometimes overlapping—groups. From such an angle, campesinos and other subaltern groups can be, and indeed are, relevant forces in the political arena.[15] Similarly, we know from those who have explored similar themes for the Central American and Caribbean regions that rural communities and their members secured varied levels of political power, constructed "transcendent identities" as tools for political change, and resisted and confronted forces of capitalism.[16] In short these studies illustrate that rural people are not only as conscious and rational as national elites and other more powerful historical players; they are also as complex and layered.

Salvadoran historiography has also begun to take note of these trends. Most recent attention has focused on the nineteenth and early twentieth centuries.

For example, Patricia Alvarenga, Eric Ching, and Aldo Lauria-Santiago have examined various networks in which Salvadoran campesinos engaged, including regional and national security forces, political machinations, and export commerce. In addition, numerous scholars have reappraised the 1932 peasant uprising and its short- and long-term consequences; in so doing they have re-incorporated indigenous and ladino campesinos into events as actors with political, social, and economic goals.[17] With regard to the mid- and late twentieth century, a few social scientists have integrated campesinos as something other than victims—as participants in the popular church and education systems, for example, and as collaborators in the armed insurgency.[18] Although scholarship on this later era has not advanced quite as far as that of the earlier period, in combination with the studies noted earlier, as well as innovations in the fields of agrarian and subaltern studies, they do suggest that a reinterpretation of the campesino's role in the Salvadoran civil war is possible.

This chapter draws inspiration from recent scholarship to further "decenter" the study of El Salvador. I first read against the grain of official data to document how a location on the margins of the nation presented local residents with unique opportunities that ultimately helped to stimulate a strong campesino rights movement. I then examine how campesinos themselves account for the evolution of that movement through the mid-twentieth century from primarily local and informal levels to more formal campaigns on both the regional and national scales. An important aspect of organization was establishing alliances with other parties. In other words, campesinos willingly engaged with both state and nonstate actors and institutions and in so doing inserted themselves—consciously and as a group—onto the national socio-political and economic scenes. As a result, the chapter reveals, northern campesinos began remapping the nation well before the arrival of liberation theology, FMLN insurgents, or civil war.

The Map Reconfigured:
The North as a Space of Opportunity

There is little doubt that, as export agriculture expanded throughout the twentieth century, an invisible yet very real border came to separate El Salvador's northern sector from the rest of the country. The apparent disregard for the north resulted in considerable adversity for its inhabitants. Yet, as African scholar Achille Mbembe has pointed out, the unequal development of space can contribute to "the emergence of cultural vectors whose influence on the reconfiguration of the map . . . is generally underestimated."[19]

Although Mbembe refers in particular to postcolonial Africa, a similar argument may be made for postcolonial El Salvador. A rereading of official data allows a reappraisal of the significance of the north to the Salvadoran nation and, moreover, offers a reintroduction of the region's campesino inhabitants as agents of historical change.

The same data that scholars have cited in highlighting the north's status as the "forgotten land" also can be used to paint a picture of a region with relative freedom and independence. Throughout the twentieth century, access to land was of paramount importance to northerners, primarily for subsistence agriculture. Although some small-scale production for export occurred, campesinos in the borderlands remained largely independent of the control of commercial agriculture. This allowed them to develop paths toward economic survival that were significantly more diverse than those followed by campesinos in regions dominated by large-scale production for export.[20]

That northerners were largely independent of the control of commercial agriculture is evident in the fact that large landholdings (and their owners) did not hold the same sway in the north as they did in other areas of the country. As chart 1 illustrates, the 1950 agricultural census placed Santa Ana and Cabañas at opposite ends of the spectrum in terms of the overall influence of large landholdings; more than five times as many fincas and haciendas existed in Santa Ana than in Cabañas, with more than six times the dedicated hectares in the former as in the latter.[21]

On the large landholdings that did exist in the north, moreover, the colonial era practice of *colonaje* was relatively uncommon. In this system, the *colono*, a permanent resident on a grand estate, received access to a small parcel of land for personal use in exchange for service on the estate, a portion of the harvest, or other payment. The colono, then, depended on the landlord not only for land and agricultural materials but also for housing and often for food. Given the dependency inherent in colonaje and the accompanying patron-peon relationship, it is perhaps not surprising that export-focused departments relied more heavily on the system than did those along the northern periphery. Indeed, as chart 2 shows, the more export oriented the department the more prevalent was the system of colonaje.

Chart 2 also shows a converse trend; in the departments where colonaje was most common, *arrendamiento* was least common. In this system, campesinos simply rented land from others. Rental agreements were usually short term — either a growing season or a calendar year — and the *arrendatarios* (tenants) paid with money, in kind, or with a combination of the two. Until later in the twentieth century, there were few laws overseeing this tenancy system; thus, renters had no guarantees that landowners would respect the contract,

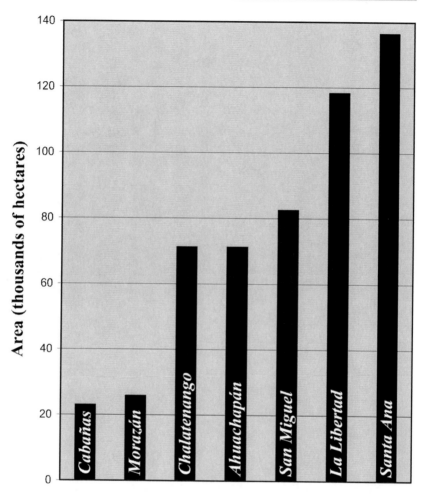

Chart 1. Large landholdings. (Data from El Salvador–Ministerio de Economía 1954)

no recourse against high rents, and no rights to claim allowances for improvements made to the land during tenancy. Despite these drawbacks, arrendamiento offered considerable benefits to the campesino. Among the most attractive aspects of the system was the fact that arrendatarios neither lived on the land nor worked for the landlord as colonos did. To a large extent, then, they were free from supervision and able to act of their own accord.

Also relatively independent were the northerners who held title to land. It is significant to note that the *propietario* (owner with title) worked more land in the north than in other areas of the country.[22] Indeed, in Cabañas,

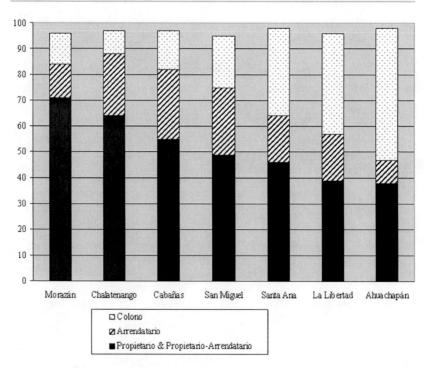

Chart 2. Tenancy on all holdings (percentage of landholdings). (Data from El Salvador–Ministerio de Economía 1967)

Chalatenango, and Morazán, nearly 70 percent of the agricultural land was worked by the propietario in 1950. In the country's coffee and cotton regions, in contrast, propietarios worked less than half of their land and relied on colonos, *jornaleros* (day laborers), and arrendatarios to work the rest (see chart 3).[23]

All the aforementioned trends become even clearer when we narrow our focus to plots of just a few hectares in size. On parcels of less than one hectare, the prevalence of propietarios in the north and colonos in the south, for example, becomes especially marked. According to the 1961 Agricultural Census, propietarios and *propietarios-arrendatarios* (those who owned land as well as rented) held between 60 and 70 percent of the smallest parcels in Chalatenango. In Ahuachapán, in contrast, colonos worked approximately the same percentage (see chart 4).

This same census indicates that, although fewer small-sized plots existed in the northern departments, rates of direct control over the land were much higher there. That is, in the north the majority of small farms were worked by owners, owner-renters, and renters. In the south, although more small plots

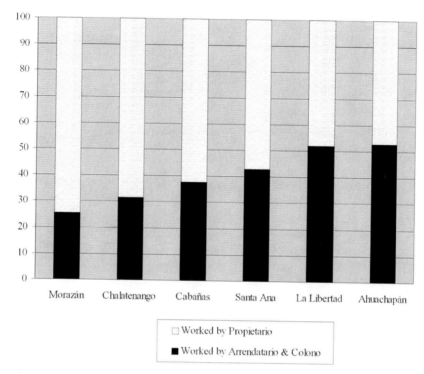

Chart 3. Who worked the land (percentage of landholdings). (Data from El Salvador–Ministerio de Economía 1954)

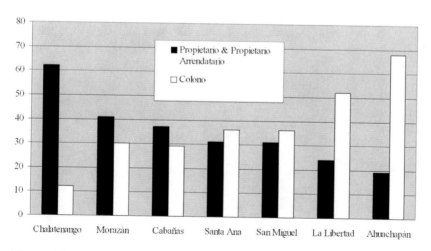

Chart 4. Tenancy on parcels less than one hectare (percentage of total landholdings in department). (Data from El Salvador–Ministerio de Economía 1967)

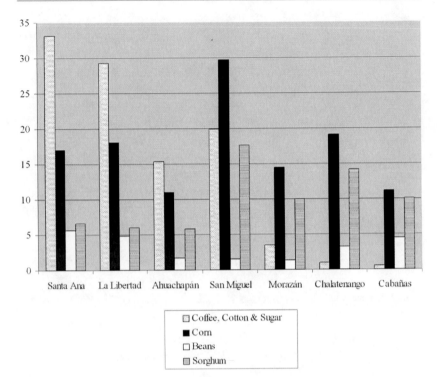

Chart 5. Export versus subsistence cultivation (thousands of hectares). (Data from El Salvador–Ministerio de Economía 1967)

were available, the vast majority of them were in the hands of colonos. Thus, poorer campesinos in the south had less control over land than their counterparts in the north.

Data on agricultural crops further support the conclusion that northern campesinos boasted more independent access to and control over the land. In Chalatenango, Cabañas, and Morazán, farmers dedicated far less area to crops such as coffee and cotton, which were typically intended for export. Instead, they turned more land over to the main subsistence crops of corn and beans (see chart 5).

Relative freedom from export pressures and more direct control over land meant that campesinos in the north enjoyed greater freedom to develop their own paths. That the north, from an early point in time, developed paths distinct from those of other regions of the country is visible in a series of land surveys sent by departmental governors to the central government in late 1879. These department-level reports included data on communal land possession and use collected by individual village councils. According to David

Remapping the *Tierra Olvidada*

Browning's analysis, these data reveal significant differences in practices and attitudes between regions. In the more fertile areas of the central and western highlands, for example, land claims were relatively small and clearly defined, whereas in the northern highlands of El Salvador, particularly in Morazán and Chalatenango, claims to common land were far more extensive. To cite just one example, the village of Nahuizalco in south-central Sonsonate claimed some twelve thousand acres of surrounding land; Tejutla, a village of about the same size in northern Chalatenango, claimed nearly sixty thousand acres.[24]

Browning attributes this contrast to differing experiences with capitalism and commercial agriculture. By the time of the survey, villages such as Nahuizalco had faced decades of encroachment by other villages as well as by large estates and individual settlers from elsewhere. Varied claims over the land had been heard time and again in the Salvadoran courts, and, as a consequence, people developed very precise understandings of what land belonged to them and what rights they had over that land. As a consequence landholders—whether individuals or whole communities—often fenced their properties to further assert ownership and control. Northerners, in contrast, tended neither to enclose their land with fences nor regulate its use to the same extent. As a consequence indigenous villagers, ladino farmers, and large landholders all tended to share the same territory. Indigenous villages in Chalatenango, Cabañas, and Morazán, for example, reported allowing cattle from neighboring ranches to graze on their communal lands. This more open conception of land use and ownership allowed local inhabitants to continue practicing traditional methods of migratory subsistence agriculture; they moved relatively freely across the land, cleared a plot, and cultivated it with the basics for a few years, then moved on to a new location.

Due to the migratory nature of farming in the north, few campesinos chose to permanently settle in their village centers; instead, they often lived on or near the lands they worked and traveled to the centers as necessary. The communities' claims to extensive tracts of land in the 1879 surveys reflected this human geography. Even if they did not formally own or even utilize much land at any given time, they regarded the areas as available to them. Had the demand for land been greater in the northern regions, as it was in many areas of the west and south, it is likely that disputes over ownership and use would have led to clearer definition of the boundaries of both common and private lands. Instead, local campesinos continued to treat vast tracts as their own domains, just as they had done for generations.

Browning's analysis makes clear that campesinos in the north both conceptualized and utilized land in unique ways. And, although he notes the continuation of traditional migratory agriculture, he does not fully recognize mobility as a resource consciously exploited by rural inhabitants. Cultural sociologists Finn Stepputat and Ninna Nyberg Sørensen, however, argue that it is necessary to consider the significance of mobility in livelihood practices. In a study of the Mantaro Valley in Peru, they reveal how peasants established and maintained high levels of mobility "between sites of subsistence production in different ecological zones, and sites of wage labour in different parts of Peru." Through the course of the twentieth century, many of the wealthier peasant families developed "dual household strategies" by setting up second homes in urban areas such as Huancayo and Lima. Urban and rural thus became "complementary spaces" for many of rural origin; families then formed networks of households, which allowed significant economic, political, and social exchanges between and among these spaces. Recognizing the "historical existence of networks of kinship and rural origin that encompass the countryside and the city . . . as well as other more distant sites," Stepputat and Sørensen maintain, offers crucial insight into people's behavior during later violent conflicts.[25]

Like the peasants of the Mantaro Valley, northern Salvadorans also developed "extended spaces of livelihood" throughout the twentieth century.[26] Movement occurred not just within their home regions but also between home and other regions of the country. Among the most ubiquitous patterns in this regard was travel to coffee and sugar estates at harvest time. Census data suggest that those who sought seasonal employment at the *cortas*, or "harvests," were not entirely dependent on wage labor; they were not colonos, for example, and they did not settle on the outskirts of estates. Rather, they combined travel to the cortas with their own agricultural work at home in the north. What developed, then, was a sort of diversification of resources. Although whole families did make the seasonal journeys, more often men went alone while women remained in the north to care for the home, children, and domestic animals. At the end of the harvest season, the small bundle of cash earned could be used to obtain agricultural supplies for the coming year, domestic materials or provisions, and, perhaps, schooling for the children.

To be sure, some people relied more heavily on wage labor than others. Some campesinos did not have access to sufficient land and could not easily afford additional rental fees. Moreover, as families grew in size and access to adequate agricultural land became more difficult and competitive, dependence on wage labor grew. Some who were formerly able to take care of basic needs no longer could do so, and as a result they became jornaleros, entirely dependent on wage labor. Those who did rely exclusively on wage labor tended to abandon the northern departments for other areas of the country. In the words of a World Bank report, the "inhospitable nature of the [northern] terrain, the historical lack of government services in the area, and the presence of greater opportunities elsewhere in the country have led to a continuing and particularly strong emigration from the northern periphery toward the center."[27] Other studies illustrate how, beginning in the 1950s, population rates in the northern departments of Chalatenango, Cabañas, and Morazán fell substantially while the areas surrounding the capital of San Salvador boasted the highest growth rates.[28]

Given that studies often emphasize how terrible conditions in the north forced people to abandon the region, it is worth taking a moment here to consider a broader context. First, El Salvador witnessed an industrial boom in the mid-1900s. The country's industrial sector more than doubled between 1942 and 1971, offering hope of employment to thousands. As a result San Salvador, where most of the new factories appeared, served as a population magnet.[29] Neither industrialization nor human migration, however, was peculiar to El Salvador during this time period. Indeed, parallel patterns were visible throughout the Latin American region. Urbanization became a major trend, especially in light of the Great Depression, which devastated Latin America's export-dependent economies. Many governments responded to the crisis by further industrializing the cities in order to produce manufactured goods formerly imported from abroad. Industrial expansion continued during World War II, contributing to a strong urban bias in terms of state investments in infrastructure and public services. During this period more than one hundred million people moved to cities such as São Paulo and Mexico City.

In light of this, northern Salvadorans' efforts to establish urban connections were not unique. A far more distinctive pattern was the extension of their spaces of livelihood across international borders. Indeed, one of the most unique aspects of life in the north was the proximity of Honduras. Many scholars have characterized this northern neighbor as El Salvador's "escape valve" into the 1960s.[30] They point out that Honduras was comparatively large, at more than five times the total land area of El Salvador, but it was seven times less densely populated. Moreover, Honduran farms incorporated less than one-quarter of the country's total land area, whereas Salvadoran farms comprised more than three-quarters of the national territory. Given the assumed availability of land, thousands of Salvadoran agriculturists crossed the border in search of the proverbial greener pastures. Others went to Honduras to sell their labor in plantations, mines, and industries. The pace of migration increased through the decades; whereas by the late 1920s some twelve thousand Salvadorans were in Honduras, by 1969 that number had grown to an estimated three hundred thousand.

There is certainly reason for scholars' emphasis on this pattern of migration. Indeed, for most of the twentieth century the Honduran government actively promoted the immigration of Salvadorans and other foreigners. In 1906 officials offered land tax free to immigrants who agreed to settle in and develop remote areas of the country. During the 1910s mining companies in central Honduras hired great numbers of foreigners, and the banana enclave of the North Coast actively recruited foreign workers, particularly Salvadorans, between 1895 and the mid-1950s. According to some estimates, Salvadorans comprised 10 percent of the labor force in Honduras as early as the 1920s. Even after 1954 when, in the wake of a series of agricultural labor strikes, legislation excluded foreign nationals from plantation jobs, Salvadorans continued to be prominent; well into the 1960s, some 30 percent of workers on Honduran banana plantations were from El Salvador, and the estimated three hundred thousand Salvadorans residing in Honduras at the time represented more than 12 percent of the total population of the country.

Yet there are aspects of Salvadoran migration to Honduras that deserve more attention. First, even as Honduran authorities and top-level officials from Standard Fruit and other international giants often encouraged the immigration of laborers, campesinos also established their own grassroots networks. Salvadorans living along the border, for example, regularly sold their wares in Honduran villages and markets, and Honduran landowners often hired Salvadoran laborers during the planting and harvest seasons. Beyond these economic connections, Salvadorans also established social links with Hondurans through cross-border friendships and marriages. Such grassroots networks remain relatively unexamined by scholars, yet they have existed since before the partitioning of the Central American isthmus into separate nation-states, and it is clear that they continued to serve as important resources for twentieth-century northern Salvadorans.

A related issue of relevance to the Salvadoran–Honduran nexus was the conceptualization of the international border itself. Government officials conceived of the border as a thin black line on a political map and El Salvador and Honduras as separate nation-states with distinct systems and peoples. Those actually living in the borderlands, however, did not distinguish between the two countries in the same way. As noted earlier, they maintained significant cross-border relations in spite of political borders. Moreover, the borderline itself was intangible in many ways. Only three official crossings existed; no other walls, fences, or distinguishing features defined the border. Without any official markings, it was virtually impossible to decipher the point at which one country ended and the other began.

Long-standing conflicts between El Salvador and Honduras further blurred the boundaries; indeed, the two republics had never agreed on an official borderline. Land and title disputes in the region dated back to the colonial period, in fact, and, although Salvadoran and Honduran officials cycled through multiple negotiations from the 1860s onward, a final resolution proved difficult to strike. Tensions erupted into overt hostilities in the 1960s, followed by more than a decade of cold war during which the two nations had no diplomatic relations and representatives of the Organization of American States oversaw the demilitarized territory in dispute. Although U.S. pressures led to the signing of a peace treaty and resumption of relations in 1980, the border delineation contest remained unresolved. At issue were six pockets of territory, known as *bolsones*, comprising approximately 420 square kilometers.[31]

What is particularly interesting about this in terms of the current study is that nearly half of the territory in dispute fell alongside El Salvador's tierra olvidada. More specifically, both countries continued to claim sovereignty over nearly 150 square kilometers between Morazán province in El Salvador and La Paz, Honduras, along with an additional 90 square kilometers between El Salvador's Chalatenango province and the Ocotepeque and Lempira provinces of Honduras (see chapter 3). This translated into a metaphorical and literal in-between land, which offered many local inhabitants additional space in which to maneuver.

For campesinos from northern El Salvador, then, Honduras was a resource they integrated into their spaces of livelihood. This, combined with the relative separation from export structures, as well as freedom from the influences of large landowners in the area, allowed northerners to sustain themselves to a large degree through the fruits of their own labor and to develop their own paths and strategies to address local problems. In short, their location on the margins of the nation did not mean complete isolation, nor did it mean that they chose to be detached or apathetic.

From *Tierra Olvidada* to *Tierra Organizada*: El Salvador's North and *La Lucha*

The north's unique position as both tierra olvidada and a space of opportunity created ripe conditions for campesino organization, mobilization, and protest. Yet many observers have subscribed to the belief that the government's violent reaction to the 1932 uprising in the western coffee districts prompted campesinos throughout the country to retreat into passivity and submission. According to this position, campesino activism remained dormant for nearly a half century, from the Matanza through the 1970s, when liberation theologians and armed insurgents coaxed them out of their stupor. Yet evidence exists that Salvadoran peasants continued to mobilize throughout this period, even if not typically in as spectacular a form as the 1932 revolt. Oral histories, scattered reports of protest actions, and the Salvadoran government's own conduct all indicate that communities in the rural north contributed to the emergence of a strong campesino rights movement that eventually came to be known by the campesinos themselves as *la lucha reivindicativa campesina* (the struggle in defense of campesino rights).

This movement began to take shape even as a measure of stability returned to El Salvador in the wake of the 1932 Matanza. Throughout the midcentury, rural poor joined together to address local-level problems. Campesino communities collaborated with each other, as well as with "outsiders," including state entities and urban-based activists and organizations. In the 1950s, campesino demands were for the most part specific and locally oriented, a community of colonos, for example, urging their employer to allow them access to land for subsistence farming or workers at a sugar mill protesting cuts in pay.[32] In the 1960s, however, both goals and methods began to shift away from the locally specific and toward the national level. Although individual landowners, employers, and politicians continued to receive attention, campesinos added new targets of discontent: the government, the economic system, the social system. Likewise, demands became broader and more intangible, for justice and democracy. At the same time, campesino actions became increasingly radicalized. By 1980, when the FMLN appeared, *la lucha* had already expanded to a nationwide struggle, a fight to place campesinos—and the "forgotten" across the country—on the national map.

Before delving into more detail, it is important to note that, in actuality, multiple campesino movements developed alongside one another. These can be divided into two general categories, which, for facility's sake, I will refer to as orthodox and progressive. The orthodox movement consisted of more conservative individuals and organizations that maintained links to the Salvadoran military government. Some of the more prominent groups within this sphere included cantonal patrols, the Unión Comunal Salvadoreña (Salvadoran Communal Union, UCS), and the Organización Democrática Nacionalista (Nationalist Democratic Organization, ORDEN). Membership in such organizations brought state-sponsored benefits, including access to land and credit, technical training, and a variety of material goods. Given this, members generally tended to back the authorities' decisions, help promote new legislation, and abstain from overt critique and protest. An essential aspect of the progressive movement, in contrast, was the overt critique of what members perceived as unjust power relations. This occurred at the local level, with protests against exploitation of seasonal migrant labor at harvest time, for example. It also occurred at the national level, with demands for change in El

Salvador's political, economic, and social systems. By 1980, associated organizations included the Unidad Nacional Obrero Campesina (National Union of Rural Workers, UNOC), the Federación Cristiana de Campesinos Salvadoreños (Christian Federation of Salvadoran Campesinos, FECCAS) and the Unión de Trabajadores del Campo (Rural Workers Union, UTC).

Scholars who have examined campesino actions during the civil war period have drawn similar distinctions.[33] Yet, when these movements are viewed within a broader time line, the distinctions between them become far less sharp. One reason is that membership was not written in stone; individual campesinos changed opinions and shifted allegiances, moved back and forth between organizations, and even participated in two organizations with apparently contradictory causes at the same time. In a similar vein, organizations adjusted their missions and tactics over time, which in turn influenced membership. Sometimes organizations overlapped and fused. And the successes and failures of one movement could influence another for better or worse. In what follows, my primary focus is on the development of the progressive campesino movement. I examine the actions of orthodox movement organizations when directly relevant.

Foundations (ca. 1940s–1960s)

Although it may seem ironic, the authoritarian Salvadoran regime played a foundational role in fomenting the progressive *lucha campesina*. Throughout the mid-1900s, administrations adopted a number of different strategies to address "the rural problem" and "the agrarian crisis." The Salvadoran president, General Maximiliano Hernández Martínez, for example, regained some support from the rural populace after his orchestration of the government's response to the 1932 uprising by condemning mistreatment of rural workers and punishing "the most egregious abusers." The Martínez administration also created the National Social Defense Board to carry out social welfare projects in rural areas. Subsequent administrations continued Martínez's efforts through successor and companion agencies that offered campesinos low-rent agricultural lots, new housing, and access to credit, among other things.[34]

As pressures on the land increased through the course of the twentieth century, Salvadoran officials repeatedly acknowledged the need for significant land reforms and, in some cases, undertook reform or distribution projects. Like the rural welfare programs noted earlier, these efforts—no matter how inadequate or unsuccessful observers deemed them to be—led to new possibilities for select groups of campesinos. The 1954 land reform program carried out by President Oscar Osorio, for example, prompted the creation of new rural communities such as Joya de Cerén in the department of La Libertad. What began simply as a new rural neighborhood of low-rent agricultural plots evolved over time into an "integrated approach to community development." Because of this unique approach, administrators of the program claimed, communities such as Joya de Cerén "would, in time, be able to solve the agricultural problem in our country, primarily in the areas of education for rural people, creating the human resources able to serve effectively in the great transformations that are currently taking place in all the countries of the world."[35]

Although El Salvador's agrarian problems continued, this integrated approach proved relatively successful. Campesinos who participated in the Joya de Cerén reform project attended trainings, acquired new skills, and developed a collective work ethic. They then put their new consciousness and skills to the test by petitioning the government for additional benefits such as access to credit and land purchase rights. As will become evident, clear parallels exist between the Joya de Cerén project and community development programs carried out elsewhere in the country in later years.

Another approach that Salvadoran officials adopted to address the agrarian crisis was the promotion of cooperatives. Although many of the cooperatives that appeared between the 1940s and 1970s further benefited those who were already quite comfortable, including the owners of large estates, the cooperative movement held significance for many smallholders and landless campesinos as well. For example, new legislation appeared on the books, beginning with Decree 113 in 1942, which promised protection of the small farmer. A decade later such promises had been incorporated into the national project, as Article 145 of the Constitution of 1950 made clear.[36] This was followed by the Salvadoran Cooperative Law of 1971, which was intended to facilitate legal recognition of cooperatives. Despite the fact that many rural inhabitants were illiterate, they would in the years to come turn to such legislation time and again in support of their claims.

Additional aspects of the cooperative movement that held special significance for poorer campesinos were the rural education programs that Salvadoran officials supported even if they did not directly conceive them. By the 1950s Salvadoran campesinos had begun attending trainings in cooperativism sponsored by the Organization of American States and the Panamerican Union. In the 1960s the U.S.-based American Institute for Free Labor Development (AIFLD) and American Federation of Labor and Congress of Industrial Organizations (AFL-CIO), in collaboration with the Salvadoran Ministry of Labor, developed an intensive four-week workshop known as the Campesino Training Program. According to a former AIFLD employee involved with the program, workshops covered subjects ranging from Salvadoran agrarian sector law and the functions and services of the various government ministries to health issues, farming techniques, and organizational methods. In the 1970s the newly established Instituto Salvadoreño para el Fomento de Cooperativas (Salvadoran Institute of Cooperative Development, INSAFOCOOP) continued these campesino training efforts by offering short courses on cooperative organization, administration, and accounting.[37] The impact of these programs is evident in the fact that graduates often went on to participate in community cooperatives or establish organizations in their home villages. By 1965 about ninety-six official cooperatives existed in El Salvador with a combined membership of over twenty thousand.[38]

Further evidence of the impact of rural training efforts and the cooperative movement in general can be found in the UCS.[39] Many of the individuals who ultimately joined the ranks of this campesino league did so because of their affiliation with AIFLD-sponsored agricultural cooperatives and peasant associations. The first of these organizations appeared in 1968, and in 1969 leaders from twenty of these AIFLD- and government-sponsored communal organizations came together to officially establish the UCS. It quickly expanded its membership from 4,000 members at its inception to 70,000 just six years later and 120,000 by 1980. The first members came almost exclusively from La Paz and Usulután, but the organization eventually counted strong bases in the western departments of Santa Ana, Ahuachapán, and Sonsonate, as well as in eastern San Miguel and La Unión. Although the UCS did have some members in the central region around San Salvador and in the northern departments, these were not particularly strong bases.

Many observers have been critical of the UCS because of its roots in and connections to Salvadoran and U.S. government initiatives. Scholars have assumed that the main purpose of establishing the UCS and allowing it to flourish was to counteract unrest among peasants in important export regions. From this perspective the material benefits of membership (land, food, housing, and services) co-opted sectors of the peasantry and, in essence, brought them under government control. To some extent this may be true. The UCS was, in fact, strongest in the areas hardest hit by the repression that followed the 1932 peasant uprising and those in which the more oppositional or radical activities of the 1970s and after were weakest. Moreover, in 1980, when Segundo Montes, a sociologist at El Salvador's Central American University, interviewed UCS affiliates, they often highlighted the material benefits of membership. After paying an admission fee, they said, "then you can be associated with the cooperative and also the evening dispensations for children, where they hand out milk, flour, oil." In addition, UCS members and their families were eligible for various types of instruction, including workshops on cooperativism, organization, hygiene, and family planning, as well as "classes in sewing and tailoring for the daughters."[40]

Yet in exchange for these and other benefits, UCS members "served as a bridge" between government officials and campesinos.[41] Indeed, the UCS played a key role in promoting and implementing government programs in the Salvadoran countryside. During recruitment trips to distant villages, for example, representatives informed prospective members not only about the benefits of affiliation with the union but also about new national laws and programs. According to one representative, "We explained some law like the agrarian transformation law. To do this we carried little books, given to us by the ISTA [Instituto Salvadoreño de Transformación Agraria] president, to explain to them about the Agrarian Transformation. We didn't get involved, we just served as advisors."[42]

It has also been shown that both the Salvadoran government and the AIFLD heavily influenced the UCS structure and particularly the organization's leadership. Authorities carefully picked UCS leaders and determined the objectives around which they received training, leading one observer to refer to the UCS as an *organización paraestatal* (parastate organization).[43] This understandably restricted the operational capacities and activities of the organization. Members sought solutions to only a limited number of "acceptable" problems, for example, and avoided conflict with the authorities as much as possible.

It may be true that the Salvadoran government determined to a large extent the scope of both UCS dissent and support at least in the initial years. Yet it is important to not lose sight of the fact that, despite the purportedly narrow nature of the organization, UCS membership was a positive experience for many campesinos. In addition to the material benefits associated with membership, involvement with the UCS had significant consciousness-raising effects in that members became well aware of their worth to the government. This was clear on a general level because the UCS was the only legally sanctioned peasant organization at the time.[44] It was also clear in specific cases such as during the 1976 agrarian transformation process when, as one campesino noted, "the whole project could fail [but] if they hold on to the UCS, it won't fail."[45]

That the UCS occupied a key position translated into a small measure of freedom for UCS affiliates to petition government officials toward certain ends. When petitions went unheeded, UCS groups began to take their claims to the streets. Efforts along these lines often were successful, in large part due to their circumscribed and focused character. For example, when UCS members

Remapping the *Tierra Olvidada*

mobilized to protest the Banco de Fomento (Agricultural Development Bank), the government's official supplier for UCS-affiliated cooperatives, for charging higher prices for fertilizer than other commercial agencies, the government eventually agreed to reduce prices to the regular public market value.[46] In a similar vein, UCS members were instrumental in pushing for legislation that protected the rights of individuals renting property. Thus, as with many other organizations during the mid- and late 1970s, the UCS shifted toward more contentious methods. Moreover, in some areas, due to a deepening affiliation with the centrist Partido Demócrata Cristiano (Christian Democrat Party, PDC), the UCS ultimately "represented one of the first alternatives to the Partido de Conciliación Nacional (the official party) [National Conciliation Party, PCN]."[47]

Thus, for many campesinos, affiliation with the UCS proved to be a positive experience not only in terms of material benefits and acquisition of skills but also with regard to economic and political awareness and involvement. Through involvement with the UCS, members gained organizational experience and witnessed change and improvement through cooperative efforts. They joined together to make demands on government entities and sometimes won concessions. In this the UCS actually paved the way for future campesino organizations. In the words of one UCS member, "I think that now the government is aware of the [rural] organizations and of the fact that the campesino is one of the pillars of progress for this country."[48]

In many ways Salvadoran government actions from the 1930s through the early 1970s sent the message that campesinos had the right to organize collectively and that government officials not only tolerated rural organization but also engaged and supported it to a certain degree. Salvadoran officials' actions—from social welfare projects to land reform and distribution efforts and from the promotion of rural cooperatives to recognition of and collaboration with the UCS—demonstrated to Salvadorans that improved working and living conditions in rural areas were not just possible; they were also necessary and just.

Official attention to El Salvador's "rural problem" clearly influenced and spurred further action by campesinos throughout the country. There are also scattered bits of evidence that campesinos organized beyond the government's direct control between the 1940s and 1960s. Various reports note actions such as squatting and land takeovers, petitions, strikes, and protests. Oral histories also reference mutual aid projects. Although the details have yet to be uncovered, it is now clear that, in spite of "the 1932 effect," campesinos did not stop organizing and mobilizing.

Formalization and Expansion
(ca. 1950s–early 1970s)

The role of the Salvadoran government in fomenting rural organization after 1932 may be considered an ironic twist of fate if, as many observers claim, official intentions were to offset unrest and pacify rural areas rather than promote mobilization and to preserve the status quo rather than alter it. The fact that most of the aforementioned government initiatives focused on areas of the country dominated by large-scale commercial agriculture suggests that such observations may, in fact, be accurate. Most of the cooperatives that appeared during the mid-twentieth century, for instance, were located in western El Salvador, precisely in those departments where the rural uprising of 1932 was most intense: Ahuachapán, Sonsonate, and Santa Ana. Land distribution projects under presidents Martínez and Osorio were likewise concentrated in export zones.[49]

Again the north remained largely beyond government attention and action. Rather than remaining passive, however, northern campesinos developed their own grassroots initiatives. Oral histories and interviews reveal that campesinos in Chalatenango, Cabañas, and Morazán formed a variety of mutual aid organizations by the 1950s and 1960s, many of which were short term, focused on specific outcomes. In El Mozote, Morazán, residents created a community council to establish a school in the town. They raised money, obtained land, and eventually built a schoolhouse. They also conducted a census of school-age children in the area and used the results to petition the government to supply the community with official teachers. El Mozote established a similar board to oversee the construction of a church.[50]

Similar projects occurred elsewhere throughout northern El Salvador. In San Miguelito, Chalatenango, an interviewee named Soledad recalled, "We made *pupusas* and cakes to raise funds, to build the bell tower and a school. We built a school that went up to sixth grade. . . . We also arranged for the church to be painted [and] we bought [our patron saint statue] new clothes."[51] The town of Portillo del Norte, also in Chalatenango, took matters into its own hands after government offices ignored petitions for a road that would connect the town to the municipal head of Cancasque. "So," another interviewee, José S., recalled, "we organized ourselves—not to earn any money but to help in an organized way, with manpower but without salary. . . . I alone worked 135 days without pay on that street, in one year. And our idea was that trucks would come to buy grain, that fertilizer would come for us to buy and not have to go and bring it back from some other place, but that it would arrive here close to the houses, right. And we were able to achieve this goal."[52]

Here José noted not only that community members constructed an important access route with their bare hands; he also emphasized that the Salvadoran government responded favorably to their activity. He reported, in fact, that once they had actually begun laboring on the road, government workers arrived to help. "Then the government picked up the project," he recalled. "And they didn't just take it up to Portillo del Norte—they took it *through* Portillo and then out the other side!"[53]

These examples illustrate short-term projects with long-term consequences. The projects bore material benefits, of course, but they also helped to generate a philosophy of solidarity among the campesinos who participated, as well as those who simply enjoyed the positive results. Perhaps the most influential aspect in terms of building confidence in collective efforts at the local level was the ability of campesino leaders and activists to successfully negotiate vis-à-vis "outsiders," whether local elites or government representatives. As José S. explained, with the road to Portillo "people started to gain more confidence in the [power of the] pueblo" and, as a result, participated more readily in later projects.[54]

These successes and the accompanying "pleasure in agency" encouraged more campesinos to participate in formalized projects with broader and longer-term benefits.[55] Men joined labor cooperatives, for example, to work their fields together. Adán, from the northern sector of Cuscatlán province, recalled, "We were a group of about 15 men who helped each other in the fields. They came to me and asked me if I would join the work group. I had many brothers and our field was pretty big [and] there was so much work to do. Together we were able to keep up more easily. . . . I joined the group and continued to help others. That's how we started to organize."[56] Walter, from Chalatenango, recalled a slightly different purpose for his work in a collective plot. "We established a collective beanfield," he explained, "which served to help those comrades [*compas*] who were unlucky, someone who had had a bad harvest, for instance, or who had a sick member of the family, so that we could give him money to buy medicines."[57] Other villages established communal stores, kitchens, and bakeries for similar purposes.

Although Salvadoran law required official recognition of all such organizations via *personería jurídica* (juristic personality, legal status), it is clear that many groups existed and functioned without this recognition. Officials clearly were aware of the existence of many acting cooperatives; one report recognized that seventy-nine agricultural "precooperatives" existed at the time with nearly three thousand members.[58] Campesinos themselves, however, did not necessarily distinguish between legal and illegal. "The cooperative," explained Amado V., "emerges out of necessity."[59]

In light of both need and the success of these mutual aid efforts, rural villages began developing more formal methods of organization and *autogestión* (self-promotion). Many towns established formal community leadership institutions known as *directivas comunales* (communal directives or councils). *Directivas* often initially served a purpose akin to work committees; that is, campesinos established councils to oversee particular projects, as occurred in the aforementioned examples of school and road building. On encountering success with their first projects, councils often continued to operate, taking on more general and all-purpose roles and directing community efforts on a variety of fronts.

Directivas, like agricultural cooperatives, contributed a great deal to the raising of campesino awareness of the marginalized position they held in Salvadoran society. Increased awareness often led to indignation, which then prompted greater involvement in campesino organizations. Rosa, a woman I interviewed, described the formation of a *directiva* in her town in northern Chalatenango as "just like the dawning of a day, the idea that a directiva was to be established . . . to organize our efforts." With the directiva in place, she continued, community members focused on "starting to build our strength to go on learning about the different ways we were being exploited, the injustices we were living."[60]

The community-elected directiva members took on specific responsibilities. The directiva in Rosa's village was typical in that it included a general secretary, a treasurer, and a sort of program director "to keep track of everything we did."[61] Other directiva activities included education, pastoral work, communications, and conflict resolution. Eventually, with the deepening of El Salvador's civil conflict, directivas added more areas of responsibility, including "propaganda" and, as chapter 2 describes, security. Those who served on the directivas often had no prior experience with such public work, and many had attended school only for a short time if at all. It was not uncommon, therefore, to have only one or two literate members on a council, and for most it was trial by fire—especially in the early years. "I always said we started from zero," one man said, "because we couldn't even draw up an agenda."[62] Despite the tricky beginnings, members quickly acquired administrative skills and developed a great capacity for solving problems in creative and community-oriented ways. Illustrative of this is the conflict resolution position, which addressed disagreements between community members through negotiation and mediation. Such an approach to problem solving further bolstered solidarity among community members, as together they sought common ground despite their differences.

Campesinos also developed and mobilized resources from beyond the borders of their own home villages. Among the most important were the alliances they established with campesinos from other villages and regions. People networked with one another during their seasonal work at the cortas, as well as while attending campesino training programs and urban markets and fairs. By the 1960s these alliances had begun to coalesce into more formal groupings. In 1965 several of these groupings held a Congreso Campesino (Campesino Congress) in Guacotecti, Cabañas. Out of such meetings emerged two of the largest and most prominent rural organizations among northerners: FECCAS and the UTC. Both of these organizations were inspired to some extent by the UCS. According to Ramón, FECCAS emerged from the need for an "organization solely representing our interests, which would be independent [from the government]; an organization that would involve the workers and peasants in the economic struggle and extend it to the political struggle."[63] In many respects, FECCAS succeeded; in contrast to the generally pro-government stance of the UCS, FECCAS developed a more independent and critical perspective on local and national issues. The founders and earliest associates, inspired by a social Christian doctrine, emphasized organizational objectives and principles that encouraged the "awakening" of the campesino population about the country's exploitative social, political, and economic systems. Whereas the UCS drew its membership primarily from small and middle-sized farmers in the south and central export regions, FECCAS attracted campesinos from some of the northern sectors as well and addressed issues of particular importance to those lowest in the national order: colonos, arrendatarios, jornaleros, and smallholders.

Like FECCAS, the UTC drew strength from Christian values, but from its very inception it was "a combative and radical organization."[64] Whereas FECCAS as an organization went through a process of transformation and radicalization in the late 1960s and 1970s, the UTC emerged out of a group of campesinos from Chalatenango and San Vicente who had already experienced such transformations on an individual level. As such, the organization "emerge[d] already with a revolutionary orientation . . . to transform the poor campesino's lived reality within the context of a national level struggle to transform the conditions of exploitation and domination to which the popular sectors found themselves submitted." In the words of Oswaldo, "We no longer wanted to be on the level of Christians and nothing more. We ha[d] to take another step."[65]

Both UTC and FECCAS spent much of the late 1960s and early 1970s defining their organizational objectives, expanding their membership bases, and solidifying their structures. By the mid-1970s, they had both emerged on the national scene with strikes and protests, as will be discussed later in more detail. Among the objectives shared by both organizations were better labor conditions and salaries, fair agricultural supply costs and land rental rates, and the legal right to organize.[66]

It must be noted that such organizations developed to different extents and at varying rates depending on local contexts. Community power relations were of particular importance in determining progressive mobilization patterns. According to Carlos Rafael Cabarrús's examination of the Aguilares area (northern San Salvador department), individuals and families with the greatest access to and control over resources such as land, water, education, and medicines often exerted significant influence over the type of organizing that occurred in a particular locale.[67] Rivalries between individuals and families also contributed to differing paths, as did kinship networks, migrant labor experiences, and connections to estates and urban areas. Given the variety of influences, neighboring villages sometimes adopted significantly different paths; even within one village, both orthodox and progressive tendencies often developed side by side. All of the communities examined by Cabarrús, for example, found proponents of both FECCAS (a progressive organization) and ORDEN (an orthodox organization). On occasion one might belong to two apparently opposing organizations at once. José R., for example, initiated a progressive Christian base community (discussed later in this chapter) at the same time he was a member of ORDEN.[68]

Despite the many variations, in terms of the north as a region a couple of general trends in progressive mobilization appeared. Villages in the departments of Cabañas and Chalatenango seem to have begun organizing into more formal associations earlier (1960s and early 1970s), whereas towns in northern Morazán did so a bit later (1979 and after). This pattern demands further examination, yet it is likely that Morazán's location even farther from El Salvador's only truly urban center, the capital city of San Salvador, was at least partly responsible for the discrepancy, for "outside forces" often had significant impacts on rural communities. Occasionally outsiders introduced new ideas; more often they simply offered new tools for discussing and explaining existing problems and new contexts within which to view those problems. Perhaps most important, however, outsiders influenced the internal power dynamics of communities. Like access to and control over water or medicine, alliances with outsiders—both individuals and organizations— represented a kind of resource; the arrival of new resources to rural communities, then, could prompt shifts in local hierarchies and alliances.[69] Many of the outside forces with which northern campesinos allied themselves in the 1960s and afterward had their roots in urban San Salvador: Acción Católica Universitaria de El Salvador (University Catholic Action of El Salvador, ACUS), labor confederations, opposition political parties, teacher and student unions, proponents of liberation theology, and the politico-military groups that ultimately formed the FMLN.[70] Generally speaking, these urban-based groups established an ongoing presence in Cabañas and Chalatenango before arriving in Morazán, which, in turn, affected patterns of local organization.

Regardless of specific timetables, it is evident that campesinos throughout the north allied themselves not only with one another but also with other sectors of society in an effort to further strengthen "the power of the pueblo." Among the most powerful alliances were those with progressive Catholics influenced by liberation theology. Although this topic has been addressed in detail elsewhere, it is worth reviewing here given its influence on and significance for the northern campesino experience.[71]

Throughout the 1960s, progressive Catholics, including university students affiliated with ACUS, engaged in mission- and charity-type projects in rural areas throughout El Salvador. Beginning in 1968 a new energy infused such work as liberation theology began to take root on the northern outskirts of San Salvador and quickly radiated outward. This new theology hit El Salvador in full force in July 1970 with the convocation of the first Semana Nacional de Pastoral de Conjunto (National Pastoral Work Week). During the conference Salvadoran archbishop Luis Chávez, his auxiliary bishops Arturo Rivera y Damas and Oscar Romero, and more than 120 religious workers and laity from all over the country discussed pastoral methods and directions in light of the Second Vatican Council (1962–65), also known as Vatican II, and the 1968 Conferencia Episcopal Latinoamericana (Conference of Latin American Bishops, CELAM) in Medellín, Colombia. Both of these meetings infused sectors of the Catholic Church with a new current of social responsibility. The meeting at Medellín was particularly important for Latin America; there bishops from the region adopted a "preferential option for the poor" and called on the Catholic Church to accompany the impoverished and marginalized in their struggle for liberation from structural injustice and institutionalized violence through the promotion of education and *conscientización* (critical awareness, consciousness-raising). Following these international leads, attendees at the Salvadoran Pastoral Week conference in 1970 pledged to promote the democratization of Church structures, the development of a "critical and liberating evangelization," the expansion of base communities, and the formation of lay leaders "who will be not only catechists but responsible individuals dedicated to the integral development of the human person and the formation of communities."[72]

"From that moment," explained Benito T., a priest who worked in Chalatenango during this period, "pastoral agents began widespread Bible distribution, not just for people to get to know it but to have it in their communities and to use it like a machete as the working tool every Christian ought to have."[73] Northern campesinos such as José S. noticed immediate changes. "Before, the priests turned their backs to us when they said mass, right. And later, they suddenly turned around to face the parish," he said. This, combined with the more widespread availability of Bibles, meant that "during mass, one already knew a bit and then learned more when the priest said mass, because one could see his face."[74] Tomás added that priests "spoke more clearly to us, not deceitfully" and stopped charging campesinos for weddings and christenings.[75]

In light of these changes, many campesinos began attending weekly meetings, known as *reflexiones*, in which they related biblical readings to historical and current events of local and national concern. Particularly influential were stories such as "Exodus," which spoke to their experience as an oppressed group. "I compared the conditions we were living in with those that I saw in the Scriptures," explained Vidal. "The situation of the Israelites for example . . . where Moses had to struggle to take them out of Egypt to the Promised Land. . . . Then I compared it with the situation of slavery in which we were living. . . . Our struggle is the same; Moses and his people had to cross the desert, as we are crossing one right now."[76]

Through such reflection many peasants met for the first time a God who sided with the poor and oppressed. No longer did peasants hear messages of passivity and submission or receive promises of heavenly rewards for a life of suffering. Instead these reflections and the Christian base communities of which they were a part fostered the development of a "community of equals." Peasants heard that it was not God's will that they be poor, and that all individuals were equal before God—from the richest *hacendado* to the most poverty-stricken campesino. "God has not made the rich, nor has he made the poor," concluded Rosa. "He has made everyone equal."[77]

Because all were equal in God's eyes, it followed that the poor possessed a basic right to organize and gesture for the improvement of their conditions and communities. As one lay pastoral team described it, "We discovered that it is not God's plan that a few people have all the land and others, like us, have nothing. God's will is not that we live in misery in this life because eternal life will be different—No! God wants us to have the right to organize and to struggle for our rights."[78] Such new understandings and philosophies further encouraged the development of local mutual aid efforts such as the building of churches, schools, and roads described earlier.

The training of lay leaders, like the pastoral team just cited, made a crucial contribution to rural communities' ability and willingness to organize in defense of their rights. Although priests and nuns initially led the reflexiones and other initiatives of the Comunidades Eclesiales de Base (Christian Base

Communities, CEBs), these groups eventually developed their own leadership, electing lay teachers and preachers known as *catequistas* (catechists), *celebradores* (celebrators), and *delegados de la palabra* (delegates of the word). Following instruction by pastoral agents, these lay leaders assumed responsibility for conducting weekly religious worship services and managing particular areas of church life such as baptism, catechism, or marriage preparation classes.

Catequistas also had opportunities for additional training at instructional centers established throughout El Salvador beginning in the mid-1960s.[79] These centers were known as *centros de formación campesina* (peasant training centers) or *universidades campesinas* (peasant universities). Each of El Salvador's five dioceses sponsored at least one center. There were also several specialized centers, including the Centro San Lucas in the city of San Miguel, which focused on health care training, another in Chalatenango for agricultural training, and two others run by and for women—the Centro de Promoción Rural in Santa Tecla (San Salvador) and the Centro Guadalupe, also in San Miguel. In addition, an itinerant team, the Centro Rural Itinerante, traveled to parishes throughout the countryside offering a variety of classes.[80]

All of these training centers shared the same overarching mission, described by a staff person at one of the centers as "to develop leadership qualities in peasants, with knowledge of the value of mutual help and of cooperative work; to train men for change, ready to form part of parish and diocesan pastoral work, putting themselves at the service of bishops and priests. Briefly: the integral training of men for liberation."[81] The core method for this training was the *cursillo*, a monthlong course of study, which, as noted by the staff person quoted here, focused on attendees' integral or holistic development. To this end courses covered a broad range of topics; in addition to biblical scriptures, attendees studied agriculture, cooperativism, health issues, leadership skills, and other themes. Walter G., a priest who spearheaded training efforts, explained in a 1981 interview that such a broad education was necessary because "the catechist, among us, is a man who not only works as a religious person but assumes leadership that is also social, including, at times, political in our rural communities."[82]

As catechists put their cursillo trainings to work in their home communities and beyond, CEB organizing spread from the more densely populated areas to the most remote hamlets. Just as formal training influenced catechists, so too did catechists influence other campesinos in these hamlets. Indeed, many campesinos traced their organizational beginnings to the influence of the catechists. Santiago, for example, recalled that the neighboring town of Portillo del Norte, Chalatenango, was one of the first in his area to establish a Christian base community; trained lay workers from there then traveled throughout the region promoting similar organization elsewhere, including his hometown: "The celebradores de la palabra who arrived to town did consciousness-raising work; they promoted organization. It was in this way that I began to work in community organizing."[83]

As Santiago's comment suggests, the organization of campesinos into CEBs had an important impact. On an individual level, affiliates gained and practiced skills in organization, public speaking, and leadership, among others. And they often referred to their early experiences with the CEBs in terms of an awakening or transformation. As one catequista from Morazán remarked about time spent at one of the peasant universities, "I was seeing everything in a different way. . . . I felt an awakening to a different world."[84] These personal changes translated into transformations for communities as well. People who had attended cursillos often developed into "organic intellectuals."[85] They returned home eager to put into effect many of the things they had discussed at the training centers. Their ideas and energy, in turn, inspired followers. In Joateca, Morazán, for example, a group of catechists worked together to establish a savings and loan cooperative for the community; Cooperative San Antonio grew and went on to receive a bank loan that allowed expansion into cattle raising and other ventures.[86] Catechists and members of CEBs also promoted the establishment or strengthening of directivas in many villages, as well as community alliances with organizations such as FECCAS and UTC. The influence of these grassroots intellectuals, along with the new resources they brought to the community by virtue of their alliances with outsiders, could alter internal dynamics, as noted earlier, thus prompting villagewide changes.

The impact of the trainings went far beyond the individual and village levels as well. The centros de formación provided spaces in which laypeople met and interacted with others from across the country. Similar to the reflexiones they conducted in their own villages, at each class meeting they exchanged stories and experiences and found that they reflected on many social issues from similar perspectives despite the fact that they were from different regions. At the training center at Los Naranjos, for example, seminars began by focusing on the "worth of the poor person." Divided into small groups, participants talked about the basic problems they faced as individuals and communities and discussed how they might overcome such problems.[87] Through such conversations, they noted striking similarities across regions and concluded that campesinos throughout the country faced the same oppression and misery, the same adversaries and challenges. Such a realization formed the basis of a new sort of class consciousness, an understanding of one's own position as part of a larger whole of campesinos.

In short, between the 1960s and early 1970s, campesinos formalized their organizing on a variety of levels. At the local level, they established mutual aid and working groups, directivas, and CEBs. At local and regional levels, they formed bases for the peasant leagues UTC and FECCAS. And through their work with these organizations and the CEBs, they became increasingly integrated at the regional and national levels. Alliances and mobility continued to play crucial roles in organizing at all levels.

Radicalization (ca. late 1960s–1980s)

The 1960s was a period of great political effervescence in El Salvador as elsewhere. Throughout the decade various sectors of society mobilized to promote their rights and demand positive change: students and educators, laborers, progressive Catholics, opposition politicians, peasants, and politico-military organizations. Many of these sectors had been active for years, often working in solitude and occasionally collaborating with one another. By the late 1960s their paths overlapped with increasing frequency. A variety of studies have examined the coalescing of the *frentes de masa* (mass fronts) and *movimiento popular* (popular movement), so I will not repeat the story here.[88] Suffice it to say that throughout the 1970s and into the 1980s the actions of individual sectors and the mass fronts they created succeeded in pushing the Salvadoran military regime to a breaking point. Within this broader context, campesinos turned increasingly radical in their actions.

It is important to recognize that campesinos moved neither lightly nor suddenly to more contentious methods; it is clear that they preferred to press for change via legal and nonviolent means such as elections, petitions, and pacific protest. The closing down of legal routes in the 1970s, however, pushed many organizations toward more drastic measures. The 1972 national elections offer a prime example of this process. Several moderate and progressive political parties founded in the 1960s joined together in the early 1970s to form an opposition coalition, the Unión Nacional Opositora (National Opposition Union, UNO), which posed a formidable challenge to the standing national party, the conservative PCN.[89] On election day, when the UNO pulled ahead in the returns, the government stopped reporting results and declared its own PCN candidate the winner. Such blatant fraud marked the turning point for many. It was "the greatest frustration of my life," said one of my informants, María. "I told myself that I would no longer participate in the elections or in anything connected to the elections."[90] Fraud at the municipal level and national levels in the 1974 and 1977 elections prompted similar reactions.

In addition to rallying behind opposition parties at election time, campesinos and their organizations continued their commitment to a nationwide *lucha reivindicativa campesina*. At the forefront of the movement during this period was the Federación de Trabajadores del Campo (Rural Workers Federation, FTC), formally established in 1976 and comprised of the UTC and

FECCAS.[91] Even a brief glimpse of the FTC's activities illustrates the affiliates' willingness to engage the Salvadoran state in peaceful negotiations. In 1976 it presented petitions to the Salvadoran Legislative Assembly requesting reform of the country's land rental laws and demanding improvements in salary, food, and working conditions for coffee harvest workers. Between 1978 and 1980 it submitted additional petitions to the ministries of labor and agriculture, as well as the Agricultural Development Bank, related to labor conditions, rural credit, fertilizer prices, and, again, land rental rules. State officials often denied or simply ignored these petitions.

In light of the state response to citizens' demands (or lack of response in the case of petitions), campesinos increasingly resorted to nonviolent demonstrations and protests. In November 1976, for example, campesino affiliates and supporters of the UTC and FECCAS staged simultaneous marches in the towns of Cancasque (Chalatenango), Ilobasco (Cabañas), Zacatecoluca (La Paz), and Quezaltepeque (La Libertad) to pressure the Ministry of Labor for a positive response to petitions previously submitted by the FTC. Although such public displays attracted attention and garnered additional support for the campesinos' cause, it also drew the ire of the authorities. They called in the military to extinguish the Quezaltepeque protest and followed up in December with military operations against numerous FECCAS and UTC bases, including Las Vueltas and Cancasque in Chalatenango.

Violence against *campesinos organizados* (organized peasants) and their communities certainly led some people to curb their activities; for many others, however, it had the opposite effect. Convinced that their demands were just, campesinos stepped up their efforts and adopted even more contentious methods. "After attempting every possible legal route to negotiate our revindication platforms," one member explained, "it was necessary to initiate other types of struggle."[92] Toward these ends they began occupying government offices, including the Ministry of Labor and the Agricultural Development Bank on separate occasions in 1978 and 1979. They also led a strike at the La Cabaña sugar mill and a series of land takeovers in at least seven of the country's fourteen departments. These actions, according to the FTC, were designed to denounce the intransigence of national officials, demand the government's response to their "just requests," and "unmask at national and international levels the demagoguery, reformist and repressive politics" of the Salvadoran government.[93]

In addition to these actions, campesinos increasingly lent support to and collaborated with other sectors during the 1970s. Affiliates of the FTC rallied in support of dozens of labor strikes in the electrical, textile, food, and mining industries. "We participated in the strikes of the workers in San Salvador, in La Diana, Fábrica de León and others," Víctor recalled. "Here in Chalate every three days we chose a delegation, some 500 people, to go to the demonstration in San Salvador. There they left in one factory, in another, and so on, so that peasants spent three days and nights with the workers. They were relieved by 500 new people."[94] Northerners also took part in the 1975 occupation of the National Cathedral in San Salvador to protest the government's violent repression of students and educators.[95]

Perhaps the most radical alliances that campesinos established during the 1970s were those with the emerging politico-military groups. Several such groups had begun to take shape in San Salvador the previous decade and formalized their associations in the early 1970s. By the mid-1970s they had moved beyond the confines of the capital city to seek bases of support in rural areas. The Fuerzas Populares de Liberación (Popular Liberation Forces, FPL), formalized in 1970, found especially strong support in the departments of Cabañas and Chalatenango. Representatives of the FPL made their first contacts with campesino communities in this region in 1972 and 1973 through shared links with progressive Catholics and members of the teachers' association, the Asociación Nacional de Educadores Salvadoreños 21 de junio (National Association of Salvadoran Educators 21 of June, ANDES). Politico-military organizations arrived in northern Morazán a bit later, in 1974 and 1975. There Father Miguel Ventura, a supporter of the CEB movement, facilitated early conversations between campesino leaders and a representative of the Ejército Revolucionario Popular (Popular Revolutionary Army, ERP), which was formalized in the first two years of the decade. Military harassment of campesinos organizados in the region, along with increased levels of violence throughout the country, provided the original impetus for the contact; catechists "sensed that they needed to link up with a broader organization that might provide them protection."[96] The organization's platforms and goals resonated with many campesinos, and they initiated collaborations of varying degrees.[97]

Throughout the 1970s, the campesinos' efforts—even with support from other sectors—produced limited success. The smallest gains, however, had a huge impact. The salary increase achieved by campesino laborers at Hacienda La Cabaña in May 1973, for example, inspired many to take their commitment to change to new levels. This is especially interesting given that some had joined the ranks of the strikers without politicized objectives. One striker recalled, "Without any political clarity we decided that we wouldn't let ourselves get screwed any longer and that we would denounce injustice."[98] The fact that the hacienda owners ultimately paid the strikers the full salary they demanded "was an example of the path that the people were constructing." That is, by joining together in defense of their rights, such as fair pay, campesinos could prompt positive change.

Campesinos encountered more hardships than gains, however, as a result of their activities and heightened profile. While they formalized their organizations, engaged in pressure tactics, and allied themselves with other sectors of the popular movement, state security forces continued to grow, intelligence networks strengthened, and the activities of vigilante groups and death squads increased. As the popular movement became radicalized, the government's responses were ever more violent. The next chapter will discuss this violence in more detail; it is important to note here, however, that petitions to government offices prompted the sack of organizational offices and the arrest and "disappearance" of leaders; protest marches and strikes invited reprisals by national security forces; and rural communities involved in any kind of organizational activities courted military operations, assassinations of individuals, and massacres of large groups.

For many people repression only served to deepen their commitment to la lucha. For others who had not yet become involved, state-sponsored violence spurred them into action. One of the men who took part in the strike at La Cabaña explained, "Due to the threats of La Cabaña's [National] Guard authorities, we saw that it wasn't just necessary to organize, but it was a serious urgency. That is when the organization [FECCAS] started to spread in this area." In this particular case the "threats" did not lead to murder, as would happen in so many other situations. They did, however, lead to blacklisting of the troublesome laborers. Such an outcome made affiliation with FECCAS and other organizations all the more appealing. Thus, even as they faced loss of employment, threats, and physical repression, campesinos did not stop pressing for change. Rather they turned to more clandestine methods of organizing. Communities established security measures, including the formation of *comisiones de seguridad y autodefensa* (security and self-defense commissions), which will be discussed in the next chapter. They also continued to build associations with other sectors of Salvadoran society. Indeed, throughout the 1970s, state-sponsored violence in many ways served to unify the myriad organizations against a common enemy. Perhaps the most obvious evidence of this was the January 1980 march of some 250,000 people under the banner "Unity of the Democratic and Revolutionary Forces." The military opened fire on the demonstrators, and the country spiraled into the era campesinos refer to as *la guerra abierta* (open war).

The Flames of Revolution

Northern El Salvador emerged onto the national scene not because of the machinations of either liberation theologians or members of politico-military organizations but rather due to the initiatives of the campesinos themselves. The north's position as the tierra olvidada on the literal and figurative margins of the nation entailed hardship, to be sure, but it also allowed inhabitants significant freedom from economic, political, and social pressures common in the rest of the country. This presented people with unique opportunities, among which was the development of extended spaces of livelihood. These spaces brought crucial economic benefits. They also entailed networking and a high degree of mobility, both of which facilitated campesino organization and mobilization through the end of the twentieth century.

Despite the assumption that the Salvadoran government's violent reaction to the 1932 uprising of agriculturists in the western districts terrorized campesinos throughout the country into passivity, campesinos in fact continued to be active. The manner in which they mobilized, however, shifted through the course of the century from primarily local levels through the 1950s to regional and national levels in the 1960s and after and from site- and sector-specific demands to more ethereal demands for justice and democracy.

Campesinos from the northern departments played a pivotal role in the formation of a campesino rights movement that by the 1970s became "a major channel for the questioning of the [authoritarian] regime" in El Salvador.[99] Although their own initiatives were fundamental in this process, alliances with "outsiders" also played an influential role. Association with progressive priests, labor unions, students, and politico-military groups such as the ERP and FPL brought new resources to communities and their struggles: material resources, rhetoric with which to discuss the problems they faced, and broader contexts in which to view the campesino struggle. Such resources helped to transform local or rural-specific grievances into national-level grievances. Through this process campesinos came to view themselves as important figures not only in terms of the campesino rights struggle but also with regard to the broader popular movement to free the country from military dictatorship and install a new government that was fair and just. In the words of one FTC document, the campesino sector was "one of the determinate and decisive forces" in the struggle for national liberation. "The flames of revolution burn once again in the rural areas of our country," the document continued, evoking the memory of the 1932 uprising. The liberation of El Salvador would depend "on this fire not being doused."[100]

2

Organizing Flight

The Guinda *System*

María C. was in her early twenties when the Salvadoran armed forces adopted a counterinsurgency strategy known as *tierra arrasada* (scorched earth). She was married and had several children, one of whom was an infant girl. One day in 1979, la Guardia—El Salvador's National Guard—attacked María's village in northeastern Chalatenango province. She and her family, along with a few neighbors, escaped into the mountains and took shelter in a *tatú*, an underground cave they had prepared for precisely this purpose. They stayed in hiding for about five days as troops scoured the area looking for the campesinos they suspected of being communist subversives. During that time, María's baby grew increasingly restless and hungry, but because María herself had had nothing to eat or drink for days she produced no milk to feed her child. The girl's cries became louder and more desperate. At one point, when soldiers drew near to their place of refuge, María covered the child's mouth with a rag to stifle her cries so that their hiding place would not be discovered. When the soldiers finally retreated and María uncovered her newborn's mouth, she found that her child was dead. María had smothered her own baby.

How could María have committed such an unspeakable act? It may seem impossible for many of us to understand. Yet María was just one of many who did so. And, as this chapter will demonstrate, such a horrible action made complete sense within a particular Salvadoran context of war flight known as *la guinda*.[1]

The literature on war displacement rarely examines the displaced themselves as actors in or agents of history. Rather the emphasis is on explicitly political actors: governments, political parties, well-organized revolutionaries, and international organizations. As studies focus on these political actors, they essentialize rural folk. Peasants appear as an indistinguishable mass of poor people forced to flee their homes; as a result, they are in desperate need of protection and assistance. They are marked by the loss of home, livelihood, family members and loved ones, representation, rights, culture, and nation. Their journey represents a radical departure from tradition; a chasm appears between "before" and "after." Often the ultimate solution is for these poor folk to wait out the war so that they may return home to their peasant ways.

Such representations assume a number of things. First, they adopt a state-centric perspective in which nations are "perceived as an organic and necessary order." The powerful hegemony of this order leads to the perception of displaced populations as anomalies, problems to be solved in the interest of preserving "the national order of things."[2] In a related vein, traditional approaches to the war displaced assume as natural and given the connections between people/citizens and places/nations. Violence and war, then, can contribute to the creation of uncategorizable peoples: the dis-placed, uprooted, stateless. In the light of these assumptions, movement is a negative event rather than a productive or creative process.[3]

These tendencies play out in the literature on Central American conflicts of the late twentieth century. This historiography presents the war displaced primarily as object populations. This is understandable to some extent; it is a relatively recent history, and therefore much of the existing literature was published during the wars by participants—governments and organizations with clear intentions of gaining support for one side or the other in a given conflict. As such, studies tended to focus on the "root causes" of conflict and displacement: government counterinsurgency tactics *or* guerrilla actions; state-sponsored death squad activity *or* international communist agitation; right *or* left. Within this trend, the majority of studies accentuated the misfortunes of the war displaced in an effort to place blame and hold some party accountable.

Equally problematic in the literature is the discussion of campesino lives in terms of "before" and "after." Flight became the dividing line between past and present; as such, it symbolized separation and rupture. The displaced entered into a fog, a holding pattern; they disappeared as campesinos and, until they returned home, existed only as refugees (read victims).

Within Salvadoran historiography this before/after dividing point was 1980. This was when mass displacements began in earnest. It was also the year in which five politico-military organizations joined together to form the FMLN. After this point campesinos literally disappear as agents. Many studies have assumed that the FMLN "was the only expression of opposition and dissent in the country, and the war between the guerrillas and the Salvadoran Army was the only arena of struggle."[4] Due to increased levels of violence, this version of history argued, civil society organizations disbanded. Campesino organizations were no exception to this assumed rule. And, although these same studies pointed to a resurgence of civil society organizations by 1984, campesino groups remained absent from the historical record. The organizations described in chapter 1—whether in the localized form of campesino mutual aid groups, directivas, or CEBs or as national groups like the UTC and FECCAS—rarely appear during the 1980s. When they do, as in the case of directivas, they appear as creations of the FMLN. Thus, throughout the 1980s, campesinos do not appear as agents; instead they are victims either manipulated by the FMLN or forced by government troops into the sad roles of internally displaced persons or international refugees.

María C.'s story provides initial insights into an alternative perspective. First, María and her family had time to escape into the mountains and evade apprehension (or worse) by government soldiers, which suggests that they had prior knowledge or warning of the troops' arrival. That her family fled to a specific and predetermined location in the northern highlands—a man-made bomb shelter—indicates a high level of predeparture preparation. Second, María and her family remained buried in their underground hideaway for nearly a week, voluntarily denying themselves water, food, sunlight, and fresh air. Moreover, María deliberately silenced her children as soldiers drew near and took extreme measures to keep them quiet even though it meant snuffing out the youngest life in the tatú. The intentional and calculated nature of these actions suggests a willingness to sacrifice, which, in turn, begs questions about rationales and objectives. Finally, it cannot be ignored that María and her companions chose to flee rather than remain in their houses and towns. Of course, in the context of civil war, fear of injury or death certainly can be motivation enough for a decision to change locations. Yet where María went and what she did (and did not do) while there indicates a level of resistance— opposition even—to the soldiers and the government they represented.

This chapter expands on the initial insights provided by María's story to make three interrelated arguments. First, it examines how campesinos organizados in El Salvador's northern highlands developed a system of community security to respond to increasing violence in the 1970s and early 1980s. Within this system, mobility—and specifically la guinda—evolved as a key self-defense tactic. Placing la guinda within the broader context of community organizations allows a reformulation of war flight; rather than a random, spur of the moment act, it becomes a deliberate maneuver and part of a larger process or system. Second, although guindas in many ways were linked to prewar mobilizations, the contexts of extreme violence and civil war prompted significant changes in the community ethos that authorized—indeed, encouraged—acts and behaviors that simply would not have been accepted in "normal" times. Violence—and specifically state-sponsored violence—blurred the social and political distinctions between campesinos and helped to tighten bonds between them. As such, a unique moral economy emerged among northern campesinos. Third, the acts undertaken in these "exceptional" times comprised a new layer of resistance to the Salvadoran government. Rather than war flight *happening to* campesinos, campesinos as individuals and groups made tactical decisions about flight in an effort not only to survive but also to continue challenging the authority and legitimacy of the state.

Civil War, State-Sponsored Violence, and *Gente Consciente*

Most scholarly assessments of El Salvador's civil war mark 1980 as the "official start" of the war. Although some campesinos contest this start date, they agree that 1980 was indeed a remarkable year. In 1980 the civilian-military junta (established in the wake of an October 1979 coup that ousted military dictator Gen. Carlos Humberto Romero) crumbled as it implemented a highly controversial land reform program. In the same year the FMLN formed and vowed to bring "peace, liberty, well-being and progress to the Salvadoran people."[5] At the same time, marches and demonstrations drew tens—even hundreds—of thousands of civilians into the streets to demand rights, protest violations, and urge the reform of El Salvador's social, economic, and political systems.[6]

The year 1980 also brought new levels of violence as "government measures and illegal repressive measures were taken to dismantle the country's legal structure and neutralize the opposition. . . . Organized terrorism, in the form of the so-called 'death squads,' became the most aberrant manifestation of the escalation of violence."[7] The murder of Archbishop Oscar Romero in March and the arrest, rape, and murder of four U.S. churchwomen by members of the National Guard in December illustrated well that no one was safe from state-sponsored terrorism. By the end of the year, more than eight thousand people had died, eight times the number murdered in 1979.[8]

Violence hit the rural population especially hard; campesinos accounted for more than 78 percent of the dead in 1980, and, through the end of the war in 1992, 95 percent of the reported acts of violence had occurred in rural areas.[9] This led the UN-sponsored Truth Commission to conclude that the

Salvadoran government's violence against the campesino population during the war was "systematic," a "pattern of conduct, a deliberate strategy of eliminating or terrifying the peasant population." Perhaps not surprisingly, the pattern was especially apparent "in areas where the guerrillas were active." The intention, noted the commission, was "to deprive the guerrilla forces of this source of supplies and information and of the possibility of hiding or concealing themselves among that population."[10]

An effect of the violence not directly addressed by the Truth Commission, and rarely given more than a passing glance in scholarly studies of the war, was the displacement of approximately one-quarter of El Salvador's population.[11] As early as 1982 the UNHCR reported assisting nearly 40,000 of an estimated 180,000 Salvadoran refugees in locations throughout the Central American isthmus. More than half of the assisted refugees resided in UN-sponsored refugee camps in Honduras alone, a subject to which I turn in later chapters.[12] A few years later, in late 1984, investigators from the UCA estimated that nearly three-quarters of a million Salvadorans had left the country for other Central American nations, Mexico, and the United States.[13]

In addition to those who sought refuge outside the country, hundreds of thousands remained displaced within El Salvador's borders. Socorro Jurídico, the legal aid office affiliated with San Salvador's archbishopric, estimated that between 111,000 and 119,000 individuals were displaced in 1981 alone. By 1984 that number had risen to nearly 500,000. The vast majority of these—nearly 90 percent—were people from rural areas.[14] Later chapters examine in detail the experience of campesinos who spent years outside El Salvador. The remainder of this chapter focuses on the internally displaced.

Rural Salvadorans had many characteristics in common, yet not all shared the same experiences of displacement. The armed forces evacuated tens of thousands of campesinos from rural zones throughout the country and relocated them to areas (both rural and urban) protected by the government. Sometimes such relocations were voluntary; at other times they were forced. Thousands more sought relative anonymity in large urban areas, especially San Salvador, which endured less violence throughout much of the 1980s. Some of these individuals and families received assistance from the archbishopric, many others lived with relatives or friends, and still others settled in shantytowns on the outskirts of the capital. In addition, hundreds of thousands of campesinos remained displaced in their zones of origin, eking out a living "on their own and with great hardship."[15]

Displacement also varied by region. The majority of the internally displaced people were "self-evacuated" campesinos in "permanently conflictive zones," including Chalatenango, Morazán, Cabañas, and San Vicente.[16] A 1982 study conducted by El Salvador's Comisión Nacional para los Desplazados (National Commission for the Displaced, CONADES) determined that these four departments accounted for nearly 60 percent of the CONADES-assisted displaced persons. These numbers stand in stark contrast to just 2.8 percent from the four western departments of Ahuachapán, Santa Ana, Sonsonate, and La Libertad.[17] The CONADES study and others conducted throughout the 1980s reveal an important trend: departments with the highest percentages of displacement were precisely those that hosted the strongest popular organizations and mobilizations in the 1970s and early 1980s. These were also the departments where the FMLN established its most secure bases throughout the 1980s and 1990s.

Such variations in experiences of displacement were in part due to the different political experiences among campesinos. Campesinos became involved in numerous activities with political relevance in the post–World War II period. These activities ranged from government-sponsored cooperatives and organizations (such as Joya de Cerén, the UCS, and ORDEN) to independent cooperatives and leagues (including FECCAS and the UTC), from the progressive CEBs to more conservative lay leadership, and from community councils to armed opposition groups. In the late 1970s and early 1980s, a general tendency emerged: campesinos who had become involved with community organizations and had taken part in the increasingly radicalized mobilizations tended to remain in the northern border region while those less committed to such activities and least sympathetic to the FMLN abandoned the area. In northern Morazán, for example, Binford estimated that some 60 percent of the prewar population either fled the area entirely or moved to municipal centers such as San Francisco Gotera.[18]

In light of this, "villages in the FMLN-controlled zones were not ordinary communities."[19] They were the *comunidades organizadas*, often comprised of the *gente consciente*—the politically conscious people committed (at least to some degree) to la lucha. Thus, it is no surprise that campesinos who remained in the north in spite of the increasingly widespread violence emphasized the fact that they were not helpless victims. Throughout the 1980s they continued and expanded on the organizational strategies that they had developed in the prewar period. Indeed, many people directly attributed their survival during the civil war to *la organización* (the organization). In the words of Domitila A., "To be able to get through these hard times, if we hadn't organized ourselves we would not have survived, because if it had been every man for himself, no one would have been saved."[20]

Mobile Communities and Self-Defense: Origins of the *Guinda* System

Just as the actions of campesinos organizados during the prewar period addressed specific needs of the rural population, so too did actions during the war respond to the exigencies of the time. In light of the increasing levels and frequency of violence in the 1970s and early 1980s, security became paramount for communities in the northern highlands. Like María C., whose story opened this chapter, many campesinos became part of an ever-evolving system of community security. Mobility evolved as a key tactic within this system.

The ability to move from one place to another was not new in terms of campesino lifestyles. For decades, economic survival for campesinos had depended on migration between one's home and various maize and bean plots, between one's rural community and urban markets in El Salvador and Honduras, and between one's own subsistence cultivation and wage labor at the coffee, cotton, and sugar harvests across El Salvador and the fruit plantations on the north coast of Honduras. Campesinos also traveled both near and far to sell and obtain products, wares, and services, including water, agricultural materials, education, and health care.

By the same token Salvadoran government and military officials had long been aware of the importance of campesino mobility and the strengths and advantages it afforded the rural population. Fear of uprisings, along with economic and political needs, prompted national leaders to institute various restrictions and controls on rural movement: vagrancy laws, prohibitions on rural collective organizing, the creation of specialized rural security forces, and requirements for identity and travel documentation.

In some ways, these efforts had a limited effect. By the late 1960s campesinos had already tapped into the tradition of movement as a resource for general collective organizing initiatives. People established connections and built alliances through the Campesino Training Program and universidades campesinas located throughout the country. And information about meetings of the UTC and other campesino groups, as well as protest actions, continued to pass between individuals on rural footpaths, at markets and religious worship, and at the rivers where people went to bathe and collect water for household use. By the turn of the decade, however, mobility had also become a physical self-defense mechanism and, as such, took on new meanings and importance. It was around this time that campesinos from northern El Salvador coined the term "guinda" to denote purposeful, temporary flight from one's home and community to evade government troops and violence.

The beginnings of the guinda system occurred in the mid-1970s when men began to voluntarily depart from their homes. By 1975 many men from northern Chalatenango no longer slept in their own houses; before dusk they headed into the mountains and woods surrounding their towns where they were less likely to be caught by the military and paramilitary forces that targeted campesinos. A similar process occurred in northern Morazán; late 1977 marked the beginning of "an all-out pursuit of catechists regardless of their political sympathies," which prompted many community leaders to go into clandestinity.[21]

In many instances it was the most overtly organized men—catechists and members of CEBs and directivas, as well as campesino organizations such as the UTC and FECCAS—who sought refuge outside the boundaries of their villages. While men headed to the hills, women initially stayed behind with the elderly and children. At first their solitude was not especially noteworthy given that, traditionally, men were often away, sometimes for days at a time, tending to the family's *milpas* (corn and bean fields).[22] Thus, the security forces initially presumed that the women were harmless and left them alone. The levels of harassment steadily increased, however, and eventually troops targeted women simply based on their kinship ties to the men who were assumed to be guerrilla collaborators or combatants. And so women, too, began to move. Some joined their menfolk in the hills at night to sleep. As Ana from northern Morazán explained, "I never wanted to sleep at home, that's why the soldiers didn't find me there when they arrived."[23] Other women joined their mothers, sisters, and aunts in other houses or towns in an effort to evade harassment. "They sought her out because she was my wife," Félix L. explained. "They said she had to turn me in and if she didn't they would imprison her. So then she had to flee, moving from house to house through the neighborhood so she wouldn't be captured."[24]

Due to harassment, many individuals and families chose to abandon their hometowns in the mid- and late 1970s. Those living in the smallest and most isolated hamlets were often the first to do so; concerned that it was too dangerous to remain secluded, they sought safety in larger population centers, including neighboring towns and municipal capitals. María and her children, for example, relocated from the small hamlet of Guacamaya, Morazán, to the nearby town of El Mozote after soldiers killed several men in her hometown, including her husband.[25] In a similar process, many inhabitants of the hamlet of Los Valles in Chalatenango relocated to Portillo del Norte, a larger town nearby.[26] This relocation process transformed many of the tiniest rural villages into virtual ghost towns. *Desierto* (deserted) and *vacío* (vacant) were common refrains among people describing the rural north during the civil war. Salvador

Cayetano "Marcial" Carpio, a leader of the FPL, described his visits to the northern war zones in a 1982 interview. "One of my strongest recollections," he said, "are the enormous stretches where villages are completely overgrown with weeds. From far off in the mountains you can see the settlements which you'll pass through. . . . And when you get closer . . . it's sad. Beautiful little houses left behind. You can see the care the peasants used to put into their homes. All this, all of it covered with weeds. All the furniture, whatever these peasants had, thrown out and burned. And most of the houses themselves burned. Over a huge area there are dozens and dozens of villages like this."[27]

By the late 1970s entire communities also began taking to the hills on temporary escape journeys. These group flights, the true guindas, ranged from a few hours and short distances to multiple years and hundreds of kilometers throughout El Salvador and beyond. Likewise, the size of groups ranged from a few families to several thousand campesinos. Although reasons for joining both short- and long-term guindas varied, nearly all campesinos cited as an important factor the increase in military sweeps, often referred to as *invasiones* (invasions).

The government's scorched earth campaigns of the early 1980s had a great impact on campesinos in the north. The drawings of child survivors of such operations graphically portray this: soldiers setting fire to a house, young girls tied up and machine-gunned to death, a man hanging by the neck from a tree limb, blows with machetes and batons, bullets flying through the air, and bombs falling from helicopters. Adults used words to draw similar pictures. "Almost everything was destroyed," explained one man. "The armed forces destroyed all the good houses, they lit them on fire or smashed the tile roofs, tore down the wooden walls and everything so they left nothing."[28] Victoria M. told of similar horrors: "They set fire to the grain. If they found a cornfield standing in bloom, they cut it down. If it was dry, they set fire to it. If they found animals, they killed them. . . . Nothing escaped from them."[29]

Understandably, the apparently indiscriminate attacks prompted great fear, which propelled thousands of campesinos out of their villages and into the rough wilderness of the highlands border area.[30] "You should have seen us in '80, running through the countryside," Paquita from Morazán said. "I was with five children—we slept by the side of a river. . . . We ran here and there to avoid death. We slept one night in a ravine [*quebrada*], and twelve soldiers so very close. . . . That's how we would pass the night, and early in the morning we would leave again."[31] Largely because of their unanticipated and frenzied nature, the sheer number of people fleeing, and the high number of casualties, the first mass guindas of the early 1980s remain deeply inscribed in campesino war memories. Chalatecos (those from Chalatenango province) clearly recall the guinda of May 1980, during which some 6,500 campesinos took flight in an effort to escape from one of the first scorched earth operations in the region. One of the unfortunate outcomes of this guinda was the death of more than 600 people at the Sumpul River. For many of those who survived the guinda and horrific river crossing, the sight and sound of the water—even twenty years later—causes great pain and discomfort. During a picnic at the river's edge with a group from Arcatao in 2003, I watched as an older campesino separated himself from the group and found a solitary seat downstream. His knees pulled close to his chest, he gazed out at the water and lost himself in thought. After I joined him, we continued to sit in silence until I said, simply, "This place must bring back memories." He nodded slowly and evenly but said nothing. The sounds of children splashing and playing in the water floated down to us from around the bend. After perhaps five more minutes of silence, he spoke. In a quiet, careful voice, he recalled the guinda of May 1980 when he survived the Sumpul River Massacre by hiding under the body of his dead wife.

Other guindas and their consequences hold similarly eminent positions in campesino memories. In Morazán the first military sweep through the northern stretches in November 1980 left some three thousand dead and pushed more than one hundred thousand *en guinda* (on a guinda) through the border region.[32] Campesinos throughout the north-central region of El Salvador recall the *guinda de mayo* (May guinda) of 1982 and the 1983 *guinda del Guazapa diez* (guinda of the Guazapa ten). Some guindas came to be known by the name of the military commander in charge of the operation, such as Chávez Carreño or Ochoa, and others the official military designation such as the 1986 Operación Fénix (Phoenix Operation). By applying names to specific incidents, Salvadoran campesinos bestowed on them the important role of referent or symbol of violence and injustice. A simple reference to *el Ochoa* or *la Fénix* serves as sort of authorization of movement; the violence perpetrated by the state dictated that they move.

In much the same way, survivors described—often in terrible detail—what happened to those who did not join the guindas. Salvador explained how on one occasion five people stayed behind in his hometown. Despite the fact that the five were "elderly, blind and crippled," soldiers "pulled them out of bed and left them in the yard, in pieces. A bit further on [the soldiers] came to another hamlet. They hung those folks up and collected everything in that house, table and bed, and they set fire to the pile. They burned those women alive. . . . That's what most motivated people to leave. Many people died there."[33] Ignacia M. from Delicias de Concepción in Morazán recalled how "the army killed two of my sons and my mother-in-law in the cottage where she lived. They burnt her with all her possessions. She was an elderly woman, seventy-five years old."[34] If state-sponsored terrorism authorized movement, stories and descriptions of this sort served as justification for departure. In other words, given the probable consequences of staying behind, campesinos deemed flight the best option. Thus, when airplanes appeared on the horizon or soldiers arrived to the area around one's village, Domitila from Chalatenango explained, "everyone left because you knew that if you stayed, you'd end up dead."[35] José agreed, "There was no other choice."[36]

It is relevant to note that not all campesinos took flight directly in response to the ground sweeps conducted by the Salvadoran armed forces. Some people identified other reasons, including a more direct targeting by armed forces and death squads. For example, in the Tenancingo district of Cuscatlán department, which borders the department of Cabañas, government soldiers imprisoned a young girl's father and three brothers, and then returned for her. "They forced me to point out people and then shot them," she explained. She and her family, along with many of her neighbors, "hadn't committed any crime—we had only tried to participate in the movement of Jesus Christ and Monseñor Romero."[37] Other testimonies offer an impression of being caught in the contest between the insurgent and government forces. A family in northern Morazán described how FMLN soldiers arrived in their town and began harassing men of military age who had completed their required stint in the national military. With the arrival of the FMLN, the family also began to fear a government attack. After carefully maneuvering FMLN gatekeepers, the family was able to leave the area. Their subsequent experience with government forces, however, was not much better; soldiers called them "subversives" and told them to "Get out of here because if you don't, you'll die too. Because the orders we have are to leave no one alive [*no dejar casa ni gente*]." With that warning, the family continued on its journey, ultimately arriving in San Salvador.[38]

It is also important to note that some campesinos made the decision to remain at home and endure. Sometimes the elderly or infirm simply could not leave. Others wanted to remain close to the grave sites of loved ones who had already perished in the violence. Still others insisted on staying to protect their houses, land, and other belongings or investments.[39] And a number of individuals and families allied themselves with the FMLN and received a measure of protection in the zones under insurgent control. Thus, although the war destroyed hundreds of towns across the northern borderlands and dozens more stood only as ghost towns, the northern border region was never fully depopulated during the war.[40] Despite these variations, a general pattern existed, for the widespread death and destruction caused by the armed forces' scorched earth counterinsurgency efforts prompted tens of thousands of campesinos to join the guindas.

Formalization of the *Guinda* System

At the time of the first massive ground sweeps in the late 1970s and early 1980s, campesinos did not yet have a defined response to them. Communities were taken by surprise; military forces suddenly arrived in town, and when the harassment and shooting commenced, people simply took to the hills without the planning and coordination of later years. Esperanza O. explained how at first "the organization was weak in the sense that we didn't have any experience, and maybe we didn't believe it, the point to which the government army was capable of killing whoever was in front of them, a child, a pregnant woman, an old man, defenseless people." Campesinos learned from their first experiences, however, and quickly adapted their strategies to the probability of additional such flights in the future. "After we saw the examples [of what the soldiers were capable of]," continued Esperanza, "we had to look for other mechanisms."[41] They began to adapt their prewar security tactics; although self-defense—survival—remained the ultimate objective, the meanings and significance attributed to that survival shifted over time. Whereas initially guindas were to a large extent an unorganized reaction to state-sponsored violence, over time and with conscious planning they became an action of resistance.

One of the first steps in formalizing the guinda strategy was for directivas to expand their work in the security realm. Many did so by creating new subcommittees specifically assigned to protection issues, including guard patrols and night watch stations. They also called community meetings to identify and ready specific places of refuge. From these assemblies arose the idea of utilizing the many natural caves scattered throughout the hills of northern El Salvador. Groups of men formed exploration commissions, which scoured the countryside in search of caves and other sites to use as possible refuges in the event of another guinda. These teams found dozens of caves; some were quite small, offering shelter to only a few people, while others were much larger, holding eighty or one hundred people. Depending on size and location, caves served for the remainder of the war as either temporary bomb shelters and hideouts from ground troops or longer-term housing for campesinos whose own houses had been destroyed in the war. In testimonies collected during the early 1980s, campesinos from Chalatenango and Cabañas frequently noted having spent several weeks or months hiding out in caves, and those from

Morazán told of living for a year or more in a series of caves in the border zone between El Salvador and Honduras.

Communities also began to design and construct their own underground caves, called tatús, as early as 1980.[42] They were typically dug vertically into the ground about two or three meters deep, with a narrower opening and wider body. Bamboo rods strategically embedded in the earth around the tatú served as *respiraderos* or air tunnels. Campesinos covered the entrances to their tatús with *tablas*, shallow wooden boxes filled with soil, stones, leaves, and brush. When the tabla was in place, it was level with the surrounding land so that "there were times when the soldiers passed right over the top of you and they had no idea that they were stepping on you." The irony of such situations was more than obvious to the campesinos. In the words of one man, "We saved ourselves by burying ourselves alive."[43]

Campesinos not only constructed their tatús "calmly, with patience"; they also took great care in choosing their locations. According to Felipe T., he and others from his town in Chalatenango divided into groups of two or three families, and then, with the help of the directiva, each group staked out a site for a tatú. Only directiva members knew the locations of all the town's tatús; a family did not share the location of its tatú with other groups because, as Santiago O. explained, "nobody knew if they would be captured by the enemy and then end up saying 'There's one.'"

Another important adaptation in campesino defense strategies at this time was the expansion of intelligence gathering into the military realm. More specifically, campesinos collected information about Salvadoran military patterns; a better understanding of official patterns increased the probabilities for successful guindas because it meant that campesinos could predict what was to come and respond accordingly. A typical military pattern consisted of a period of exploration followed by a bombing run and, finally, invasion by ground troops. "They did two hours of exploration, the small planes first," explained Elías M. "They explored the terrain in the area where the guerrillas were. Then came the A37s—the bombings, right? The indiscriminate bombings. . . . Each plane threw 22 bombs, they were 250-pound bombs." Elías's wife Catalina continued, "When you heard the helicopters, everyone left the houses."

As these comments indicate, campesinos became remarkably adept at identifying military patterns. They were able to tell the difference between various types of airplanes and helicopters by sound as well as sight. Likewise, campesinos could distinguish battalions not only by uniform insignia and type of helmet but also by the sound of their guns, the boot prints and spent ammunition the soldiers left behind, and the graffiti and torture marks they inflicted on human bodies.[44] Such distinctions were crucial. The Batallones de Infantería de Reacción Inmediata (Rapid Deployment Infantry Brigades, BIRIs) were among the few companies that attacked at night, and they were known to be especially savage in their treatment of campesinos.[45] In a similar vein, different aircraft served different purposes. Some delivered 500-pound bombs while others dropped 250 pounders; some carried troops while others sprayed defoliants such as white phosphorous and napalm. Identifying such specifics enabled campesinos to make better decisions regarding guindas: when to leave, how far to go, how long to stay away. "We were always forewarned," José R. said. "We'd always know about an invasion that was coming." The arrival of helicopters at the military garrisons signaled the movement of troops in and out of the zone, he continued. In addition, directivas from different areas would provide tips to one another regarding troop movements.[46] Amado V., noting similar tactics, recalled, "When there was an exploration, we had already figured out that . . . within three days, the military operation would hit. If we saw airplanes doing fly-overs, either in the day or at night, then we started preparing the conditions [*preparando las condiciones*]."[47]

In many ways preparation grew easier with experience. That is, with each flight cycle campesinos acquired new tricks and strategies to facilitate survival and ease hardships en guinda. For example, people initially brought animals with them to carry and provide milk for the children. Quickly, however, they realized that the animals made the campesinos an easier target: they were often big and slow moving and loud, they left tracks that were difficult to conceal, and they were impossible to hide. Another early lesson emerged from experiences when multiple thousands traveled together; the large groups drew attention more easily and attacks on these *hormigueros* (literally "anthills") inevitably resulted in a high number of casualties.[48] In an attempt to avoid more unfortunate outcomes, campesinos began traveling in much smaller groups; this facilitated quick, quiet movement and made detection more difficult. Estimates of the number of campesinos en guinda at any one time varied, yet by examining the many different numbers a general trend does emerge. When describing the guindas of the early 1980s, campesinos often offered numbers in the thousands or tens of thousands. The same campesinos distinguished guindas of the mid-1980s by the number of families that participated: ten, fifteen, or perhaps twenty-five. We can attribute this reduction in the size of guindas at least in part to the utilization of tatús and caves for protection; after all, a finite number of people could fit into each space. José G., who recalled his own community divided into groups of ten families—about a hundred people per group—offered further explanation: "Only a few families, in small groups, to not have such a conglomeration of people because it was easier to defend a few people in many different places than to have a huge group of people in one single spot."[49]

Here it bears mentioning that FMLN soldiers sometimes helped protect campesinos en guinda. They did so both directly, by accompanying them, and less directly through the provision of information on government troop movements. Although I will discuss campesino–FMLN alliances in more detail later, it is relevant to note here that in the first years of the 1980s, FMLN battalions often traveled side by side with the mobile communities and thus provided significant protection. In 1984, however, things changed. As El Salvador became one of the world's largest recipients of U.S. military assistance, the government shifted to a "low-intensity warfare" strategy that entailed carrying out massive air campaigns (often followed by ground sweeps) in the northern departments.[50] The government's shift in tactics, in turn, prompted the FMLN to make the transition to smaller, more mobile units that carried out quick and irregular strikes against government forces and installations. In addition the FMLN sought to expand both the military and political fronts of the war to new sites, including the capital San Salvador and its environs.[51] These strategic changes made it impossible for the guerrillas to travel with and protect large groups of civilians. And this, in turn, affected the size and operation of the guindas.

As with the size of the guindas, experience prompted other changes. Over time a system of norms emerged, which passed from the more knowledgeable and organized campesinos to the less experienced via modeling, informal conversations, and formal workshops or presentations known as *orientaciones* (orientations). Part of the duty of orientation leaders was to convince the more hesitant community members to join upcoming guindas. Most instruction, however, focused on preparatory initiatives of benefit to the community as a whole such as the design of exit strategies and additional security tactics. For example, in addition to securing new sites of refuge, communities also defined specific escape routes. As one campesino put it, "We already had figured out which way we'd get out."[52] Many set up meeting points at which community members en guinda would convene after the immediate danger had passed. They also stashed water and food reserves in *buzones*, hidden receptacles or locales along designated guinda routes, and identified prime locations for *postas* (guard posts, sentries) on roads and paths leading into villages and high atop surrounding hills. The sentries typically formed a wide circle around the town, thus ensuring that the community would receive forewarning of an attack regardless of the direction from which government forces arrived. The sentries, in turn, devised numerous systems to spread the word about approaching troops.[53]

People also learned through experience and orientations how to prepare for guindas on individual and family bases. Given that reliable food sources were rare in the mountainous terrain, campesinos paid much attention to food preparation. To avoid lugging the traditional *comal* (a large, round pan made of thick clay used for toasting the staple campesino meal of corn tortillas), some campesinos made a sort of travel comal out of tin, which was much lighter and shatterproof. They also learned how to prepare foods that would not spoil quickly, including *tortilla dura*, a biscuitlike tortilla that can last for months. Many women began to make enough tortillas for several days at a time rather than per meal as was traditionally done. They packaged the extra tortillas with other easily transportable rations, such as crackers, candies, sugar, and salt, and kept them accessible in case of an emergency departure. Similarly, many packed *maritates*, bags containing a change of clothing, perhaps a thin hammock, and some sort of blanket or covering. Some also collected medicinal herbs and prepared natural remedies to help them through the hardships of flight. Families kept such things at the ready for the next guinda; this way, even when taken by surprise, they could grab the essentials on their way out the door. Some families even assigned the task of collection to specific individuals.

In addition to these preparatory efforts, campesinos learned how to behave appropriately while on the move. Many of these norms entailed blending in with their natural environment as much as possible. They learned where and how to travel in order to cover their tracks. "We walked at night," Jose R. explained. "Those hikes took place in darkness, and if it was winter time we had to bear the storms. During the day we were in hiding."[54] In addition, because government troops typically kept to higher ground, deep ravines offered substantial visual and auditory cover. Therefore, campesinos en guinda followed the "ravines, the deepest gulches" whenever possible. Water, too, helped campesinos cover their tracks, and so they often sought out "the ugliest routes," the places where "soldiers wouldn't go" or, according to one man, places where "you had to have balls" to get through.[55]

Campesinos adopted many other tricks for safe travel. They generally avoided using tarps as shelters during guindas; not only were their typically bright colors easily visible from a distance but the plastic material also made considerable noise when rustled by wind or pelted by rain. Likewise, because smoke and flames were easily visible from the air, one had to avoid lighting fires unless absolutely certain the situation was safe. "You don't even smoke cigarettes because the smoke can be detected," noted José R. "You stay in darkness, you don't make any noise, you don't light flashlights, nothing, not a thing."[56]

In a similar vein, campesinos were to wear clothing *de color de monte*, colors that matched their natural surroundings—shades of green and brown. If a white or brightly colored shirt was all one had, Amado V. explained, "what we did was to stain it with colors from the trees—for example we ground up the peel of the *nance* fruit and with that we painted our shirt. . . . Or we would grind up bits of the forest and, with that, camouflage ourselves with green."[57] Some people also attached leafy branches to their bodies to further blend in with their environment.

Although white and other colors were not formally prohibited, campesinos used both formal and informal channels to encourage each other to maintain as low a color profile as possible. Those who did not learn this particular strategy through orientations quickly picked it up while en guinda, as the more experienced campesinos did what they could to enforce this and other norms. Domitila A. explained, "If someone saw you with light-colored clothing, 'Take it off!' [they would urge you]."[58] And one usually did so for it became clear that lives depended on it.

Following these norms "was part of the security and safety for yourself and for others," Roberto A. explained, and if you did not comply "you were committing an offense against [*estaba atentando contra*] your own life and against the rest of the group."[59] Roberto's choice of the verb *atentar* is noteworthy here. It carries a hostile weight similar to the English verb *attempt* (as in "to make an attempt against"). Yet, the Spanish term moves beyond animosity and aggression to denote illicit or illegal acts committed against principles or authorities. This turn of phrase is particularly interesting given the collective nature and subaltern context of the Salvadoran guindas, for it belies the existence of significant tensions within the northern population and guinda groups.

Just as rural communities before the war were "dynamic entities whose identities and lines of unity or division were constantly being negotiated," so too were the mobile communities of the guindas.[60] Tensions existed, certainly, between genders and families but also between individuals and groups with varying political commitments. Frictions affected behavior on the ground and often produced schisms visible in local geography. For example, campesinos who participated in the guindas were critical of those who abandoned the rural zones; these were "the people who did not organize," who were committed neither to campesino rights nor to the broader Salvadoran liberation struggle. Those who remained in northern Morazán often labeled families that had abandoned the rural zones for San Francisco Gotera as *orejas* ("ears" or spies) for their known or presumed collaboration with Salvadoran government forces.[61] Those who stayed behind, in contrast, "resisted a bit."[62]

If political tensions were visible in local and regional physical geographies, so too were they visible on a national scale. Whereas campesinos organizados from Morazán tended to ally themselves with the ERP, campesinos from Chalatenango and Cabañas leaned toward the FPL. To be sure, there were exceptions to this trend, and the other three guerrilla factions gained some campesino support as well. Generally speaking, however, ERP ideologies and actions predominated in the northeastern corner of the country and the FPL (the larger of the two factions) held sway in the north-central and northwestern areas.

The language used by campesinos to describe their experiences also offers insight into some of the political tensions within the populations en guinda. Some were quite passive in their speech, as in *nos llevaron* (they took us) and *nos orientaron* (they oriented us). The frequency of this kind of language suggests that a number of campesinos felt pressured, even coerced, to join the guindas and abide by the norms. On the other end of the spectrum was an active and dynamic rhetoric, as in *nos organizamos en guinda* (we organized ourselves during the guindas) and *nos apoyamos uno al otro* (we supported each other). Occasionally campesinos adopted an oppositional stance. Several people noted with pride how they had outsmarted government security forces by *jugando la mica*, evading capture by successfully playing a sort of cat-and-mouse game. In a similar vein, some campesinos referred to the Salvadoran armed forces as "the enemy"; to defeat this enemy one had to evade the military sweeps, survive the bombings, and return home alive. Félix L. put it most eloquently, perhaps, when he explained that the gente consciente "knew perfectly well that we had come to the mountains to struggle, to work, to organize ourselves in every possible way in defense of our own pueblo."[63]

Understandably, political differences could erupt into outright conflict on occasion. Yet, for those who joined the guindas, organization and unity were crucial not only to individual survival but also to the survival of entire communities. Although campesinos did not always share the same levels of political consciousness or even the same ideologies, the guindas allowed them to develop "a common material and meaningful framework for living through, talking about, and acting upon social orders characterized by domination."[64] Given the extreme violence associated with the military sweeps and the subsequent hardships of the guindas, it became relatively easy to define oneself as a victim of repression. It followed, then, that victims would blame the perpetrators of that repression for their suffering and loss. In this way, government security forces did indeed become an enemy to campesinos en guinda even for those who would not necessarily use such a label to describe their aggressors.

This development of a relational identity parallels a shift in solidarity consciousness, and both were in large part due to the new and rather narrow focus of collective organization that emerged in light of the guindas. Before the guindas, campesinos often could choose to contribute (or not) to a variety of community efforts, including agricultural perquisites, workplace improvements, and access to resources—in short, a broad range of civil and labor rights issues. During the guindas, however, the sole concentration was on survival, the fundamental right to life. Such a narrowly focused objective in many ways served to blur distinctions and divisions between campesinos, which in turn fostered a stronger communal ethos.[65]

To be sure, campesinos felt a significant degree of pressure to follow the norms. It was rare, however, for people to highlight behavior that challenged the norms; those who did clearly harbored resentment toward the misbehaving individuals. Sebastián S. remembered one woman who would neither hide from the airplanes nor remove or cover her white shirt. "You guys are wimps [*miedosos*]," she claimed and remained where she was. "And, look," he pointed out, "they bombed us; they lit up the entire mountain."[66] When people refused to follow the established norms, they ran the risk of drawing negative attention to the communities en guinda. Indeed, to purposely not remove a bright shirt or disregard other norms translated into a sort of moral transgression or crime. (Recall Roberto A.'s use of the verb *atentar*.)

Compliance with the norms was crucial to the success of the guinda system. Indeed, to survive within the guinda context one had to think and act not only in terms of one's self and family but also in terms of the group with which one traveled, as well as the broader campesino population in the area or region. To not do so could mean the difference between life and death not only for one's self and family but also for the entire community. This moral economy, to adapt E. P. Thompson's term, often forced individuals to make major sacrifices for the good of the whole.[67]

María C.'s story, which opened this chapter, highlights one unfortunately common sacrifice: the asphyxiation of children. When campesinos found themselves in caves and tatús hiding from government forces, the cries of hungry, scared, and otherwise uncomfortable children could betray both the presence and the specific locations of the mobile communities. Because silence was so essential to survival, adults frequently had to cover children's mouths to stifle their cries with the unintended result of smothering some children to death.

In later years, as international support networks expanded (see chapters 4–7), campesinos acquired new resources to help them—and their young children—survive the guindas. A number of substances were used to release children into temporary sleep during times of extreme danger. Some campesinos referred to "special drinks" given to children, which probably contained some form of medication or liquor. Others recalled giving children a minuscule amount of diazepam, a sedative used to treat anxiety. Still others, like Josefa R., highlighted how medics or nurses "gave them an injection so they'd sleep—who knows what it was, but they ended up sleeping like little angels."[68] The drugging of infants and children served dual purposes. Children who slept, of course, were spared much of the terror of military attacks. At the same time the relative quiet of the sleeping children helped to relieve some of the adults' own anxieties about being discovered by government troops.

En guinda, however, resources were hard to come by, and specialized and costly items such as pills and injections were even more so. Most campesinos, therefore, relied on other means to keep children quiet, including covering their mouths with a hand or rag. On occasion, as noted earlier, the children suffocated. Nearly all campesinos who spent time en guinda recalled such instances. Juana A. remembered how "in just a short while where I was, three died. We were in the mountains hiding and in a really tough spot when the kids were crying and the enemy was coming closer. They covered their mouths and the children ended up dying right there."[69] Being in such a "tough spot" forced people to make seemingly impossible choices. And yet, as José R. described it, people "decided to smother their little ones. This decision is reached because they are surrounded by the enemy and there are hundreds of people, and if a child is crying and the enemy discovers them, then everyone dies. That's why it has even become possible for parents to decide to smother their children. It's very sad. But they do it save a whole group."[70]

Another sacrifice, far more common, for those hiding in caves and tatús was to forgo water and food so as to not risk drawing attention. Carmen O., for example, recalled how she and her companions en guinda refused to venture out of their tatú for several days in a row despite great thirst and the fact that they could hear a stream not far away. "If they saw us," she explained, "they would look for everyone all over this part of the mountain."[71] In other words, although it was likely that they would have been able to get to the water and back without incident, the possibility of discovery—and what that would mean for other groups hiding in the same area—persuaded them to remain in hiding.

Other campesinos told similar stories of waiting out hunger and thirst. Some adults remembered squeezing water and sweat from their shirts to at least wet the children's mouths; others drank their own urine when the thirst became unbearable. A few, such as Josefa R., recalled not feeling any hunger when in the tatús. "You didn't get hungry," she said. "One could pass even eight days without eating a thing, surviving on fear alone."[72]

Conditions within the tatús were often horrible, which heightened the sacrifices that campesinos made for the greater good. During the dry season, heat inside the tatús could become nearly unbearable. In interviews, campesinos described the sensation of being "fried" or "cooked alive" and having to strip down to their underwear in hopes of a bit of relief. In a similar vein, the wet season's constant rains caused many tatús to flood, submerging those inside for days on end in several inches, or even feet, of muddy water, like hogs in a muddy pen, several people noted.

When campesinos eventually emerged from their tatús and caves, their bodies served as symbols of the sacrifices they had made while in hiding. The longer they remained hidden, the deeper the lack of food, water, fresh air, and sunlight inscribed themselves into the flesh and the more arresting their appearance became to others. Domitila A. recalled how one family in particular looked after spending fifteen days buried in an underground tatú. "The earth was already consuming them," she said. "Without spirit, they couldn't even get out of there; they were like walking dead. And the tiny children already with distended bellies, because they weren't eating. No energy—nothing— they kept fainting. It was terrible. The people looked like they were dead, their faces like cadavers."[73] Many others had observed similar scenes; a common refrain among campesinos was that the longer you spent underground the more the earth "robbed" you of energy, of life.

These kinds of sacrifices clearly required tremendous dedication and commitment to one's campesino companions. Whereas some observers may consider such selfless actions a form of heroism, Salvadoran campesinos referred to them, along with the careful observation of the guinda norms, as discipline (*disciplina*), a strategy crucial to the guinda system. In the words of one man, "The principal weapon that we had for our own self-defense was discipline."[74]

Just as discipline was crucial to the success of guindas, so too was leadership.[75] Similar to the preflight period, individuals both volunteered and were chosen by others as leaders to address the community's needs and make decisions based on the best interests of the group. People often described these leaders as the most awake (*despierto*), denoting both intelligence and *consciencia* (literally "conscience," but used to refer to sociopolitical consciousness and awareness) as well as physical alertness. Guinda leaders, or *responsables*, were the organic intellectuals described in chapter 1. They typically had previous experience with community organization and often had held positions of authority in CEBs, directivas, cooperatives, or campesino unions. Many had undergone weeks or even months of cooperative or lay leadership training. As a result of their experience, these responsables generally commanded significant respect in the community; when they made a decision and put it into action, José R. noted, "people always responded."[76]

In addition to the general leadership of the guindas, many committees continued to operate even while communities were in motion, although their precise roles shifted and evolved in response to changing circumstances. Exploration committees, for example, continued to determine safe routes. During the day, while the group took cover and rested, a few responsables would explore the surroundings and determine which direction to take the following night; they would then return to the group and pass the information on to other responsables, who would lead the group as directed while the first responsables rested. Such a pattern continued each day and night for the length of the guinda, with multiple leaders sharing responsibility for exploring the terrain and guiding the group to safety.

With time, as guindas lasted longer and groups traveled greater distances, new tasks arose such as food detail: collecting supplies from reserves that had previously been hidden in the hills; finding water sources; and gathering mango, papaya, and other fruits. Special commissions sometimes descended into towns in order to obtain supplies. On the rare occasions when the campesinos had a bit of money, these commissions would travel to towns considered "friendly," where they would purchase a few basic provisions. Other times they went into towns to *requisar* (requisition, expropriate). On these operations, commission members entered town under the cover of night; when they found a supply of rations such as corn or beans, they packed it up to take back to the community en guinda. Occasionally they were able to find animals, including pigs and cows, to provide meat for those en guinda. The campesinos' use of the term "requisar" is interesting in that it has a strong military connotation. In fact, FMLN soldiers also conducted *requisas*, and their practices certainly influenced the actions of northern campesinos, as I will discuss later. Yet most campesinos presented requisas as a consequence of war and need, a defensive move. As one observed, "We saw ourselves forced to steal corn."[77]

In addition to food detail, security tasks also shifted in response to the exigencies of lengthier guindas. Campesinos formed mobile guard units, which accompanied the groups en guinda. These guards moved at a slight distance from and in a rough circle around the group. Although they did carry weapons—usually machetes, *corvos* (an implement like a machete but with a curved blade), sticks, and rocks but a few small firearms as well—defense typically meant quietly warning the group of approaching danger, which would enable a shift in route. Another kind of guard functioned when the groups en guinda rested or remained in one location for an extended period of time. When a family or group fled to its designated cave or tatú, for instance, someone (usually an able-bodied male, often childless) remained outside the site to keep watch. Elías M. explained, "One always stayed outside. In the case of some surprise, if they didn't kill him, he ran, but his family stayed there, protected. If he detected approaching soldiers, he quickly ran to tell his family: 'Maintain your discipline [*mantenga la disciplina*] because they're coming by here. I'm taking off; I'll be back later.' They knew that when the soldiers leave, I come back again [to let them know] 'The military is gone, it's clear, you can come out.' I'd open the *tabla* and they would come out."[78] Sometimes a guard might allow only adults without children to emerge for a quick breath of fresh air; at other times he might allow everyone to come out after warning the children that they should play in silence. A guard was also responsible for erasing the group's tracks and camouflaging the entrance to the hiding place. As one campesino put it, "If I didn't, anyone who passed by would discover my refuge."[79]

Refuge Points and Alliances

Just as campesinos shifted what they did and how they did it, they also adjusted where they went. More specifically, they established a series of refuges to respond to the various types of operations launched by the Salvadoran armed forces. The first refuges were caves and tatús, which campesinos utilized for protection from short-term ground invasions conducted by relatively small battalions. When soldiers occupied towns or regions for weeks or months at a time, however, it simply was not feasible for campesinos to remain *encuevados* (encaved) or *entatuzados* (encaved in tatús) for such long periods of time. They therefore traveled ever greater distances and stayed away from home for longer periods of time. During these extended guindas, campesinos established temporary resting points at houses in abandoned villages along their flight paths, in deep ravines or caves in the hills, and in other hard to reach locations where they erected *zanjas*, huts or lean-tos camouflaged with sticks, brush, and other natural materials and occasionally plastic sheeting.

After about 1982 some of these temporary resting points evolved into semi-permanent bases known as *puntos de refugio* (points of refuge). Depending on troop movements and combat locations, campesinos could move between these various sites. The best known were those at which large groups were able to remain for significant lengths of time, perhaps six months, two years, or even four years, before moving to another, more secure location. During these periods of relative calm, campesinos recovered some of the organizational initiatives that had suffered in the process of constant movement. As one man from Morazán described it, "There'd be a few months between operations, [when] the people who'd stayed put, all dispersed, would come out of hiding and work for a bit, grow something to eat. And when the next operation came, the people went back again to where they were a bit safer, where the army wouldn't find their families."[80]

Many of the most populated refuge points were located high in the mountains surrounded by extremely difficult terrain. One such site, frequently referred to in interviews among campesinos from Chalatenango and Cabañas departments, was El Alto. Thousands convened at El Alto during the 1980s; it was high in the mountain range known as La Cañada in a well-forested area that offered significant privacy from military overflights. Even if they were detected, the location would be difficult to reach on foot and virtually inaccessible to helicopters due to the rough terrain. These features, said Elías M., transformed El Alto into "a very small island" of safety.[81]

An additional security feature of El Alto and many other refuge points was a strategic location near FMLN encampments. The close physical proximity enabled campesinos to take advantage of and benefit from guerrilla efforts, including intelligence gathering and guard patrols. In a similar vein, many refuge points also existed within the zones under FMLN control ("liberated zones" in campesino organizado parlance, "red zones" in government lingo). This reveals another important aspect of the guindas: although overt and formal alliances between civil society organizations all but disappeared with the increase in violence in 1981 and 1982, campesinos continued to ally themselves with others when possible and beneficial. For those who remained in the rural north, self-preservation took precedence, and alliances that helped them in this endeavor grew in importance. It is within this context that the insurgent forces of the FMLN became a crucial support to campesinos.

It is important to reiterate that the FMLN meant different things to different people. The FMLN was not a single entity but five different organizations with five distinct backgrounds, political philosophies, and geographies of influence; just as the FMLN was diverse, so too was the campesino population. Add to this mix the extreme volatility of wartime life in El Salvador and it is understandable that each community, family, and individual had unique, ever-evolving relationships with the insurgents. As Elizabeth Wood has illustrated, campesinos in Usulután and Cuscatlán had multiple levels of association with FMLN forces, ranging from nonparticipation combined with a sort of resigned tolerance to collaboration of various stripes or actual incorporation into the FMLN ranks. Many campesinos shifted between levels; others remained at the same level.[82]

Documents and interviews with campesinos from El Salvador's northern departments collected both during and after the war reveal a similar pattern. On one level campesinos presented less than flattering or even wholly negative opinions of the FMLN.[83] Some blamed FMLN soldiers for various forms of mistreatment, including death. One man, for example, claimed that the guerrillas forced people to kill their children. "I know because I saw it," he said. "I observed a grand injustice: with the people there, enduring hunger, they [the FMLN] required the dad to kill his boy. They put the little one like this, they put his hand like this, they pressed down on his mouth, his nose. He suffocated. That's how he suffocated."[84] This same campesino also described the inequality he experienced at one of the FMLN-run clinics. "My two oldest boys were dying, they were going to die of hunger but they wouldn't give us any medicine. There was a woman who was responsible for the medicine; she wouldn't give us any. She carried it with her, she gave it to other people but she never gave us even one pill, and my children dying of hunger and sickness." In contrast, if anyone was recognized as an FMLN combatant or officer, "they attended to him very well. . . . They gave him juice, good food and everything."[85] A woman from Morazán painted a similarly negative picture of the FMLN soldiers who came to town and harassed the locals. Notable in her portrayal, however, is their mistreatment of women. "They asked for money," she said, "and they asked for girls too. And if you didn't give them the pretty one, they'd kill you."[86]

A more ubiquitous complaint against the FMLN insurgents was that they forcibly recruited people into their combatant ranks. In fact, a formal recruitment campaign ran between March and September of 1984; although it increased the number of combatants, it also "provoked massive resistance on the part of the subject population."[87] Thousands of people left the FMLN-dominated zones in the north to avoid incorporation and subsequently denounced the recruitment campaign to representatives of international agencies at refugee camps outside of El Salvador as well as at camps for the internally displaced in San Salvador and other cities.[88]

Another segment of the Salvadoran campesino population did not critique the FMLN directly, yet the language used by these campesinos implied distinctly uneven relations. For example, as noted earlier, people occasionally spoke of "others" as the decision makers and directors. Phrases such as *nos orientaron* (they oriented us) and *nos trajeron* (they brought us) implied that they lacked control over their actions. The speakers typically did not identify FMLN combatants as the leaders or directors; rather, they referred to an ambiguous party, which may have been the FMLN or another individual or group. A common statement like *nos sacaron en guinda*, for example, could be understood as either "they pushed us into a guinda" or "they took us on a guinda." If the former, it typically referred to the government troops involved in the military operation that had prompted flight. If the latter, it referred to either campesino *responsables* or FMLN soldiers accompanying a mobile community.

Much more common in documents and interviews were representations of the FMLN as a sort of big brother. Within this layer of association, campesinos highlighted the protection offered by FMLN soldiers. Uberlinda Q., for example, described how guerrilla guards often first warned communities of coming government sweeps and then provided security during the *guindas*: "They told us when the operation was coming: 'Get out,' they told us. 'Look, the operation is coming from such-and-such a place, so retreat.' . . . They loaned us security in part to make sure that we would leave. . . . Yes, they provided protection."[89] Many chronicles also included variations on the theme of *rompimiento de cerco* (breaking the military cordon). When a group *en guinda* found itself trapped on all sides by government troops, FMLN soldiers would begin shooting elsewhere to break the circle and allow the campesinos to escape. Occasionally people described a much more intimate kind of protection-related relationship in which guerrilla soldiers helped to establish and train *milicias civiles* (civilian militias), which would help with the protection of populations *en guinda* and serve as a sort of bridge between civilian populations and the FMLN.[90] As Vicente, a community leader in charge of self-defense, explained, "The guerrillas patrol the places where the enemy might penetrate. Those of us on security detail, along with the *milicias civiles*, remain in a constant state of awareness; we take note of everything that is different or strange, and then let the guerrillas know."[91]

Although Vicente's comments reveal close connections between civilians *en guinda* and the FMLN with regard to security issues, other campesinos noted that the FMLN offered other forms of support as well. Some described how, in the hardest of times, the FMLN provided food for groups *en guinda*. Others spoke of the medical aid received through the FMLN, which included treatment of wounds and illnesses, training provided by medics, and contributions of supplies for first aid kits.[92] Still others remembered how, when things were a bit more calm, the FMLN would sponsor *fiestecitas* (little parties) to instill hope and *ánimo* (spirit, energy, courage) in the population. Norma, one of my young hostesses in a small village in Chalatenango, described what a delight it was to hear music, dance, and simply enjoy life for a while. Particularly exciting, she thought, was dancing with the handsome FMLN soldiers. Other people I spoke with, who were older and more involved in community organization efforts during the war, remembered the importance of these gatherings not only for release and renewal but also because they served as an attractive introduction to collective organization for individuals not yet committed to such efforts.

But if some campesinos perceived the FMLN as a big brother who "in many ways took care of the people," others considered themselves and the FMLN as partners and collaborators.[93] Resurgence of local government initiatives in the northern zones in the mid-1980s highlights this "professional relationship."[94] Although campesinos had begun to organize their communities prior to the formation of the FMLN and the onset of civil war, many aspects of that organization suffered during the guindas with the constant movement from place to place. As the FMLN established "liberated territories" across the northern fringe of the country in the early 1980s, campesino communities gained a new measure of stability. Settling at semipermanent refuge points within the zones under FMLN military control meant fewer sweeps and incursions by government forces. This, in turn, allowed campesinos to recuperate some of the organizational initiatives that had suffered during constant movement.

After 1982, campesinos at refuge sites in FMLN territories began to resurrect the directivas. Although the specifics of self-government structures varied between different sites, they held much in common with the directivas of the 1970s. Most directivas involved numerous positions, including those of president, vice president, and responsables for numerous areas such as organization, health, production and distribution, education, security and self-defense, social welfare, and legal matters. Members of the refuge communities elected people to these positions at general assemblies. Directivas maintained communication with each other through subregional governments, which emerged as the refuge communities grew and directivas became more organized. Subregional governments improved coordination and collaboration on various projects, in the areas of health and education, for example. Directivas also communicated with other civil society organizations (which once again flourished after 1984) through local advisory councils on which sat representatives from teachers', women's, and workers' organizations among others.[95]

The FMLN certainly was not passive with regard to civilian organizing; rather, the various factions of the FMLN encouraged and even directed civilian organization within its zones of influence. Just as initial contacts between campesinos and insurgents differed from place to place, so too did the guinda era relations between grassroots governments and guerrilla forces. In northern Chalatenango and Cabañas, where comunidades organizadas and campesino organizations were especially strong and active during the 1970s, mobile communities revived the directivas by 1982. The FMLN faction that predominated in the region, the FPL, supported and encouraged these organizations—and even bestowed on them the revolutionary title Poderes Populares Locales (Local Popular Powers, PPLs)—yet directivas remained relatively autonomous from this and other insurgent groups. According to Facundo Guardado, of rural Chalatenango origin and a founder of the FPL, "local civilian government . . . [was] not dependent on the FMLN."[96]

This was less the case elsewhere, however. Orlando R. from Aguilares noted that FMLN militia participated "as members or delegates" at community assemblies and directiva elections.[97] And in Morazán the ERP maintained strict oversight of civilian organization. Although campesinos there had previous experience with directivas, CEBs, cooperatives, and other forms of collective action, directivas apparently did not reemerge among the mobile communities at refuge points until 1984 when "the ERP created a model of organization and assigned political activists to work with civilians in order to concretize it." According to Leigh Binford, the ERP promoted participatory democracy but to a limited degree. Guerrillas "colonized the commanding heights of civilian organization" through control of directiva elections; they also "designed strategy and tactics, and advised, praised and sanctioned civilian administrators." At the same time, because the ERP could not supervise every level and each step of civilian organization, "a substantial degree of autonomy existed at the local level."[98]

Regardless of the sentiments toward and levels of association with the FMLN, it is crucial to note that nearly all campesinos made a clear distinction between themselves as a civilian population and the FMLN as armed insurgents. Indeed, campesinos took pride in being unarmed and highlighted their nonviolence. As one man explained, although campesinos were part of the revolutionary movement, "we had no weapons; the weapon we had was our mouth, our ability to speak."[99] Those who did carry weapons—and guns in particular—often deemphasized their importance. A member of a guard patrol, for example, might refer to his *pistolita chiquita* (tiny little pistol) or he might highlight that there were only two guns to protect a group of one hundred or more. Many who carried weapons further distinguished themselves from the armed insurgents by emphasizing how they simply did not use their weapons. Whereas the purpose of the regular guerrilla army "was exclusively to annihilate and recover weaponry from the [government] army," one campesino explained, the popular civilian militias "served . . . as defense for the communities. . . . They served as the periphery without shooting."[100]

Debates surrounding the requisition tactic described earlier further illustrate the campesinos' preference for nonviolent tactics even in the midst of war. Insurgent troops also conducted requisas and on occasion collaborated with the civilian population to carry out such operations. Yet even in such instances campesinos did not discuss requisition as an offensive war maneuver. Instead they defended their expropriations using moral rhetoric. Vicente, for example, described how joint civilian-guerrilla requisas worked: "Everyone goes, very ordered indeed! We take over the pueblo and organize a meeting. The guerrilla takes care of security. So the *masa*, the people from the PPLs and the civilian militias, about 200 people, we go to *requisar* at the houses that belong to a member of ORDEN, of a [death] squad or the military. We drag everything we find to one spot [*a una bodega*]."[101] In this brief description Vicente divides participants into two distinct groups: the FMLN soldiers, who secured the locale militarily; and the civilian population, which carried out the requisa. He also highlights the fact that requisas targeted only specific members of the government's security forces and their affiliated vigilantes (death squads and ORDEN). As the civilians raided these individuals' properties, they carried out a sort of "popular justice"; because they themselves had been mistreated by government troops, the campesinos argued, it was only fair that they receive this sort of compensation. In a similarly morally upright manner, some claimed that they took only from towns that had been forcefully depopulated; the supplies would have only gone to waste otherwise. And many maintained simply that "stealing out of necessity is not bad."[102]

It is interesting to note that at the same time campesinos admitted to significant overlap between themselves and the FMLN in the northern refuge sites, they also drew a sharp contrast between their own requisition tactics and those of government troops. Whereas campesino requisition commissions were discriminating in their choice of targets, government soldiers plundered wherever they set foot. Likewise, if campesinos stole in order to survive, soldiers did so with the explicit intention of causing injury and hardship. They did not steal out of need, as evidenced in the fact that soldiers usually razed or burned crops and slaughtered chickens and cattle but did not take with them any of the spoils.[103]

Along with justifying requisitions on moral terms, campesinos also noted the guilt that accompanied the tactic. Such feelings make perfect sense given that the campesinos en guinda had long lived in poverty and knew well the importance of a harvest no matter how meager. Moreover, according to the Catholic faith held by the majority of campesinos organizados, stealing was a sin. The feelings of guilt and the justification of requisas are further important to note because they highlight the campesinos' continued preference for nonviolent methods of resistance and survival.[104]

The distinctions that campesinos drew between the FMLN and themselves further illustrate a common perception among campesinos that civilians and guerrilla soldiers were two parts of a greater whole, la organización. Both campesino civilians and guerrillas belonged to it, yet it was greater than either group on its own.

From Reaction to Resistance:
A Combative Mass Movement

There can be no doubt that the violence and war of the 1970s and 1980s brought immeasurable pain, suffering, and loss to the campesinos of northern El Salvador. But theirs is not a simple story of victimhood. As this chapter has illustrated, campesinos responded to increasing levels of harassment and violence by adjusting their community security tactics. The flights from home that came to be known as guindas eventually—and surprisingly quickly—became a learned, conscious, and planned strategy of survival. Campesinos never knew exactly when a military sweep would occur, yet they prepared themselves well for such an eventuality. They learned to interpret military patterns and predict attacks. They designed emergency exit routes, constructed tatús and other hiding places for people and supplies, prepared special foods, and prepacked items to facilitate survival while en guinda. Within the context of the guinda system, moreover, campesinos established strategic alliances with other campesinos, with collaborators and combatants of the FMLN, and, as the following chapters will illustrate, with international aid workers inside and outside El Salvador.

Taken together, this evidence directly counters the traditional image of refugee flight: poor rural folk fleeing their homes blindly and managing to survive only through sheer luck, God's intervention, or outside assistance. Moreover, a longer historical view erases the presumed division between "before" and "after" by highlighting two crucial continuities between campesino actions during the prewar period and during flight.

First, northern campesinos continued to utilize mobility as a resource, although the meanings ascribed to that resource shifted over time. Chapter 1 described how, during the nineteenth and early to mid-twentieth centuries, northern campesinos secured "extended spaces of livelihood" through physical movement, travel, and migration. The present chapter revealed how they adapted this pattern of movement during the late twentieth century. In response to rising levels of violence against organized campesino communities in the 1970s and early 1980s, individuals, families, and entire communities moved. They left their homes at night to sleep in the mountains, they relocated to neighboring villages and the homes of family and friends, and they formed mobile communities that traveled en guinda throughout El Salvador for weeks and months, even years. With the development and formalization of the guinda system in the early 1980s, mobility took on new significance. Civil war—and, more specifically, state-sponsored violence—stripped down "livelihood" to its barest meaning: survival, the ability to remain living in spite of the civil war that raged around them, in spite of the individual and group targeting by ORDEN and death squads, and in spite of the military's scorched earth tactics. Remaining alive in the northern *tierra olvidada* thus became an overt challenge, an action taken in order to spite the Salvadoran authorities.

In short, mobility became a conscious act of moral and political resistance. In this, Salvadoran campesinos had much in common with the Guatemalan Comunidades de Población en Resistencia (Communities of Population in Resistance, CPRs) of the 1980s and 1990s. Although we still have much to learn about the CPRs, existing research recognizes not only the suffering of those in flight but also their conscious resistance to Guatemalan government and military efforts to, at best, relocate and reeducate them or, at worst, eradicate them. These studies also note that the CPR organizations were independent of the insurgent forces operating in Guatemala at the time; although members of the CPRs may have held similar dreams and goals for their communities and nation, and although they may have interacted with guerrilla groups, their organizational efforts and initiatives remained distinct from those groups.[105] Given the similarities between these two Central American cases, it is curious that observers have recognized rural Guatemalans' actions as autonomous resistance but dismissed rural Salvadorans' actions as the result of manipulation by the guerrilla groups. It is high time to acknowledge the independent efforts of Salvadorans even as we admit that many did indeed cultivate relations with the insurgents. As Jeffrey Gould has demonstrated in the case of Nicaragua, and as others have illustrated for Mexico and elsewhere, autonomous action and relations with bandits or rebels are not mutually exclusive.

A longer historical view of the Salvadoran case also reveals that campesinos continued their commitment to *la lucha* even during the period of *guerra abierta* in the 1980s. Notably, the majority did not demonstrate their commitment by taking up arms against the Salvadoran military. Rather, they developed the *guinda* system; by evading death and refusing to leave their northern highland communities, campesinos refused to recognize or submit to the authority of the Salvadoran government. The extremes to which they went in this endeavor were evident in their willingness to abide by the unique moral economy of war flight, a system of norms that dictated what had to be done or accepted for the sake of preserving life and community. In times of maximum risk this moral economy required absolute silence and extreme deprivation. It also necessitated the reversal of normal morals and values; campesinos scavenged grains, livestock, and other basic supplies from rural houses and communities, and parents like María C., whose story opened this chapter, stifled noisy children even if it threatened their young lives. But *guindas* were, simply put, exceptional measures for exceptional times, and as a result new justifications emerged for behaviors that campesinos did not normally condone.

If refusal to abandon the northern regions of the country was one method of demonstrating their continued commitment to la lucha, association with the FMLN was yet another. Regardless of the specific levels at which individual campesinos collaborated with the FMLN, the very fact that communities en guinda established sites of refuge in areas with a significant FMLN presence literally marked them as targets of the Salvadoran regime. Moreover, as the FMLN used military might to physically remove government authorities from northern communities in the early 1980s (mayors abandoned their constituencies, for example, and the armed forces retreated to points farther south), mobile campesino communities moved into these "liberated territories" and began constructing grassroots governments.[106] These governments were unique not only in their location beyond official control; they were also "collective and cooperative experiences."[107] As both experiences and structures, the directivas, PPLs, or *autogobiernos* (self-governments)—whatever designation one wishes to use—further illustrated campesinos' commitment to la lucha. Not only did they contribute to the disarticulation of the standing regime; as local formulations of participatory democracy, these governments also signified the possibility of a more just and equitable future. They were, in other words, the seed of the new El Salvador.[108]

In essence, campesinos who chose to remain in the north and *guindear* (run or flee) during the 1980s comprised a combative mass movement. They were a movement in two senses of the word: both physical mobility and a collective, organized effort toward specific goals. And they were combative in that they opposed the Salvadoran regime and contributed in various ways to its disarticulation and eventual downfall.

Mobile campesino communities dealt one blow to the Salvadoran regime by refusing to abandon northern territory. Choosing to settle within conflicted zones or areas under FMLN control—even temporarily—represented yet another strike. Perhaps the heaviest blow came, however, when mobile communities—tens of thousands of campesinos—established refuge sites beyond the nation's borders in Honduras. It is to that subject that I now turn.

3

Internationalizing
La Guinda

A Thin Black Line?

Gladis G. remembers exactly when and how the civil war arrived at her hometown of La Hacienda in northern Chalatenango, El Salvador. It was mid-December 1979. The Salvadoran Army and National Guard, along with paramilitaries from ORDEN, began forcefully dislodging people from nearby villages. About four hundred campesinos from these villages descended on Gladis's town of La Hacienda, where they stayed for a few weeks before moving on to Las Aradas, a hamlet of perhaps a dozen houses located on the banks of the Sumpul River. Initially Gladis and others from La Hacienda decided to stay home, but a few months later a new wave of violence hit. "*La guardia* [the National Guard] came, shooting first and then ransacking houses and stores. . . . They tore down the doors with machetes, they killed the animals, and the people who stayed in their houses, the little old people who couldn't run, they pulled them outside at bayonet point and beat them."[1]

That was in March 1980. In late April, when la guardia started to kill, Gladis and many of her neighbors decided to leave La Hacienda. They, too, headed toward the hamlet of Las Aradas, and along the way they joined up with others from many other area villages. By the time they reached their destination, the group had grown to over five hundred. In the days that followed, campesinos continued to arrive at Las Aradas so that by mid-May the tiny village on the border with Honduras hosted nearly fifteen hundred people.

Then, on 14 May 1980, as the campesinos at Las Aradas breakfasted on corn tortillas, the ambush began. Barely had someone yelled "Here comes la guardia!" when the ground troops were upon them. The campesinos scattered, attempting to escape, but soldiers knocked them down with kicks and blows, bayonets and bullets. Witnesses later recounted the worst of what they saw: soldiers slicing open the bellies of pregnant women, fetuses and infants thrown into the air and bayoneted, genitals cut off of men and boys, girls and women raped. As these horrors occurred, many campesinos threw themselves into the river and tried to reach the opposite shore, only to be carried away by the swollen current or pegged midstream by machine-gun fire from helicopters circling above. Those who made it to the other side were turned back by Honduran soldiers. "They started to push us back by force and to shoot," recalled Gladis. "And then people ran back to the Salvadoran side, where they were massacred by the army." By the time the "human carnage" slowed in midafternoon, along the banks of the Sumpul River between Santa Lucía and Las Aradas, more than six hundred people lay dead.[2]

This incident, which quickly came to be known as the Sumpul River Massacre, in many ways marked the beginning of a new era of El Salvador's civil conflict. It was one of the first military operations that left indisputable evidence of the negative consequences of the counterinsurgency strategies adopted by the Salvadoran armed forces. The tactics, which included broad-scale ground sweeps through rural areas, placed campesinos directly into the military's gun sights. Between 1980 and 1984, in fact, massacres like the one at Sumpul became almost commonplace, leading the UN Truth Commission on El Salvador to the conclusion that the number of group executions "is so high and the reports are so thoroughly substantiated, the Commission rules out any possibility that these might have been isolated incidents. . . . Everything points to the fact that these deaths formed a pattern of conduct, a deliberate strategy of eliminating or terrifying the peasant population."[3]

The Sumpul River Massacre also helped to spark a new international focus on El Salvador's civil conflict. This was the first time that the crisis had so obviously bled beyond national borders, and, largely due to the efforts of priests and religious workers from the Honduran Catholic Diocese of Santa Rosa de Copán, news of the incident spread throughout the Americas and Europe. Journalists, governments, and nongovernmental organizations began exploring the realities of the civil conflict with vigor; many focused in particular on state-sponsored terror, and critiques of the Salvadoran government grew ever harsher as officials denied the events at Sumpul in spite of eyewitness testimonies and visual evidence obtained by Hondurans and foreigners alike.[4]

A related level on which the Sumpul River Massacre marked the start of a new era in El Salvador's civil conflict was that, although Salvadorans had been seeking refuge in Honduras for months, the ambush of May 1980 created the first large group of internationally recognized Salvadoran war refugees.

Among them was Gladis G. Amid the chaos of that day she managed to escape to the Honduran town of Guarita. Gladis and others like her at dozens of Honduran border towns first recounted their experiences to Honduran campesinos, priests, and religious workers and soon to international journalists as well. "There was an invasion of journalists, from all over the place," recalled a Honduran priest who spearheaded the Honduran Catholic Church's investigation into the massacre and its subsequent public condemnation of it. "The facts surrounding the massacre became the focal point of international attention. Journalists came from every country."[5]

International reporting on the plight of the Salvadoran refugees in Honduras attracted the attention of aid and solidarity groups, which then came to Honduras to lend assistance to the local organizations already working in the area. By January 1980 Médecins Sans Frontières (Doctors without Borders, MSF), Catholic Relief Services, World Vision, and many others were among those aiding the refugees. By mid-1981 the UNHCR had negotiated agreements with the Honduran government and began to officially coordinate refugee relief efforts.

It cannot be denied that these organizations played a critical role in helping Salvadoran campesinos weather the civil war period. Without the food, shelter, clothing, and medical attention provided by international agencies, many Salvadorans simply would not have lived to witness the signing of the Peace Accords in 1992. It is equally critical to recognize that the international humanitarian aid regime functioned on the basis of a number of assumptions.[6] First, the very foundation of the aid regime was that the Salvadoran campesino refugees were victims swept up in the chaos and violence of war and had been driven from their homes against their will by forces beyond their control or comprehension. From this perspective leaving one's home appears only as the result of frenzy, fear, and panic and leaving one's country as an act of desperation. In other words, Salvadoran campesinos fled across the border suddenly because they had no other choice.

Following this train of thought, arrival in Honduras symbolizes the consummate form of escape, illustrating not only the campesinos' desire to escape a military sweep or save their lives but also their intention to find greener grass and simply leave the war behind. Scott Wright, a Catholic lay missionary from the United States, expressed this assumption clearly when he described Salvadoran border crossers as "a people on the march, trying to survive, hoping to reach a promised land."[7] Annette Wenzel, a nurse from West Germany, offered a similar interpretation; the first days were especially difficult for newly arrived refugees, she said, because "they had hoped that, by fleeing to Honduras, they would find better conditions. . . . But, many times it wasn't like that. It was a huge shock for them."[8] Such comments reveal how Wenzel, Wright, and many other aid workers perceived the international border as a slim black line on a political map. They assumed that as Salvadorans stepped across that line they moved into territory of an entirely different color.

A closer look at cross-border war flight from the perspective of the people who made the journey problematizes this thin black line, our modern conception of political boundaries. This chapter examines the mobile communities' extension of the guinda system across an international border to reveal more continuities than discrepancies. Rather than expecting significant improvements in their life situations, Salvadoran campesinos knew that arrival in Honduras promised more hardship and suffering; repression against them continued, though often from different sources and in alternate forms. But if repression continued, so too did the campesinos' organizational efforts and resistance.

Discovering Honduras

More than one million Salvadorans crossed international borders to establish refuge points outside their native country.[9] Costa Rica became a refuge point in 1980 when 200 Salvadorans occupied the Costa Rican embassy in San Salvador and successfully negotiated an airlift transfer. Before too long more than 3,000 Salvadorans had made their temporary homes in Costa Rica. In a similar vein, the Panamanian government invited the relocation of approximately 600 campesinos from northern El Salvador who had been captured by the Honduran military. Nicaragua ultimately hosted around 24,000 Salvadoran refugees and Belize approximately 8,400. An additional 200,000 Salvadorans trekked even farther north to Mexico and another half million to the United States.[10]

The focus of this chapter is the more than twenty-four-thousand Salvadorans who crossed into Honduras, where they established a series of refuge points on Honduran territory all along the border with El Salvador (see map 2). These villages and UNHCR-supported camps evolved into strategic sites from which the campesinos—now known as refugees—continued la lucha. Such strategic positioning was at first largely accidental. That is, although Honduras and the border zone in general quickly became integral to the guinda system, the first groups of Salvadorans to be recognized as refugees in Honduras did not intend for Honduran towns like Los Hernández, Mapulaca, Colomoncagua, and La Virtud to become the crucial refuge points they ultimately became.

Map 2. Refugee zones. (Map by Pamela Larson, Augustana College)

The fact that during 1979 and 1980 many campesinos crossed back and forth across the border without settling in Honduras supports the idea that Honduran towns were initially considered in much the same way as caves and tatús were—as temporary hiding spots.[11] Testimonies and interviews reveal how campesinos often escaped military sweeps through the far northern regions of El Salvador by crossing into Honduras, where they waited until the immediate danger passed before returning to their sites of refuge in El Salvador. The story of Gladis G., recounted earlier, offers one example. When she and her companions first arrived in Las Aradas, they knew they were on the border with Honduras because at that point the river served as the delineation between the two countries. They did not, however, know that they were going to cross into Honduras until the chaos of the ambush on 14 May 1980. Somehow Gladis made it across the river and escaped undetected into the woods on the other side. The next day, however, she and several others returned to the Salvadoran side because they "didn't know the land" and feared the Honduran soldiers. They headed back toward Gladis's home town of La Hacienda but learned from others on the way that dozens of Salvadoran soldiers "were waiting for those who had survived the massacre." So they turned around and, as she put it, "decided to seek refuge in Honduras." They crossed the border once again and eventually settled with other Salvadoran refugees on the outskirts of the Honduran town of Guarita.[12] Another campesino, Suyapa, shared a similar story but highlighted the intentionality behind the decision to cross the border. "We left temporarily, only to wait out the worst of the military operations," she explained. "But when the operations were over, well, we were from El Salvador, our roots, our culture, and our country is El Salvador, right. So, they were moments of, well, temporary refuge."[13]

When discussing the integration of Honduran sites into the guinda system, it is crucial to note that the border between the two republics was not delineated at this time. Only three official crossings existed; no other walls, fences, or distinguishing features defined the border. Without any official markings it was virtually impossible for anyone to decipher the point at which one country ended and the other began. Towns on both sides were equally small, widely dispersed, and, in general, beyond the margins of government maps. And topography helped little in determining whether one was in El Salvador or Honduras. Despite the fact that a mountain range divided the two countries, a ground-level position did not always afford the necessary perspective; the rugged terrain, trees, and fog and mist at higher altitudes made it difficult to ascertain one's whereabouts. Such a task was further complicated by the fact that Salvadorans en guinda typically moved only at night.[14]

Long-standing conflicts between El Salvador and Honduras further blurred the boundaries; indeed, the two republics had never agreed on an official borderline. Land and title disputes in the region date back to the colonial period, in fact, and, although Salvadoran and Honduran officials have cycled through multiple negotiations since the 1860s, a final resolution had proved difficult to strike. In 1969, tensions erupted into what was subsequently dubbed the Hundred-Hour War. No clear winner emerged, and a decade of cold war ensued. In 1980, with prompting from the United States, relations between the two countries began to warm once again, although border delineation remained an issue. By 1985, Honduras and El Salvador had turned over the case to the International Court of Justice in The Hague.

What is particularly interesting about this in terms of the current study is that nearly half of the territory in dispute was alongside El Salvador's tierra olvidada. Specifically, both countries continued to claim sovereignty over nearly 150 square kilometers between Morazán province in El Salvador and La Paz, Honduras, along with an additional 90 square kilometers between El Salvador's Chalatenango province and the Ocotepeque and Lempira provinces of Honduras. Many of the known guindas occurred in or passed through these *bolsones* (pockets), as the disputed zones are called. Moreover, Salvadoran campesinos established the vast majority of their semipermanent points of refuge either inside these bolsones or on Honduran territory surrounding them.

Although observers long have conjectured about the possible political motives behind this, it is important to consider that, historically, campesinos from northern El Salvador did not distinguish between the two countries in the same way government officials, international observers, and political maps did. As noted in chapter 1, campesinos in the region actually have a long history of cross-border relations regardless of national political and geographic boundaries. Honduran and Salvadoran campesinos married and raised families together. Hondurans came to El Salvador to sell their wares at market and seek medical care, and Salvadorans went to Honduras for land and work.

Given the history of cross-border relations, it should not be surprising that the first Salvadorans to settle in Honduras during the civil war period simply did not locate themselves in either country; instead they described wandering through a sort of no-man's land, which they referred to alternately as *la zona fronteriza* (frontier or border zone), *las fronteras* (the borders/boundaries/frontiers), or *la periferia* (the periphery). As Luis explained, the border problem was a "government thing" and northern campesinos simply went about their business. They "just weren't obsessed with where to draw lines."[15]

That the first groups of Salvadorans to become long-term refugees in Honduras located themselves in this sort of extended tierra olvidada indicates that they did not cross the border explicitly in search of better conditions. Even had they intended to arrive and settle in Honduras, they knew from their generations of cross-border relations that the economic and political environments of the Honduran border zone were no better than those on the Salvadoran side. In fact, many observed that conditions in Honduras were worse than in El Salvador. Militarization of the border zone, moreover, meant that border crossings became increasingly perilous. As Gladis G. and others learned at the Sumpul River in May 1980, campesinos no longer had only Salvadoran soldiers to fear; Honduran officials also posed a threat.

Indeed, the Honduran government did not welcome these thousands of Salvadorans with open arms. Despite the fact that officials repeatedly avowed that their role was "apolitical" and "purely humanitarian" in addressing the "refugee crisis," political interests clearly spurred many government policies and practices. Government documents from the period reveal that Honduran officials distinguished Salvadorans from the other refugee groups in the country; whereas the refugees from Nicaragua, Guatemala, and Haiti were "*nonnational groups* that have no effect on the life of the country," Salvadorans comprised *a special, national group* that posed multiple threats to the Honduran nation.[16]

Several major concerns stemmed from the history of tense relations between Honduras and its southern neighbor. Officials feared, for example, that Honduras was being "invaded by a needy Salvadoran population in search of new economic horizons."[17] In other words, Salvadorans were not considered true political refugees but rather "elements whose lives and properties are not at risk." These economic migrants, officials claimed, played the role of refugees as "a method of getting into Honduras in order to make a new life in our territory. . . . They are people who came to Honduras already decided and convinced that they would remain living in the country."[18] Officials also feared a repeat of the 1969 Hundred-Hour War. As long as the Salvadoran conflict continued to spill into Honduras and the disputed bolsones, this threat remained. As one pro-government source explained, the border zones occupied by Salvadoran refugees were being used by both the FMLN forces and Salvadoran government troops; consequently, Honduras found itself "in disagreeable situations since, on the one hand, it cannot permit that its territory be used as a safe and inviolable asylum for the guerrillas and, on the other hand, neither can it tolerate that it be considered a hunting ground by the neighboring country's government forces."[19] The refugees were at the center of the problem; the location of their camps and bodies in the border region offered too many options to both the FMLN and the Salvadoran government forces and too few to the Hondurans. The continued presence of Salvadoran refugees in Honduras, then, threatened to "turn into the friction point that will lead once again to an armed confrontation between the two countries."[20]

The Honduran government also viewed these concerns—and sought solutions to them—within a cold war context. Anxieties about the international spread of communism (a fire fanned by U.S. advisers in the region) led many officials to view the FMLN—and, by extension, Salvadoran campesinos from rebel-held zones—as "reds."[21] Indeed, throughout the 1980s Honduran officials criminalized the Salvadoran refugees for what they perceived as intimate connections between the refugee camps and the FMLN guerrilla forces. "There are only guerrillas living in the refugee camps," claimed Colonel Flores Auceda at a 1984 meeting of the Honduran Comisión Nacional de Refugiados (National Commission on Refugees, CONARE).[22] Other political figures argued that even if the Salvadorans were not combatants themselves they were "connected to terrorist militants. Even a family relationship could indicate that they have a moral commitment that leads them to participate in such activity."[23] According to this perspective, Salvadoran guerrillas used the refugee camps as strategic sites in which to rest and recuperate from injuries; to recruit and train new soldiers; produce boots, uniforms, and other items for combat; broadcast propaganda from a secret FMLN radio station; and transfer and store weapons and other supplies received from "communists" in Nicaragua and Cuba.[24] The national and regional news media reiterated such allegations in articles boasting headlines such as "Farabundo Martí Barracks in Refugee Camps," "Subversives Capture Support Destined for Refugees in Honduras," and "FMLN Traffics Weapons from Nicaragua through Camps in Honduras."[25]

Given all this, it is perhaps not surprising that the Honduran government resisted offering refuge to Salvadorans. Honduras was not a signatory to the Geneva Convention Relating to the Status of Refugees (1951) or its Protocol (1967). This meant that the UNHCR had a limited capacity to act independently within Honduras. It also meant that Honduran officials retained considerable leeway in determining the terms and conditions under which the UNHCR could operate in Honduran territory. Officials had initially negotiated agreements with the UNHCR for assistance with multiple waves of Nicaraguan refugees in the mid-1970s. As the decade progressed, large numbers of Salvadorans and Guatemalans arrived, and the UNHCR expanded its aid efforts to include these groups as well. The Honduran government was slower to recognize the new groups; official acknowledgment of the Salvadorans as refugees did not come until the UNHCR had been providing assistance to them for more than a year.

In light of the perceived dangers represented by Salvadoran refugees, the Honduran National Security Council insisted that officials "manage the situation in the most intelligent manner."[26] Strict control and oversight were essential, and so in its negotiations with the UNHCR the Honduran government made its official recognition of the Salvadorans as refugees contingent on their confinement to designated zones controlled by the Honduran military. By 1983 the UNHCR had relocated the majority of the Salvadorans dispersed along the border to five official refugee camps: La Virtud (serving between 3,000 and 10,000 refugees at any one time); Colomoncagua (sheltering around 8,400); Buenos Aires (200 to 300); San Antonio (approximately 1,500); and Mesa Grande, which ultimately absorbed the population of the La Virtud camp, making it the most populous of the camps (around 11,500).[27]

Per Honduran rules, these were "closed camps."[28] Officials closely monitored all movements made by refugees: no one could enter or exit the refugee camps unless "duly authorized" by both national immigration officials and local military commanders; travel between the different camps and subcamps required a written pass even when the distance was but a few hundred yards; and ever-changing curfews prohibited many things after hours, including the use of lighting and movement between tents. Other efforts to track and control the Salvadorans included the regular collection of census data from each of the camps and the stipulation that even emergency medical evacuations required military oversight and accompaniment. Moreover, officials declared it illegal for Salvadorans to attend schools in Honduras, participate in local markets, purchase land, or establish *colonizaciones rurales* (rural colonizations or settlements). Persisting concerns that Salvadorans would use their refugee status as a "foot in door" for Honduran citizenship led the National Congress to rewrite the Constitution to further clarify Honduran citizenship require-ments and explicitly exclude children born to refugee parents.[29]

Although Honduran officials working with the Salvadoran refugee aid regime maintained that they had only the best humanitarian intentions, it is clear that they also had significant political concerns. They sequestered Salva-dorans in isolated locations, confined them in militarized camps, and placed severe restrictions on their activities and lives. The primary intention behind these policies was, no doubt, to exert as much control as possible over a popu-lation that officials perceived as a threat to national security. It is also likely that officials intended (or at least hoped) that the harsh conditions at the camps would dissuade other campesinos from deciding to cross the border. Although this may have been true to some extent, Salvadorans continued to cross the border by the hundreds—even thousands—throughout the 1980s. Moreover, the Honduran government's "closed camp" policies ultimately served the mobile communities' interests very well.

Integrating Honduras into the *Guinda* System

The strategic importance of Honduras as a refuge point grew in 1981 and 1982 as the UNHCR established official refugee camps and the international aid regime solidified. Campesinos still in El Salvador began con-sciously integrating Honduran refuge points—and the people who worked there—into the guinda system. In fact, Honduran towns and refuge points evolved into semipermanent refuge points largely due to the attention and aid bestowed on the Salvadorans, first by Honduran campesinos and local orga-nizations and later by international entities. In other words, although the cam-pesinos were initially in search of temporary respite from the dangers of counterinsurgency operations and military sweeps, the arrival in Honduras of international attention allowed the formation of new alliances and resources.

Campesinos came to consciously and purposely integrate Honduras into the guinda system. Interviews and testimonies indicate that, in contrast to the first arrivals, later arrivals to Honduras often planned their journeys from the point of departure. According to Manuel, "It was completely structured."[30] Preparation for cross-border guindas proceeded in much the same way as for any other guinda. In recognition of the unique nature of an international trek, however, some individuals chose to bury or sell their belongings rather than carry them en guinda or leave them behind unprotected. Interviewees also de-scribed how men often accompanied their wives and children to refuge zones in Honduras, and then returned home to northern El Salvador to guard their houses and fields or collaborate more closely with the FMLN. Women offered similar stories about taking elderly mothers and fathers to the camps. Some campesinos described going to the refugee camps for a while, then returning to El Salvador.

Intentional arrival in Honduras is also visible through the campesinos' use of both the FMLN and international aid workers. Mass guindas to Honduras usually occurred with the knowledge of the FMLN; to be sure, any movement through FMLN-controlled territory had to be negotiated with commanders. Insurgents also frequently traveled with the mobile communities in order to ensure their safe arrival in Honduras. Indeed, after 1984 the various guerrilla bands began to actively promote Honduras as a refuge point as the FMLN shifted from a "war of position" to a "war of movement." Combatants and collaborators planned mass departures and accompanied groups of campesinos to the border to be collected by international workers, who would then take them to the UN-sponsored camps in Honduras. Collaborators traveled through the region familiarizing people with the refugee camps and working to convince them to join the planned guindas headed in that direction. Esther, a campesina who worked such rounds in northern Chalatenango, explained that "it was negotiated and everything because they [FMLN commanders] saw that with a ton of people it was hard to move around. Okay, first because they had to be combating with the enemy, right? Attacks, confrontations— that was one thing. Another was the question of food; it was really difficult to be able to plant food crops. So all of these things forced us to get the people out. That was it, yes, planned." According to Esther, FMLN commanders "just sent me a note telling me how many people were coming . . . and that I should try coordinating them so they could cross to the other side." Meanwhile commanders also made contact with international aid workers in Honduras to let them know to expect the arrival of another group of refugees.[31]

The extent to which these coordinated flights to Honduras were FMLN driven or campesino initiated is difficult to determine. Even the various FMLN affiliate organizations differ on this point. Those from the ERP, for example, claimed that campesino flight to Honduras was purely an FMLN operation. Those from the FPL, in contrast, indicated that the FMLN simply educated campesinos about the flight option and then accompanied and protected those who chose to go to Honduras. Differences of opinion existed within each group as well; some from the Resistencia Nacional (National Resistance, RN) claimed that the FMLN planned and directed every cross-border guinda while others described mere accompaniment.[32]

In addition to working with the FMLN, campesinos en guinda often coordinated their activities with the workers and volunteers of international aid agencies. Internal documents of several agencies indicate that, on at least some occasions, those fleeing were able to inform aid personnel of their imminent arrival at a specific town or landmark. Such communications traveled through the Salvadoran Red Cross and Honduran Green Cross, as well as through FMLN channels. An international presence at the designated site afforded the campesinos a layer of protection against harassment from Salvadoran and Honduran troops. By about 1982 even those Salvadorans who left home with little preparation or planning integrated international aid workers into their guindas. They knew that these workers regularly scoured the border area in search of newly arrived refugees; indeed, the UNHCR designated a number of "roving officers" specifically for this purpose. The campesinos, therefore, penetrated as deeply as possible into the border zone, and then waited in hiding for these officers to pass by, collect them, and escort them to the official camps. The numbers frequently surprised aid workers; one source noted that on one occasion they "expected perhaps 50 and then 100 or 200 refugees emerge[d] from hiding."[33]

It is important to recognize that many campesinos resisted joining the guindas to Honduras. Campesino leaders and FMLN affiliates who encouraged people to depart for Honduras often encountered opposition and sometimes aroused hostility and anger. "Some of them ended up mad at me," said Esther with a sad smile. She remembered one elderly woman in particular who grew increasingly indignant. "I am not tired!" she yelled at Esther. "How can you even think that . . . I would throw myself into those places as if I were a hog in a pen?!"[34]

This woman and most of the others were clearly aware that to set forth on a journey across the border would bring an uncertain future. Many preferred to remain with the mobile communities in El Salvador where, even if life was by no means easy, they at least knew more or less what to expect for the foreseeable future. Moreover, they knew that the border zone was risky and crossing the border could be treacherous given that security forces from both countries continuously worked to flush out "subversives" in the region. Newly arrived refugees and roving aid agency personnel frequently reported encountering corpses of campesinos in the border area. Although the exact number of dead and missing is impossible to ascertain, a few agency estimates corroborate refugee testimony. In the first six months of 1981 alone, for example, one aid agency reported finding 150 "atrociously mutilated corpses" on the Honduran side of the border; another source reported 172 corpses for the same time period. On the basis of such reports, AW calculated that more than 2,000 Salvadoran refugees had been assassinated along the border between January 1980 and July 1981, with several hundred others detained or disappeared.[35]

The roads and paths leading to Honduran towns—and to the official refugee camps—were equally dangerous. As in El Salvador at the time, many Honduran border villages had some sort of fixed military presence: a command office, barracks, or simple guard post. Therefore, Salvadoran campesinos who descended from the mountains in search of relief in Honduran towns faced the probability of being intercepted by soldiers—if not at a roadblock—and then at a guard post at town entrances and exits. Without proper identification and migration documents, the incoming Salvadorans risked harassment, deportation, arrest, and, as indicated by the numbers above, even death. It was for these reasons that aid agencies initially designated roving officers to make the rounds of the border zone.

Those who sought refuge in Honduras during the mid and late 1980s also were aware of the risks and dangers of life inside the refugee camps. Unlike the earliest refugees, they received news about the refugee zones and therefore knew that—despite the growing levels of aid—the situation in Honduras was less than ideal. Information about the camps traveled through campesinos, aid workers, and the FMLN. On a near daily basis, people chose to leave the camps and return to El Salvador. On occasion family members visited their loved ones in the camps. The FMLN's own messenger system reached into the Honduran camps. And representatives of aid organizations moved through the border zone, interacting with campesinos and FMLN combatants and collaborators. Through all these methods, those still in northern El Salvador learned about the harsh realities of life in the refugee camps.

Despite these dangers, tens of thousands opted to join the cross-border guindas. They made this decision for a variety of interrelated reasons. Understandably, people were weary. As the years passed and the war continued with no end in sight, the guinda cycle grew increasingly difficult to sustain in northern El Salvador. There were fewer ways to produce or obtain enough food for survival, and napalm and other chemicals made both food and shelter more difficult to find. Points of refuge in Honduras offered a relative sense of stability. Arrival at UN-sponsored refugee camps in Honduras meant that they could stop running for a while, rest, and regain their health. This was especially important for children and the elderly, who comprised a large percentage of the refugee population and suffered the most during the extended guindas. To be sure, life in Honduras was not entirely safe. Yet by 1984 the dangers faced there were in many ways more predictable, and therefore more manageable, than those in El Salvador. The possibility or promise of FMLN protection and accompaniment on cross-border treks also likely persuaded people to join.

Particularly influential in peoples' decisions was a strong sense of solidarity within the mobile communities. Campesinos knew that there was a certain degree of both strength and safety in numbers. Although while en guinda they preferred to move in small groups, they also had experiences in which numbers tipped the scale in their favor. In interviews and testimonies, campesinos offered examples of group protests that spurred positive outcomes, which might include a group of women gathering at a military post to demand the release of a prisoner or dozens of children swarming around government soldiers, harassing them until they abandoned the community. In such cases, "because there was a big block of 100 people, with that number, well, they didn't kill us."[36] Thus, as reception centers in Honduras evolved into semipermanent sites of refuge, and as the population of those sites grew, more people were drawn across the border.

The attraction of the refugee camps intensified throughout the mid-1980s as the Salvadorans living there gained international recognition not only for their status as refugees but also for the strength of their organization. As the refugees' international profiles rose, campesinos still in El Salvador learned about their new international allies as well as the new resources available through these agencies and individuals. This, too, prompted people to make the journey.

Organizing Exile: Salvadoran Refugees in the Closed Camps of Honduras

Life was far from easy for those who chose to cross the border into Honduras. The military cordons around the camps—which involved not only chain-link fences but also guard posts at the one official entrance/exit in each camp and troops stationed around the circumference—along with the twenty-four-hour military surveillance and ever-changing regulations, entailed serious security risks.[37] Simply stepping outside camp boundaries—especially after curfew—could lead to arrest, disappearance, and even death. To cite just one example, in February 1982 Honduran soldiers detained two male refugees near La Virtud for not carrying identification (despite the recognized problems with documentation procedures in the camps). During the night, the men's screams emanated from the barracks as soldiers interrogated and tortured them. The next day Honduran officials claimed that the two had tried to escape; one man supposedly had been killed during the attempt, and

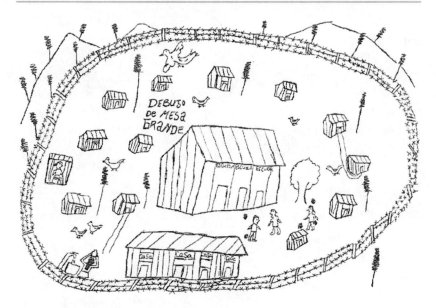

Fig. 1. Mesa Grande refugee camp. (Reproduced from SJDPA 1994)

the other was reported missing.[38] Not only did refugees need to be careful to not overstep camp boundaries; they also had to be wary of incursions by Salvadoran and Honduran security forces. On some occasions, incursions resembled covert military operations as soldiers and others attempted to "pass as refugees" and infiltrate the camp ranks as spies. In May 1981, for example, there were several reports from refugees that members of ORDEN had tried to join the lines of refugees waiting for food distribution. More often, however, incursions entailed more obvious strategies: air patrols over refugee zones, military occupations of the same zones, and foot patrols through the interior of camps. The arrival of soldiers in refugee zones frequently was a precursor to violence, including the ransacking of tents, warehouses, and voluntary agency offices; strafings; and, in the refugees' terminology, abductions and disappearances.

Reports of such harassment pervaded documents produced by refugees throughout the 1980s, and interviews, songs, and writings from the period clearly reflected the Salvadorans' sentiments. Refugees frequently likened the camps to prisons. A child's drawing from the Mesa Grande camp illustrates this well; in the picture, a massive barbed wire fence encircled the camp, dwarfing all the people and tents inside (see fig. 1). The song "Poder volar" (Able to Fly) expressed similar feelings: "We don't want to be closed in / like little birds in a cage. / They sing and move their wings / wanting to be free and able to fly."[39]

Perhaps not surprisingly, the Salvadorans as refugees held Honduran government and military officials largely responsible for their confinement and its associated difficulties. Rather than remaining apathetic, they went to great lengths to defend themselves as individuals and as a community and to maintain as much control over their surroundings as possible. It can be argued, in fact, that many refugee-related decisions made by the Honduran authorities ultimately backfired in that rather than depoliticizing the refugees they actually encouraged an internal, self-reflexive gaze, which, in turn, strengthened the Salvadorans' resolve, collectivity, and power.

Defining the Community

Just as campesinos turned to their advantage their isolation in El Salvador's tierra olvidada, so too did the closed refugee camps of Honduras produce significant advantages for the Salvadoran campesino refugees. For instance, Salvadorans in many ways had no choice but to see and define themselves in contrast to others. Norberto A., one of the foremost songwriters among the Salvadoran campesinos, illustrated some of the tensions involved in this process of self-definition in a song that mirrors a conversation between a *guanaco* (slang for "Salvadoran") and a *catracho* (slang for "Honduran"), with the latter criticizing the former for abandoning his country to live in the refugee camps:[40]

> The catracho treated him badly;
> stop your stories, you're a guanaco
> I'm a Catracho,
> go to your own land if you're such a man
> There is nothing to keep you here . . .
> don't get mad that I tell you
> your work is worthless . . .
> and here they pass their time so well
> lazy every day, dancing their time away.

Norberto's song depicts the tensions not only between Salvadorans and Hondurans but also between Salvadorans who stayed in El Salvador and those who crossed into Honduras. Part of the song, in fact, argues that the refugees continued to support the popular movement and the liberation of El Salvador from the camps of Honduras:

> Over there, bombs
> Here, potatoes
> here there is work,

I need nothing more;
it's better to labor in the workshops
or on the tents;
I contribute in the tailor shop
in the schools
and once in a while in the gardens.
And that is how I spend every day
you know nothing about my commitment.

Although the subject of commitment to El Salvador will be explored in more depth in later chapters, it is important to note here what Norberto's song tells us: that Salvadoran refugees continued to identify themselves as Salvadoran, albeit a unique type of Salvadoran given their location in exile.

Salvadorans further defined their own community by emphasizing the commonalities among themselves. They all shared common experiences of poverty and repression in the preflight and guinda periods. They found themselves in similar circumstances in the camps: suffering from traumas of flight; grieving the loss of family, friends, and homes; living dozens to a room in substandard housing; eating the exact same foods; catching each others' illnesses. They also worried about threats from the same "enemies," soldiers from both El Salvador and Honduras. And they shared the same hopes for peace and plans to return home to El Salvador.

This "sameness" helped focus activities in the camps. Given that the international aid regime covered the basic needs of the refugees, including food, shelter, and clothing, individuals and families no longer needed to direct their energy toward those ends in the same manner as before their flight or during the guindas. The "release" from traditional obligations, along with their isolation from the Honduran host society, allowed Salvadorans the space, time, and energy to direct toward other ends. As a result, in the "protected spaces" of the refugee camps, organization was able to flourish as never before.[41]

Managing the Basics

Many observers commented on the organized nature of Salvadoran refugee camps as early as 1981 (before the international aid regime was fully established), and commendations continued throughout the 1980s. "I was constantly amazed," wrote a pastor from Pennsylvania of his visit to the Colomoncagua camp, "at the strength of the refugees' organization and their ability to make decisions by consensus."[42] In this, Salvadorans distinguished themselves from the Nicaraguan and Guatemalan refugees in Honduras at the time. "Those who were best organized," admitted Abrahám García Turcios, Honduran army colonel and the head of CONARE, "were the Salvadorans."[43]

Unfortunately, most sources to date have offered little sense of the extent to which such initiatives came from the refugees themselves. Some simply expressed an amazement bordering on disbelief at the refugees' achievements. As one observer wrote, "With each day that passes one sees with more admiration how these humble people, nearly all of them illiterates, peasants, have been able to achieve a level of organization that is truly exemplary."[44] Others tended to hold international agencies responsible for all aspects of camp organization. And, as noted earlier, Honduran and Salvadoran officials chalked the refugees' organizations up to manipulations by the FMLN insurgents. In the words of García Turcios, "Guerrilla commanders had absolute control over the refugee camps."[45]

When told from the refugees' perspective, however, the story is quite different. Campesino refugees highlighted their own role in the organization of life in the refugee zones and pointed out that, in fact, they had organized themselves before international aid arrived. Just as they arranged their crossing of the international border, so too did they manage to effectively address their needs once in Honduras by successfully drawing on preestablished connections with Honduran campesinos to negotiate living arrangements and work agreements. During this early period it was not unusual to see upward of forty people residing in the humble houses of Honduran campesinos. Most Salvadorans helped their hosts with subsistence plots and household tasks, and some of the earliest refugee arrivals also found work in the fields of local large landowners.[46]

Salvadorans welcomed the Honduran campesinos' hospitality, of course, and particularly so considering that many arrived at their sites of refuge with little more than the clothes on their backs. Yet they also made clear that they did not passively accept assistance from their Honduran counterparts. On the contrary, as a Morazán man explained, from the very first day "we started to organize ourselves to form little groups and through them be able to resolve our problems."[47] These "little groups" certainly paralleled the various committees and commissions of both the preflight and guinda periods. Of course, arrival in new surroundings entailed plenty of adjustments, including eventually "how to administer the few resources that the humanitarian and solidarity organizations brought."[48]

Salvadorans referred to these aid agencies in much the same way as they did the local Hondurans; they clearly appreciated the assistance provided by the aid groups but placed their own personal efforts at the center of the narrative. Necessity, they argued, prompted them to take action, particularly with regard to the most basic issues: shelter, food, health, and security.

Refugees described, for example, how the need for shelter prompted the election of construction coordinators and the formation of work crews.

Fig. 2. Corn for tortillas, communal kitchen, Colomoncagua refugee camp. (Photo by Steve Cagan)

Coordinators and their crews negotiated with locals and aid groups for necessary supplies, such as tools and nails, and collected wood from local forests. Over time they replaced crude emergency shelters with more sturdy structures of wood, canvas, plastic, and sheets of corrugated metal. Construction crews also designed, built, and maintained considerable infrastructure projects, including classrooms, health clinics, latrines, and water systems.[49]

In a similar vein, necessity prompted the formation of crews responsible for the acquisition, preparation, and distribution of food. At first there were not enough supplies—utensils and comestibles—to satisfy the great need. But the refugees did the best they could with the little they had, and, as one refugee at Colomoncagua said, "we began at the bottom, and little by little we got a pot or a dish and kept working" to feed everyone.[50]

As the number of refugees in Honduras continued to grow, international food donations increased; eventually Salvadorans received weekly deliveries of rations. In response they established committees to handle the receipt of goods, as well as their storage, preparation, and equitable division. Kitchen work teams, comprised primarily of women, spent much of the day preparing corn tortillas (see fig. 2); at mealtime, then, they distributed the tortillas and other food items to their compatriots (see fig. 3). Refugees at La Virtud established a

Fig. 3. Food distribution, Colomoncagua refugee camp. (Photo by Steve Cagan)

rather unambiguous method of distribution. One observer noted that "in the morning, the refugees left a container in a line, the committee filled it with a ration proportional to the size of the family and at meal time the families returned to collect their containers filled with food."[51]

Salvadoran refugees in Honduras considered that their heavy dependence on donated food supplies, while necessary, was an unnatural and unwelcome condition. In testimonies taken at the time, as well as in postwar interviews, Salvadorans repeatedly highlighted the forced isolation in the camps imposed by Honduran government policy and enforced by military vigilance. They also frequently noted that their access to Honduran markets had been purposely blocked and land for tilling denied. They often lamented that the small gardens they planted around the camp perimeter did little to contribute to the great need within the camp. These sentiments contrasted sharply with idealized recollections of bountiful harvests in their homeland of El Salvador. Such commentary indicates that, if conditions had permitted, most Salvadorans would have preferred to work the land to provide their own food.

Equally noteworthy is the fact that, although the rules established by the Honduran government forced refugees' reliance on donated food supplies, Salvadorans did not adopt an attitude of passivity or dependence. Rather the refugees continued to act independently and in creative and resourceful ways. To cite just one example, addressing the need for household utensils, refugees established a unique sort of recycling system. For instance, they "established . . . a metalsmithing workshop where they made jugs from empty cans of cooking oil."[52] Additional evidence of their resourcefulness can be found in their vegetable gardens. Shortly after the refugee camps were established, a Honduran remarked that it would be impossible to plant anything on the steep hills within the refugee camps. Within the first year, however, the Salvadorans constructed a series of terraced gardens where they planted vegetable gardens to augment their diet (see fig. 4).

Closely linked to both food and shelter was the issue of health, a major concern that demanded concerted attention from the start. Salvadoran refugees recognized the indispensable medical assistance provided by University of Honduras health brigades and other voluntary agencies such as MSF and Concern, an Irish aid organization; interviews and written documents from the period are replete with the refugees' expressions of appreciation. Even more common in these same sources, however, are descriptions of their own roles in improving health conditions in the camps.[53]

Particularly important were the *guardianes de salud* (health custodians or wardens), who visited a set number of tents daily to monitor the health of residents and, when necessary, make referrals for consultation with the

Fig. 4. Agricultural terraces, Colomoncagua refugee camp. (Photo by Steve Cagan)

international doctors. Committees of guardianes also educated their compatriots in the refugee zones about the importance of personal and environmental hygiene. For example, they decorated the camps with colorful drawings and carefully scripted texts informing people of the benefits of latrines, hand washing, and boiling water. Guardianes also helped establish task forces to address the sanitation needs of the camps such as removing trash and debris from public pathways, cleaning the latrines, and collecting garbage for proper burning (see fig. 5).

Refugees also highlighted the role of the nutritionists who, working with professionals from international organizations, identified various levels of malnutrition and, using rations of fruits, vegetables, meat, eggs, and dairy products, developed supplemental diets for each level. The positive results of the refugee nutritionists' efforts prompted the UNHCR and other organizations to offer additional assistance, and soon nutrition centers could be found throughout the refugee camps.

Safety concerns also prompted refugee organization and action from the start. Just as they had at home and during the guindas, refugee men formed *grupos de vigilancia* (vigilance groups) and took turns patrolling the camps in order to inform the community about the movement of troops around the camp circumference, suspicious behavior, and impending incursions. Similar to the early warning systems of the guindas, emergency communications systems existed in the camps so that all inhabitants could be contacted within

Fig. 5. Cleaning crew, Colomoncagua refugee camp. (Photo by Steve Cagan)

ten to twenty minutes. Refugee security guards also kept formal watch over all camp entrances and exits; they warned residents of potentially dangerous visitors and on some occasions even blocked the entry of especially problematic individuals. This happened in May 1981, for example, at La Virtud. When a Datsun with Salvadoran license plates arrived to the camp entrance, members of the refugee security group recognized two of the passengers, José Angel (a member of the Salvadoran National Guard) and Alejandro Roje (the mayor of Victoria, Cabañas). These men had been responsible, the refugees said, for multiple murders in Cabañas. The refugees vociferously opposed their entry into the camp, and in the end the van was not allowed to enter in spite of written authorization from Honduran immigration and military authorities.

Collective organization among Salvadoran refugees expanded well beyond the issues of security, shelter, nutrition, and health. In fact, these work areas were part of a much broader organizational structure that became clearer and more formalized as the years passed. Chart 6 illustrates how Salvadorans in Honduras established an entire system of self-government in the refugee camps. Upon first arriving at the UN-sponsored camps, the refugees used the geography of the camps to define several levels of administration. *Colonias* (neighborhoods) were groups of ten adjacent houses, and approximately ten colonias comprised a subcamp. The hundred or so refugees within each colonia then established committees to address their various needs, including

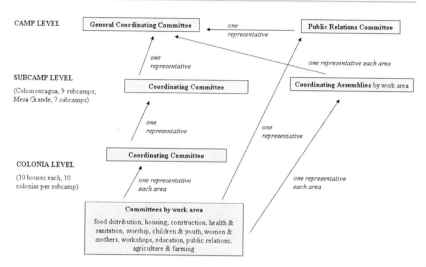

Chart 6. Refugee governance structure.

construction, agricultural production, education, food preparation, health care, religious worship, security, and child care. Elected representatives from each of these work areas served on a colonia-wide coordinating committee. Each of these committees, in turn, elected one representative to serve on a subcamp coordinating committee. These subcamp committees then sent one member to the campwide coordinating committee. The refugees also established coordinating groups for each of the work areas (education, agricultural production, and so on), thus ensuring parity of services across the entire camp.

Documentation from the 1980s reveals that communication and coordination also occurred between the various Salvadoran camps in Honduras despite officials' efforts to isolate Salvadorans. Representatives from the Colomoncagua and San Antonio camps often coauthored materials, including calendars, public announcements, and newsletters. Representatives from Mesa Grande, Colomoncagua, and San Antonio worked together to produce *INFORESAL*, a cross-camp informational magazine complete with editorials, news stories, comics, and calendars of events. Representatives from each of the camps also orchestrated multiple mass protest actions, including a 1989 hunger strike involving dozens of refugees across the three camps.

Managing the Moral Boundaries of Community

Much of the documentation produced by refugees in Honduras portrayed them as an extremely close-knit community, a united front. They shared experiences of poverty, marginalization, and repression at home in rural El Salvador; they all grieved for their loved ones lost to violence and civil war; and they faced the same risks and dangers in exile. They all held the same social, political, and religious values and the will to strive toward common goals. Descriptions of public assemblies in the refugee camps paint a picture of full collaboration, with all inhabitants present, each individual having the opportunity to voice his or her opinion, and everyone casting votes in camp elections. Descriptions of committee work follow a similar vein: everyone cycled through the various duties, and everyone had the opportunity to develop and practice organizational and leadership skills.

Closer examination reveals, however, that multiple tensions existed among the refugees. As noted in previous chapters, campesinos organized at different rates, for various reasons, and with multiple collaborators. In spite of this variety, several trends in geography and politics were evident. The western refugee zones, comprised of Mesa Grande, La Virtud, and their environs, hosted Salvadorans primarily from the departments of Chalatenango and Cabañas, who often were associated with the FPL and to a lesser extent the RN. Campesinos from Morazán, where the ERP predominated, tended to seek refuge in the eastern camps of Colomoncagua, San Antonio, and Buenos Aires. These different political preferences traveled with campesinos across the border and into the refugee camps of Honduras. At Mesa Grande, both FPL and RN influences and affiliations existed and sometimes flared into conflict. As a result the camp developed geographic divisions, with individuals strongly affiliated or allied with the RN in one location and those linked to the FPL in another.

In the eastern refuge zones it appears that fewer overt frictions occurred. This may have been due in part to the heavy influence of ERP high officials. With a reputation for being the most militant and strict of the FMLN affiliates, ERP influence may have helped to keep discord to a minimum. The comparative "harmony" of the eastern refuge zones was also likely a result of the fact that very early on, campesinos of differing political tendencies had settled in separate camps. More to the point, when campesino supporters of the government clashed with supporters of the popular movement and insurgents in the Colomoncagua refugee camp, Honduran and UN officials simply relocated the former to a camp established specifically for this purpose. This camp, Buenos Aires, was quite small and located on the edge of the town of Colomoncagua rather than at a great distance. "This is where refugees who were fleeing from the guerrillas came; they were allied with the government," explained Colonel García Turcios. "We couldn't have them together because if we did, there were problems."[54]

In addition to political tensions, interpersonal conflicts plagued the refugee camps. People undoubtedly brought with them old resentments and disputes, and new ones arose in the camps as a result of living in such cramped quarters. In response, campesino refugees established Secretarías de Conflictos (Conflict Resolution Commissions) whose members "had to keep watch in order to help resolve family problems. If there was some dispute with the neighbor, one sat down with the family and then looked for a solution so that they wouldn't have any more problems."[55]

According to women who spent time in the refugee camps, marital disputes were among the most common problems. Although there is no doubt that such problems existed prior to flight, it is important to note that the circumstances of exile altered gender roles and, in particular, introduced new expectations of women.[56] Women outnumbered men in the refugee camps, sometimes three or four to one. The skewed demographics, along with the "liberating" effects of popular education, Christian reflection on the Bible, and interactions with the international aid regime, prompted women to take on more public roles in the camps. As refugees, then, women participated in community life and moved into leadership positions to an extent far beyond what they previously had done at home in northern El Salvador. Their male partners did not always approve of these activities and often harassed and abused them as a result.

From the perspective of the women, men's behaviors were at the root of the problem. For example, although alcohol was prohibited in the refugee camps, many men managed to obtain liquor through the black market encircling the camps, and drunkenness worsened patterns of physical abuse. Beyond this, women simply pointed to the prevalence of *machista* (male chauvinist) ideologies and practices, claiming that men believed women to be inferior, did not respect women or women's work, and often maintained multiple sexual relationships while expecting women to stay behind closed doors.

And so the women took matters into their own hands. They established Committees for Women and Mothers to address issues specific to these groups such as maternal health and child care. These committees soon became integrated into the general camp government structure. At Mesa Grande, the women went one step further and established an all-woman security patrol, which they called the Batallón Pacho (Pacho Battalion). The choice of title alone reveals some of the deep tensions that gave rise to the battalion, for *pacho* is a slang term that refers to an indolent or cowardly man or, taken one step further, the lack of male genitalia. The Batallón Pacho paid special attention to men who drank excessively, mistreated their wives and children, or used their leadership positions as a way to exert power over women or demand sexual favors (this was particularly evident among those who had responsibilities in the workshops and food storage and distribution centers). The women of Batallón Pacho "began to restrict these kinds of situations," explained one former member. "Many times, when they found men who had their partners and families, and they found them 'in the act' with other women, sometimes they detained them, this group of organized women. They detained the men and even imprisoned them for up to three days—until the UNHCR intervened [and] came as a mediator, right, so that the conflict could somehow be resolved."[57] Other former members of the battalion did not recall UNHCR representatives intervening; a bit of time in confinement, along with a stern talking-to, they said, often straightened out the problem. In a similar vein, the Batallón Pacho also bridled "loose behavior" among the women who "liked to go and sleep with the Honduran soldiers."[58]

The activities of the Batallón Pacho at the Mesa Grande camp provide insights into a process that occurred on a broader level in all the closed refugee camps: the defining of the exile community through the drawing and maintenance of that community's borders. If Honduran officials controlled the physical borders of the refugee camps, the campesino refugees controlled the moral boundaries. When individuals did not stay within those boundaries, they suffered the consequences meted out by their compatriots, sometimes by members of subgroups such as Mesa Grande's Batallón Pacho and other times by the general camp leadership. "When someone made a mistake or committed a crime" at Mesa Grande, explained Rosa, "we got together, we made them see what they had done wrong, and we sanctioned them."[59] Thus, people who had misbehaved sometimes spent days locked up in the aforementioned "prisons," storage sheds or classrooms modified for individual confinement. It is worth noting, however, that the delinquents were never entirely confined; according to Rosa, doors and windows remained open and visitors came and went at will. To a large extent, then, the prisoners stayed inside of their own volition as they listened to their consciences. In this way camp prisons served as a sort of theater of punishment, a space in which to publicly display the individuals who misbehaved; embarrassment and humiliation pressured those who had committed offenses to repent and to mend their ways. The refugee leadership also utilized other publicly visible sanctions, including the assignment of particularly unpopular duties such as cleaning the camp latrines. These kinds of sanctions not only punished the guilty; they also served as a warning to others about the consequences of trespassing against group expectations. "A sanction," Rosa concluded, "was a lesson."

Thus, like the norms that developed during the guindas, exile had its own norms. And, as they had done during the guindas, refugees continued to police each others' behaviors in the refugee camps. Not only did they keep an eye on social relations, but they also regulated political matters. As the next chapters will illustrate, Salvadoran refugees remained committed to their homeland and la lucha, the popular struggle to liberate the country from oppression and tyranny. They viewed many of their activities in the camps—news magazines, workshops, literacy training, and local government itself—as tasks that supported the struggle in both the short and long terms. Although refugees came to expect each other to actively participate in these various activities, the historical record makes clear that not everyone did so in ways deemed proper by the majority. Yet, rather than ignoring or covering up the existence of malcontents in the camps, the refugees purposely identified them through songs and other media. Some pieces depicted *los haraganes* (good-for-nothings, loafers) in general as outsiders, people who did not contribute to the community but instead threatened the collectivity. As "El corrido de los haraganes" (The Song of the Haraganes) warned, "Great laziness is an enemy / that can lead us to be criminals / so that by turning us into vice-draggers / we lose our fear even of killing."[60] In other instances refugees pointed out problematic individuals by name. A July 1988 communiqué from Mesa Grande, for example, announced the names and aliases of three "antisocial subjects" who had purposely "fomented the intranquility of the refugee community" through scandalous and criminal behavior, including alcohol consumption; disrespecting women, children, and the elderly; collaboration with the Honduran military; and the murder of a member of the camp coordinating committee.[61]

In much the same way as the prisons, these songs and other media served to publicly scorn problematic individuals. Identifying people in this way often prompted action, and it is toward this end that the refugees undoubtedly designed many of their statements. In other words, given enough pressure from refugees and sympathetic aid agency personnel, the UNHCR and Honduran officials would remove problematic individuals from the camps.[62] In some cases officials transferred such individuals to other refugee camps or, in special cases, to sites outside the refugee zones. After the three "antisocial subjects" murdered the committee member at Mesa Grande in 1988, for example, refugees pushed for their expulsion from the camp. María, who lived at Mesa Grande for nearly a decade, recalled frequent occasions on which whole families were removed from Mesa Grande and one particular incident when the problematic group did not move to another camp but rather "to the Honduran interior." In a similar vein, problems at Colomoncagua in 1985 prompted the transfer of several refugees to Mesa Grande. And, as noted earlier, officials once removed several hundred Salvadoran refugees from the Colomoncagua camp and installed them in an entirely new and separate camp at Buenos Aires. Other *indeseables* (undesirables) were relocated to Bolivia, Canada, and elsewhere.

It is important to note that clandestine "policing" occurred among the refugees in Honduras. Some expulsions, for example, occurred under the official radar. According to former refugees interviewed during the postwar period, the refugee community frequently treated haraganes with such repudiation and contempt that they ultimately chose to leave the camps of their own accord. As Rosa recalled, "A lot of the refugees who started to act different, we just ran them out of the camps. We repatriated them."

In some cases it was simply easier for the refugee leadership to deal with especially sensitive political issues in a clandestine fashion. Refugee association with the FMLN insurgents was one of these issues.[63] It was common knowledge that the FMLN sent individuals to the camps for various reasons; but because not all refugees supported the FMLN to the same extent, the camp leadership designated specific committees to quietly handle relations with guerrilla representatives. Members of these committees often had collaborated with the FMLN in northern El Salvador before flight and during the guindas; many also had family members who had chosen to join the insurgents either as soldiers or as support personnel. These committees exchanged news and information, as well as supplies, with guerrilla representatives. Understandably, these transactions could not occur just anywhere at any time; they had to be carefully planned and orchestrated so they would be seen neither by officials nor by unsympathetic or uninformed refugees and aid personnel. "When people informed officials that they had seen others leave the camps at night with suitcases, they [the refugee leaders] had to hold meetings to let everyone know that these were our people," explained one woman. When that did not solve the problem, she continued, "we began to work at night more so that the population wouldn't have reason to criticize us."

Another method of internal management deserves mention here, although the details are far from firm. According to numerous sources, the refugee leadership occasionally used murder to address particularly problematic situations and individuals. Understandably, this was not a topic often broached by Salvadoran campesinos in either documents or interviews. Yet numerous observers reported the phenomenon, among them Hondurans, Salvadorans, internationals, government and military officials, refugees, and aid workers. Regardless of the truth behind the claims, even rumors that murder had occurred, or threats that it might occur at any moment, served a powerful function in terms of maintaining a desired level of order among the refugees. Indeed, an unverifiable account of such severe punishment could take on a life of its own, serving as a constant reminder to the refugees that there were rules to follow and consequences for not following them.[64]

Thus, the boundaries of life in exile were imposed not only by the Honduran government but also by the refugees themselves. Just like during the guindas, a kind of moral economy functioned in the refugee camps, and a system of norms evolved that was peculiar to the wartime experience of exile. This system intentionally stifled internal differences and dissent to strengthen the group's public profile. As the next chapters will illustrate, emphasizing their unity, in turn, helped to attract new allies among the international aid workers and visitors to the camps.

Although the initial arrival of the mobile communities in Honduras may be considered accidental, Salvadoran campesinos soon chose to take advantage of the situation and began to establish semipermanent refuge points on Honduran territory. Settling on the other side of the border did not entail escape from danger and repression; the Honduran security forces collaborated closely with Salvadoran forces such that campesinos came to consider both as threats. To counter these threats and address their short- and long-term needs in exile, Salvadorans did what they had been doing for years: they organized.

Just as they did during the guindas within Salvadoran territory, campesinos in Honduras established a variety of work crews and committees to address the everyday needs of the community. These bodies evolved into a complex system of self-government similar to the PPLs of northern El Salvador at the time. As with any community, there were both leaders and followers and mechanisms of internal control.

In addition, alliances continued to prove crucial. As mobile communities made their journeys into exile, they called on support from the FMLN as well as international aid workers and solidarity networks. In the refugee camps Salvadorans rallied their new international allies through public denunciations, petitions and letters, and a variety of other nonviolent pressure tactics. The longer they remained in Honduras the more astute they became at utilizing these allies and the resources they proffered. This maneuvering of the international aid regime is the subject of the next chapter.

4

 The Politics of Exile

On 25 November 1987 retired Honduran army colonel Abrahám García Turcios made a memorable trip to the Colomoncagua refugee camp in Intibucá, Honduras, where thousands of Salvadoran campesinos had been living since 1981. The colonel, head of CONARE, arrived at the camp unannounced in an unmarked vehicle. He spent some time with representatives from the UNHCR, perhaps further dickering about the details of the "Memorandum de Entendimiento" (Memorandum of Understanding) signed by government and UN officials in June of the same year. At the close of the meeting, the colonel climbed back into his car, ready to return to his Tegucigalpa office three hundred kilometers to the east. As he rounded a curve in the dirt road leading to the camp exit, however, García Turcios found his path blocked by several hundred Salvadorans demanding an impromptu meeting.

Elected representatives of the refugee community had been trying for weeks, in fact, to arrange a meeting with García Turcios in order to discuss numerous concerns they had regarding plans outlined in the "Memorandum"; of particular concern was the Honduran government's proposal to replace internationals with government-appointed delegates. García Turcios had already reneged on the proposed meeting several times. As a result the refugees likely interpreted the secrecy of his visit to the Colomoncagua camp on that November day as proof that he had no intention of meeting with them at all.

But the refugees would not allow García Turcios to ignore them. So they blocked his exit. While some refugees hoisted picket signs and banners calling for internationals to remain in the camp, others approached García Turcios's vehicle and urged him to meet with them before he left the camp. Still the colonel refused, and, rather than get out of his car, he attempted to drive straight through the crowd, wrenching down banners and forcing people to scatter. The Salvadorans remained resolute, however, and they closed in on the vehicle until it barely crawled along. When they began to place rocks around the tires in an attempt to completely halt his progress, Colonel García Turcios flew out the car door, brandishing a pistol. The sight of the gun sparked panic among the refugees, and in the ensuing confusion the colonel withdrew from the camp, threatening immediate action in retaliation for the refugees' refusal to accept the authority of the Honduran government.[1]

This incident was not the first of its kind. Nor was November 1987 the first time that García Turcios had uttered such a warning. In fact, concerns about the management and control of Salvadoran refugees had plagued Honduran officials since the late 1970s when campesinos from El Salvador began to illegally cross into Honduras in search of a temporary respite from the violence raging at home. As noted in the preceding chapter, the Honduran government had resisted formally acknowledging the Salvadoran campesinos as refugees for several reasons, including historic animosities toward their southern neighbors and new concerns regarding the international spread of communism. Between 1980 and 1982, however, the UNHCR successfully negotiated a series of agreements with Honduras that allowed Salvadorans to stay in Honduras but placed financial and administrative responsibility on the UNHCR. The Honduran government remained the ultimate authority in all things related to Salvadoran refugees. Because these campesino refugees "endanger the country's national security," the Honduran National Security Council announced, "[we must] manage the situation in the most intelligent manner."[2]

But if Honduran officials perceived Salvadorans as threats, the Salvadorans in turn perceived García Turcios and other Honduran officials to be in the same league as the Salvadoran armed forces and death squads—in short, as threats to their individual and communal well-being. Salvadoran campesinos had considerable experience with state-sponsored marginalization and repression from the economic deprivations of life in the tierra olvidada to the military's scorched earth campaigns to the collaboration of Salvadoran and Honduran soldiers in "cleansing" the border region. Life in exile in many ways continued in the same vein. Campesinos in Honduras faced not only the physical and psychological effects of political violence and war; they also had to confront anti-Salvadoran propaganda, exclusion from official decision-making circles, military incursions into the refugee camps, arrests, tortures, executions, and deportations.

It was a combination of overt and covert threats that prompted the Colomoncagua representatives to request a meeting with Colonel García Turcios in late 1987. According to the Salvadorans, the "Memorandum" signed by Honduran and UNHCR officials in Geneva threatened to consolidate Honduran control over the refugee camps and their inhabitants, as well as international aid efforts, which would only increase the already high levels of harassment and prompt more violations of their rights as refugees and as humans. Further convincing the refugees of the hazards foretold by the "Memorandum" was the fact that UN and government officials considered unnecessary and invalid any counsel from the refugees themselves; some, like García Turcios, even went to great extremes to avoid any discussion with the refugees. The Salvadorans insisted that their voices be heard; they were, after all, best positioned to fully understand and respond to the problems and needs of the refugees. When officials refused to listen, however, they found alternate ways to prompt discussions.

This chapter examines the "negotiations" among Salvadoran refugees, UN and Honduran officials, and international aid workers, focusing in particular on issues of control and authority. Although Salvadorans did not arrive in Honduras carrying suitcases of clothes or boxes of kitchen utensils, many—if not most—did bring with them a certain level of sociopolitical awareness, as well as significant organizational skills and sensibilities. Previous chapters illustrated how campesinos responded to challenges through local, regional, and national organization. This chapter expands the discussion to an international level by exploring how these same campesinos, once in Honduras, responded to the unique contexts and circumstances of life in exile. Not only did they draw from previous experience at home and en guinda; they also integrated international solidary workers and agencies into their defense systems and organizational schemes. Through the use of strategies both old and new, the Salvadorans succeeded in maintaining a great deal of control over their spaces of refuge.

Allying with *Los Internacionales*

Salvadoran refugees were well aware that international attention produced tangible results. This became profoundly clear during some cross-border guindas; foreign observers not only accompanied campesinos, but some also literally carried them across the border. At the Sumpul and Lempa rivers, for example, foreign nationals swam across the river with children on their backs while pushing others across on inner tubes and logs. Once in the refuge zones of Honduras, campesinos found that the presence of people from other countries—especially the United States, Canada, and northern European nations—significantly curtailed the behavior of the Honduran and Salvadoran security forces, in effect protecting refugees from harassment,

Fig. 6. Refugee embroidery. *From top*: "Thank you Solidarity for the help you provide to Salvadoran refugees in San Antonio"; "Salvadoran refugees in Colomoncagua Honduras. We ask for more international assistance for the whole community and to advance in our work process." (Photos by Steve Cagan)

arrest, and even murder. In the words of one former refugee at Mesa Grande, "When [foreigners] were there, they [government forces] mistreated you, but they didn't kill you."[3]

It should come as no surprise, then, that Salvadoran refugees integrated these foreigners into their camp security systems in a number of ways. International aid workers and observers spread testimonies, accounts, and *denuncias* (denunciations) across the globe and in so doing drummed up additional support for the refugees. Their own firsthand observations added weight to the refugees' versions of events, which many outsiders refused to believe. After one U.S. aid worker provided testimony about a military incursion into the La Virtud camp in July 1981, a high-level UNHCR representative admitted to her, "It is so important that a North American witnessed it because this makes the testimony verifiable."[4] Thus, international witnesses pushed the refugees' concerns farther and to higher levels of government and nongovernment agencies. This was especially important considering that Salvadoran and Honduran officials and news media consistently portrayed Salvadoran refugees in the worst light possible. It was precisely for this reason that refugees sought alliances with many aid workers and visitors.

In order to utilize their international allies to their full potential, Salvadorans studied them and, just as they had done with the Salvadoran armed forces during the guindas, identified patterns. Similar to the campesino movement in El Salvador, aid agencies also occupied positions along a progressive/orthodox spectrum. Refugees were careful to detect and foster relations with agencies and individuals with philosophies paralleling their own, that is, toward the progressive end of the spectrum. These the refugees labeled *los internacionales* (the internationals); they were the solidary witnesses, the allies in the refugees' various struggles, from short-term efforts to improve conditions in the camps to long-term campaigns against relocation or in favor of repatriation to the ideal solution of peace and justice in El Salvador.

An important part of the refugee–internacional alliance was the fact that los internacionales proffered the refugees an extremely valuable tool: information. Employees affiliated with UN programs, for example, typically rotated from camp to camp, spending several weeks to two months in each.[5] Upon their arrival at a camp, they would reveal information about their previous post through expressions and assumptions, as well as words and deeds. Aid personnel and visitors also had access to resources unavailable to the refugees, including ham radios, telephones, faxes, and cables; not surprisingly, refugees frequently overheard information being passed between aid workers through these media. In late 1981 and early 1982, for example, refugees in the La Virtud area learned via two-way radio transmission that their compatriots in nearby villages had been forcefully relocated to the new UNHCR-sponsored camp at Mesa Grande. After the transfer of each group they heard "discouraging descriptions" of the new location, which spurred higher levels of resistance to official relocation efforts.[6] Los internacionales also carried messages between family members and friends in different camps and introduced oral and written reports and news about foreign opinions and actions regarding events in El Salvador and the situation of refugees in Honduras.

Los internacionales also brought with them information about international law. From them Salvadorans learned not only about their rights as refugees in light of international agreements such as the 1951 Geneva Convention and its 1967 Protocol; they also learned that it was the internationally sanctioned responsibility of the UNHCR to protect those rights and assure the safety of refugees. Salvadorans would make good use of such information throughout their time in exile.

The Politics of Refugee Aid

Between the late 1970s and the mid-1990s, Honduras hosted more than seventy thousand refugees from other Central American and Caribbean nations.[7] As one of the poorest countries in Central America, Honduras had few resources to draw from to sustain its own population let alone such a high number of foreign squatters. Thus, the Honduran government relied heavily on international aid, most of which funneled through the UNHCR. The UNHCR, in turn, depended on dozens of Honduran and international voluntary aid agencies, including the Comité Evangélico de Emergencia Nacional (Evangelical National Emergency Committee, CEDEN), Caritas, World Vision, the Mennonite Central Committee, Concern, emergency brigades from the medical school at the Universidad Nacional Autónoma de Honduras (National Autonomous University of Honduras, UNAH), Catholic Relief Services, MSF, and others. Although all these agencies generally shared the same basic humanitarian intentions, each approached their work from different—and sometimes quite opposite—directions. Inevitably, this led to tensions.

The very structure of the aid regime produced frictions as each organization sought to establish hegemony over specific camps or areas of refugee aid. At the top of the regime hierarchy, the UNHCR found itself in a sort of catch-22; because Honduras was not a signatory to the Geneva Convention and Protocol Relating to the Status of Refugees, UNHCR personnel associated with the Honduran mission had no juridical framework that would allow deeper intervention or more concerted action with regard to, for example, Honduran military patrols through the refugee camps or the detention of refugees. In large part due to this, voluntary aid agency evaluations of the UNHCR ranged from neglect and unconcern to dismissive and patronizing. Agencies complained, for example, that the UNHCR operated in a very closed fashion; rather than allowing cooperative decision making, the UNHCR worked on a bilateral basis with individual agencies. Such private negotiations produced a wide chasm between the UNHCR and field agencies to the point that the last place a UNHCR mission chief would inquire for a place to stay overnight was with the Caritas office.[8]

Agency personnel also found fault with the UNHCR's administration procedures. "It is getting increasingly difficult to work with the UNHCR," wrote Caritas volunteer Yvonne Dilling in 1984. "The red tape involved . . . is not just a nuisance—it is costing lives." She described how, despite the conditions of extreme privation in the refugee camps, the UNHCR insisted on formal project proposals to spell out the need. Moreover, proposals needed to be typewritten and submitted in multiple copies. "Without formal requests," claimed Dilling, "they cannot manage to bring in a truckload of vegetables."[9]

Despite these and other frustrations, voluntary agencies acknowledged the UNHCR's international prestige and influence and therefore sought formal affiliations with the organization. Such official association, they felt, would provide the optimum in physical protection for their staff and volunteers. Although most voluntary agencies provided identification papers for their staff and volunteers, such papers paled in comparison to those endorsed by the UNHCR. Therefore, when asked, agency personnel often indicated that they were UNHCR employees even if they did not have the official paperwork to prove it. Yet the UNHCR did not always acknowledge them as UNHCR affiliates. This was of particular concern for Honduran nationals working with more progressive organizations, including Caritas and CEDEN, who were at special risk for retribution from the Honduran military. Fear of the Honduran security forces was by no means specious, as the assassination of Caritas employee Elpidio Cruz in November 1981 illustrated. In light of the risks of involvement with refugee aid, the UN's disparate treatment of internationals and Hondurans exacerbated tensions between voluntary agencies. Frustration and distrust abounded as agencies and individuals accused each other of receiving preferential treatment or collaborating with one or another "enemy."[10]

Along with structural issues, frictions based on politics, religion, and social practices were routine and at times pressed the humanitarian aid regime to the brink of collapse. Perhaps the most exemplary case of this was a contest between the orthodox Christian evangelicals of World Vision on the one hand

and the progressive Catholics of Caritas and CEDEN on the other.[11] From the beginning of the Salvadoran refugee crisis, World Vision's anticommunist stance deeply affected its participation in the aid network, as personnel from the organization believed that through their work they would not only spread the gospel to the refugees but also "stop the communist enemy who ruined everything in the area."[12] Political and religious doctrines led World Vision to denounce Roman Catholic ecumenism in general and in particular "revolutionaries from the Diocese of Santa Rosa" (Caritas), as well as the other "socalled Christian groups [that] are in fact agents of international marxism" (CEDEN).[13]

It appears that World Vision found some success in reducing the influence of these organizations on the refugee aid network. When the UNHCR began officially sponsoring the Salvadoran refugee assistance program in 1981, it contracted with CEDEN as the primary aid coordinator, thereby ousting Caritas from a position it had occupied since the first Salvadoran refugees arrived to Honduras in the late 1970s. The UNHCR based this decision at least in part on government pressures to *not* extend an offer to Caritas, as the Honduran newspaper *La Tribuna* reported: "From today forward all refugee assistance efforts will be channeled through CEDEN and not through Caritas as had been occurring. The government has placed restrictions on the activities of the latter organization due to the fact that it is coordinated by the Diocese of Copán, which denounced the massacre at the Sumpul River."[14]

Given the overlaps between World Vision attitudes and Honduran government policies, many observers believed the two to be collaborating in a campaign to not only oust "undesirables" from the aid network, but also to place World Vision in the coordinating seat. Almost immediately after CEDEN had been contracted by the UNHCR, in fact, high-ranking Honduran military officers expressed their dissatisfaction with CEDEN and its supporting agencies and announced their intention to entrust administrative authority for the refugee aid program to a different organization. Around the same time a World Vision publication claimed that the Honduran government had "asked World Vision to take a leading role in the assistance granted to refugees."[15]

Numerous aid organizations opposed this move. Officials at CEDEN argued that World Vision was unworthy of such a high-profile position due to both its religious proselytism in the refugee camps and its broader penchant for *manejo político* (political maneuvering). They pointed first to World Vision's questionable politics and procedures. "These people had been employees of the Department of National Investigation, the DIN," explained Nidia of CEDEN. "So they were people who were turning Salvadorans in. And to put them in the camps, as promoters, brought us some incredible political problems. . . . We found out that their people, well, they were doing national security work, *inside*."[16] They also pointed to World Vision's "sketchy" past, highlighting in particular its involvement in U.S. counterinsurgency efforts in Indochina, Cambodia, and Somalia and linking specific personnel to the U.S. CIA.[17]

As CEDEN officials began taking action to dismiss World Vision from the aid network, World Vision employees collectively resigned from the aid program, charging that the CEDEN leadership did not respond to the organization's needs and interests.[18] Weeks later, in March 1982, the Honduran government announced that it would not reauthorize CEDEN as the principal coordinating agency for the UNHCR-sponsored refugee aid program. Following this news, CEDEN virtually collapsed. The conservative members of the board of directors forced out numerous liberal employees; dozens of others chose to leave of their own accord.[19]

The Honduran government's decision to not renew CEDEN's authorization as the coordinating agency, combined with World Vision's withdrawal and CEDEN's internal crisis, meant that the refugee aid regime virtually imploded. The UNHCR headquarters in Geneva dispatched a special emergency team to Honduras in April 1982 to negotiate a solution and help repair the damage. After three months, however, the mission remained incomplete, compelling the UNHCR itself to assume the primary coordinating role, which it continued to occupy through the early 1990s. Although this was not the UNHCR's usual practice, it appeared to be the only way to work in the tense environment in Honduras.

As this episode suggests, the Honduran government also played a key role in humanitarian aid operations. Chapter 3 noted how officials repeatedly performed acts of sovereign control precisely out of concern that the presence of so many poor squatters threatened national sovereignty; they mandated the rounding up of refugees and their concentration into camps isolated from true Honduran citizens, thus creating "spaces of exception." At the same time they reconfirmed state control over those spaces through security cordons around camp perimeters, the collection of biographical information (in essence census data) about the inhabitants, military patrols through the camps, and the arrest of suspected subversives. Despite these and other control efforts, authorities remained apprehensive about the Salvadoran camps. In January 1985, in fact, a Honduran delegation traveled to Geneva to discuss matters with UNHCR authorities. The delegation's typewritten agenda for the weeklong series of meetings emphasized the "control of refugees," with specific items including camp infrastructure, procedures for determining refugee status, and voluntary repatriation. At the bottom of the page a delegation member hand wrote an additional item: "Problem of security: state within a state."[20]

Honduran authorities perceived the Salvadoran camps as a "state within a state" not only due to the high levels of organization and mobilization among inhabitants but also because of heavy international influence. The multitude of international agencies working with the refugees were causing "huge problems for the country" by discriminating against Hondurans in hiring, for example, and by failing to establish "a connection between national development plans and the refugees' existence."[21] Moreover, foreign nationals controlled so much of the camp administration and functioning that, in the words of one official, "the Camps enjoy a kind of extraterritoriality into which Honduran authorities are unable to enter."[22]

The UNHCR was especially problematic for authorities. Although it was crucial in providing much-needed financial and material aid, Hondurans claimed that it had "transformed itself into a superagency [*superagencia*] and it has played a more predominant role in Honduras than in other neighboring States in the region."[23] Its personnel presumed authority over not only the refugees but also over the territory inhabited by the refugees; in so doing, UN representatives "impede[d] the involvement of Honduran authorities in the control, administration and supervision of these camps."[24] When Honduran authorities attempted to assert their right to rule over the camps, they found that "UNHCR functionaries become even more resistant."[25] Others made more subtle allusions to the UNHCR's power; in a memorandum to the National Security Council, for example, the Honduran Ministry of Foreign Relations referred to the refugees in Honduras as "the UNHCR's refugees."[26]

If concerns ran high regarding the UNHCR's impugning of Honduran sovereignty, even more troublesome was the fact that voluntary aid agencies contracted by the UNHCR were "riddled with Marxists, Leninists, Maoists and every kind of element identified . . . with the ideas of the left and ideologies ostensibly inclined toward totalitarianism."[27] Work in the Salvadoran refugee camps, they claimed, served both as a stepping-stone into direct combat on behalf of the FMLN and as a cover for less direct methods of assistance. This perception is wonderfully illustrated in the editorial cartoon described in part in the introduction to this book. A few additional details about the cartoon are relevant here. Not only does the artist represent the refugee camps as resting grounds for insurgents; he also questions the intentions of the aid organizations working in the camps (see fig. 7). From the right edge of the frame, two long arms reach out toward the guerrilla-refugee. One offers a cocktail, complete with fancy straw: the forearm reads ACNUR (the Spanish acronym for UNHCR). The other arm, labeled CEDEN, presents a platter on which a huge roasted turkey lies steaming and delicately garnished. The cartoon's caption reads "Care for an appetizer?" Thus, this cartoon not only associated the Salvadoran refugee camps with criminal behavior; it also portrayed national

Opinión

5 DE FEBRERO DE 1982

A BOQUITA QUE QUERES:

CAMPAMENTO DE REFUGIO

ACNUR

CEDEN

Rowi

Fig. 7. "Care for an Appetizer?" (Drawing by Roberto Williams [Rowi], reproduced from *Diario La Prensa*)

and international aid agencies as willing accomplices in the FMLN's "crimes."[28]

To counter concerns about the "extraterritoriality" of the Salvadoran refugee camps, officials closely regulated the national and international agencies lending aid to the Salvadorans. All aid personnel relied on the Honduran government not only for general authorization to work at the refugee camps but also for daily permission to access the border region and the camps, travel across the country from one camp to another, and collect or deliver aid materials. Foreign nationals were in a particularly dependent position; they were required to renew their visas every three months and could be denied visas and deported from the country at any time for any reason.

Perhaps not surprisingly, personnel from international agencies frequently critiqued "the constant control of the Government."[29] The frequency of criticism suggests that Honduran officials found at least some measure of success in its efforts to maintain control over the refugee zones. Nonetheless, they remained ever concerned about their participation in camp affairs and, as a result, launched myriad campaigns to "Honduranize" the aid system; the 1985 special delegation to UNHCR headquarters in Geneva and the negotiation and signing in 1987 of the "Memorandum of Understanding" offer just two examples. The Hondurans' concerns were well founded, for their control was far from complete.

Maneuvering the System

As illustrated earlier, the politics of refugee aid produced a volatile atmosphere. Salvadoran refugees certainly knew this and, indeed, turned such tensions to their own advantage. On both individual and group bases, they identified fissures between personnel and agencies and then inserted themselves into those chinks in order to play one side against another. In essence they sought to use one party in an "official dispute" as leverage in their own struggles to obtain concessions from authorities and gain short- and long-term benefits. For this to work refugees also had to carefully manage information about themselves.

Utilizing Fissures

Time and again Salvadoran refugees turned to one group to critique and press for changes in another. From the very start of their exile, they turned to aid agencies and the UNHCR regarding harassment by Salvadoran and Honduran security forces. Both orally and in writing, refugees repeatedly denounced a variety of attacks, harassment, and mistreatment. At first they tended to focus their denunciations on Salvadoran aggressors rather than Hondurans. As described in chapter 2, they were able to distinguish between the various Salvadoran forces with relative ease; in contrast, they either were unable to or chose not to highlight Honduran forces with equal precision. With time, however, the refugees began to publicly denounce Honduran military and government officials as well. Although incidents of physical harassment topped the refugees' lists of complaints, they also spoke out and took action against disagreeable policies and procedures forwarded by Honduran authorities.

Early in their exile experience campesinos came to understand the UNHCR as "the *only* authority" in matters related to the safety and protection of refugees. They used this new knowledge, along with the rhetoric of international law and human rights, to press individual representatives, as well as the institution as a whole, to comply with their protection mandate.[30] They invoked the high commissioner's authority by sending their grievances directly to UNHCR headquarters in Geneva. Their letters decried the abuses and repeated "attacks against our dignity" by Honduran immigration and military officials and requested that the commissioner send additional protection officers to the refugee zones.[31]

The refugees' efforts occasionally produced results, as when, at the refugees' prodding, the UNHCR convinced Honduran officials to allow international workers to remain overnight in the camps. Often, however, refugee demands went unheeded.[32] In light of this, Salvadorans turned their critiques and protests directly against the UNHCR. The names of particular employees and examples of their failures to fulfill their obligations began dotting refugees' letters, petitions, and paid advertisements: Leila Lima's "inability to do anything" and "mocking attitude," the "lies" of Roberto Rodriguez Casasbuenas, and the "false promises" of Denis Van Dam and Serge Ducas were among those called out.[33] They also took aim at the UNHCR as a whole, focusing in particular on the institution's failures to comply with its mandate. In March 1988, for example, the Coordinating Council of Refugees at the Mesa Grande, Colomoncagua, and San Antonio camps wrote, "We consider the UNHCR to be an organization delegated by the United Nations to guarantee and protect the lives and human rights of refugees. The UNHCR should—given the way the Government and military authorities behave and treat the refugees [and] understanding how we are disrespected in our lives and human rights—strengthen its presence and not passively accept any steps that reduce its protection role. . . . We Salvadoran refugees [demand] that the UNHCR does not passively accept the diminishment of its protection role and at the same time that it reinforces its presence in our camps 24 hours a day to fully comply with the role delegated to it by the United Nations."[34]

Repeated complaints and demands along these lines illustrate the refugees' disillusion; despite the promise of its mandate, the UNHCR was *not*, in practice, the ideal protection authority. To help remedy their situation, Salvadorans mustered the support of international observers, visitors to the camps, and sympathetic voluntary agency personnel. Pressures from these sources could prompt the UNHCR to behave in ways amenable to the refugees by sending more protection officers, for example, or encouraging the Honduran military to soften curfews or lift bans on deliveries and travel.

Salvadoran refugees also utilized divisions within the aid regime to counteract individual workers and entire aid agencies that they perceived as threatening to the refugees' social or political objectives. In some instances they highlighted the misdeeds of particular individuals. As with campaigns against the haraganes within their own community, refugee drives against specific aid workers led to positive results on more than one occasion. In late 1984, for example, Colomoncagua refugees and their supporters launched a protest campaign against the local protection officer. This UNHCR employee's misdeeds included leading a Honduran lieutenant, two armed soldiers, and an immigration official to a Salvadoran refugee in the hospital. Not surprisingly, the patient objected to the visit given that his hospitalization was due to a severe beating by Honduran soldiers. In response to the refugees' protests, the UNHCR removed the officer from Colomoncagua and reassigned him to a desk job in Tegucigalpa.[35]

In other cases refugees questioned the actions and motives of entire agencies. A particularly tense relationship existed between Salvadorans and the MSF. The refugees' frustrations with the MSF began as early as 1982 or 1983 when the organization did not sign on to a letter prepared by relief workers and delivered to UNHCR headquarters in Geneva opposing plans to relocate the refugees deeper into the Honduran interior. Refugees claimed in their publications and letters to international solidarity groups that all the relief agencies working with them in Honduras had supported their decision to remain where they were except the MSF. Thus, although refugees recognized and appreciated the important medical aid provided by MSF doctors, they critiqued the MSF as an agency for not siding with them in this important struggle.

Problems arose once again in the mid-1980s. According to an MSF employee, in 1986 the agency became "concerned by the elevated drug consumption rate and the levels of health care and caloric consumption, which were higher in the camps than among the surrounding population." After investigating the situation, and in an effort "to standardize . . . medical assistance in accordance with public health guidelines used in refugee camps around the world," the MSF recommended closing the camp nutrition centers. The refugees, with the support of another aid agency, Concern, not only refused to close the centers but also made counterdemands for additional quantities and types of medications and for more health-training opportunities. The MSF refused and, in light of "the superior health status in the camps," interpreted the refugees' actions as evidence that they had been siphoning health supplies to FMLN insurgents.[36]

Curiously, the refugees' version of events did not even address the possible closure of the centers. Instead they claimed that MSF doctors sought to restrict the refugees' participation in the supplementary nutrition program. A communiqué from Colomoncagua to government officials and international solidarity groups, for example, explained that "in light of the discussion about the supplementary diet for the malnourished, sick and pregnant, [the MSF] took a position opposing the refugees' own dispensation of the donated vitamins and medications" despite the fact that a recent delegation from UNHCR's headquarters in Geneva had authorized them to administer the resources.[37]

This communiqué was part of a broader campaign of denunciation against the MSF. Refugees commented on the situation in their camp publications, sent letters to renowned international figures, and even filmed a video, which they distributed clandestinely to camp visitors. With time the campaign widened even further to target the UNHCR, which, refugees claimed, planned to reduce food rations and medical aid in an effort to force repatriation. "Poor health," San Antonio strikers told the UNHCR, "is a clear expression of contempt toward us, trying to force us to repatriate."[38]

When these actions did not produce the desired results, refugees turned to more drastic measures; in July 1988 nearly three hundred refugees at the Colomoncagua and San Antonio camps launched a hunger strike, which they designated the Ayuno contra el Hambre y la Represión (Fast against Hunger and Repression). Although a hunger strike against hunger might appear oxymoronic, scholars have illustrated that such protests "can be used to great symbolic effect." For example, in prisons—perhaps an appropriate parallel to the closed refugee camps in Honduras—"the emaciated body and the suffering of the hunger-striking prisoner destroying his/her own body, transforms the prisoner from a criminal to an almost sublime and purified figure."[39] In a similar way, Salvadoran refugees used their own bodies to protest against camp authorities. The refugees' action implied that anything but a positive response to their demands—for continued food and medical aid and against forced repatriation—would result in greater suffering for an already vulnerable population.

It was precisely through such use of their bodies that refugees prompted a resolution to the conflict with MSF. In addition to the public relations campaign, hunger strike, and protest marches through the camps, the refugees decided to physically block MSF personnel's access to the camps. As they refused workers entry, they publicized their demands that another agency take over coordination of health services. In November 1988 the MSF withdrew from the Salvadoran refugee aid program.[40] The refugees also remained where they were, in the camps; they were not forced to repatriate.

This episode is instructive on several levels. First and foremost it highlights the refugees' insistence on being agents rather than objects. The refugees considered the MSF threatening because the agency intended to remove Salvadorans from an important community function. Refugee notices portrayed this as a paternalistic move, claiming that the MSF wished to remove Salvadorans from such positions because as refugees they either should not do such work or were incapable of doing it in the "right" way.

Fig. 8. "Brother Solidarity, our aspiration is: to repatriate as a community. Let's work together to contribute to creating the conditions." (Reproduced from the refugees' newsletter *INFORESAL* 4, no. 3)

This series of events also reveals how refugees played one agency off another. The refugees first used the UNHCR (which had authorized refugees to distribute resources) against the MSF (which intended to *de*authorize them from distributing resources). In a similar vein, refugees found allies with Concern employees and volunteers, who refused to close the nutrition centers despite MSF's recommendation. Ultimately both the MSF and the UNHCR became targets while refugees addressed communiqués "to the grand National and International Solidarity movement, to humanitarian organizations, ecumenical church Movements, non-governmental organizations, to friendly governments, to the workers of the world."[41] Internal UNHCR documents make clear that "some NGOs" joined the refugees in leveling accusations against both agencies.[42]

Finally, this episode provides insights into how refugees presented themselves before the world. In every action that refugees took before (and for the benefit of) "outside" audiences, participants adopted a sort of role or persona that would help push the intended message as far as possible. Those who engaged in the hunger strike, for example, appeared as victims of policies forced on them by the authorities. The medical evacuation of one female striker—"in view of significant weakness"—no doubt emphasized the vulnerability of the refugees and in so doing rallied the most empathetic observers.[43] In other words, refugees presented themselves in particular ways in search of specific outcomes. The next section explores this practice in more detail.

Staging for Success

As Marc Edelman acknowledged about his work *Peasants against Globalization*, "I certainly 'stage' the words of some of the protagonists, but they were also asking—indeed, demanding—to be 'staged,' to be subjects of history and of the history that I was writing." He also recognized that the Costa Rican peasants he interviewed considered him "at least in part as a useful resource." Edelman's education and sympathies, along with his foreign ties and involvement in the world of publishing, meant that peasants staged themselves appropriately to his presence; peasant assemblies were, therefore, "part theater, with some of the drama directed at observers like me rather than peasant participants."[44] Salvadoran campesinos in exile similarly staged themselves for successful encounters with the international humanitarian aid regime. Evidence of this can be found in the fact that Public Relations Committees shared the top tier of the refugee government hierarchy with the Campwide Coordinating Committees (see chart 6). The Public Relations Committees determined which visitors could speak to the various refugee committees and which refugees would represent the community to visitors.

Remarked a Honduran priest who worked closely with them, "The refugees did not speak to just anybody."[45]

And all this had a purpose. In their interactions with outsiders, the refugees played different roles in order to gain allies and obtain both short- and long-term benefits. Two of the most common roles were *victim* and *paladin*. Each encompassed multiple layers: strategic decision making within the refugee community, particularly by the leadership; information management; and public relations campaigns.

Before delving into these strategies, two caveats are in order. First, as we have already seen, Salvadorans did not simply bare their hearts and souls to anyone who appeared before them. Second, it must be made clear that to highlight this sort of role playing is not intended to minimize the very real traumas that Salvadoran campesinos experienced as a result of the civil war, nor do I intend to argue that Salvadorans fabricated stories in order to manipulate their international supporters. Their stories were true and their experiences real, indeed. Rather, my goal here is to illustrate how Salvadoran refugees transformed their often grim reality into an advantage by strategically emphasizing certain pieces of that reality while downplaying others. In short, the following discussion intends to demonstrate the agency and protagonism of Salvadoran refugees even as it highlights their uses of victim narratives.

Perhaps the most frequent staging strategy employed by Salvadoran refugees in Honduras was to "play the part of the victim." This role included various layers and themes, as Salvadorans listed their sufferings (as campesinos, as refugees, as children and women) and accentuated their political naïveté and devout religious nature. The refugees' main objectives in touting their victimhood were to make their abusers and opponents appear even more unethical and to gain the sympathies and support of international observers in order to turn situations to their advantage.

Salvadorans depicted themselves as victims in two distinct arenas: as campesinos in El Salvador and as refugees in Honduras. On the one hand they repeatedly detailed the horrors of El Salvador's civil war. Using such words as *sacrificio* (sacrifice) and *pérdida* (loss), they described the violence of landowners, soldiers, and death squads; they commemorated especially traumatic events such as the disappearance of family members, massacres, and the bombing of their villages. In some ways exile to Honduras was simply an extension of these wartime experiences. The refugees were quick to point out, for instance, that Salvadoran military battalions and vigilante groups continued to consider them subversives and guerrilla sympathizers and sought them out in the refugee camps just as they had done before in their places of origin. In many other ways, however, exile was a completely unique experience, and so the Salvadoran campesinos also highlighted the persecution they experienced as a direct result of their new status as refugees. As noted earlier they depicted themselves as animals locked in a cage or prisoners in a cell. They argued that their cramped quarters in closed camps under military surveillance placed them at extremely high risk—for disease, certainly, but also in terms of manipulation by their captors, as when government and UN officials cut off their food supply to force them to relocate to another site. Salvadorans capitalized on this victimhood by employing both past abuses and fear of future abuses as evidence in their various arguments and struggles. Repeated military incursions into the refugee zones, for example, proved their need for protection. Similarly, as part of their opposition to relocation to other sites within Honduras, they emphasized their fears of repeat appearances of ORDEN or even mass extermination.[46]

To accentuate the harshness of the abuses and hardships they endured in the camps, the Salvadorans made themselves appear as innocent and harmless as possible. They described themselves as *gente sencilla*, uneducated simpletons who knew little about anything but working the land. They also emphasized their piousness. They formed Bible study groups; they built *casitas de devoción* (little devotional houses) and attended services led by Honduran priests and refugee lay leaders; they tacked pictures of the pope on their walls; and when Honduran soldiers tore down their signs and banners memorializing slain archbishop Oscar Romero, refugees at San Antonio responded by publicly condemning the military for "tromping on our religious faith."[47]

As further evidence of their innocence, Salvadoran refugees stressed the skewed demographics of the camps and specifically the high numbers of seniors, children, and women. Although men did reside in the camps—as pictures and audio recordings from the period demonstrate—the refugees chose to downplay their presence and instead highlight the less suspicious and more vulnerable groups.[48] The verses of the song "Pueblo sin cabeza" (Pueblo without a Head) offers just one example of such practice: "This genocidal junta / does not respect our lives, / it orders the assassination of the elderly / . . . women and children."[49]

Formal denunciations issued from the camps often highlighted the brutalization of refugee children. In January 1988, for example, Colomoncagua refugees called attention to a military incursion during which Honduran soldiers registered all educational materials in the camp schools. During the incident, soldiers attacked various young adults and beat a seven-year-old child.[50] Another public denunciation from Colomoncagua, in March 1988, reported that Honduran troops had captured four refugee boys between the ages of eight and ten and taken them to the military base at Marcala. There soldiers bribed the children with candy, beer, money, and promises of good food to answer questions about the camp's organization and leadership.[51] In a similar vein, many public denunciations focused on the sexual nature of offenses committed against children and women in the camps. In the wake of military incursions into the camps, refugees often accused soldiers of raping refugee women, and, in April 1988, refugees at San Antonio denounced several cases of soldiers showing their penises to underage refugee girls.[52]

By focusing attention on women, children, and the elderly in these ways, the refugees utilized the experiences of these subgroups to emphasize the innocence and vulnerability of the refugee community as a whole. They then turned this vulnerability to the community's advantage. This pattern is especially clear in the context of the continuous threats of relocation to other sites in Honduras; refugees based their opposition to relocation on the negative effects that a move would have on their most vulnerable members. Refugees at the camp of San Antonio, for example, argued against their proposed relocation to the Mesa Grande camp because, they wrote, "We would not adapt well to the climate because it is very cold and the children and elderly would die."[53] In fact, numerous refugees—most of them infants and elderly—had died during the forced move from La Virtud to the newly established Mesa Grande camp in late 1981 and early 1982; this fact was clearly not lost on those facing relocation in later years. Also effective were women's own testimonies; female refugees often confided to international visitors that they had suffered miscarriages during the forced move to Mesa Grande and feared that pregnant women and their unborn babies would suffer the same fate if forced to move again. Highlighting these especially grim aspects of their lived experience evoked the empathy of the visiting internationals, which, in turn, spurred international support and strengthened the refugees' opposition to relocation.

Another way in which the Salvadorans turned innocence and vulnerability to the advantage of the refugee community was by employing children in camp security systems. The longer they lived in exile and the more exposure they had to internationals, the more they learned about international law; children, of course, were especially protected subjects under such laws, and so refugees consciously and strategically utilized children in both their informal vigilance habits and formal security patrols. Whole classrooms abandoned their schools in order to prevent their compatriots from being removed from the camps by Honduran or Salvadoran troops. Felicita, a young refugee at the La Virtud camp, recalled one occasion in particular: "We were in the camp school, around ten in the morning, when we saw that the soldiers grabbed a man on the other side of the hill. Then all of us, the students, went after them, right, so that they wouldn't kill him. And then, when they saw that we were following behind, the soldiers yelled at us that they were going to kill us too and we didn't pay any attention to them, always a big mob of kids following them. From there we crossed some gullies near the camp, and there some internationals arrived, and the soldiers had to let the refugee go."[54]

Along with these active protection maneuvers, children also served as scouts, collecting as much information as possible about military actions and behaviors toward the refugees. When Honduran soldiers took a refugee prisoner at the La Virtud camp, for example, a little boy kept watch. He followed them to the town command post, climbed a tree so that he could see over the high walls surrounding the post's grounds, and saw the soldiers torturing their new captive. He then took this information back to the refugee leaders and internationals in the camp. In a similar vein, small children often carried messages from one subcamp to the offices of international aid organizations located in other subcamps. One U.S. aid worker recalled several incidents in which young boys interrupted meetings of agency personnel to deliver news of military incursions into the camps.[55]

These kinds of security actions illustrate the refugees' strategic decision making on two levels. First, in light of international law, they knew that children could "get away with" things that adult refugees—and men especially—could not even attempt. Second, they understood that the presence of international aid workers significantly curtailed the behavior of government and military representatives and, in turn, protected the refugees from harassment, arrest, and even murder. In sum, Salvadorans applied both the perceived innocence of children and the immunity of international workers to the benefit of the whole community.

Refugees also claimed innocence in the realm of politics. Indeed, they frequently emphasized in themselves and their community a sort of inherent inability to be associated with politics in general and insurgent warfare in particular. Many also commented on their illiteracy and lack of education more broadly. When accused of providing logistical and material support to the FMLN guerrillas, the refugees flatly denied any involvement and made the prospect appear ridiculous and even illogical. A female refugee at Colomoncagua, for example, recalled how she and her companions responded to charges that they stored weapons for the guerrillas: "We told them we were just defenseless people, children, women, elderly, and that the majority were children, why would we have any weapons?"[56] A handwritten letter from the refugees to solidarity groups expressed similar thoughts in an especially vivid manner: "At this time [the UNHCR] appears with a list of 64 brothers who, according to the UNHCR, said persons collaborate with the Salvadoran guerrillas. In light of the fact that these brothers that they mention in such a problem are women children elderly over 70 years old, sick people, invalids, cripples without feet, and some even have already died they live in their graves! Unless today in these times the dead must abandon their graves and go out to collaborate with the guerrillas of the world!"[57]

In fact, as noted earlier, Salvadoran refugees did maintain connections with the FMLN. Just as their levels of association had varied in El Salvador, so too did the depth of involvement vary between individual refugees and their camps. It is safe to say, however, that the majority of the refugees (with the exception of those at Buenos Aires) identified with the basic principles of the FMLN's struggle and therefore were at least partially sympathetic if not active contributors. Although the refugees did not easily reveal their FMLN connections to international visitors, many of the songs and poems they created and performed in the camps contained undercurrents of these affinities. Some pieces simply portrayed the FMLN in very positive terms as liberators and heroes: "you, the one we awaited . . . / that you would free us from this chain . . . / it is you valiant guerrilla."[58] Others utilized rhetoric typical of the radical leftist cadres, with terms such as *yanqui* (Yankee), *imperio* (empire), and *imperialismo* (imperialism) used in relation to the United States and *tiranía* (tyranny), *oligarquía* (oligarchy), *burguesía* (bourgeoisie), and *dictadura* (dictatorship) referring to the ruling elites of El Salvador. These labels contrasted sharply with their own self-classifications as *obreros* (workers, laborers), *proletariado* (proletariat), and *pobretariado* ("pooritariat").

Refugee writings also often reflected inside knowledge of both the FMLN structure and its victories and losses. Some songs referred to the various FMLN departmental fronts by name; others commemorated specific FMLN combatants and collaborators who had died "in the name of the pueblo."[59] Other writings could be interpreted as explicitly linking the refugee population with the guerrilla forces through references to FMLN-supported organizations in the zones of control, including the Poderes Populares Locales and the Bloque Popular Revolucionario. Other authors called on their compatriots in the camps to *componerte* (get yourself together, get well) so that they could return to the struggle.[60] And, according to the song "Valiente Guerrillero" (Valiant Guerrilla), one refugee may well have been part of the FMLN ranks:

> I am not from here
> I am pure guerrilla
> I come from faraway lands
> to fight for the workers . . .
> When I arrived in this land
> they called me the stranger:
> "what are we going to do
> now with so many guerrillas?"[61]

Such references were intentionally ambiguous, however. "Valiente Guerrillero" certainly may have alluded to an FMLN soldier residing in the Mesa Grande camp, but it may also have referred to that soldier's relocation from one department to another within El Salvador. Similarly, the calls to componerte may simply have been an effort to revive a faltering sense of collectivity among refugees.

Whether or not insurgents actually spent time in the camps is beside the point; what is relevant here is that both subtle and explicit connections did indeed exist between the refugees and the FMLN forces. The fact, then, that the refugees publicly denied these links provides further evidence of their strategic decision making and staging tactics. The Salvadoran campesinos knew that they had much to lose if they openly admitted and publicized their relations with the FMLN; they were well aware that their continued refugee status—and concomitant international attention and material and financial resources— largely rested on their political innocence. Therefore, they took great care with all information relating to the FMLN. While "odes to the guerrillas" such as those quoted earlier may have been regular fare in the camps, artists performed them only for select audiences. In many cases refugees had set their new lyrics to traditional folk songs; this allowed them to switch back and forth between new and old versions, replacing any questionable lyrics with more conventional ones depending on each particular audience. And refugee commissions worked with FMLN representatives in a clandestine fashion, often under the cover of night.

A crucial aspect of the Salvadorans' information management was the concerted and public negation of all commentary that connected them to the FMLN—whether the slight aspersions expressed by the UNHCR or the conservative aid agency World Vision or the explicit accusations from Honduran, Salvadoran, and U.S. officials. To all remarks refugees responded individually by claiming innocence and naïveté. They also responded on a collective level; refugee committees issued a number of statements during the 1980s that countered their opponents' claims. Again they emphasized their innocence by noting the skewed demographics of the camps and the community's religiosity. Interestingly, they not only denied the accusations; they also demanded proof from their accusers, behavior not usually associated with ignorant and passive victims. For example, during a 1988 visit to Mesa Grande, UNHCR associate director Phillipe Levanchy noted with surprise and dismay that he had seen a paid advertisement signed by the FMLN indicating its relations with the refugees. The Coordinating Council of Refugees for the Mesa Grande, Colomoncagua, and San Antonio camps promptly published a communiqué in response, declaring, "We are even more surprised about the declaration, and it worries us that he links us with the guerrillas since this argument will only serve those who wish to repress us . . . [We declare] our insistence to Mr. Philippe Levanchy that he present us with that paid advertisement of the Salvadoran guerrillas."[62]

Although Salvadoran refugees were especially careful with the details of their FMLN relations, they also took care with other kinds of information. Sometimes they deliberately avoided sharing news with international workers and visitors, even the most sympathetic ones. During their first few months at Mesa Grande, for example, dozens of refugees, and in some cases entire families, secretly returned to El Salvador rather than remain in the new camp. One incredulous U.S. aid worker admitted, "We were completely unaware of it, until they didn't show up to collect their weekly food provisions. The rest of the refugees kept their secret."[63] Although in some instances such secret keepings may have appeared to be unintentional or accidental, they were often in fact carefully constructed and managed information campaigns designed to help the refugees obtain important concessions and benefits.

These information management efforts make clear that even as the refugees highlighted their victimhood, they were not "just victims." They also promoted and asserted themselves as an organized and capable community of Salvadorans that managed many successes in the face of hardship. Although these more heroic narratives are examined in the next chapters, for present purposes it is relevant to note how, in letters and commentary to international solidarity groups and UNHCR representatives, Salvadorans touted their self-built camps and listed their organizational successes. One such message read, for example, "We have focused the majority of our efforts on building new houses, health centers, education, nutrition, evangelization centers, we have farms, gardens, potable water, streets, and other areas that serve our community."[64] Their work was so great, they argued, that Honduran officials wanted to remove the refugees from the border camps in order to take over the camp infrastructures for use as military bases. The refugees opposed relocation in part because they had accomplished such remarkable things in their actual locations, things that simply would be impossible to reproduce in another site. Interestingly, these heroic narratives often accompanied victim narratives. Refugees closed their long list of successes with statements such as "In the event of a relocation we are no longer able to do new constructions" and "We do not have enough labor power because we are only women, elderly and children and we are not self-sufficient enough to start new agricultural productions because we don't have the skills."[65]

The community pitched by Salvadorans was not only material and infrastructural; it also enveloped moral aspects. Refugees described a deepening of the sense of belonging, a sort of collective identity based on the traumatic experiences of the past, hope in the future, and united will in the face of present challenges. Refugees evoked this collectivity in their writings and speeches when they described how they maintained and defended their community. They emphasized to international visitors how they all shared both opportunities and duties; everyone took turns in the production workshops, for example, learning and practicing new trades such as tailoring and machinery repair. Similarly, the community took responsibility for war widows and orphans. Their care was an important duty. "The unity that our pueblo wants goes far beyond our own family," explained a Colomoncagua refugee. "We all form one large family by virtue of being Salvadorans."[66]

Refugee studies scholars long have noted the aid regime's attempts to depoliticize refugees and reduce them to "bare life."[67] More recently they have also begun to recognize and explore the "layered sovereignty" of refugee camps, as well as the varied ways in which refugees "strike back" with their own politics.[68] This chapter reveals that the Salvadoran case has much to offer these discussions.

As elsewhere, the refugee aid regime in El Salvador was highly politicized despite claims to the contrary. Salvadoran campesinos knew this and often turned it to their advantage. They identified which aid agencies and associates were most amenable to their own goals and objectives, fostered relations with them, and employed them as allies. Likewise, they identified which agencies would be more adversarial toward their goals and engaged in concerted campaigns against them. In efforts to abet (or obstruct) certain behaviors or force negotiations with officials, refugees (with their allies) engaged in a variety of pressure tactics, including letter-writing campaigns, protest marches, sit-ins at agency offices, and hunger strikes. With such actions, it is important to note, refugees continued a long tradition of activism. Just as they had been marginalized at home in El Salvador, so too were they excluded from official circles in Honduras. And just as they had struggled to make their voices heard in El Salvador, so too did they demand recognition and involvement in their Honduran environment.

As refugees in Honduras, Salvadorans discovered and utilized new resources. Even as officials from the UNHCR or the Honduran government refused to engage with refugees as agents, many international audiences would. In light of this, refugees geared many of their writings and other presentations toward los internacionales: aid workers, journalists, human rights observers, visitors to the camps, and others they perceived as allies. In addition they made good use of a new rhetoric acquired during their exile experience—that of international human rights. In their various presentations, moreover, refugees consciously performed particular roles in an effort to enhance their messages. To highlight harassment or poor living conditions in the camps, for example, they adopted the role of victims, and to counter official plans for relocation of refugees they emphasized the community as a victor over adversity in their original locales.

In short, through a combination of both old and new strategies, Salvadoran refugees succeeded in maintaining significant control over their spaces of exile. As the next chapters detail, this control, this production of a unified front, entailed significant internal work as well.

5

Salvadorans to the Soul

Citizen Refugees and La Lucha

A new trend emerged in the refugee camps of Honduras by 1982: the Salvadoran campesinos' self-documentation or the recording of thoughts and opinions about themselves, their experiences, and their goals and objectives. As previous chapters illustrated, many Salvadorans who eventually fled to Honduras had participated in consciousness-raising initiatives prior to flight: agricultural cooperatives, mutual aid groups, community councils, CEBs, and peasant leagues. Although records of some such initiatives exist to this day—accountings of specific cooperatives, for example, and the paid advertisements of the UTC—there is a serious paucity of documentation from individual campesinos. Illiteracy, lack of material resources, and the daily demands of tending to crops and putting food on the table meant that during the prewar period most northern Salvadoran campesinos were either unable or chose not to document their experiences.

Circumstances changed during the 1980s, however, and while in exile in Honduras many campesinos became able and willing to express themselves in writing. This was due not only to the new literacy skills gained through the popular education system (discussed in more detail in chapter 6) but also to the various new "freedoms" that Salvadorans enjoyed while in Honduras in spite of the many heavy restrictions of life in the closed refugee camps. As has been noted, their exclusion from Honduran labor and agricultural markets forced them to rely almost exclusively on international donations of food and other supplies, which meant that they did not have to work in the same way or to the same extent as they had done at home. This, in turn, meant that Salvadorans had more "free" time and space to dedicate to other activities, including literacy training, community organization and development initiatives, the arts, and other forms of self-expression. As a former Mesa Grande refugee explained, although "to a certain degree we were like prisoners [in the refugee camps and] we had no freedom, we did have freedom of expression and organization."[1] In short the Salvadorans' seclusion in closed refugee camps contributed to their ability and willingness to put their experiences and opinions into words.

Constant international attention made a crucial contribution to the Salvadorans' self-documentation. Citizens from all over the world worked alongside Salvadorans in Honduras, and journalists, church workers, human rights monitors, and representatives of foreign governments also made regular visits to the refugee camps. Whereas at home in El Salvador campesinos felt silenced or simply ignored, in Honduras they were often the center of attention. People arrived with notebooks, cameras, and tape recorders in hand; they actually *wanted* to meet the refugees and hear their stories. The international refugee aid regime, moreover, placed a high value on the written word. Representatives of the UN, for example, demanded regular written updates on UN-funded projects in the camps and required refugees and aid workers alike to submit typewritten, formal proposals when requesting funds for new projects. Likewise, journalists and other visitors to the camps not only sought firsthand accounts through oral testimonies and interviews but also collected as many refugee-produced documents as possible.[2]

And so Salvadoran campesino refugees began to document their experiences, both orally and in writing, for their new global audience. They kept logs and calendars in which they recorded incidents of harassment and abuse. They produced newsletters, magazines, and daily news shows. They posted signs and banners throughout their camps, condemning mistreatment and publicizing their opinions and stances. And musicians and word artists created songs and poetry to perform for visiting delegations. Through these various methods of documentation, as well as their accompanying actions, the refugees presented their community *as a community* to outside observers. As explained in chapter 4, they "staged" themselves for the international aid network with the intention of gaining allies in their struggle to protect and defend their community in exile.

Just as the refugees' self-documentation galvanized international solidarity consciousness about victims and refugees of war, so too did it galvanize politico-cultural consciousness among the Salvadoran campesino refugees themselves. An illustration in a 1982 manual used by camp schoolteachers (refugees themselves) offers a vivid outline of this process (see fig. 9). The line drawing depicts a Salvadoran campesino crossing a rapid-flowing river. On the

Fig. 9. "A New Man." (Reproduced from the teacher's manual of the Salvadoran refugees at Mesa Grande and Colomoncagua, "Manual para instructores populares," 1982)

first shore, labeled *analfabetismo ignorancia* (illiteracy ignorance), the campesino sits on a rock. He looks deflated, and his clothes are tattered and torn. On the opposite shore, however, he is *un Hombre nuevo* (a New Man). There he walks tall and proud in crisp, clean clothes, a new hat, and boots. The campesino's bridge to this better future consists of two large rocks labeled *leer la realidad* and *escribir la historia* (read reality, write history). The message is powerful: despite physical separation from their homeland, campesino refugees continue to consider themselves Salvadoran.

This chapter and the next examine the stepping-stone bridge of this illustration. Whereas chapter 6 focuses on the refugees' process of writing history, this chapter explores how refugees analyzed the contemporary reality of El Salvador, as well as their own roles in that reality. I first examine the refugees' assessments of the overall state of their homeland and their evaluations of the central players on the ground: the Salvadoran government and the FMLN in-surgent forces. I then examine how campesino refugees perceived themselves in relation to these players and their homeland in general. As a whole the chapter demonstrates that despite physical separation the campesino refugees considered themselves to be citizens of El Salvador. As "citizen refugees" they were not only entitled to many thus far unrecognized rights and freedoms; they also had duties and obligations to their country and therefore defended it even while outside its borders. In other words, they continued their engage-ment in la lucha, although the specific roles they played in the national libera-tion struggle shifted with exile.

Before delving into an analysis of the self-documentation, it is important to recognize that refugee writings are highly politicized. Again, Salvadorans were not all of one single mind, as we have seen; they had differing political af-filiations, and they responded to the exigencies of war in different ways. Some differences played out in the migration patterns of rural inhabitants. Whereas some campesinos chose to remain in the northern provinces of El Salvador, others relocated to urban areas of the country or moved closer to military sta-tions; individuals and families based their decisions on political affiliations, kinship networks, and environmental and economic factors. Due in part to this process of self-selection, the campesinos who remained in the north and those who chose to guindear to Honduras generally held similar perspectives in that they supported many of the goals and ideals of the FMLN even if they did not always agree with the insurgents' tactics.

Although common ground did exist, tension and conflict formed part of daily life in the refugee zones of Honduras. Yet the moral economies of flight and exile mitigated differences. Thus, the oral and written documentation produced by Salvadorans in the Honduran camps did little to address discord and instead presented a universal, often heroic narrative. The analysis offered here describes this universal narrative forwarded by the most active and vocal community leaders—the organic intellectuals.

A *Patria* Stained Red

Refugee writings reveal a continued interest in and commit-ment to El Salvador. It is clear that Salvadorans in Honduras followed closely the events back home. As they tracked the military contest between govern-ment forces and the FMLN, a distinct pattern of interpretation emerged; whereas the government (writ large) was criminal, the FMLN represented hope. Indeed, for many the promise of change and the very future of their homeland was tied closely to an FMLN victory. The refugees' sights were on a "new" El Salvador in which the leadership would be legitimate and morally upright and where peace, justice, and equality would reign. They viewed the civil war as a necessary evil, a process of liberation from tyranny, a transition toward this new and free El Salvador. The hardships of civil war—perhaps one's own run-ins with security forces, certainly the deaths of family and friends, as well as the abandonment of one's home for life en guinda—were an important part of this national transition. Salvadorans also viewed their own exile in this light, as a sacrifice of great significance in the larger struggle for progress.

From their sites of exile in Honduras, Salvadoran refugees remembered their homeland with great fondness. El Salvador was, explained one poem, "a very small country / but of great worth."[3] In their writings, refugees exalted the natural beauty of their country—the grand volcanoes, green forests, and deep blue lakes, the fat harvests of coffee and cotton. Many poems and songs contrasted these homegrown glories with the bleak existence of the refugee camps in Honduras. As Ramiro wrote from the Mesa Grande camp in 1982:

> Do you remember, compañero?
> In the houses of our towns,
> in the orange trees,
> in the thickets,
> many birds sang . . .
> In Mesa Grande
> not one bird has sung.
> The hills have not flourished.
> Where, compañeros?
> This is rustic land.
> Not one single crop has it borne . . .
> Do you remember well?
> It was a garden of many flowers.
> With its colorful clothing
> it was like a Pipil garden.[4]

In a similar vein, refugees often expressed strong desires to return to El Salvador in the not so distant future. Many poems, songs, and drawings offered hopeful images of this homecoming such as the sun rising into a new dawn and birds taking flight.

Of course the refugees realized that the *patria* (homeland, mother- or fatherland, nation) they extolled and to which they planned to return was a far cry from the El Salvador of contemporary times. Not surprisingly, they lamented the pain and damage that war continued to inflict on the Salvadoran land and people. Nearly every song and poem written by campesinos in exile made reference to generalized destruction and death. Many also evoked startling images of blood. One poet referred to El Salvador as "a Patria stained red with the blood of so many murdered innocents." Another grieved, "Our Patria of El Salvador / is a river of pure blood / that day after day rises." Still another likened the body and spirit of El Salvador to a bloodied cadaver:

> The image of El Salvador
> is terribly disfigured,
> her beauty is a cadaver
> left by the Armed Forces.
> Her face is unrecognizable
> covered, bloodied.[5]

As this last excerpt indicates, the refugees in Honduras held Salvadoran officials responsible for the extreme physical and spiritual damage to the nation. Indeed, refugee estimations of the ruling regime—along with its military and elite allies—were extremely low. The animal metaphors used by the refugees to refer to both the government in general and specific officials clearly illustrate this grim view: gorilla, ape, mosquito, lizard, fox, dragon, and rat. As one might guess, all these terms carry derogatory meanings in colloquial Spanish. Both *gorila* and *gorilón* (gorilla, ape) often refer to thugs or bodyguards. In a number of Latin American countries, the terms also refer to armed forces— and government forces in particular—that violate human rights. *Zancudos* (mosquitoes) are parasitic individuals who live large by sucking the blood and life from others. A *lagarto* (lizard) is a lowly individual, one who lacks honor and modesty. In Central America a lagarto can also be a selfish or indulgent person, especially with regard to food. Anyone with a particularly voracious appetite might also be called *un dragón* (dragon), and in a similar vein, *lobo* (wolf) refers to one who drinks too much, a drunkard. *Dragón* also signifies someone who is especially fierce and cruel. As in English, *rata* (rat) carries multiple meanings: someone who is mean, stingy, or tight-fisted or, more generally, a despicable character.

Refugees often combined these colorful metaphors with more direct commentary on government impropriety, deceit, and irresponsibility. In oral interviews and written works, they described government functionaries as gluttons for food, liquor, and women. They were also *grandes bandidos* (great bandits), *magos* (magicians), and tricksters. The song "Carro choco" (Crooked Car), written by Norberto A. at the Mesa Grande refugee camp, offered perhaps one of the most vivid analogies assessing the Salvadoran leadership:

You can see that it's wobbling
the wheel of the *Choco* car,
it only goes backward,
stop already, I know it is crazy . . .
the brakes are failing.
This circle, circle, circle
does not look where it goes,
is it that the brakes don't work
or is it the guy who's driving.[6]

The refugees believed that it was this uncontrolled speeding along without regard for life or limb that resulted in the greatest harm to the Salvadoran nation
and threatened its very survival. Direct evidence of this behavior could be
found in the government's indiscriminate use of chemical weapons, which, according to the refugees, was poisoning the "dear mother nation" and turning
her into a barren woman. Death squad killings, bombing raids, and scorched
earth campaigns were further contributing to her ruin.[7]

   This reckless behavior also prompted the refugees to refer to Salvadoran
political and military representatives as *drogados* (drugged), *tomados* (drunk),
and *locos* (crazy). Campesinos offered long lists and intimate details of "crazy"
behaviors. The most common examples offered by campesino refugees in all
parts of Honduras were that soldiers imitated lost and crying children to lure
campesinos from their hiding places; soldiers killed pregnant women, slit
open their bellies, and removed the fetuses to feed to the dogs; soldiers killed
men, cut off their genitals, and stuffed them in the dead men's mouths; and
soldiers tossed infants into the air to use as bayonet targets.[8] Refugees also
pointed out that Salvadoran soldiers behaved recklessly even beyond the borders of their own country; they consistently violated Honduran sovereignty
and international law, charges that will be discussed later in more detail. Refugee documents also contained reports of Salvadoran soldiers dressing as civilians, and even as women, in an attempt to gain entrance to the refugee camps
and infiltrate the refugee community.[9]

   These comments about the Salvadoran authorities' excess, trickery, and
lack of respect for the citizenry point clearly to the base opinion among refugees in Honduras that the ruling regime of El Salvador was, simply put, illegitimate. One writer drove home the spurious nature of the national leadership by
placing quotation marks around the word "government," as in "the Salvadoran
'government.'" Another belittled officials by referring to them as *hombrecitos*
(unmasculine, infertile men, literally "little men"). The most common tactic
employed by the refugees, however, was to attach derogatory adjectives to the
various terms of government, as in *la junta genocida* (the genocidal junta).[10]

This illegitimacy went beyond political machinations such as managing elections. It was also amoral. They got their way not through honesty and forthrightness but through deceit and trickery. Government officials pretended before the world to be righteous while they treated their own people with unspeakable cruelty. They referred to their form of government as democratic, yet they denied the majority of citizens a voice. They purported to be Christian, yet at the same time they tortured, maimed, and killed.

The refugees' depiction of the Salvadoran government as amoral and illegal stood in stark contrast to their depictions of the FMLN insurgent forces. Although campesinos held varying levels of identification with the insurgents, only the more positive renditions appeared in the writings of refugees. Some songs and poems lauded the guerrilla soldiers directly as liberators and heroes: "you, the one we have awaited / you would free us from this chain . . . / it is you valiant guerrilla."[11] More often, however, the refugees expressed support for—even idealized—the struggle for justice in general rather than the insurgent forces in particular. From this perspective the FMLN was one part of a larger movement to save El Salvador; la lucha encompassed all sectors of Salvadoran society, including peasants and laborers, students, educators, and professionals. Each of these sectors contributed to the struggle on a number of fronts, including the political, economic, social, legal, and military. The FMLN, of course, contributed largely to the military struggle; the insurgents were the ones who took up arms in the name of the larger struggle.

Many Salvadorans held the FMLN in such high esteem precisely because the insurgents took up arms and sacrificed themselves on behalf of the Salvadoran nation in general and the poor in particular. Although the refugees highlighted their own peaceful nature and insisted that they themselves did not bear weapons, they supported the FMLN's decision to do so given the lawless and misbegotten nature of the standing government. The refugees further justified the FMLN's guerrilla warfare by placing it within the historical tradition of peasant resistance. Indeed, they pointed to the very name that los muchachos, or "the boys" of the FMLN, took for themselves as evidence of their pedigree: Augustín Farabundo Martí, martyred leader of the 1932 uprising in western El Salvador, lived on in the Farabundo Martí National Liberation Front of the 1980s.

Thus, in many ways the FMLN represented hope for the Salvadoran refugees in Honduras. Like Martí and his comrades of the 1930s, the contemporary insurgent forces had the power to stand up to the ruling regime. In contrast to Martí, though, the FMLN also had the power to win. By the early 1980s the insurgents had already forced the ruling regime out of its corner; their success was evident in the very fact that El Salvador was embroiled in a civil war. Despite very concerted efforts by the Salvadoran government and military—and in spite of the virtually unlimited backing from the U.S. government—the FMLN and the broader opposition movement persisted and, indeed, continued to gain new ground. And so the refugees eagerly awaited the ultimate victory: the liberation of El Salvador from despotic rule. Poetry and songs written and performed in exile frequently referred to the *nuevo día* (new day) and *nuevo amanecer* (new dawn) that awaited the nation. Thenceforth, equality and justice would reign, and the proverbial table would be set for all:

> The table is for all
> of those who are suffering,
> the crippled and the lame,
> the ugly and the handsome
> as well as the high officials
> everyone together will eat.[12]

As they awaited this final victory from the camps, the refugees closely and anxiously followed the FMLN's exploits and government responses. At the Colomoncagua camp, the refugees' Social Communications Committee monitored commercial radio programming in Honduras and El Salvador (including Voice of America, La Voz de Nicaragua, and the FMLN's own Radio Venceremos) and compiled news bulletins for the camp. Each of the many Colomoncagua publications carried news sections that kept the refugees in touch with the goings-on of the FMLN. The fifth edition of *Comunidad en desarrollo* (Community in Development), for example, announced that thirty-two injured FMLN soldiers had been safely escorted out of El Salvador by the International Red Cross.[13] Another Colomoncagua publication, *La Patria en lucha* (The Patria in Struggle), provided FMLN military briefings in each edition, listing the numbers and ranks of government soldiers killed or imprisoned, the weapons captured, and enemy targets destroyed.[14] Refugees at Colomoncagua also learned about the FMLN through the Social Communications Committee's bulletin boards and oral news reports, as well as through television broadcasts (see fig. 10). Publications from the Mesa Grande camp featured similar news briefings.

As the refugees followed events in El Salvador, they praised each FMLN military success as an important step toward the popular movement's ultimate goal: the liberation of El Salvador. Songs and poems written by refugees often referred to these advances. "El taconazo" (The Kick), for example, paralleled a string of FMLN victories throughout the country to a scoring streak in a game of *fútbol* (soccer).[15] In a similar vein, "La consigna del FMLN" (FMLN Slogan)

Fig. 10. News bulletin board, Colomoncagua refugee camp. (Photo by Steve Cagan)

described "the progress of our pueblo" and noted in particular that 90 percent of the territory in Chalatenango province was under FMLN control by mid-1983. These plaudits stood in stark contrast to the refugees' evaluations of any advances made by the Salvadoran military. The latter actions they usually portrayed as massacres, unnecessary bloodshed. "La mecha encendida" (The Burning Fuse), for example, featured two government excesses: the assassination of Archbishop Oscar Romero in March 1980 and the Sumpul River Massacre in May of the same year. Another common strategy employed by the refugees to express their contempt for the government forces—and to contrast them with FMLN troops—was to simply use terms such as *asesinos* (assassins) and *tiranos* (tyrants) in lieu of *army* or *government*.[16]

The FMLN and the Salvadoran government were not the only participants in Salvadoran affairs, however. Refugees also highlighted the role of the mobile communities that remained in northern El Salvador. More specifically, poems and songs noted with optimism the PPLs established by campesinos in the FMLN regions of control. Just as occurred with refugee organizations, campesinos displaced within El Salvador took turns serving on the various committees that comprised the PPLs such as production and commerce, legal and social affairs, self-defense, and education. From the refugees' perspective these groups were the basis of a new and representative system of government. Norberto A. explained:

Thousands have already died
for the pueblo to establish a new government.
Now we are going to carry it forward
it is formed by the [Local Popular] Powers;
there is a secretariat
for the revolutionary government.
So that you know, and don't cry anymore
it is a government for the poor.

As this song implies, the PPLs were evidence of the positive changes that were already beginning to occur in the Salvadoran countryside, and they would ultimately replace the standing regime. Indeed, refugees pointed out that in the *zonas liberadas*, or "liberated zones" under FMLN control, the PPLs had already displaced official government representatives. In the words of the song "Carro choco": "how nice, how beautiful / the roads now are new / the Choco car doesn't come here anymore." As refugee writers and performers made clear, what distinguished the PPLs from the official government of El Salvador was their consideration for the poor. Indeed, the PPLs *were* the poor, the peasantry, the laborers. Because they were of the masses, they were best able to address the needs of the majority of Salvadorans, from the basics of food and shelter ("They keep watch to ensure that promises are fulfilled / that there are enough supplies") to the more ethereal self-esteem ("They are responsible / for the strength and courage of our pueblo").[17] The PPLs, in alliance with the FMLN and the popular movement more generally, would lead the country in new directions or, as Norberto A. put it, "row the boat of liberation."

Salvadoran to the Soul

In their analyses of Salvadoran affairs, refugees presented events not as happening far away or "over there" but, rather, as immediate in both space and time. Likewise, they themselves were not outsiders, mere observers of events; they were, instead, part of the mix. As such they consciously marked themselves and their spaces of exile as Salvadoran.

Documents produced by refugees in Honduras highlighted their personal identification with El Salvador. As time passed and the campesinos came to understand that their exile would be much longer than they had initially anticipated, the emotional weight of physical separation grew heavier. As Alejandro, a refugee at Mesa Grande, lamented in December 1982:

[El Salvador's] sun still warms our veins;
this sun that each day
rises and hides behind these mountains of Mesa Grande,
behind these great walls of scorched earth
that rise up like insurmountable giants
isolating us from our land
to the point of ripping out our souls.[18]

At the same time, as if to counter the weight of the separation, refugees made clear that exile—no matter how long—was only a temporary state of being. To this end, it is important to note, Salvadorans nearly always employed the phrase *estar refugiado* rather than *ser refugiado*. Both phrases translate into English as "to be a refugee" or, literally, "to be refuged." In Spanish, however, *ser* denotes a permanent state of being while *estar* is much more temporary or transient. The refugees' preference for the phrase *estar refugiado*, then, indicates their conception of exile as a temporary state of being. In a similar vein, refugee writings made repeated reference to *el retorno*, the ultimate return to their homeland. Indeed, Salvadoran refugees insisted on return not as a possibility but, rather, as an inevitability, and focused much of their attention and energy on that eventuality.

Further evidence that Salvadoran peasants perceived exile as a temporary situation can be found in the fact that the vast majority did not reground themselves in Honduras. That is, they did not press for Honduran documentation such as work visas, residency papers, or citizenship for their children born in the camps. Although Salvadorans initially recorded births and deaths in the civil registries of the Honduran towns nearest to their sites of refuge, the Honduran government prohibited this procedure by mid-1980. At that time, representatives of the UNHCR began keeping a separate registry, copies of which they delivered to the Salvadoran consulates nearest the refugee camps. It is telling that the refugees neither opposed this change in policy nor demanded to be listed in the Honduran registries.[19] Similarly, most refugees did not actively seek resettlement outside the refugee camps, nor did they seek integration into Honduran communities or markets. In fact, Salvadorans actively opposed efforts to relocate them to a different region of Honduras where they ostensibly would have enjoyed greater freedom of movement, more land for farming, and better economic opportunities. Likewise, they resisted the involvement of Honduran government ministries in refugee camp operations and affairs despite the new resources and opportunities that officials promised to introduce.

That the Salvadorans did not wish to anchor themselves in Honduras does not mean that they did not identify with their spaces of exile. On the contrary,

Salvadorans embraced their sites of exile. They did so, however, not as Honduran sites but, rather, as extensions of their homeland, El Salvador. Settling into the official, UNHCR-sponsored refugee camps—whether at La Virtud, Mesa Grande, San Antonio, or Colomoncagua—meant claiming the space as not only belonging to them but also identifying it as specifically Salvadoran. Refugees insisted on flying the Salvadoran rather than Honduran flag, and some named their spaces after important Salvadoran figures, including slain archbishop Oscar Romero, who was especially beloved for his work on behalf of El Salvador's poor.[20] Moreover, they marked their territory as Salvadoran by carving *hecho por salvadoreños* (made by Salvadorans) into the drying cement of the foundations and walls of newly erected warehouses, latrines, and other infrastructure (see fig. 11).

The refugees also continued to observe important Salvadoran holidays. Many of the dates they recognized were specific to the war and their personal experiences as refugees. The refugees at Mesa Grande commemorated the massacres at the Sumpul and Lempa rivers. Refugees at Colomoncagua and San Antonio commemorated the massacre at El Mozote. Those at Mesa Grande also commemorated the various start dates of the large guindas that eventually brought them to Honduras, including the *invasión* (invasion) of Santa Marta, Cabañas, in March 1980, and the *famosa guinda de mayo*, or "famous" guinda of May 1980 in Chalatenango. All the refugee camps held special religious and cultural ceremonies on 24 March in memory of Archbishop Romero, who was slain on that date in 1980. Perhaps most striking, however, is the fact that the refugees also observed Salvadoran Independence Day.

Through these various inscriptions Salvadorans endowed their spaces of exile with critical personal meaning, which, in turn, helped them to re-establish the boundaries of their community. As they took control over the definition and operation of the space, they further strengthened their own self-identification—now not only as members of a specific rural community of campesinos but also as a community of refugees, a community of Salvadoran citizens in exile. Furthermore, claiming a piece of Honduran territory as Salvadoran and associating it with important Salvadoran figures and dates sent a clear message to observers that they considered their sites of refuge to be extensions of their homeland.[21] As such they served as a kind of collective resistance to exile and the imposed identity of uprooted people without territory.

Just as they identified their spaces of exile as Salvadoran and defended them as such, so too did they define *themselves* as essentially Salvadoran. That is, in spite of their position outside national borders, they never stopped "being Salvadoran." Curiously, even though the refugees had low opinions of generations of national leaders, they still continued to identify with and even

Fig. 11. "Made by Salvadorans" etched into a wall at Mesa Grande camp. (Photo by the author)

embrace various aspects of the state system. Many refugees expressed belief in the Salvadoran Constitution, for example. They explained that the document itself was decent, but the leaders of the country ignored or abused it, as illustrated by the popular saying among Salvadorans that "The Constitution of the Republic of El Salvador is like a prostitute because everyone violates/rapes her."[22] In the refugees' estimations, however, the Constitution, like a woman, was worthy of defense. Most refugees also supported elections even though many had boycotted the Salvadoran elections of the early and mid-1970s. Again it was not the system itself that was corrupt but rather the acts of fraud committed by the leadership that rendered election results unfair. Refugees pointed to their own elections of representatives within the camps, as well as those among the PPLs in the FMLN-controlled areas of El Salvador, as proof that election processes and results could be just and fair.

The refugees were also very strong proponents of documentation. This is especially remarkable when we consider the fact that many campesinos possessed no personal identity documents prior to flight. Lack of money and the inaccessibility of many municipal and national offices deterred peasants from obtaining official birth certificates or photo identity cards. Moreover, such documents were often simply unnecessary for life in rural areas of the country.

While in exile in Honduras, however, documents took on new importance and meaning. This shift may be partially related to the fact that many campesinos received documentation from the UN that identified them as war refugees under the protection of the UNHCR. The legal weight of this documentation quickly became clear; having a refugee card could mean the difference between life and death for those detained by authorities inside or outside the boundaries of the refugee camps. Aid agency records offer multiple accounts of Honduran officials releasing detained refugees after aid workers presented their documentation. Having official Salvadoran documentation, then, became an increasingly important goal for the refugees because it conferred (or confirmed) legal rights as citizens and thus was another tool the campesinos could use to counter their marginalization and challenge the standing Salvadoran regime. With the help of international aid workers, therefore, refugees began to press the Salvadoran government for official identity documents. This pressure increased after 1985 as groups of refugees planned and prepared for their return to El Salvador. As chapter 6 will show, this national documentation became a critical rallying cry during the grassroots repopulation movement.

The refugees' writings and testimonies, along with postwar interviews, illustrate other ways in which Salvadorans perceived their emotional, physical, and legal attachments to the nation of El Salvador. Nearly all spoke of the land and crops, domestic animals, houses, and family members they had left behind when they fled and their intention to return home to them. While in exile they struggled to remain as close as possible to El Salvador by resisting relocation away from the border and teaching Salvadoran geography and history. These actions and attitudes served to minimize the separation from their homeland and, concomitantly, to maintain their connection to the nation. It is interesting to note that in interviews, former refugees described how some of their compatriots had left the refugee camps for other locations in Honduras. These people did not *want* to be Salvadoran, they explained, and so had renounced their citizenship by moving deeper into the Honduran interior. In contrast, those who remained in the refugee camps near the border had chosen to retain their Salvadoran citizenship. They were the true Salvadorans, or *salvadoreños hasta el alma*, Salvadorans to the soul. According to this logic, then, citizenship was an individual choice and not something that any government official could take away. Defining one's self in contrast to others in this way emphasized physical proximity to El Salvador as a key factor in determining "Salvadoranness" and citizenship. Such definitions, moreover, strengthened the unity among the Salvadorans who chose to remain in the refugee zones.[23]

As citizens of El Salvador, the refugees believed, they had many legal rights: access to land and the rights to vote in free and fair elections, earn a living wage, and organize, among others. Unfortunately, the country's governing elite had long denied campesinos these rights. The guindas and exile offered incontrovertible evidence of this exclusion. But the denial of rights did not mean that the rights did not exist; indeed, the refugees believed them to be definite and real. They pointed to the Salvadoran Constitution and international human rights law as confirmation, and they demanded that Salvadoran leaders recognize these rights. Throughout their period of exile, then, Salvadoran campesinos wrestled not only with the Honduran government and the UNHCR but also with the Salvadoran government. The remainder of this chapter will explore in more detail the ways in which refugees, from their sites of exile in Honduras, engaged Salvadoran officials and the Salvadoran nation in general.

Contributions from Exile

The campesino refugees in Honduras believed that their Salvadoran citizenship bestowed on them not only rights and freedoms but also certain duties and obligations. In the contemporary context of civil war, these duties became even more critical. As noted earlier, the majority of Salvadoran refugees viewed the war and la lucha as necessary parts of the transition to a "new dawn" of peace and prosperity. Active involvement in this process was a patriotic obligation expected of everyone from university professors and the FMLN high command to factory workers and the poorest of campesinos.

The refugees made clear that they, too, were active participants in the national sphere despite their physical location beyond the nation's borders. "Just because we are refugees / doesn't mean we will forget / all the suffering / that exists in El Salvador," explained one poet. Another writer argued that he and his compatriots had sought refuge precisely so that they would be able to continue the struggle, writing, "the campesinos, / fleeing from suffering / and pain, / sought refuge / to continue their work." Many refugees also pointed to their location in the border region as proof of their continued commitment to and involvement in Salvadoran affairs. They explained how they had resisted plans by UN and Honduran officials to relocate them deeper into the Honduran interior. Such plans, the refugees argued, were developed with the specific intention of separating them from the struggle going on in El Salvador or, in the words of one refugee, "to confuse us [and] make us forget about the blood that has been shed." But the refugees refused to forget, and they resisted relocation precisely "so that they will not separate us from our struggle for liberation."[24]

References and examples along these lines highlight how the refugees sought to maintain an active presence in and connection to their homeland while at the same time defending their decision to seek refuge in Honduras. They came to see themselves not only as involved but also as key contributors—even leaders—of the Salvadoran struggle. As early as 1982, in fact, refugees began referring to their unique and historic role. "Conscious people are always needed to take charge of historic tasks," explained the popular teacher's manual referred to earlier. "We do not want to waste time while we are refugees. . . . [We are] accomplishing something important and historic."[25] The refugees also drew parallels between their own work and that of important Salvadoran figures, including Archbishop Romero. Refugee writings frequently likened their exile to Romero's martyrdom. In both cases a force beyond their control had separated them in body from the struggles occurring in El Salvador—"You, Monseñor Romero / they sent you to heaven / and they sent us to this land"—but, like Romero, neither their spirits nor their voices could be silenced.[26] To the refugees, both exile and death represented duties and sacrifices to the nation. Such sacrifices would live on in the nation; just as Romero's voice and spirit was a seed that would grow and give strength to the Salvadoran people, so too would the refugees' exile have long-term meaning and significance.

The refugees' important role in the national struggle was closely related to their status as refugees and their physical location outside the nation. In essence, by occupying fringe territory, they transformed themselves into a sort of rearguard that defended the nation. This national defense took several different forms. First, from both sides of the border they served as witnesses to the atrocities committed against El Salvador's poor majority. Testimonies about their various guindas provided detailed, firsthand evidence of the Salvadoran security forces' excesses: repression and harassment, torture, disappearances, and massacres. In addition, from their sites of refuge in Honduras, campesinos kept close vigil over El Salvador's northern region. They were able to see planes flying low over the hills, dropping bombs on the rural communities they had left behind. They watched as helicopters delivered government troops in circles around specific targets. In one instance several refugees at the Colomoncagua camp observed as government soldiers stealthily snaked their way through the river valley below the refuge—stealthily, that is, until one of the men accidentally stepped on a *casabobos* (land mine, literally "dummy hunter"). The explosion drew more refugees to the vantage point at the top of the hill, and the small crowd watched the soldiers below screaming and scrambling to take cover from the attack they believed was upon them.[27]

But the refugees did not simply watch such incidents; they also took action to stop them. Specifically, they denounced the Salvadoran government and military through all sorts of written formats that reached international audiences: calendars, letters, petitions, newsmagazines, posters, and drawings. Each of the camps compiled a monthly calendar in which the refugees recorded the attacks they had witnessed. An excerpt from Colomoncagua's December 1983 *Calendario* reads as follows:

November 27—Around 3 in the afternoon on Sunday, a massive bombing campaign began around Torola, a town located in N. Morazán. From Picacho, a small mountain near Colomoncagua, one could see the planes launching bombs. The bombing lasted approximately 3 hours.

December 12—All morning one could hear intense bombings throughout N. Morazán . . .

December 20—. . . one could hear powerful bombings around the civilian populations of San Fernando, Perquín, and Torola. In the morning from the camps one could see four planes that, two by two, dedicated themselves to bombing the towns of San Fernando and Torola. One plane dropped 31 bombs. . . . This could be seen perfectly from the camp.

December 21—Bombing continues in the same towns, in N. Morazán . . .

December 23—Throughout these days (22, 23, 24) there is a massive military operation in northern Morazán . . .

December 26—All morning, mortars fall over N. Morazán, especially over Perquín. . . . It has not been a very happy Christmas.[28]

For visitors to the camps, refugees used performance pieces—songs, poetry, and theater sketches—to similar effect. Eventually, they also held marches, sit-ins, hunger strikes, and other protest actions. With their writings and actions they worked to raise international awareness of the continued violence being inflicted on their compatriots who remained in El Salvador. If the refugees' denunciations had the desired effect, then international observers would speak out and place pressure on Salvadoran officials to do certain things or behave in certain ways such as curtailing their military operations. As a result northern El Salvador would be spared further destruction.

Vigilance and denunciation served not only as a sort of protective shield over their homeland; these acts also protected the cross-border path for new arrivals to the refugee camps. This was of special interest to many of the refugees given that military operations and guindas frequently separated families; those who made it safely to the camps awaited the day when their lost siblings, children, and cousins would arrive. During the mid- and late 1980s, moreover, the refugees received frequent visits from family members who had chosen to remain living in El Salvador; violence in the border region put those treasured visits—and the lives of the visitors—in jeopardy.

Although the international attention generated by the refugees' denunciations may have reduced the number or intensity of military actions in the border zone, it did not halt them completely. The refugees, therefore, once again adjusted their tactics. Initially they focused principally on the illegalities of Salvadoran military actions; not only did government forces attack innocent civilians, the refugees claimed, but they also violated Honduran national sovereignty. Refugees pointed out that many Salvadoran military operations originated on Honduran soil. In July 1981, for example, refugees reported that more than a thousand Salvadoran soldiers had arrived by air transport in the Honduran border town of Los Patios, then crossed back into El Salvador to attack the FMLN.[29] Likewise, calendars from the early years in exile frequently listed the dates and times when Salvadoran planes flew low over the refugee camps, then crossed back over the border to carry out bombing campaigns in the northern rural areas.[30] In light of such incidents the refugees urged Hondurans to take a stand. "Do not let the Salvadoran army infiltrate," they wrote, "because this is a violation of Honduran territory. We are concerned about the sovereignty of our Honduran homeland. We are refugees in Honduras."[31]

Eventually Salvadoran refugees shifted away from targeting only Salvadoran forces to emphasize the relationship between Salvadoran and Honduran forces. It is worth noting here that in October 1980 Salvadoran and Honduran officials signed a treaty reestablishing the diplomatic relations that had been interrupted during the 1969 Hundred-Hour War. Despite the fact that the Lima Treaty, as the agreement was known, did not settle the border delineation dispute, it did set the groundwork for military collaborations between the two countries.[32] Salvadorans in the refugee zones of Honduras perceived this cross-border collaboration as a dangerous kind of collusion designed in large part "to impede, through every means possible, the arrival of new refugees."[33] From this perspective the policies and procedures set by the CONARE also comprised part of the sinister plan. The lights-out curfews imposed in the refugee camps, for example, were intended to hinder recent border crossers' ability to find the refugee camps at night, which was precisely when most sought refuge.

To counter these intentions the refugees began to actively protest Honduran-Salvadoran military collaborations. In September 1982 the high commissioner for refugees, Poul Hartling, received a petition signed by more than 5,700 refugees at Mesa Grande, asking him "to denounce before the world the Repression of the Honduran government against the Salvadoran refugees, to denounce also their collaboration with the Salvadoran National Guard even to the point of intervening in our country."[34] In a similar vein, calendars and letters sent by Salvadoran refugees to international solidarity groups between the mid- and late 1980s frequently reported cross-border operations and requested assistance in countering the negative effects of such incidents. As time passed, the refugees' actions became increasingly bold. As noted in chapter 3, they coordinated marches and other actions to protest repression and make demands of officials. One of the more extreme actions along these lines was a June 1988 hunger strike, which united refugees at the Mesa Grande, Colomoncagua, and San Antonio camps in protest against, among other things, the increased involvement of the Honduran military in Salvadoran affairs.[35]

Refugees also framed their resistance to relocation within their role as protectors of the border region. The issue of relocation away from the border and into the Honduran interior surfaced repeatedly during the 1980s, and with each new rising Salvadorans offered new arguments against it. Between late 1981 and early 1982, despite widespread opposition, UNHCR and Honduran government officials succeeded in relocating the majority of the refugees who had settled in La Virtud, Guarita, and surrounding areas to the newly established refugee camp of Mesa Grande. Shortly thereafter, in 1983, the Honduran government announced that Salvadoran refugees at the Colomoncagua and San Antonio camps, along with those at Mesa Grande, would be relocated to Olanchito in the western province of Yoro. According to officials, the decision to relocate the refugees had been taken "with the intention of ensuring increased protection and security." At the new site, moreover, the refugees "will be able to achieve self-sufficiency in terms of subsistence and they will have more freedom of movement. . . . All of this will allow them to live a more dignified and normal life."[36]

Such promises did not convince the refugees. "They have told us better protection, more freedom, better lands, promises that they will never fulfill," wrote the Colomoncagua refugees to international solidarity groups. "We already know this from our brothers at La Virtud who were relocated to Mesa Grande where they did not fulfill those promises."[37] In addition to such statements about previous deception, the refugees argued against the move based on safety concerns and the desire to preserve the relatively sturdy infrastructures they had managed to establish at the refugee camps.

Most intriguing, however, is the fact that they also began to express concerns about the relocation as "part of the political intervention of the United States government."[38] According to the refugees at Colomoncagua, "The general objective of the North American embassy in Honduras and the high command of the armed forces of this country is to clean this zone and to take over these camps for military operations and to achieve a direct U.S. intervention in El Salvador."[39] As evidence of this conclusion they pointed to the Centro

Regional de Entrenamiento Militar (Regional Military Training Center, CREM), which began operations at Puerto Castilla, Honduras, in June 1983. Although ostensibly a "technical center" for the Honduran armed forces, it was clear to many insiders, as well as external observers, that it was a Washington initiative established "so that the Pentagon could train Salvadoran soldiers without increasing the number of U.S. military advisers in El Salvador."[40] The refugees knew that Puerto Castilla and the CREM were only about sixty miles from Olanchito, where they were to be relocated; in letters to internationally renowned figures, including Queen Sofía of Spain and the First Lady of France, "Sra. Mitterand," they capitalized on the threat that such proximity entailed. "If in that very place they have their bases for training Salvadoran soldiers . . . then what will that mean for our future security and freedom???" wrote Colomoncagua refugees to international solidarity groups in November 1983.[41] A couple of weeks later another letter carried a similar statement: "If in this same country there are support bases where they train Salvadoran soldiers—like the case of Puerto Castilla!!! For this reason, the deeper they take us into Honduras, the greater our insecurity will be."[42]

The Honduran government ultimately decided against relocating the refugees to Olanchito, but just a few years later, in 1987, officials announced a new plan; Salvadorans at the Colomoncagua and San Antonio refugee camps would be moved to the Mesa Grande camp. Once again the refugees took a strong stance against the new plan. "The principal reason for the Relocation and Repression," claimed the editorial highlighted on the cover (see fig. 12) of a 1988 issue of the refugee magazine *Patria Nueva* (New Patria), "is to clean the border zone of Refugees and Honduran villagers because we are a bother to the involvement of the Honduran military in the Salvadoran conflict. All of this is part of the North American plan for direct intervention in our patria, which would bring as a consequence the lengthening of the war, affecting the Honduran pueblo as well, distancing the possibility for Peace in El Salvador and regionalizing the conflict."[43]

In light of the tremendous consequences that a direct intervention would entail, the refugees announced that they would, at all costs, remain where they were in order to protect themselves, their camps, their patria, and their compatriots. In the words of one poet: "they will never see us on our knees . . . / we will defend our refuge and the people / and this land should not be used for intervention."[44]

It is obvious that the refugees' roles as witnesses and protectors would have been severely curtailed, if not insolvent, without international support. The refugees themselves knew this, and, as argued in chapter 4, they "staged"

Fig. 12. "Yankee Objective: Depopulate the Border." (Cover illustration from the refugee journal *Patria Nueva* 3, no. 5 [1988])

themselves and their arguments appropriately, that is, in ways that would garner the most favorable attention and backing. The Salvadoran campesinos in
Honduras viewed this process of representing El Salvador, and especially the
poor majority, before international opinion as a direct contribution to the
struggle for Salvadoran liberation. Through their testimonies and interviews,
performance pieces, letters, denunciations, and newsletters, refugees contrasted the present and past circumstances and behaviors of the Salvadoran
peasantry with the attitudes and actions of government and military forces.
When internationals took action based on the negative image of the authorities painted by the refugees—for instance, by condemning military abuses
before international assemblies at the UN and the Organization of American
States or before state and national congresses and governing bodies—the refugees were successful. Condemnations and pressures from solidarity groups
helped the Salvadoran popular movement and sped along the process of national liberation.[45]

Beyond witnessing and representing Salvadorans in the court of world
opinion, refugees in Honduras also saw themselves as agents of positive
change. They considered their actions within the sphere of the refugee camps
as preparation for El Salvador's "new dawn." Specific programs in the camps
were preliberation reconstruction efforts and therefore *aportes a la lucha* (sup-
portive action in the name of the national struggle). Refugees viewed their efforts in this light quite early in their exile, as we can see from this excerpt of a
poem written in 1983 by a group of refugees at the Mesa Grande camp:

> We have already set the foundation
> for a very solid consciousness,
> at least in terms of everything that describes
> our role as refugee
> Looking out over the border of the camps . . .
> we learned more in depth
> where our position really is
> in the reconstruction of our country.
> Can we reconstruct it here in Mesa Grande?
> . . . Here—we agree—we can prepare ourselves
> and many, yes, many have prepared ourselves well.[46]

As these lines indicate, many refugees considered their position in Honduras
to be uniquely important because, in their sites of refuge, they had begun to
"set the foundations" and prepare themselves for El Salvador's new dawn. One
of the ways they did so was through the camp workshops. Each of the refugee
camps had a system of *talleres* (workshops) where refugees produced clothing

Fig. 13. Kerchief embroidered by refugee: "Shoemaking workshop . . . Salvadoran refugees in Honduras, we do not accept violent repatriation or relocation. Colomoncagua 1987." (Photo by Steve Cagan)

and shoes, kitchen pots and utensils, and other needed items (see fig. 13).[47] The talleres became a source of great pride for the refugees; not only did they help sustain the camp population, but they also taught skills that would be valuable in the eventual reconstruction of El Salvador. The refugee leadership even initiated a kind of lottery system that allowed almost everyone in the camps the opportunity to cycle through each of the workshops and learn the skills and trades, including mechanical engineering, business administration and accounting, carpentry, shoemaking, tailoring, and crafts. The lottery itself stood as an example of things to come in the new El Salvador; according to the refugees, it was democracy at work. It contributed to the sense of collectivity and equality among the camp dwellers and even, they pointed out, gave rise to an interesting shift in traditional gender roles; women began working in the metalwork and mechanics workshops while men began sewing clothes and, for a short time, making tortillas in the communal kitchens. (The latter did not last long, both the women and men laughed, because people were far too hungry and the men far too slow in feeding them.)

Along with the workshop systems, refugees considered education to be a crucial and foundational task. Although the camp education systems will be discussed in more detail in chapter 6, it is worth noting here that, according to the refugees, education contributed not only to personal liberation, as individuals learned to "read reality"; it also aided in collective liberation. In the words of Cristóbal, an adult student at Mesa Grande, literacy classes helped campesinos "discover the truth," which, in turn, helped inspire them to work toward and "realize our dream." His "Poema dedicado a todos los refugiados" (Poem Dedicated to All Refugees) explained:

> Since we have always wanted to escape exploitation
> and that is what we will learn by studying with the literacy classes
> we must study with determination while we are refugees
> so that when we leave here we will not be same terrorized people.
> We must all insist on moving forward with this great literacy movement
> to offer a contribution toward our liberation.[48]

From this perspective, education countered negative patterns of the past and established new, cooperative patterns. Campesinos would carry these new patterns with them into the future, and on their return to El Salvador they would become the leaders and teachers that, as one source promised, "our pueblo will need so much."[49] In essence, then, scholastic efforts in the camps—from teachers and students alike—served as practice and preparation for the eventual homecoming. As such, they comprised both a personal and a patriotic duty.

On an even broader scale, the refugees viewed their overall camp organization in a similar light as an important *aporte*. Many Salvadorans repeatedly emphasized the fact that as refugees they did not give in to *asistencialismo*, a term they adopted to describe passive acceptance of and reliance on international aid.[50] Rather they embraced the collective way of life that was in many ways encouraged (or perhaps forced) by the very nature of the closed refugee camps. They developed an entire system of camp government, with committees to address the needs of the community from food storage and preparation to latrine cleaning and camp security, from news distribution and libraries to religious worship and child care. They held public assemblies, voted for representatives, and negotiated with each other and outsiders. They honed these organizational skills and, when necessary, revamped their structures for more efficient and effective service.[51] All this they did with a dual purpose: first, to improve the quality of life in the camps and in the border region in general; and, second, to prepare for their eventual return to El Salvador. "The experiences with community management that we are acquiring here," explained the popular teacher's manual, "will serve us well when we return to El Salvador. There, we will have many duties of popular participation. That is why we should practice here our own participation and collective responsibility."[52] A Mesa Grande poet agreed: "What we are experiencing and learning here at Mesa Grande / we know that it will help us . . . / when we return to our country, because working [together, collectively] / we become better organized."[53] As these lines indicate, Salvadoran campesinos continued to view communal organization and collective labor as crucial steps toward a more promising and productive future in El Salvador.

While in exile in Honduras, Salvadoran campesinos prepared and distributed myriad written documents: letters, petitions, denunciations, newsletters and magazines, calendars, reports, poetry, autobiographical sketches, and more. Although in many contexts such documentation warrants little attention, for Salvadorans the process of writing was a political act and, as such, an action of protest against a history of marginalization, as well as against a national leadership that did not represent the interests of the majority of Salvadoran citizens. Writing signified access to the basic education denied to them in the northern highlands of El Salvador, and it publicly exhibited the voice and presence of the campesino population. At no other time in the history of El Salvador did campesinos, individually and as a group, enter so prominently into the written historical record.

Through their writing, Salvadoran refugees clearly and directly expressed their opinions of themselves, others, and their Salvadoran homeland. They followed events, determined the Salvadoran regime responsible for the horrors of war, and repeatedly emphasized the immoral and deceitful behaviors of political and military officials. The time had come, they believed, to oust the country's illegitimate leaders and usher in a new era of peace and justice. In this struggle for national liberation, the FMLN led the way militarily while the mobile communities—both in El Salvador and beyond its borders—helped to bring about political change.

Through their analyses of events, Salvadoran refugees demonstrated a continued connection with and commitment to El Salvador. Rather than consider themselves outside the nation, they saw themselves as important contributors to and even leaders of la lucha. They defended national territory and placed pressures on the Salvadoran regime by drawing international attention and solidarity. And they set foundations for the new El Salvador in the camp workshops and schools and through their camp management and leadership structures.

Being able to understand current events—and engage in those events as well—was a potent tool of change. As the "New Man" sketch illustrates (see fig. 9), reading reality comprised half of the bridge over "a river of pure blood." As the next chapter demonstrates, citizen refugees also crossed to the other half of the bridge: writing history. By combining the two stones campesinos would cross that raging river and carry their patria into a new, more prosperous future.

6

(Re)Writing National History from Exile

Declining Aid in the Name of the Nation

"Most Excellent Madame Minister of Public Education," began a 25 July 1987 letter from the Salvadoran refugees to the Honduran minister Elisa Valle Martínez de Pauveti. The letter continued, "We have been informed that the United Nations High Commissioner for Refugees has designated additional budget funds to the area of education in our camps. These funds would be used to increase the number of certified teachers for the children in our camps. Although we are always interested in improving our children's education, we believe that the educational needs of our fellow Honduran pueblo are greater than our own." For this reason the refugees had decided to pass on the offer of additional assistance. They informed Martínez that they had already requested that the United Nations funds be channeled to the Honduran Ministry of Education for use in the Honduran villages neighboring the refugee camps. "As refugees," the letter concluded, "we aspire to neither wealth nor privilege at the cost of the Honduran people, and our only desire is to return to a new El Salvador filled with peace and love."[1]

This letter to Minister Martínez de Pauveti followed closely on the heels of the "Memorandum of Understanding" signed by Honduran and UN officials just a few weeks earlier. The memorandum set forth new guidelines for the management of the refugees in Honduras, with Honduran officials moving into a dominant position. Although the memorandum as a whole caused great worry among the refugees, of particular concern was article 5, which announced that "Honduran teachers, under the supervision of the [Honduran] Secretary of State for Public Education, will be in charge of educational programs [in the refugee camps]."[2] This announcement prompted a series of mobilizations among Salvadoran campesinos in the refugee camps. Committees prepared letters for Minister Martínez, as well as the high commissioner of the UNHCR, Jean-Pierre Hocké, to announce their decision to pass the offer to the Honduran campesinos. Letters to international solidarity groups explained that "the rural schools in Honduras are in need of many teachers. As campesinos, we are always concerned about the situation of our Honduran brothers, since it was they who received us at the border when we came fleeing from El Salvador."[3] The refugees also placed paid advertisements in Honduran newspapers to publicly affirm their intention to transfer the promised funds directly to the Honduran Ministry of Education. And, as described in chapter 4, the "Memorandum" prompted sometimes violent confrontations with officials, including Colonel Abrahám García Turcios of CONARE.

This decision to pass on additional funds and support for education in the camps is rather surprising given how diligently Salvadoran refugees worked over their years in exile to secure assistance, improve conditions in their sites of refuge, and advance their various organizational efforts. Why would they now refuse aid?

The short answer to this question is that the citizen refugees considered education to be a crucial component of their role in El Salvador's national liberation struggle. As the preceding chapter illustrated, Salvadoran refugees in Honduras remained deeply committed to El Salvador despite their physical location beyond the borders of their patria. Borders were in many ways irrelevant for them. They defined their spaces of exile as extensions of El Salvador, they defined themselves as essentially Salvadoran, and they considered it their duty as Salvadoran citizens to do whatever they could to bring about El Salvador's "new dawn." Although much of the refugees' attention and energy focused on the big picture—transforming El Salvador into a peaceful and just nation—they also recognized the value of the smaller, individual contributions to this goal, which calls to mind the image that introduced the previous chapter, a campesino crossing into a new and prosperous future over a stone bridge. In the sketch, the campesino evolves from an illiterate and ignorant person into a "New Man" by learning to "read reality" and "write history." The two stone steps clearly represent the campesino's process of personal transformation, of *conscientización*, the development of critical consciousness. Education, in a variety of formats, formed the backbone of this personal transformation process in the refugee camps of Honduras.

This chapter examines in more detail the Salvadorans' commitment to conscientización while in exile, focusing in particular on *educación popular* (popular education). It reveals how the patterns introduced in the previous chapter—including continued identification with their patria and an accompanying sense of obligation and duty—appeared not only in the context of contemporary events but also in the study of the past.

To Educate Is to Transform

In a 2003 interview, Rosa, a Salvadoran campesina from the northern fringes of Chalatenango, recalled the civil war. She described the horror and anguish of her own experience: escaping the government's scorched earth operations, surviving a massacre, witnessing the death of family members, deciding to leave her homeland, and living in a crowded and dirty refugee camp in Honduras. But the war was not all bad; interspersed with Rosa's painful recollections were many positive points. The civil conflict led to stronger sentiments of solidarity among Salvadoran campesinos, for example, and a higher level of participation in local and national issues. Women discovered new leadership roles. More educational options existed. People made new friends from different regions of El Salvador and from all over the globe. "The war has been so difficult, since wars are never good," Rosa concluded. "But maybe for us it has been a school."[4]

Many others echoed Rosa's conclusion, highlighting the wealth of knowledge gained from experience. Indeed, learning infused every aspect of the northern campesino experience during the mid- and late twentieth century. Between the 1950s and the 1970s, campesinos throughout El Salvador gained experience with organizational methods through agricultural cooperatives, campesino training programs, and CEBs. These experiences influenced northern campesinos; many went on to establish mutual aid groups and directivas in their own villages and to become active in la lucha on both the local and national levels. Between the late 1960s and mid-1980s, as levels of violence in the countryside increased, northerners adapted their defense strategies, created new systems like the guinda, and continuously adjusted their systems based on trial and error.

Another system that evolved during the guinda era was educación popular. This was a grassroots system of education that both responded to and integrated the circumstances and realities of campesino life. "In the times of the guinda," explained María C., "in the places that the people went to, the ministry [of education] didn't do what it was supposed to do as the ministry; they were afraid to send teachers. So the people, considering the necessity—there were so many children and nobody was teaching them how to read or write— picked out a few people who were able to [read and write] a bit."[5] These selected individuals typically had only a few years of formal schooling themselves, but they taught "what little [they] knew" to others who knew less. These *maestros populares* (popular teachers), as they were known, held classes outside under the trees or, when possible, in homes or other buildings. Classroom sites were always close to a cave or tatú; when some threat arose, classes stopped, and everyone scampered to the designated hiding site. When necessary, teachers led their students on guindas away from the community or refuge point and deep into the mountains. "This is how they continued their studies," Uberlinda Q. said. "Studying for a while, then hiding for a while. In class one day and then, 'There's a military operation! Let's get out of here!' That's the way life was."[6]

In the refuge zones of Honduras, more formal systems soon evolved. As early as 1982 the four major refugee camps in Honduras—La Virtud, Mesa Grande, Colomoncagua, and San Antonio—boasted various education committees, teacher training programs, and primary schooling for both children (kindergarten through sixth grade) and adults (first through fifth grade).[7] Although international visitors to the camps frequently commented about the high level of refugee involvement in general camp operations, they touted the popular education system as one of the most successful areas of communal life. International observers pointed in particular to the refugees' achievements in the area of literacy. According to one survey, whereas 80 percent of all Salvadoran refugees were illiterate on their arrival in Honduras, by 1987 only 15 to 20 percent were unable to read and write. Others simply noted the high numbers of students—approximately ten thousand—who successfully completed one grade level each year. Another oft-cited statistic of success is the number of trained refugee teachers. One source noted, for example, that by 1989 four hundred teachers had been trained at Colomoncagua alone; another reported that in any given year more than five hundred instructors worked throughout all the camps.[8]

Popular education in the refuge camps went far beyond the basic skills of reading, writing, and arithmetic; the system also highlighted individual and community transformation through *concientización*. Indeed, a guiding principle of the system was *educar para transformar* (educate to transform). In the words of Equipo Maíz, a Salvadoran NGO that emerged out of the popular education movement, popular education was "radically transformative" precisely because it utilized "the peoples' daily practices, their immediate reality [as] the point of departure" for personal conversion. These personal conversions, when linked to broader liberation struggles, led to the transformation of society as a whole.[9]

Salvadoran campesinos who spent time in the refugee camps of Honduras support this conclusion. In fact, many referred to their experiences with popular education as a sort of awakening or rebirth. Whereas before they had been ignorant and resigned—*gente sencilla y pasiva* (simple and passive folk)—their new mentality was one of knowledge and participation; they had become *civilizado, politizado, conscientizado* (civilized, politicized, conscious, aware). In documents produced in the camps, literate campesino refugees encouraged their compatriots to continue their own educations, for the time had come to *despertarse* (wake up) or *levantarse* (stand up, rise up) and "emerge from the shadows / that strap us." As one poet wrote:

> In school one learns to read
> in school one learns to sing
> it is the source of knowledge
> of the simpletons who will awake . . .
> this is true, school will wake us up
> we do not want to be the simpletons . . .
> of a new pueblo that will move forward.[10]

As these lines suggest, the awakening prompted at least in part by popular education—the shift from "simpletons" to "new pueblo"—in many ways meant the campesinos' further realization of the value and power of their own voice and presence.

Conscientización infused popular education at every level in the refugee camps. Small children, for example, drew pictures in class as one method of "talking about" and understanding their experiences of war and exile. For older children and adults, "dialogue, social critique and the problematization of reality [became] the tools of learning."[11] Popular teachers built these "tools" into their lesson plans, as is evident from the manuals used during adult literacy campaigns in the refugee camps. One handbook begins by posing general questions that speak to the campesino refugees' reality, including "Who are we?" and "Where are we?"[12] The book goes on to identify in the answers to these questions a variety of "generative" words and phrases, that is, words from which discussions arose and on which lessons relied. For instance, the popular teacher's manual recorded the following as the response to the question "Who are we?": "Salvadoran refugees, men and women campesinos who need work, assistance and security." Teachers then used the key words in this answer as the basis for reading and writing lessons. Students learned all the vowels through the word *refugiados* (refugees) and the difference between the consonants *v* and *b*—which in some spoken Spanish are virtually indistinguishable—through

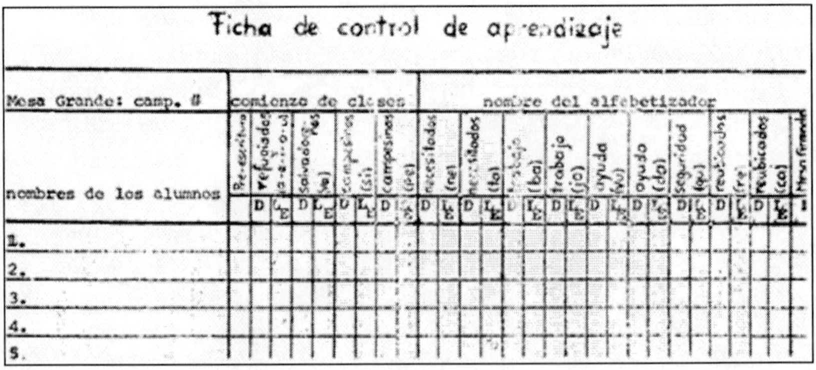

Ficha de control de aprendizaje

Mesa Grande: camp. #	comienzo de clases	nombre del alfabetizador

(Handwritten grade sheet with columns for syllable/sound words and D / L / E marks; rows numbered 1–5 for nombres de los alumnos, all blank)

Chart 7. Instructor's grade sheet for pronunciation lesson, Mesa Grande camp. (Reproduced from the teacher's manual of the Salvadoran refugees at Mesa Grande and Colomoncagua, "Manual para instructores populares," 1982, private collection)

the words *salvadoreño* (Salvadoran) and *trabajo* (work, labor). The other words helped students learn to speak, read, and write additional syllables and sounds, as illustrated in chart 7. Lessons based on the question "Where are we?" used the words *reubicados* (relocated), *campamentos* (camps), Mesa Grande, Honduras, *lejanos* (distant, far away), *familia* (family), *esperanza* (hope), *regresar* (return), and *patria* (fatherland, homeland) in a similar way.

As teachers and students reviewed each word, they covered far more than correct spelling and how to identify syllables. They also discussed the meanings of the words and explored how each related to the campesino refugees' everyday lives. Popular teachers referred to this pedagogical method as *alfabetización integral* (integrated, holistic literacy training). "We study themes that are relevant to our lives," their manual explains. "We always think about the things that we read and write [and] reflect on why things are the way they are."[13] Rosario, who worked as a popular teacher in Honduras, described how a word as simple as *casa* (house) generated discussions about the refugees' lived reality. "With the word 'house,'" she said, "we could put 'Maria's house.' Then we could say 'the burned-down house.' Then it said, 'Maria's house was burned down.'"[14] Further discussion would then lead to who was responsible for burning the house and why they did so. In a similar vein, when learning to read and write the word *refugiado*, teachers and students discussed what a refugee is and explored the many reasons why they had sought refuge in Honduras. For the word *soldado* (soldier), another teacher described asking his students "'What do soldiers do? What do they do to us?' And we start motivating people. 'Why? Who? Why did they drive us here?'"[15] Through these kinds of conversations refugees came to better understand their reality, gained practice in speaking about it, and began identifying ways to improve it. In short, "By talking about words, we raise our own consciousness."[16]

In both oral and written form, then, words became another means through which Salvadoran campesino refugees continued to discover themselves and their human potential. By speaking their words, they named their world and, in so doing, transformed it.[17] This pattern appeared earlier when refugees at La Virtud named their refuge site Campamento Monseñor Romero. Such naming entailed processes of not only identifying and defining their site of refuge as Salvadoran but also of asserting their control over that space.

In much the same way, Salvadoran refugees referred to the education system in the refugee camps as educación popular and their teachers, los maestros populares. The choice to identify their system as "popular" marked it as distinct from "classical" or state-sponsored education. Highlighting the system's grassroots beginnings further empowered campesinos to claim full ownership over not only the system but also their own education in general, as well as their unique perspectives on the world. In the wartime context this staking of claims had serious political implications.

The Political Implications of Popular Education

Chapter 1 revealed how patterns of Salvadoran national development contributed to the marginalization of northern campesinos from the economic, political, and social realms of national life. Similar patterns emerged in chapter 4, which described how UN and Honduran officials excluded Salvadoran refugees from policy discussions and decisions. But these chapters also revealed how campesinos took action on various levels, how they claimed their rights, and how they asserted themselves as Salvadoran citizens and refugees. Popular education in the Honduran camps certainly played a role in empowering campesinos toward these ends, for it enabled them to systematically explore patterns of marginalization and exclusion—their history as well as their impact on the present.

One of the first chapters in the popular teacher's manual focused on the very subject of education in El Salvador. Texts noted the high level of illiteracy in the country and pointed out that in rural areas like Chalatenango rates were three to five times higher than in the capital city of San Salvador. But the manual urged popular teachers to move beyond merely stating the existence of this problem; they should also explore with their students answers to the questions "Why?" and "Who's responsible?" and "What can we do?" Through a series of lessons, students came to see their own illiteracy as a consequence of the conditions in which they lived: rural schools were few and far between, the cost of uniforms and supplies were high, children had to work in order to help maintain their families. Further exploration revealed that these "conditions of misery" were not a natural state of being; rather they were imposed by the wealthy and powerful. As the manual explained, "Certain people have never been interested in having educated workers. They paid illiterates less. Illiterates are not as aware of their rights. Illiterates knew little about the causes of their misery. Illiterates only rarely sought to improve their situation. These people were also not interested in building schools in the countryside or sending teachers to the rural villages because a mass of illiterate people is less likely to demand improvements or to oppose inequalities."[18] According to this line of analysis, education was not a privilege, as campesinos previously had been led to believe. Rather it was a fundamental right that the Salvadoran elite had intentionally denied the rural poor.

As campesino refugees began to perceive education as a right, laying claim to their own education gained in importance. When viewed from this perspective, the very founding of an educational system that was beyond the reach of government officials was a purposeful political action. At least in part because of this, Salvadorans took great care to ensure that they, not outsiders, were at the forefront of educational programs in the refugee camps. Outsiders provided substantial support, of course, from pencils, paper, and blackboards to *técnicos* (technical experts) who helped with teacher training and professional development programs. Refugees were well aware that educational efforts would not have been as successful without outside aid. Yet the refugees had their limits; they drew the line not at any particular level of assistance but rather at specific modes of delivery.

Many of the international aid workers who engaged in the realm of education did so within the context of a progressive aid philosophy that emphasized *acompañamiento* (accompaniment). Largely for this reason Salvadoran refugees perceived these individuals and their organizations as allies in their struggle and accepted all that they had to offer (and often asked for more). Refugees categorized the Honduran government, in contrast, as an intruder and staunchly resisted all attempts by Honduran officials to become involved in the camps' educational efforts. At the very foundations of the refugees' opposition was the "dictatorial" nature of the UN–Honduran plan outlined in the "Memorandum of Understanding"; far from an offer of assistance, it was a unilateral announcement that the Honduran Ministry of Public Education would assume direct control over the refugees' education.

The nature of the announcement provided much fodder for the Salvadorans' public relations campaign against the "Memorandum" in general and Honduran involvement in refugee education in particular. Refugees distanced themselves as much as possible from the "Memorandum" by highlighting the fact that "the agreement between the UNHCR and the government of Honduras [was] planned without the participation of us and the aid agencies." With this statement, they also set the stage to charge the Honduran government with planning to simply replace the refugees' education system with the Honduran state program. This made no sense, Salvadorans argued, in part because they "already have an educational program . . . that we ourselves have developed over the past six years and that has worked very well up to now." The program was exceedingly successful, they explained, precisely because "it allows us a high level of participation as well as training for refugee instructors; we have achieved a great deal in terms of literacy and teaching of our communities."[19] All of this would be in jeopardy if placed in the hands of Honduran officials.

A Honduran state education program in the refugee camps was also highly inappropriate given the fact that the refugees were Salvadoran citizens who at some point in the near future would return to their homeland. In light of this impending return, it was crucial for them to continue with their Salvador-specific lessons. And just as a Salvadoran map was the only suitable method of teaching students the geography of their home country, only teachers from the Salvadoran campesino refugee community were truly qualified to teach in the camps. For this reason the refugees were particularly critical of article 5 of the "Memorandum of Understanding," which announced that Salvadoran teachers would be replaced with Hondurans. "We are always striving to further develop our community in all respects," the refugees countered. "But we do not consider this project to be beneficial for our development given that it establishes a total dependence on teachers that are not from the community."[20] Not only would such an exchange exclude Salvadorans from program administration; Honduran teachers would also create a moral and ideological distance between the Salvadorans and their homeland in much the same way that relocation farther from the border would result in physical distance. And so the Salvadoran refugees held tightly to their own teachers, who were "born of the same pueblo," for "we do not come from another place, we are Salvadorans."[21]

With this we begin to see that the refugees' reasons for defending popular education went far beyond the desire to provoke the authors of the "Memorandum of Understanding." It was also about defending their community—not only as refugees but as Salvadoran citizens. As noted earlier, popular education in the camps played an important role in empowering students. Precisely because the system was beyond the influence of government officials, it was a space in which the refugees could explore and analyze their experiences of marginalization and oppression. Popular teachers and their students together learned to read El Salvador's reality and place themselves into the national story not simply as victims of war but as contributors to and leaders of the struggle to create a new and better patria. In the popular education context, however, it was not enough for campesinos to recognize and act on current realities; it was also necessary to place those current realities within a historical context. As the popular teacher's manual explained, "Alfabetización integral means we say the word, we make our voice heard, we read reality and we write history."[22]

And write history they did; historical narratives permeate the documentation produced by Salvadoran refugees in Honduras. Not surprisingly, these versions of national history contrasted sharply with "official" versions. They did so on two levels. First, refugees highlighted their marginalization from the economic, political, and social realms of national life. Campesinos across El Salvador suffered immeasurably as a direct result of this purposeful exclusion: the ruling elite dispossessed them of their land; forced them to work under inhuman conditions for paltry remuneration; charged them prohibitively high prices for basic foodstuffs and agricultural inputs; and blocked their access to education, health care, and other state services. The civil war—with its death squads, bombing raids, and scorched earth campaigns—was simply the most recent expression of this pattern and their exile the literal and figurative proof of official disregard. The patterns of marginalization and exclusion were, however, much older than the civil war. Refugees traced these patterns back through many generations, drawing direct links to and parallels with the Matanza of 1932 and the 1969 war with Honduras, as well as other regional and world events.

At the same time, the refugees' historical narratives revealed an accompanying pattern of peasant challenge to the elite-imposed "national order of things."[23] As campesinos re-remembered and literally rewrote Salvadoran national history from their sites of exile, they tied together the threads of the past and present and, in so doing, placed themselves squarely within a long tradition of peasant resistance. Thus, even while literally and physically separated from their nation, they countered their marginalization by writing themselves into El Salvador's national history not merely as witnesses but as participants and protagonists.

Documenting Tradition

Educación popular helped refugees understand that illiteracy was not the campesino's natural state of being; rather it was a condition purposely imposed on rural inhabitants by El Salvador's wealthy and powerful, a tradition as old as the nation of El Salvador. Through their studies and accompanying self-documentation, refugees identified many such traditions and, in so doing, wrote a unique new version of Salvadoran history. The citizen refugees' perspective on history contrasted sharply with the version put forward by the Salvadoran state. Although campesinos occupied a central role in both "state" and "popular" narratives, they did so in very different ways. State versions presented campesinos either as violent rebels and threats to national security or as helpless victims acted on or manipulated by outside forces. The refugees' narratives, in contrast, placed campesinos at the center as historical agents.

Two events figured especially prominently in the refugees' historical narratives: the 1932 Matanza and the 1969 Hundred-Hour War between El Salvador and Honduras. In each of these events the refugees not only found evidence of the ruling elite's mistreatment of campesinos; they also discovered a tradition of popular resistance.

Refugees as the Heirs of Farabundo Martí and the Martyrs of 1932

After the stock market crash of 1929, deteriorating labor and living conditions in El Salvador prompted a "remarkable and unprecedented outpouring of protest and organizing by rural workers."[24] Campesino efforts focused primarily on improving labor conditions, establishing a livable minimum wage, and the right to organize. The government met campesino petitions, protests, and strikes with increasing force. After an estimated eighty thousand farm workers took to the streets of San Salvador in May 1930, President Pío Romero Bosque (1927–31) outlawed organizing and rallies. When the protests continued, Romero and his successor, Arturo Araujo (March–December 1931), began relying more heavily on Salvadoran Army and National Guard units to quell the unrest—in many cases, by opening fire on the protesters.

Peasant mobilization climaxed on the night of 22 January 1932, when tens of thousands of campesinos and workers launched a rebellion in the central and western regions of El Salvador. Armed with machetes, sticks, and a few rifles, they occupied several towns and a few isolated police posts and military barracks. According to most accounts, General Maximiliano Hernández Martínez, who had assumed the presidency just weeks before following a military coup that deposed Araujo, responded swiftly and decisively; on his orders the National Guard and local military and police forces marched through the countryside and systematically targeted all those suspected of participating in the rebellion. Although the military had regained control of the region within a matter of days, eyewitnesses reported that indiscriminate killings of peasants continued for weeks thereafter, especially in the heavily indigenous municipalities of the west. This "grotesque" revenge, for which President Martínez earned the nickname "El Brujo" (The Sorcerer), resulted in so many thousands dead that burial became impractical; fearing epidemics, the Salvadoran Department of Sanitation ordered the incineration of all corpses. In the end an estimated thirty thousand perished, the vast majority of them campesinos.[25]

Many observers at the time did, in fact, recognize as legitimate the discontent that gave rise to the rebellion. The renowned Salvadoran social critic Alberto Masferrer, for example, decried the country's landownership structure as "feudal" and called for a serious land reform that would benefit the country's campesinos. In a similar vein, the commander of Canadian marine troops that landed at El Salvador's port of Acajutla around the time of the uprising reported that rural working conditions there were "not in fact far removed from slavery."[26] Yet where others saw class exploitation, the Salvadoran elite perceived benign paternalism. From this latter perspective the January revolt represented an unwarranted attack against beneficent patrons, "a dangerous lunacy in the simple minds of the peasants caused by the preachings of the Communists that tricked them."[27] The double offensive—of disloyal peasant and communist—posed such a threat to the national order that elites called for it to be met with the harshest punishment. The Matanza launched by "El Brujo" Martínez was nothing, if not that.

Fifty years later many Salvadoran elites continued to rationalize the slaughter as a necessary and successful political tactic, one that quelled popular unrest and brought the country a half century of stability. In this sense the Matanza was an important turning point in Salvadoran history. Scholars have tended to agree; while their approaches to the events of 1932 have grown much more complex and layered through the years, they continue to highlight the uprising and its aftermath as a landmark in Salvadoran history and collective memory. Sociologist Jeffery Paige, for example, describes the uprising and its aftermath as "the defining event in modern Salvadoran political history," and Héctor Pérez-Brignoli concludes that it "conditioned political life in El Salvador between 1932 and 1980."[28]

Salvadoran campesinos living as refugees in Honduran camps during the 1980s also viewed the 1932 Matanza as a sort of watershed, but, not surprisingly, their rationales were very different than those offered by scholars or the Salvadoran elite. Interestingly, their narratives of events did not place the military's atrocities at the center of their discussions; the real value of the period could be found instead in the successful gathering of popular forces behind a common goal. That the military bridled the uprising so quickly did not mean that it was a failure; nor did it mean that the peasant movement was vanquished, as elites contended. On the contrary, according to the refugees, the movement that began in the early 1930s continued to grow and gather strength through the decades until it exploded onto the national scene once again in the 1960s and 1970s.[29]

The civil war, then, was in many ways simply an extension of the events of the early 1930s. The desperate economic conditions that drove so many thousands to revolt in the wake of the stock market crash continued to saddle the majority of the Salvadoran populace, and the social and political promises of the late 1920s had been broken by the Martínez dictatorship just as subsequent military regimes had repeatedly dashed all hope and promise of fair elections and reform. The mobilization of all sectors continued, and the military used the same terror tactics to counter the unrest. Refugees highlighted three patterns in particular, all made notorious by the Salvadoran National Guard and its supporters during the Matanza: tying captives' thumbs behind their backs; hanging dead bodies from tree limbs along well-traveled roads; and decapitations followed by the public display of the severed heads, as happened with Agustín Farabundo Martí, the most famous of the leaders of the 1932 uprising. Such tactics were not successful, the peasants were quick to point out, as "far from deterring the advance of [the organizations of the rural workers], it has achieved the contrary effect. It has increased peoples' resolve to continue forward." The blood shed by campesinos in the 1980s joined with that of 1932, and transformed "into a source of inspiration, stimulation, and the energy to continue forward."[30]

In spite of their exile the Salvadoran refugees in Honduras considered themselves to be part of this long-standing tradition of peasant activism. Indeed, they presented themselves as descendants of the martyrs of 1932. As such, they were also heirs to the movement founded by these national heroes and Agustín Farabundo Martí in particular. In the words of a refugee poet:

> I come to tell you the (hi)story
> of a martyr who has already died;
> he left us his example,
> because he will live on in la lucha.
> He was a valiant man
> his name was Farabundo.
> We have read his story
> and the example he gave us . . .
> Martí's body died,
> but he left us his example
> that we will follow . . . [31]

Campesinos followed Martí's example through involvement in peasant rights struggles, as well as the broader national liberation movement. Involvement with peasant unions, for instance, was a mark of great courage and dedication, especially in light of the fact that the Salvadoran government had deemed such behavior illegal since the uprising of 1932. Participation in mutual aid groups, agricultural cooperatives, and CEBs was also highly respected, as was (for many) association with the insurgents. Exile itself became a badge of pride as refugees highlighted the work they did in the camps to raise international awareness of the situation in El Salvador and press for the dissolution of the Salvadoran regime.

For the refugees in Honduras, then, the contemporary civil conflict—which encompassed campesino and popular mobilizations, the guindas, and their own exile—was in many ways an extension of the events of the late 1920s and early 1930s. From the past to the present, Salvadoran campesinos joined forces to demand fair consideration. And, from past to present, members of the oligarchy, along with military and political authorities, tried desperately to quash them.

The 1969 (B)Order Wars

On 14 July 1969 the Salvadoran armed forces launched a surprise attack on their northern neighbor, Honduras. The air force bombed airports and other targets in Tegucigalpa, San Pedro Sula, and Santa Rosa while troops invaded and occupied Honduran towns all along the border. Four days and approximately a thousand casualties later, pressures from the Organization of American States and the United States government prompted first a cease-fire and then the withdrawal of Salvadoran troops from Honduran territory. This war quickly became known as both La Guerra de 100 Horas (the Hundred-Hour War) for its length and La Guerra de Fútbol (the Soccer War) for the accompanying altercations between fans and players of the Salvadoran and Honduran soccer teams during the Central American playoffs for the World Cup competition.[32]

As with the 1932 Matanza, both elite and campesino versions of the 1969 war placed Salvadoran campesinos at the center of the narrative, albeit in very different ways. In the elite narrative, campesinos appeared simply as the victims of Honduran excesses. According to government, military, and press reports, Hondurans had systematically swept through their border region territory in the weeks prior to the military engagement, violently dispossessing Salvadoran immigrants of their land and belongings and forcefully expelling them from the country. In the process these "defenseless peasant families" suffered all manner of "crimes against dignity and arbitrarities," including theft, arson, rapes and other denigrations of women, child abduction, and murder.[33] In a public address on 14 July, Salvadoran president General Fidel Sánchez Hernández announced that the exodus had exceeded seventeen thousand people, with thousands more "dead, in various places in Honduras, or they are being hunted like wild beasts in the mountains, or they can be found in the concentration camps."[34]

Such persecution was particularly egregious, Salvadoran elites believed, because many of the targeted campesinos had owned and farmed land in Honduras for decades, had married and raised children with Honduran nationals, and had, for all practical purposes, become part of local Honduran communities. But, interestingly, the value of these immigrants went far beyond community membership, as a colonel in the Salvadoran military explained:

The avid adventurers of new horizons arrived in [Honduras]. . . . New nerve to confront the vicissitudes of destiny bursts from the fighter man, tenacious and decided, who ultimately becomes a strong labor model for his counterparts in that new environment. . . . A large part of the products of daily consumption were due to the efforts of the Salvadoran peasants who left sweat and energy in the soil of the Central American paladin. . . . These agricultural pioneers arrived not to conquer lands but to improve them, to prepare them to be able to labor on them, to make them produce the maximum of the best fruits and to convert them into accessible places of progress and civilization.[35]

Like this colonel, other Salvadoran officials lamented that instead of rewarding the immigrants the Hondurans persecuted them "for the simple fact of their nationality."[36] The result was an "orgy of blood," a campaign of extermination that prompted the Salvadoran minister of foreign relations, Francisco José Guerrero, to file a formal complaint with the Inter-American Commission on Human Rights in which he accused the Honduran government of "acts in violation of human rights, constituting genocide."[37] According to Salvadoran officials, then, Honduras carried the full blame for the war; Salvadoran military action was not unwarranted aggression but rather "an act of legitimate defense" designed to "guarantee the lives and belongings of our compatriots in Honduras."[38] In the words of the Salvadoran president, "No nation that values its own dignity can permit its own children to be massacred with impunity."[39]

These "children"—these Salvadoran campesinos—viewed the 1969 war in a completely different light. From their perspective, the 1969 war with Honduras was another watershed incident that, like the 1932 Matanza, revealed the Salvadoran national leadership's deception, excess, and base disregard for campesinos.[40] Contrary to official versions of events, campesinos did not hold the

Honduran government accountable; rather they believed that the Salvadoran government had instigated the conflict on both the diplomatic and military fronts. They also countered official assertions that the mistreatment and expulsions of Salvadoran campesinos from Honduras was the main issue of concern by pointing out that the Salvadoran armed forces did not immediately respond in June when the expulsions first began. Instead the military launched its offensive only after thousands of campesinos had already streamed back across the border and into the northern Salvadoran departments of Morazán, Chalatenango, and Cabañas. According to campesinos, this delay proved that the government did not act to support or protect the affected "refugees" but rather ordered military attacks on Honduras with the intention of stopping the cross-border flow and forcing the Honduran government to continue hosting the immigrants.

Campesino narratives of 1969 further countered official versions by arguing that the war was, in effect, a smokescreen for the government's true objective: the militarization of the northern border region in order to control an increasingly mobilized peasant population. As described in previous chapters, many of the campesinos there had begun to organize into mutual aid groups, agricultural cooperatives, and peasant leagues during the 1960s and had started to press government agencies for assistance and even broad reforms. Given the increasing incidents of peasant mobilization and protest, the sudden military presence in the region could not be simply coincidence, especially coming, as it did, on the heels of decades of disregard. "The objective was something else, right," explained a former refugee from northern Chalatenango. "It was as if they maybe wanted to display the weaponry that they had because El Salvador, it already . . . had symptoms of organization. So they wanted to demonstrate that they had weapons and we could be squashed."[41] A campesino from a nearby town concurred and highlighted the way the Salvadoran government had framed the situation: "To see the governments, they had defined their objectives; because a war was going on with Honduras, one shouldn't show opposition within the country then. And one didn't even know why these situations arose. But they infused you, well, that we had to defend our sovereignty, and that these were attacks against the people, and that we had to defend ourselves. But the truth is that around here there was a question of intentions, that is, with the intention of terrorizing the civilian population as well. They had the objective of instilling fear in people, that if one got involved in things, that's what would happen."[42]

The government did, in fact, present the war with Honduras as a noble defense and even used the "national emergency" label to justify the suspension of constitutional guarantees—a measure that was, the president declared, "indispensable to preserve internal order and national security."[43] Many campesinos considered this heroic rhetoric a sham, an attempt to divert attention from the real objective of the war. According to one man, "Many lucid people understood what the connection was, of wanting, for example, to confuse people and justify military preparedness. . . . But the objective was something else. It was to restrain the organization of the people."[44]

In this sense the war of 1969 was inextricably linked to the civil war of the 1980s in that it marked the start of the trenchant militarization of the border region; it was not meant to address any threat posed by the Republic of Honduras but instead to keep vigil over the comunidades organizadas. Campesinos described how, after the Hundred-Hour War, pockets of troops remained stationed throughout the area: "They had a stable presence there, right. They maintained a more permanent vigilance in the border zone."[45] One former refugee described in a particularly dynamic way the encircling of rural villages in Chalatenango by Salvadoran troops. Shortly after the 1969 war, she explained, "in a village named Quipur, they had left a military post. *Nearby*. But they *changed* it. . . . They put it *closer, right in front*. But that wasn't the objective. More than anything it was because they had begun to see that the people had started to get organized. And it was more to control the people and keep vigil over the people who had organized."[46]

These comments illustrate how government "deception" regarding the 1969 war was an important sticking point for the Salvadoran campesinos who crossed into Honduras in the 1980s. Some expressed this in very unequivocal language. One man stated, for example, "It was a deception that they told the whole population. . . . They made us believe it was a war about a ball game, but those were just manipulations of never telling them [campesinos] the truth."[47] According to another, the government "always uses war as a smoke-screen so that you cannot see the real reasons."[48]

Many campesinos pointed out how this pattern of government deception continued into present times with the questionable Lima Treaty in particular. As previously noted, Salvadoran and Honduran representatives suddenly signed this treaty in October 1980 after a decadelong cold war that had begun with the incidents of 1969. Refugees and many international observers argued that the agreement was primarily of a military nature given that it did nothing to resolve the economic and border delineation issues. They supported this conclusion with evidence drawn from the cross-border guindas. Survivors of the Lempa and Sumpul massacres, for example, emphasized the presence of soldiers of both the Salvadoran and Honduran militaries and described being literally caught between two armies as they attempted to flee to safety by crossing the rivers. Even Salvadoran children depicted this trap in vivid detail in

Fig. 14. Las Aradas, the Sumpul River Massacre. (Reproduced from SJDPA 1994)

their drawings (see fig. 14). In the lower-right-hand corner of a drawing by a child from Chalatenango province, we see Salvadoran soldiers shooting at campesinos as they flee toward the Sumpul River. On the opposite side of the water, Honduran soldiers patrol the border and, in the sky above the river, the Salvadoran air force targets campesinos as they attempt to cross the river.

Refugees also argued that the Salvadoran security forces' frequent incursions into the refugee zones of Honduras were a direct result of the Lima Treaty. According to one of the refugees' newsletters, *INFORESAL*, the treaty gave Salvadoran troops permission to enter Honduran territory; incursions into the camps were usually a joint effort, with Honduran troops accompanying Salvadoran troops as they patrolled the camps. On some occasions, however, Honduran military commanders ordered their troops to remain in their barracks during the entire time that Salvadoran soldiers were patrolling the camps. Further evidence of military collaboration was the training of Salvadoran soldiers at the Regional Military Training Center in Puerto Castilla, Honduras.[49]

Salvadoran authorities, in contrast, made no explicit connections between the civil war of the 1980s and the 1969 war with Honduras. Nor did they make reference to the increasing levels of campesino unrest within their borders. (They did, however, notice and comment on such unrest within Honduran borders.) Yet Salvadoran campesinos were at the center of the official narrative—not as aggressors but rather as innocent victims. The rescue mission for these humble "children," moreover, unified the nation as nothing before had done. As President Sánchez Hernández announced at the close of the war, those so unjustly treated by the Hondurans "have given life to a new Salvadoran nationality. . . . 'Fraternity' will never again be a word without meaning among us."[50]

From the campesino refugees' perspective, the 1969 war only served to further divide the nation. Whereas Salvadoran campesinos had already been economically and socially marginalized by the elite, with the Hundred-Hour War they became physically marginalized as well in two senses. The ruling elite attempted not only to halt the return of immigrants from Honduras but also to curtail the organization and mobilization of campesinos in the northern reaches of the country. Herein lies the real crux of the refugees' narratives of 1969: the activity of the campesinos was strong enough to merit the concern and attention of elites and government representatives. Thus, campesinos were at the center of events not as victims but as agents.

Tracing Patterns beyond the Nation

The Salvadoran refugees living in Honduras during the 1980s also placed these patterns of marginalization and mobilization into broader geographic and temporal contexts. Documents produced in the refugee camps linked campesinos to indigenous resistance to conquest and colonization, Salvadoran independence from Spain, the struggles of oppressed groups elsewhere in the Americas and the world, and figures of importance in Roman Catholic religious traditions.

Themes of conquest and independence run squarely throughout Salvadoran refugees' writings and presentations. Many drew a very direct connection between their own experiences and those of their counterparts of the eighteenth and nineteenth centuries. That is, struggles against exploitation began "in the beginning against the Spanish invaders who stole their lands." After independence, Salvadoran peasants continued to fight "against the creole landowners and later against the coffee oligarchy."[51] The same exploitation that occurred during the nation's early years continued into present times; likewise, campesinos continued to struggle against mistreatment and marginalization. The civil war of the 1980s, then, was in many ways an extension of the struggle for independence. In the words of one refugee poet:

> On the 15th of September
> eighteenhundredtwentyone
> they won their independence
> those who raise their fist.

Today they raise it once again
to free us from the yoke.[52]

Salvadoran refugees emphasized that independence from Spain did not necessarily mean freedom from foreign influences. Their writings, in fact, decried the fact that *extraños* (strangers, outsiders) continued to meddle in Salvadoran affairs well after independence. Indeed, many poems and songs likened the current "enemy" to the Spanish conquistadors. One poem, for instance, lamented that outsiders had taken control of El Salvador's best land, leaving little for the Salvadoran campesino:

> Upon the high volcanoes
> you can see green coffee fields
> and in the lowest lands
> you can see the cane fields;
> in the coastal plains
> the white cotton fields.
> The owners of these crops
> none is from El Salvador;
> when the harvest comes
> they take it to other countries
> because from there are the owners
> of the good and best lands.
> The Salvadorans always
> work the worst;
> the products of our land
> are not enough to live on;
> this is why the peasants
> die from so much suffering.[53]

Outsiders did not come to dominate landownership or economic relations in El Salvador in the same way as in other neighboring countries, including Guatemala and Honduras. Campesinos, however, could point to the family names of many of the wealthiest and most prominent landowners—D'Aubuisson, Dalton, Hill, and Duke, for example—as proof of their nonnative and non-Hispanic heritage. Moreover, as the poem implies, campesinos were well aware that the vast majority of El Salvador's produce found its way to foreign lands. From the perspective of the campesinos, this export focus was essentially equivalent to outside ownership of the land.

Many other poems and presentations focused explicitly on the role of the United States of America. The unhealthy alliance between the "creole bourgeoisie" of El Salvador and "Yankee imperialism" began in 1932, and with each passing decade the United States had became more intricately involved in Salvadoran affairs.[54] By the 1980s, campesino refugees were pointing to the Salvadoran state's relationship with the United States as further proof of the government's pattern of *engaño* (deception) of the Salvadoran people. Although the refugees' poems and songs frequently referred to the "Yankee invader" and "Yankee oppressor," the real culpability rested with the Salvadoran government for having no spine and allowing the United States to virtually take over the country.[55] The title of one poem even referred to El Salvador as a "pueblo without a head." This same poem lamented the lack of true leadership, which was particularly evident in the various fraud-filled elections:

> They cannot trick the pueblo
> with the electoral trap . . .
> Yankee imperialism
> in the urns of this pueblo
> with all of its crazy orders [*mandracados*].[56]

Another poem noted that "the people spoke [to the government] without weapons" for too long without adequate response, so now "the people no longer believe in elections." Refugees pointed to the fraudulent elections of 1972 as particularly disillusioning and to those involved as "the magicians / and crazy 'politickers' / that try to deceive the whole world."[57]

Most troublesome for the campesinos, however, was the fact that the Salvadoran government had come to rely so exclusively on the United States to train, equip, and advise the Salvadoran military and security forces. The armed forces had always been capable of savagery, as the 1932 Matanza demonstrated, but U.S. training, according to the campesinos, only served to further pervert them, causing ever more harm to the nation:

> Our land of El Salvador
> has turned into a river
> of the blood of the men
> whom Reagan sent to be assassinated.
> This genocidal junta
> does not respect our lives
> it orders the assassination of elderly
> women and children.[58]

Along the same lines, refugees condemned the government for sending Salvadoran troops to the U.S.-owned and operated CREM in Puerto Castilla, Honduras. And, finally, the refugees listed the very real consequences of the Salvadoran government's dependence on the United States: fighter jets, Huey helicopters, and bombs and other ammunition carrying U.S. insignia, as well as the training of the elite BIRIs, which many peasants ranked alongside the death squads.[59]

Salvadoran refugees in Honduras portrayed heavy foreign influences—whether Spanish colonialism or U.S. imperialism, economic, political, or military—as harmful to their patria. The way to save the nation from this malady was to install a popular government created by and for the people. The FMLN, many of them believed, intended to do just that, and, as noted earlier, refugees pointed to the PPLs as evidence of the positive change that a revolutionary government would bring. Images of hope surfaced frequently in this context: the boat of liberation, the dawning of a new day, a supper table set for all, and birds once again beginning to sing.

Salvadoran refugees often pointed out that they shared their histories of both U.S. imperialism and Spanish conquest with other nations across Latin America. In their self-documentation, they identified not only as campesinos, refugees, and Salvadoran but also as Central American and Latin American; as such they were also part of a broader Latin American tradition of popular resistance to oppression. One of the texts in a popular teachers' manual, for example, included the declaration "I am Latin American, / it matters not from what country, / I want my continent / to live happily someday." Although the handbook does not specify the author of this piece, those familiar with the Latin American *nueva canción* (new song) movement may recognize it from the song "La segunda independencia" (Second Independence) by the Chilean group Inti-Illimani. The Salvadorans' use of these song lyrics exemplifies the refugees' sense that common experience united peasants across Latin American borders and created a unique bond of solidarity.[60]

Many refugee texts emphasized the Nicaraguan connection in particular; in addition to praising the Nicaraguan revolution as a successful model, refugees noted that El Salvador and Nicaragua had participated in a historic cultural exchange. Augustín Farabundo Martí, hero and martyr of the 1932 Matanza, traveled to Nicaragua in the late 1920s to join Augusto César Sandino's fight against U.S. forces; Sandino's heirs—the Sandinistas and their supporters—returned the favor in the 1980s by traveling to El Salvador to assist Martí's heirs in their struggle for liberation.[61] Former refugees spoke very highly of one such individual, Jesús Rojas, who spent years working with the FMLN in the department of Chalatenango before he was killed by U.S.-trained forces in an ambush in 1991.[62] By the late 1990s Rojas had become a local legend; all Chalatecos—regardless of age—seemed to be able to freely recount the story of the ambush, as well as the aftermath, when guerrillas from another FMLN post moved in, collected Rojas's body, and buried him in a secret place until

Fig. 15. Memorials to Jesús Rojas. *Clockwise from top left*: Jesús Rojas silhouette on the wall of a home in Arcatao, Chalatenango; memorial at site of the ambush in which Rojas and his companions died; official stamp of Arcatao's directiva; and the new Colonia Jesús Rojas in repopulated Arcatao. (Photos by the author)

they were able to clandestinely pass his remains to his family in Nicaragua. In addition, peasants erected a large memorial at the site of the ambush on the now well-traveled road between Chalatenango City and the town of Arcatao near the Honduran border. Locals gather at the monument each year on 11 April, the anniversary of the ambush, to pay tribute to Rojas and the others who died in the attack.[63] To this day the repopulated town of Arcatao continues to hold Rojas in especially high esteem (see fig. 15). As the community rebuilt following the war, it decorated walls throughout town with the silhouettes of various locals who gave their lives to the struggle; Rojas's image is among them. Moreover, Arcatao's Directiva Comunal adopted the formal name Asociación

Comunal Héroes 11 de abril (Communal Association "Heroes of 11 April") and christened one of the first rebuilt neighborhoods "Colonia Jesús Rojas."

This kind of veneration exemplifies a common idiom among Salvadorans, referred to by one refugee as "the motto of the good Central American": "Between spouses and siblings, let no one interfere."[64] This same sense of solidarity extended well beyond the American continent, however. A number of poems and songs from the period referred to Vietnam in particular. One pointed to both the role of the United States and the unstoppable strength of the popular opposition: "No, no, no to intervention . . . / If they don't go, they'll go through what happened in Vietnam."[65]

Another significant connection Salvadoran refugees made across both time and space was a comparison of their own experiences with biblical stories. The *iglesia popular* (popular church) was a great influence in this regard. As noted in chapter 1, during the late 1960s and 1970s a faction of the Catholic Church in El Salvador adopted new methods of spiritual work that made the Church truly accessible to the masses for the first time. Among these new methods were the creation of rural CEBs and the training of lay pastoral agents who, among other things, facilitated group readings and reflection on the Bible. These *reflexiones* continued in the refugee zones of Honduras as the campesinos interpreted their past and current situations in light of biblical scriptures.

Not surprisingly, the refugees emphasized the theme of suffering and particularly the trials associated with exile. At one of the first worship services at the La Virtud refugee camp, for example, the *celebrador de la palabra* (celebrator of the word, lay preacher) compared the refugees' crossing of the Lempa River to the Hebrews' crossing of the Red Sea. As one put it, "Yahweh opened the water so that the people of Israel could cross safely out of Pharaoh's land and escape Pharaoh's army. Similarly, Yahweh guided the bullets of those [Salvadoran Army] helicopters so that of 3,000 [campesinos who crossed the river], very few were killed." At another service, a delegate further contextualized their refugee experience in this way: "Moses wasn't able to lead the people immediately into the Promised Land; they spent forty years in the wilderness first. Even afterwards they were recaptured many times. We know what they felt when they said, 'We hung up our harps and wept because we could no longer sing our songs in a foreign land!'"[66]

In a very similar vein, the refugees also compared themselves to Jesus; both were "strangers expelled from our land by foreign forces." But with suffering came hope. Despite the hardship and pain of exile—or perhaps because of it—the refugees believed that Jesus was resurrected in them. As one elderly refugee explained, "We carry on with his work of building a better world where justice dwells and suffering is ended."[67] They also pointed out with pride that

Jesus was born of a campesina woman and compared Mary's travails to those of Salvadoran campesinos:

> The son of the peasant woman . . .
> born of the working class
> of the most humble people,
> of the most heavy work,
> the shoulder blistered from hauling wood;
> Mary with her child
> working night and day
> in the duties of the kitchen
> ironing at night
> earning food
> for her child,
> oh campesina.[68]

Thus, in their historical narratives, Salvadoran refugees in Honduras drew important connections to other oppressed groups and nations. The threads of solidarity crossed geographic borders to include Nicaraguans, other Central Americans and Latin Americans more broadly, and Vietnamese and other foreigners. The threads also linked Salvadorans to the distant past and specifically to the conquest, colonial period, and biblical times. Their narratives, then, placed them squarely within an extended pattern of peasant resistance.

For Salvadoran campesinos, the popular education system offered many tools that were necessary to successfully cross to a new and better future. On both the individual and collective levels, popular education in all its forms—literacy training, Christian reflection on the Bible, skills acquired in the camp workshops, and general self-government—promoted transformation from "ignorant simpletons" to "conscious" and politically aware citizens. Of course many had begun their transformative journeys at home in El Salvador through involvement with agricultural cooperatives, CEBs, directivas, and peasant unions. Others began their journeys during the guindas. Still others did not begin until they arrived at the refugee camps of Honduras. In all cases, as Salvadorans experienced these transformations they gained new awareness of the "national order of things" and the accompanying patterns of marginalization and discrimination. In the refugee camps they began to record their experiences and construct an alternative national order of things, one in which campesinos past and present were active participants and agents of positive change.

7

¡Retorno!

The Grassroots
Repopulation Movement

On 9 April 1986, representatives of the Honduran and Salvadoran governments and the UNHCR met in San José, Costa Rica. On the agenda for the day was the issue of repatriation, the return to El Salvador of the more than twenty thousand Salvadoran campesinos who had been living in refugee camps in Honduras for years—some of them for more than half a decade. This particular meeting was historic in many ways. It was the first time Salvadoran and Honduran officials had met face to face specifically to discuss the situation of Salvadoran refugees in Honduras and the eventuality of their return to El Salvador. This in itself was no small feat given the history of tense relations between the two countries.

This was also the inaugural meeting of the newly established, UNHCR-sponsored Comisión Tripartita (Tripartite Commission), the overarching goal of which was to lay the groundwork for and promote the voluntary repatriation of Salvadoran refugees. No such commission had ever existed in Latin America despite the near continuous presence of refugee crises in the region since the founding of the office of the UNHCR in 1950 and the subsequent approval, in 1951, of the international Convention Relating to the Status of Refugees. In terms of setting a precedent and finding "permanent solutions" to the problems facing Salvadoran refugees, Tripartite Commission members certainly had their work cut out for them.

They began their work at this first meeting by setting forth the fundamental bases for the repatriation process. According to reports from the period, members agreed that (1) repatriation must be of a voluntary and individually expressed nature (2) the process should be nondiscriminatory (each and every person had a right to return and live in his or her country of origin), and (3) it should happen in a gradual manner in order to allow for careful planning, preparation, and execution. Commission members also decided on the need for specific programs designed to facilitate both repatriation and reinsertion into Salvadoran society, although the details of such programs would have to wait for subsequent meetings.

In the meantime, unbeknownst to Tripartite Commission members, refugees at the Mesa Grande camp had established their own commission. The Comité de Repoblación (Repopulation Committee) had held meetings, organized work groups, and gained a wide range of allies among groups inside El Salvador and around the world.

On 10 January 1987 the Comité members informed the UNHCR of their plans to return home. Their Proyecto de Retorno (Return Project) announced, "We are Salvadoran, and we have the internationally recognized right to return to our country under the conditions presented in this project." Among the listed conditions were that the campesinos would return en masse to locations of their choosing in El Salvador, on their journey they would be accompanied by international and national support groups, and they would not be detained or harassed in any way. Salvadoran officials and the UNHCR would work together to provide the returnees the necessary immigration and identity documents. And once they were in Salvadoran territory, government and military officials would respect the campesinos' rights to live and work as civilians, which meant that no military posts would be established in their repopulated communities, repatriates would not be forcibly recruited into the armed forces or be required to establish civil defense patrols, and their towns would not be subjected to bombings and strafings. "These conditions are logical and negotiable," the Comité concluded. "We hope that the negotiations occur and the project is approved in the shortest amount of time possible."[1]

The refugees' announcement took officials by surprise. The Tripartite Committee had met but twice by that point and had only begun to debate the particulars of a plausible official repatriation program. Although internal documents reveal that UNHCR representatives immediately began making arrangements in response to the refugees' announcement, Salvadoran authorities were less receptive. The Salvadoran defense minister, General Carlos Eugenio Vides Casanova, argued before UNHCR representatives that the "present moment is not the appropriate for this purpose." In addition to the war, he said, the country faced a severe economic crisis due to a recent earthquake, price declines in principle export products, and the arrival of thousands of deportees from the United States. Perhaps more to the point, however, Vides Casanova claimed that the Mesa Grande proposal had "evident political motivations" and was a ploy of the FMLN guerrilla forces.[2] Given this, the Salvadoran government rejected the platform presented by the Mesa Grande refugees and, in fact, pressured others, including the UNHCR and international agencies, to dissuade the refugees from their plan.[3]

Over the ensuing months, government and refugee representatives debated the repatriation through news media and the UNHCR. It was not until September—more than nine months after receiving notice of the refugees' plans—that the Salvadoran government began to negotiate directly with the refugees. In a series of meetings at Mesa Grande and in the nearby Honduran town of San Marcos, officials tried first to persuade the Comité to abandon its plans and then to limit the operation. The Comité refused to accept the government's conditions, and as October dawned about a quarter of the refugees in the camp began packing their few belongings and breaking down their shelters in anticipation of a midmonth return. They were ready to go home, they said, and they would do so on foot if necessary.

On the morning before the departure date set by the refugees, Salvadoran officials met with the Comité de Repoblación and other followers of the return plan. Officials urged the refugees to delay their plans and once again insisted that repatriation be "gradual and ordered" rather than "massive and spontaneous." Refugees responded with angry shouts: "When you bombed us out of our houses it wasn't gradual or orderly!" Made nervous by the uproar, the government delegation abandoned the meeting with admonishments that "we do not respond to this kind of disorder, these attempts to squeeze the government."[4]

Given the "imminence" of the refugees' return, UNHCR representatives in Honduras promptly arranged an "urgent meeting" with Salvadoran officials. For seven hours they debated. In a cable to headquarters, UNHCR representatives described the eventual resolution: "Finally, given the deadlock in discussions UNHCR requested that [Salvadoran] President Duarte be contacted directly to ascertain the position of the authorities at the highest level. . . . Following consultations . . . President Duarte as Commander in Chief of the Armed Forces and with the full knowledge of the Military Command expressed his agreement to permit the Mesa Grande refugees to return to their villages of origin."[5]

The next morning, 10 October 1987, more than four thousand campesinos began their journey back to El Salvador, where they repopulated five villages in northern Chalatenango, Cabañas, and Cuscatlán. Over the next two years, six additional mass returns occurred, involving some fourteen thousand Salvadoran campesinos.

Studies of these returns have followed similar patterns to those of war flight and exile; the return to one's homeland, ironically, represents yet another "historic break" in campesino lives.[6] One study proclaimed that the "repatriation of these refugees to El Salvador . . . represented an awakening of a peasant population."[7] In the words of another, the refugee experience, combined with repatriation struggles, "helped the displaced begin to recognize themselves as human beings."[8]

The displaced continue to be displaced from the official story. They are relegated to the sidelines in the preparation and execution of repatriation and repopulation projects. Perhaps this is not surprising given the standing that government and UN officials proffered refugees during the Central American refugee crisis of the 1980s. The Tripartite Commission, for example, did not include representatives of the refugee population, nor did the proceedings of the first CIREFCA, sponsored by the UNHCR in 1989.[9] People included in such working groups, and scholars who utilize documentation produced by them, tend to adopt the "official" view. From this perspective a refugee who returned home "owes it all to CIREFCA," and the high number of campesinos who took part in the mass repatriations to El Salvador measures the success of official efforts. A Honduran member of the Tripartite Commission, for example, concluded that the commission gave "the refugees a greater incentive for their return home and offered guarantees for their safety."[10]

But Salvadoran campesino refugees believed otherwise. They knew that the first CIREFCA was convened *after* thousands had already returned home. And, they said, the Tripartite Commission's "firm guarantees" regarding security were empty promises: "In the Salvadoran reality, there exists no possibility for establishing guarantees for the pueblo that lives in El Salvador, much less for the refugees repatriated from Honduras."[11]

The following pages examine this "underside" of the repopulation of rural El Salvador. As previous chapters have shown, Salvadoran campesinos responded to exclusionary tactics through organization and mobilization. They demanded participation and, despite many restrictions and risks, they struggled to maintain as much control as possible over the policies and procedures affecting their lives. And when officials ignored their calls to negotiate—as they often did—the campesinos turned to high-profile protest actions. This chapter continues to highlight the campesinos' agency, focusing in particular on the development within the displaced communities of a grassroots repopulation movement. Campesinos built this unique social movement on decades of experience in their hometowns, on the guindas, and in camps. As with numerous other initiatives, they achieved significant successes. They repopulated locales within conflicted zones in the midst of civil war before the signing of the Peace Accords and before peace negotiations between the FMLN and the government had begun in earnest. And they did so on their own terms.

This chapter also argues that this grassroots repopulation movement altered the political and social landscapes in El Salvador. It forced Salvadoran officials to recognize campesinos as agents, civilians, and citizens of the nation. Within the resettled villages, moreover, campesinos established and nurtured alternative structures that directly challenged the nation's traditional social, political, and economic relations. Finally, by insisting on their rights as civilian citizens to live in the rural north, and through their alternative structures, Salvadoran campesinos helped drive forward a national peace process.

Repopulation as Resistance

Voluntary repatriation was not a novel idea at the time of the 1987 mass return from Mesa Grande. Honduran authorities had encouraged repatriation programs since 1981 when the government officially recognized the Salvadorans as refugees. In a similar vein, UN officials promoted voluntary repatriation as a "durable solution" to refugee crises around the world; they even offered financial incentives, as well as logistical support, for individuals and families that chose to return to El Salvador. According to UNHCR documents from the period, dozens of people took advantage of the agency's offer each year.

These documents also reveal that many more refugees opposed repatriation. In response to Honduran campaigns promoting repatriation, for example, refugee communities announced that they would not leave until "peace with justice and dignity" reigned in El Salvador. The conditions were not yet safe for them, they argued. One letter to the UNHCR stated, "We wish to return to our country; but not in the circumstances that the Salvadoran pueblo now lives, where every day the numbers of internally displaced rise and the massacres of civilian populations, tortures and imprisonments by the government's military [continue]." As proof of the dangers that awaited them in El Salvador, they listed the "violations against the dignity" of six men who had repatriated in previous years and had subsequently been imprisoned or killed.[12]

In addition to these very real dangers, refugees claimed that repatriation plans being discussed by government and UN officials were part of a plan to oust them from the border zone in order to further militarize the region. Refugee publications often placed official repatriation plans within the context of

U.S. aggression in the region. From this perspective, resistance to repatriation and continued witnessing on the border were important contributions to El Salvador's liberation struggle.

There is no doubt that the moral economy of the camps played an important role in fostering opposition to repatriation during the early 1980s. The more politicized refugees placed significant pressure on others to decline the UNHCR's offer of individual voluntary repatriation assistance. On occasion they went to extremes to prevent their compatriots from leaving the refugee camps. When a group of twenty-five refugees at the San Antonio camp indicated to UNHCR representatives in May 1988 that they wanted to return to El Salvador, they "insisted that their decision not be made known to the refugee community, for fear of reprisals." The UNHCR quietly made arrangements, but at the time of departure "a crowd of refugees" gathered to prevent the group from leaving the camp. In a cable to headquarters, UNHCR field representatives reported that the crowd, "armed with sticks, knives and machetes," staged a violent attack. One man "was carried away by the crowd, badly beaten and virtually taken hostage. Similarly, one other young voluntary repatriation candidate was impeded to leave the camp and three women did not dare to turn up for repatriation." Two days later, when the representatives finally gained access to the "hostage," he no longer wished to repatriate. "It was obvious that [he] made this statement under pressure," UN officials reported. "His mouth was still swollen from the beating up. . . . Moreover, he seemed to be under the effects of drugs."[13]

If the moral economy of the refugee camps dictated against voluntary repatriation, then why did more than four thousand Mesa Grande refugees decide to return home in 1987? There can be no doubt that by 1987, Salvadorans were weary of exile. Many of them had been living in the closed camps of Honduras since the UNHCR began sponsoring them in 1981 and 1982. Before that, many had spent two or more years in Honduran villages along the border. Most had been en guinda—in one form or another—since the late 1970s, some even earlier. Just as weariness of life in constant movement initially prompted many to cross the border into Honduras, so too did fatigue of exile induce the return journey.

The poor camp conditions contributed to this weariness. The closed camps had never been pleasant of course. Yet after 1986, budget and program cuts heightened difficulties. Although the UNHCR argued that aid had been reduced due to a global financial crisis, the refugees perceived it as part of a long-term "policy of repression" intended to starve them out of the camps and out of Honduras. In light of this, many felt it was simply better to return to El Salvador than endure conditions where they were.

Perhaps foremost in many refugees' decisions regarding repatriation, however, were political considerations. We have seen that Salvadorans occasionally resorted to violence to keep their compatriots from leaving the camps. In other instances the refugee community "kept the secret" about groups that repatriated without the assistance or even the knowledge of aid personnel. These two behaviors, when placed side by side, indicate that refugees often perceived repatriation as a political act. Thus, as the circumstances within El Salvador shifted, so too could the refugees' ideas regarding returning home.

In fact, by the mid-1980s, refugees began to note changes in the Salvadoran context. Although the civil war in El Salvador continued (government and Salvadoran forces had been in a stalemate since at least 1983), the "demonstration elections" of 1984 had brought José Napoleón Duarte to power.[14] During his campaign as the PDC presidential candidate, Duarte had promised to end the work of death squads, submit the military to civilian authority, and support a "national dialogue." Apparently true to his word, he arranged the first round of face-to-face talks between the government and the FMLN soon after taking office. Although the negotiations collapsed after only two meetings, "democratization" continued to be a theme throughout the Duarte years (1984–89).

Among those who began testing this new political opening were the internally displaced populations. They did so by repopulating areas of the country that the military had forcefully depopulated in previous years. A catalyst for this migration was Salvadoran Catholic Church officials' decision to relocate thousands of "internal refugees" who had been living in more than a dozen urban refuges operated by the Church. One of the first projects organized by the Church was the repopulation of Tenancingo in central Cuscatlán department. This gained a high profile in both national and international news in light of the Church's negotiation of agreements with the FMLN and government officials; both parties to the conflict agreed to respect the repopulation site as a demilitarized zone. In January 1986, fifty-six families returned to rebuild the town.[15] Other relocation and repopulation projects followed, and by 1987 only one Church-sponsored urban refuge continued to operate.

Concerned about the paternalism evident in the Church's decision and actions, a number of people living in the urban refuges responded by taking matters into their own hands. In July 1984, four hundred families gathered at a forum "to talk about the Church's decision to relocate us and decide what to do. We decided to form an organization . . . to find a way together to solve our problems. . . . We formed CRIPDES [Comité Cristiano Pro Desplazados de El Salvador (Christian Committee of Displaced Persons of El Salvador)]."[16] The purpose of this new organization was to promote repopulation and relocation,

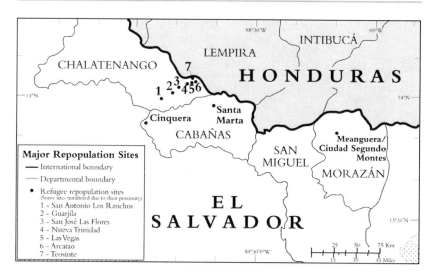

Map 3. Major repopulation sites in northern El Salvador. (Map by Pamela Larson, Augustana College)

coordinate aid to these communities, and raise awareness about the challenges facing them. Two years later CRIPDES represented approximately 350,000 displaced persons and coordinated work in twenty-seven communities in five of the country's fourteen departments.[17]

But in 1986 the war continued, and there was no end in sight. Given this, and in the wake of "Phoenix," another high-profile counterinsurgency operation, CRIPDES sponsored a national assembly in May 1986 to assess options and determine long-term solutions to the problems facing the displaced. Out of that assembly a new organization emerged: the Coordinadora Nacional de Repoblamientos (National Coordinator of Repopulations, CNR). Whereas CRIPDES would continue addressing general issues facing both displaced and repopulated communities, the CNR would focus on organizing displaced persons' return to and repopulation of their places of origin. Its representatives dove into their work, and a short month later 120 families left the Calle Real camp in San Salvador to repopulate San José Las Flores in Chalatenango. There they were joined by some 500 others who had been living en guinda. The following month, July 1986, CNR coordinated another 500-person repopulation at San Antonio El Barillo in Cuscatlán. Such projects continued for the next several years (see map 3).

The work of the CNR, CRIPDES, and the Catholic Church gave strength to the many "silent" repopulations that were occurring at the same time.[18]

These were typically smaller groups—perhaps just a few families—that decided to stop leading the guinda life. Some joined previously repopulated communities; others returned to abandoned hamlets. Unlike the Tenancingo or San José Las Flores groups, these silent repopulations counted on neither assistance nor publicity. Yet they contributed a great deal to the growth and expansion of the grassroots repopulation movement. According to one calculation, between twenty and thirty thousand people repopulated communities in northern Morazán alone between 1985 and 1987.[19] Although these "silent" movements were especially risky for campesinos, all repopulations faced serious dangers, including direct targeting by the military. Still people continued to filter back into the northern regions. The message was clear: people were going home.

People en guinda had often returned to their villages for varying lengths of time. The repopulations were different in that they were intended to be permanent; once resettled, communities resisted being dislodged. As such, they posed a considerable challenge to the Salvadoran regime. Up to that point, government troops had deliberately depopulated vast areas in an effort to isolate the FMLN from civilian supporters. Officials then justified intensive bombing campaigns and other counterinsurgency operations by saying that civilians no longer existed in the conflicted areas. As Coronel Sigifredo Ochoa Pérez reported to journalists in 1985, "In these zones, there are no civilians. There are only guerrilla groups, so we keep them under intense fire."[20] Repopulations countered such claims. The communities organized, built highly public profiles, and attracted sustained international attention. In light of this attention, it became increasingly difficult for the government to oust people using the scorched earth tactics of earlier years. "The people were organized and counted on international recognition," said one CNR founder. "To deny the repopulation would have been very shameful for a government that claims to be democratic. We (the CNR) would have ensured that the international solidarity networks would find out."[21] Thus, even as the military sought to "illegalize" civilian life in conflicted zones, repopulators struggled to "legalize" it.

Neither the repopulations nor Duarte's democratic rhetoric were lost on Salvadoran refugees in Honduras. This changing context at home, combined with the deterioration of conditions in the Honduran camps, prompted many to consider returning home a viable option by 1986. Refugees at Mesa Grande began to mobilize toward that end. A group of adult literacy students rallied with the following verse:

> Let us orient ourselves . . .
> Let's pack our suitcases

—with our abilities
—with our experience
—with our conscience
and let's carry them home
take to the pueblo that awaits us
everything we already have contributed from Mesa Grande
to participate in the construction of our future.[22]

As these lines indicate, many refugees were ready to take their political commitments and contributions to yet another level.

Preparing the Conditions

If internally displaced populations "broke the ice" of the repopulation movement, refugees in Honduras pushed the movement to full tilt.[23] They did so by forcing the Salvadoran government to negotiate with them and recognize them as agents, citizens, and civilians. It is here, perhaps, that the campesinos put their status as refugees to greatest use. Throughout their time in exile, they had been "subjects" of the humanitarian aid regime. This brought attention and publicity. But their status as refugees also conferred special rights under international law. Salvadorans pressed such recognition to full advantage during the repatriation process.

A group of Mesa Grande refugees was the first to organize a grassroots repopulation project, which they branded *retorno* (mass return) rather than "repatriation" to distinguish it from official projects. They would not have known it at the time, but they established a two-phase course that all subsequent groups would follow. The first phase entailed clandestine organization and planning. Proponents of retorno worked to raise awareness within the refugee population of the benefits of returning to El Salvador. When enough people had signed on to the idea, they established an organizational structure to design a plan and carry it to fruition. An important part of this underground phase was lining up allies to financially and physically accompany them on the journey home. During the second phase the refugees went public with their plans. They announced their intentions to officials, engaged in negotiations, and when necessary launched protest actions. Throughout both phases the strategic management of information was crucial to success.

Phase One: Operation Underground

Each retorno began at the initiative of a small group of refugees who felt the time was right to return home. This group then "started to consult with the people, presenting them with the idea of returning."[24] The preparations that refugees undertook at this point closely paralleled the actions they had taken years before as they prepared for the guindas. It appears, however, that preparing the conditions for return to El Salvador entailed far more tension, as proponents of the retornos exerted pressure on the more reticent refugees to compel them to sign on to the campaigns. The Mesa Grande refugee population, for example, was deeply divided with regard to plans for the first mass return. International observers reported in January 1986 that one group (about 40 percent of the camp population) was promoting a "massive and immediate" retorno while another (the remaining 60 percent) felt it was "not time yet." Those who had opted in, moreover, did so "with glorified expectations" because the Comité de Repoblación "provided incomplete and sometimes false information to people to convince them to repatriate." Although the Comité eventually "calmed down a bit," tensions lingered.[25] According to one report, "Those who are going to stay behind fear that they will be pressured. . . . Although the majority want to return, there are some who have more fear than desire. Many say, 'We don't want to be the first or the last.'"[26]

It also appears that the first retorno strained relations between the different camps in Honduras. As noted in previous chapters, refugees at Mesa Grande, Colomoncagua, and San Antonio often synchronized denunciations, publications, and protest actions. Much of their coordinated effort had been to counter Honduran officials' relocation and repatriation campaigns. Suddenly refugees at Mesa Grande announced their intention to return home while at the same time refugees at Colomoncagua continued to speak out against "forced repatriation."

It is probable that this split corresponded at least in part to divisions within the FMLN regarding the viability of repatriation. The precise stance that the FMLN high command took will remain unclear until its internal documentation becomes available to researchers. It is no secret, however, that ideological and procedural differences existed among the five bands of the insurgent coalition and that "each party . . . did what its leaders interpreted as the reality."[27] And the leaders clearly differed in their opinions regarding displaced populations. An ERP commander, for example, stated that the mass repatriations from the Colomoncagua camp "were part of a totally deliberate political strategy." Walter, an officer from the RN, disagreed. "That we went there [to the camps] and we told them 'do this'—that's a lie," he said. Instead "the people" were responsible for deciding to return home and organizing to make it happen. The FMLN coordinated its activities with such sentiments; the "General Strategic Counter-Offensive" plan developed by the high command, for example, included a discussion of repopulation. Yet this was not the driving force behind the retornos. Rather, a cadre named Walter said, the Honduran refuges were "concentration camps" and people there simply "couldn't stand it anymore."[28]

This contrast between the ERP and RN representatives' narratives is especially intriguing in light of events on the ground. Whereas refugees from Mesa Grande (the majority of whom endorsed the RN or the FPL) initiated return projects in late 1986, those in Colomoncagua (many of whom endorsed the ERP) did not begin returning until late 1989. Moreover, available documentation from around the time of the first retorno reveals that UNHCR and voluntary agency representatives spent considerable time discussing the Mesa Grande refugees' decision and plans with those at the Colomoncagua camp while also relaying the Colomoncagua refugees' rationales against returning to those at Mesa Grande. Furthermore, records show that some people in the Colomoncagua camp transferred to Mesa Grande in order to take part in the first retorno. All this suggests that the ERP may have had not only a more strict policy regarding repatriation but also a more direct role in the return process from Colomoncagua.

Regardless of the root of the initial plans, FMLN leaders and combatants certainly influenced the execution of all retornos. At the very least, refugees planning to return to northern El Salvador had to negotiate with insurgent leaders to ensure safe passage to and respect for their repopulation sites. Additional discussions were often necessary in light of the fact that most sites were in territory controlled by the FMLN. "Yes, we negotiate with the FMLN," one man from Morazán explained. "We have to do it. They are one of the authorities we have to deal with."[29]

If the first group to return from Mesa Grande was not a picture of perfect unity, subsequent groups also faced challenges. A volunteer with the Maryknoll order foreshadowed one difficulty at the time of the first Mesa Grande retorno in 1986; she had, she said, "a deep fear that the exodus will lead to chaos in the camp. Many of the most *capacitados* are leaving."[30] The use of the term *capacitado* here is important, as it may refer to practical training or skill level, as well as to political awareness and commitment. Although "chaos" did not engulf Mesa Grande after its most committed leaders returned to El Salvador, it does appear that collective organization in the camp declined to some extent and that organizers of later retornos struggled to cultivate a sense of unity. For example, they created dozens of silkscreened posters promoting retornos (see fig. 16), and, as still visible on Mesa Grande's now crumbling walls, painted murals entreating refugees to "*¡Incorpórate!* Sign on to the 2nd [or fourth or fifth] retorno!" Voluntary aid agency and UNHCR documents reveal another

LAS CONDICIONES PARA REPA—TRIARNOS HAY QUE

CONSTRUIRLAS

TRABAJEMOS JUNTOS PARA

LOGRARLAS

REFUGIADOS EN COLOMON. JUN. 89

LA ALEGRIA ES: RETORNAR EN COMUNIDAD

LUCHEMOS PARA LOGRARLO

Fig. 16. Three posters promoting repatriation read:
(*left above*) "We must construct the conditions to repatriate. Let's work together to achieve them. Refugees
at Colomon. Jun. '89"; (*left below*) "Happiness is returning as a community. Let's struggle to achieve it.
Colomon. Jul. '89"; (*above*) "Brother refugee: Organization guarantees our security. Colomoncagua April—
'89." (Photos by Eric Ellefsen)

possible strategy: protest actions. In response to a June 1988 hunger strike in Mesa Grande (a parallel to the Ayuno at Colomoncagua and San Antonio referred to in chapter 4), a UNHCR representative notified headquarters that "some of us believe this movement is nothing but a way of getting adhesion and solidarity of whole Mesa Grande population, who, after massive repat in October 1987, remained predominantly indifferent to community and political matters."[31]

In short, the "founders" of each retorno project adopted different methods to attract followers. As the number of adherents grew, they established an organizational structure to formalize and carry forward a plan. They formed committees, conducted surveys, considered their options, and developed guidelines for action. The first Mesa Grande group, for example, formed a Comité de Estadísticas (Statistics Committee) to conduct surveys about who wanted to return to El Salvador and where they wanted to go; the committee drew from this information to identify five specific locations for repopulation: Santa Marta, Copapayo, Arcatao, Las Vueltas, and San Antonio Los Ranchos. Once the sites had been specified, the refugees organized into affinity groups—one for each of the five communities to which they would return. Each group then established its own coordinating committee, which, in turn, elected representatives to the campwide Comité de Repoblación.

Later repatriates had a distinct advantage over those who went before, in that they could draw from previous experiences; toward this end they carried out exhaustive evaluations of prior retornos to help inform their debates and eventual platforms for return. Those who initiated the second retorno from Mesa Grande, for example, requested and acquired reports from the directivas of the first five return sites as early as January 1988; in February they reviewed and analyzed those reports and, with the results in mind, began elaborating their own formal plan for a mid-August journey home.

Later retornos also drew from previous experiences in order to adjust their strategies and prompt better results. After the first retorno, platforms for return became much more specific and detailed. All platforms included the same basic conditions: the return to locations designated by the returnees, as one group, accompanied by internationals and free from harassment. But, whereas the first Mesa Grande retorno platform included only eight points, the official announcement for the second retorno from Mesa Grande listed thirteen demands made directly to the Salvadoran government, with seven additional demands made to the UNHCR.

Reports of multiple difficulties experienced by repopulators in their Salvadoran communities also prompted participants in later retornos to more thoroughly plan new repopulation sites before leaving the refugee camps.

In several cases, teams of refugees visited the repopulation sites prior to the retorno in order to evaluate the location and determine the needs of the community. For all retornos after 1987, organizers established contacts with Salvadoran communities neighboring the intended repopulation sites. The directivas in these communities, along with CNR affiliates, often helped make arrangements in advance of the retorno. In May 1990, for example, the directiva in the repopulated community at San Antonio Los Ranchos began working with committees at Mesa Grande to prepare for a mass return to the nearby town of Nueva Trinidad. In a similar vein, the repopulated community at Santa Marta, Cabañas, negotiated a rent-to-own agreement with the owner of some nearby property so that a group of refugees returning from Mesa Grande could establish the village of Valle Nuevo.[32]

Those who returned to Morazán province from the Colomoncagua refugee camp in 1989 offer perhaps the best example of a preplanned repopulation site. While still in Honduras, the refugees not only sought concessions from Salvadoran, Honduran, and UN officials through their return platform and subsequent negotiations, but they also planned economic and social projects for their community-to-be at Meanguera. An important part of this planning process involved the physical layout of the community itself. In terms of housing, a committee of refugees drew up a blueprint for the type of housing to be built in the new settlement. A construction crew then built a model house in the Colomoncagua camp, sought feedback from the refugee community, and adjusted the original blueprint according to the comments they received. In terms of the village as a whole, another committee of refugees, in collaboration with city planners and architects in their international solidarity network, created a diagram of the repopulation site complete with schools, parks, gardens, production facilities, and warehouses.[33]

In addition to communitywide preparations, people also prepared for retornos on individual bases. Some actions revealed just how heavily the decision to return weighed on them in light of the dangers involved. The Maryknoll volunteer quoted earlier, for example, remarked to her colleagues that refugees who planned to return to El Salvador with the first retorno insisted on being formally baptized or married before their departure; they were, in effect, resolving their status with the Church because they feared what would happen to them in El Salvador.[34]

The underground planning phase entailed far more than this internal work. An additional, crucial aspect was a quiet public relations campaign to garner support and allies. In El Salvador, refugees established support networks that included former refugees and internally displaced persons living in newly repopulated communities; faith-based groups such as the Catholic

Church's Diaconía, CEBs, and NGOs such as CRIPDES, CNR, and the Patronato de Desarrollo de las Comunidades de Morazán y San Miguel (Community Development Council of Morazán and San Miguel, PADECOMSM) provided crucial assistance with planning and fund-raising, as well as coordination of accompaniment and reception.[35] In addition, these organizations closely followed each return journey in order to denounce obstacles and harassment. Denunciations typically took the form of paid advertisements in the Salvadoran media and communications with international solidarity networks. Occasionally activists from these NGOs took more radical actions, including the occupation of the National Cathedral on at least one occasion.

Although Salvadoran NGOs helped to coordinate international accompaniment, refugees also worked this angle. It is important to remember that the initial contacts were quite secretive. "Dear María," wrote Julio G. to an international ally in July 1988. "On behalf of the Comité de Repoblación we would like to let you know that we need you to give publicity to all the solidarity people you think convenient. And who can accompany us on the second retorno from Mesa Grande to our country. . . . We are unable to specify the departure date, but we ask that you be ready for sometime between the tenth and twentieth of August."[36] Refugees sent letters like this one to hundreds of individuals and organizations in the months before each retorno. Refugees sought support from those who had visited or worked in the refugee camps, had accompanied their compatriots on earlier return journeys, had offered donations, or had otherwise shown solidarity with the Salvadoran campesinos over the years.

The amount of documentation generated by solidarity organizations can be used as one measure of the refugees' success in gaining allies in their endeavors to return home. Public and private collections in the United States reveal a plethora of national and local organizations—including the SHARE Foundation, Catholic Relief Services, American Friends Service Committee, Lutheran World Federation, and National Council of Churches—that supported the Salvadoran grassroots repopulation movement. Numerous specialized support groups also appeared on the scene, including the Going Home Interfaith Campaign and Voices on the Border. These organizations, like their counterparts in other countries, promoted congressional resolutions, paid for advertisements, and sent letters and telegrams in support of the refugees' platforms. Members also raised funds for the returning families and sent delegations to El Salvador and Honduras to pressure for support prior to the retornos, as well as to provide accompaniment during the actual return journey. Likewise the UNHCR archive holds hundreds of petitions and letters from nurses, boy scouts, businessmen, teachers, and others in Spain, Germany,

Canada, the United States, Sweden, France, and many other countries. Prominent individuals around the world lent their names to the support efforts: bishops and archbishops, members of Congress, rock music idols, and other internationally renowned figures, including the Holocaust survivor and writer Elie Wiesel.

Phase Two: Going Public

After the first phase of quiet internal and external public relations, the refugees took their campaign into the public realm. They did so first by presenting officials with their return platforms and then by engaging them in indirect and direct negotiations.

The refugees' information campaigns were carefully and deliberately constructed and managed. They intentionally staggered publicity about their plans so that the Salvadoran government was the last to know. According to Alejandro, who served on the first Mesa Grande Comité de Repoblación, first they informed international solidarity groups, then local humanitarian workers, and last the UNHCR and Honduran and Salvadoran governments. According to one campesino, "The thing was that we always had a secret information venue; we didn't give everything out at once. . . . More than anything, we publicized our plans internationally. . . . The UNHCR was not willing to negotiate given the conditions in El Salvador because the government then—of Napoleón Duarte—wouldn't give the green light for us to return. . . . So that's why we hid—why we, um, publicized our information internationally. . . . We began the campaign outside and announced our return date *before* giving it to the government. . . . So when we told [officials], we'd already publicized it abroad."[37] From Alejandro's point of view, managing the information in this way ensured a wide international base of support, which forced all parties, and the Salvadoran government in particular, to take the refugees' demands seriously.

Honduran government and UNHCR documents reveal that this practice was in fact successful in terms of placing officials on the defensive. A series of UNHCR cables from July 1988 illustrate the extent to which officials had to scramble in response to the refugees' demands. The cables referred to refugee plans for the second mass retorno from Mesa Grande, which had been under way for months. By 10 May 1988 the Going Home solidarity group was fully aware of the refugees' plans and already had initiated a "one million seeds of hope" fund-raising campaign.[38] Yet two months later neither the UNHCR nor Salvadoran officials knew for certain. A UNHCR cable from 2 July 1988 described a telephone conversation between the chiefs of UNHCR missions in Honduras and El Salvador, Leila Lima and Roberto Rodríguez Casasbuenas, respectively, in which Lima suggested that a "massive repatriation could take place July." Several days after that conversation, Rodríguez and the Salvadoran vice minister of foreign affairs initiated talks about the "increasing rumors" of the "potential return" of Salvadoran refugees from Honduras.[39] Officials reported similar "indicators" for other repatriations as well.

Once the word was out, refugees and officials began to negotiate. Documents from the period reveal that Salvadoran officials wrangled with UN and Honduran officials, and both UN and Honduran officials worked directly with the refugees. However, Salvadoran government representatives resisted direct interactions with the refugees until days, even hours before planned departure times. Instead they negotiated through the UNHCR and media outlets.

The initial response from Salvadoran officials to each retorno announcement was a resounding no. The country was still at war, they said; therefore, they could not guarantee the protection "beyond what was possible in a country at war," especially in the conflicted zones to which the refugees wished to return.[40] Numerous officials, especially those of the military, presented the refugees' plans as FMLN maneuvers. In 1988, for example, Army Commander Iván Reynaldo Díaz claimed that "the communist leadership is trying to create a ring around the department of Chalatenango, relocating villages of supposed displaced or repatriated persons in order to convert them into terrorist refuge areas."[41] The following year, Interior Minister Francisco Merino announced that there was a "terrorist plot" to pressure repatriation from Colomoncagua in order to utilize the newly returned population in "subversive actions."[42]

The refugees responded with paid advertisements, petitions, and letters. Some letters they sent directly to the Salvadoran president or the UNHCR. Many more they addressed to their international allies in hopes that they, in turn, would pressure officials. What they had done for years in the refugee camps they continued to do throughout the repopulation movement: stage themselves as victims. Explanations for why the time was right for return highlighted the deteriorating living and security conditions in the camps and listed the increasing difficulties facing them at Mesa Grande: physical and mental health problems due to overcrowding, increased military incursions and harassment by Salvadoran and Honduran security forces, and a general sense of imprisonment. Many also lamented that children born in the camp had never known freedom. In addition the UNHCR had begun to cut parts of the refugee assistance program. Refugees blamed these cuts, and specifically those in the areas of food aid and protection personnel, for ratcheting up feelings of frustration and desperation in the camp. Representatives of the UNHCR explained that the reductions were part of a strategy to address a global UN budget crisis, but the refugees remained suspicious.

The refugees also continued to paint themselves as politically innocent. Much of this work entailed countering official "disinformation campaigns" that claimed the FMLN was controlling the retornos and repopulations. In an open letter to Interior Minister Merino, for example, Colomoncagua refugees stated, "At no time are we under FMLN plans as you asserted yesterday to the press; we consider that your declarations only jeopardize our organization and the very process of repatriation."[43] On a more general level, refugees returning from Mesa Grande remarked, "We have no cause to defend, we are on no one's side. We are poor people, peasants and workers. All we want to do is to return home to work and live in peace."[44]

Throughout the indirect negotiations with Salvadoran officials, refugees utilized a moral rhetoric that emphasized both their own rights as humans, civilians, and Salvadoran citizens and the duties and "moral obligations" of the Salvadoran state. The first group to return from Mesa Grande began the pattern with demands such as these before President Duarte: "It is our legitimate right as Salvadorans to return to our country [and] the government you represent is morally obligated to provide us a satisfactory answer to our desire to return."[45] Refugees embraced the images that the Duarte government presented of itself and consciously utilized them as tools to promote their own position in favor of return. They often did so by pointing out discrepancies between officials' words and actions. They noted, for example, that Salvadoran officials had publicly announced that the refugees were welcome to return home and that El Salvador was now a democracy and moving toward peace. Officials had already launched various campaigns, moreover, for the return and integration of refugees and the internally displaced, including Chalate '88 (Chalatenango 1988) and Unidos para Reconstruir (United to Reconstruct). Yet when the refugees in Honduras decided to take the government up on its offers, officials charged them with collusion in terrorist plots and purposely impeded the grassroots return projects. They pointed out as well that resettled communities were suffering repeated bombings, strafings, and other forms of harassment.

To further the power of their moral rhetoric, refugees integrated important new developments into their rationales for retorno. When they became aware that the UNHCR had established an office in El Salvador to assist with repatriation plans, they made use of this information. Likewise, they acquired a copy of a Plan for Repatriation document prepared by the Chief of the UNHCR mission in El Salvador, Roberto Rodríguez Casasbuenas, and referred to that plan in their own discussions. Perhaps most beneficial, however, were high-profile events occurring at the regional level. The signing of the Central American Peace Plan in August 1987 in Esquipulas, Guatemala, was one such event. President Duarte's signature on that plan, known as Esquipulas II, signified the Salvadoran government's commitment to seeking solutions to the ongoing civil conflict in El Salvador, and, although resuming negotiations with the FMLN was one component of the solution, so too was the return of citizens from their wartime refuges abroad. Refugees planning retornos made good use of this information in their campaigns. As a Mesa Grande visitor noted, "Esquipulas II served as a breath of fresh air. . . . One could say that the peace plan accelerated the preparations."[46] In a similar vein, organizers of the fourth retorno from Mesa Grande used a September 1988 meeting at Tela, Honduras, as a pressure point. As they wrote in their public announcement: "[We] consider that the accords of the recent meeting of Central American Presidents in Tela, Honduras, open a climate of hope for all of Central America. These same agreements respect our voluntary decision to return to our country and call on the Salvadoran government and Armed Forces to commit themselves to not placing obstacles of any form or under any pretext against our arrival and our desire to remain in the repopulated areas of our choice."[47]

References to such meetings implied that refugees were well aware of the agreements reached by the parties involved—particularly those accords relating to refugees, the internally displaced, repatriations, and repopulations. By placing their own retornos within such high-profile contexts, refugees not only boosted their justifications for return; they also publicly associated their grassroots movement with peace efforts. Indeed, refugees frequently noted their intentions in this regard (see fig. 17). "As Salvadorans we must help bring peace," declared one group from Mesa Grande. "We are peasants and the way we struggle to achieve peace is by planting our crops on our lands and demanding that our lives be respected."[48] Such rhetoric, particularly in light of ongoing regional peace initiatives, made it difficult—and potentially very embarrassing—for the Duarte government to oppose the return of the refugees.

Although officials ultimately authorized most of the mass returns, authorization did not mean a favorable response to all the refugees' specific demands. Officials found two of these demands particularly problematic: the refugees' decision to return to their places of origin in the rural north and the size of the returning groups.

Each of the retorno platforms announced the specific locations to which the refugees would return. The vast majority of these were in northern conflicted areas or zones under FMLN control. Salvadoran officials inevitably opposed the repopulation of these locales and countered with options for integration into government-sponsored resettlements at a variety of "haciendas": Valle Verde and Popayan in Cuscatlán, Normandía and La Cuchinama in Usulután, Zamora in La Paz, and several in Sonsonate. Since the early 1980s the government had launched numerous programs to address the problem of

SOLUCION PERMANENTE
PARA LOS REFUGIADOS ES :
REPATRIARNOS EN COMUNIDAD.

Fig. 17. Communal assemblies, Colomoncagua camp. *From top*: "We wish to repatriate voluntarily; not due to pressure by aid cuts"; "Permanent solution for the refugees is: To repatriate as a community." (Photos by Steve Cagan)

the displaced, including Project 1,000 (1982), the National Plan (1983), Well-Being for San Vicente (1983), United to Reconstruct (1986), and Chalate '88. Resettlement efforts within these broader programs often shared a two-pronged strategy: *limpiar* (to clean) areas of the FMLN and to subsequently repopulate them with people sympathetic to the government. In a process similar to the Guatemalan military's creation of "model villages," the Salvadoran military closely controlled the resettlement process to ensure proper sympathies. In the words of one government employee, "The armed forces have information about people. . . . They decide who goes and who does not."[49] Once they were in the resettlement sites, moreover, the armed forces monitored inhabitants and compelled their participation in civil defense patrols and other counterinsurgency projects.

These kinds of obligations undermined civilian support for government resettlement programs. Statistics make abundantly clear that the vast majority of refugees distrusted the government's offers; although refugees voluntarily repatriated each month from the Honduran camps, just 5 percent opted to do so through government programs.[50] Despite this, officials insisted with each retorno announcement that the armed forces would "install repatriated persons in places assigned by the Salvadoran government and not where the leaders of the communities say."[51]

Refugees developed detailed arguments against the government-proposed locales. To counter resettlement in the coastal lowlands, for example, they argued that it would be impossible to survive there due to the lack of land and employment connections, their ignorance of the labors of the sea so prevalent in the region, and the fact that they simply were not accustomed to the climate. More frequently, however, refugees countered with an unwavering insistence on the sites that they themselves had identified. These were, they claimed, their *lugares de origen* (places of origin). Some owned land there; others had access to the lands they had previously rented. Many had old work connections at area farms and ranches. Most important, however, they *chose* to live in these locations, and the Constitution of El Salvador and international law recognized a citizen's right to choose his or her domicile.

Another contentious issue was the size of the returning groups. Salvadoran officials demanded "ordered" repatriation, that is, the return of small groups over a series of weeks or even months. The refugees insisted, however, on retorno as one large group and offered numerous reasons for this. On a practical level, refugees argued that time was of the essence. Organizers of the first Mesa Grande retorno calculated that were they to return in groups of one hundred, as the government suggested, it would take thirteen days to complete the repopulation of just one community, Santa Marta, and another fifteen days for

Copapayo. At such a slow rate, they calculated, it would take years for all four thousand refugees to return home. This was simply unacceptable. Moreover, refugees timed their retornos to coincide with the agricultural seasons. Delaying departure of some or all of the returnees would mean being unable to plant adequate maize and bean plots before the arrival of winter rains. This, in turn, would jeopardize their very survival.

Refugees also argued for mass returns with moral rhetoric. They were a community, they said, and as such could not be divided without dire consequences. Project leaders pointed out that a high percentage of those who planned to return were widows, orphaned children, the elderly, and "invalids." If these special groups returned without the support of the entire community, they would end up as *mendigos* (beggars). Retornos as planned by the refugees themselves would avoid such sad consequences: "Only with the support and solidarity of the community will we be able to resolve the assistance problem of these sectors."[52] The refugees' international allies echoed the call; only large-scale returns would "guarantee the cohesion of the communities [and] avoid renewed 'dismembering' of their extended and adopted families."[53]

The most commonly cited reason for returning en masse was security. Once it was certain that a particular group would indeed return to El Salvador, government officials did what they could to convince returnees that government-controlled areas were safer. As a member of the first Mesa Grande Comité de Repoblación recalled, during one such meeting "this military man said quite a bit, 'The armed forces, we are now protecting the population, there is a democracy. . . . It is no longer the same as when you took off in flight and a few soldiers . . . didn't follow orders, they did unjust things with you. That's why you are here. But today, no; today we're protecting you.'"[54] But distrust of the Salvadoran military ran deep in the displaced population. Refugees knew, moreover, of the difficulties faced by earlier repatriates, including arrests and interrogations regarding their activities prior to seeking refuge in Honduras and in the camps. Such harassment, in fact, prompted dozens to return to the refugee camps in Honduras. Refugees were also well aware that repopulated communities suffered constant harassment, including bombings, arrests, killings, and economic and aid blockades. In light of the security risks, they insisted on returning as one large group.[55]

From Negotiation to Direct Action

In letters, petitions, and meetings, refugees demonstrated willingness and good faith attempts to negotiate with government and UNHCR officials. Several groups adjusted their list of demands through the course of negotiations. Others agreed to postpone their departure for various reasons, including promises of face-to-face meetings with high-level Salvadoran officials. But the refugees' patience had a limit. When it was clear that officials did not intend to meet them on level ground, the refugees once again shifted to more contentious actions.

Protest actions were quite common in the refugee camps. Just as they protested mistreatment by Honduran authorities and insisted on involvement in the day-to-day operations of the camps, so too did refugees demand to be heard with regard to repatriation. When ignored, they often responded with verbal protests, as on the occasion when the Comité de Repoblación and its followers at Mesa Grande greeted Salvadoran officials' proposals with shouts and jeers.

They also responded with physical action. A closer look at negotiations on the issue of documentation offers a striking example. The first group to return from Mesa Grande demanded that "legal arrangements should be resolved as quickly as possible" at the border. The actual border crossing, however, took over twenty-four hours, which forced thousands of refugees to spend the night in the buses that had been contracted by the UNHCR for the journey and on the ground outside. The second group to return from Mesa Grande, therefore, insisted that documentation arrangements take place in the repopulation sites themselves rather than at the border. The night before their scheduled departure, when a Salvadoran government delegation arrived at Mesa Grande to collect immigration forms from those planning to travel the following day, the refugees simply refused. They referred to their original platform and indicated that the UNHCR had the relevant information; if government officials wanted that information prior to their arrival at the repopulation sites, the refugees maintained, they could access it through the UN.

The third group to return made additional adjustments. Reports from the first repopulated communities had trickled back to Mesa Grande; despite the guarantees and efforts of Salvadoran and UN authorities, the reports said, the majority of the returnees had not yet received official documentation in the form of national identity cards. In an attempt to avoid a similar outcome, the organizers of the third Mesa Grande retorno demanded that all participants receive documentation prior to departure from the refugee camps. On the planned day of return, 17 October 1989, the Salvadoran government still had not provided documents. Not wanting to delay their departure any longer, three hundred refugees broke through a military cordon at the camp entrance and marched five hours to the town of San Marcos. There one group protested at the UNHCR office while other contingents occupied the city plaza and a nearby church. According to witnesses, UNHCR and Honduran military officials threatened to refuse water and food to the refugees unless they re-turned to Mesa Grande. Rather than dispersing the protesters, such threats prompted the refugees to launch a hunger strike "for the unfulfillment (*incum-plimiento*) of our return project."[56] Shortly thereafter eight religious workers from the United States and Canada joined the strike. These various acts of protest—by refugees and their international allies—combined to force re-sponses from the UNHCR, Honduran church and military officials, and Sal-vadoran government authorities; within a week the various parties had nego-tiated a new agreement to allow the refugees "provisional documentation" before they departed for the border. Once the refugees received this documen-tation, the third mass retorno from Mesa Grande officially commenced.

Well aware that physical protest actions could produce positive results, ref-ugees often used them during the journeys back to their communities in rural El Salvador. These en route protest actions were designed both to avoid some of the problems of earlier retornos and to force authorities to comply with predeparture agreements. During the second Mesa Grande retorno in 1988, for example, a large portion of the bus caravan was detained at the border while those who had already crossed the border continued on their way. A represen-tative of the Comité de Repoblación traveling in the official UNHCR vehicle with the first group noticed the apparently purposeful separation and de-manded that everyone return to the border to wait for the rest of the caravan so that the group could travel—as previously agreed—as a single, intact group. Later on during the same journey, returnees headed for the town of San Anto-nio Los Ranchos in Chalatenango detained their caravan when they discov-ered that their food supplies had not yet been delivered. The UNHCR repre-sentative accompanying the convoy scrambled to resolve the problem, making phone calls and traveling to various locations in El Salvador for meetings with military, government, and church officials. Despite promises from all sides, the returning refugees refused to board the buses and continue en route until the delivery trucks joined their caravan.[57]

Similar actions occurred during every other retorno around such issues as the routes to take, road conditions, military harassment, documentation, welcoming and thanksgiving masses, and accompaniment by internationals, church representatives, family, and friends. By blocking roads or occupying churches and refusing to get on or off the buses at strategic points in the jour-ney, campesinos used the power of their physical presence to compel UNHCR and Salvadoran officials to respond to their demands. Even if the eventual out-comes of such actions were not always ideal from the campesinos' perspec-tives, the very actions served to put officials on the defensive—a worthy goal in and of itself.

Refugees at Colomoncagua pushed protest actions to new levels in late 1989 through an "unauthorized" retorno. The Colomoncagua refugees had announced in May 1989 their intention to return to the area around Meanguera, Morazán, later that year. Through months of negotiations, the Tripartite Commission reached an agreement, which a UNHCR official subsequently presented to the refugees. The refugees accepted, and the departure date was set for mid-November. On 11 November, however, the FMLN launched a major military offensive, dubbed la Ofensiva Final (the Final Offensive), which affected all regions of El Salvador. In response the Salvadoran government recalled its delegation from Colomoncagua and indefinitely suspended the repatriation. The refugees, for their part, did not accept this unilateral decision. They immediately organized a work group of about two hundred people to return to Meanguera clandestinely, on foot via a *punto ciego* (blind spot) on the border; once at Meanguera the group would begin preparing the location for the others' eventual arrival. On 18 November, after a brief confrontation with the Honduran military, this group left the Colomoncagua camp, passed through town, and began climbing into the mountainous border region. They crossed the border without incident and two days later arrived at Meanguera, where they began preparing the land for cultivation and community infrastructure.[58]

In December a similar retorno occurred—again without authorization from the Salvadoran government and, as a result, also without UNHCR assistance. This time around, however, the Honduran government, through CONARE, provided dozens of trucks to help transport people and belongings to the border. "Colonel García Turcios always caused problems for us while we lived as refugees," one repatriate remarked. "But now here we are, moving hand-in-hand toward the border."[59] Salvadoran officials often characterized such unauthorized returns as an "invasion" and claimed that refugees were returning to enlist with the FMLN.[60] Yet in late December, Salvadoran government representatives returned to Colomoncagua to continue negotiations with refugee leaders. Following these talks, in the first months of 1990, the remainder of the refugees at Colomoncagua returned home.

This series of retornos from Colomoncagua demonstrates the extent to which Salvadorans would go; once they decided that the time was right to return, they moved toward that goal in a definitive and determined way, sometimes in spite of Salvadoran government directives. To be sure, those returning feared what might await them in El Salvador. Yet the returns also brought relief. "Of course we're afraid of [the bombing]," one returnee said, "but you become brave out of fear itself. . . . If we die, we'll die in our own country. And that's what we want. Because I don't want to die in some other place, fleeing."[61] Also, for many, the retornos and repopulations inspired hope.

Contested Sovereignties

By 1990, mobile communities—groups en guinda, the internally displaced, and refugees living abroad—had repopulated dozens of villages in rural El Salvador. This grassroots social movement had significant impacts on both rural communities and the nation. For most Salvadoran campesinos, repopulation was an impressive victory in the most basic sense: they returned to more permanent settlement. After years on the move or a decade in exile, going "home" was an important achievement in and of itself. For the most politically committed campesinos, however, repopulation held great political significance as well. Through the repopulation movement, they forced the Salvadoran regime to recognize them as agents, citizens, and members of the national body. By going home they reclaimed fundamental civil rights.

As noted earlier, Salvadoran officials characterized some of the mass repatriations from Honduras as "invasions." In a sense this is true—not only for retornos from refugee camps but for the repopulation movement more generally. That is, despite resistance and outright opposition from Salvadoran government and military officials, campesinos succeeded in "conquering" not only physical sites of resettlement but also the more ethereal right to exist as civilians in a war zone. However, because campesinos (often literally) had to break through official resistance, they asserted their citizenship through what was basically a forced physical presence. Indeed, refugee committees in charge of the retornos billed repatriation as a conquest; declarations of "Long live the conquest of our places of origin!" accompany many statements from the period.

Returning home, then, signified yet one more phase in a long struggle of resistance against an authoritarian regime. Rather than the "hidden transcripts" and more clandestine forms of resistance of previous years, however, campesinos involved in the repopulation movement challenged the Salvadoran regime directly and in multiple ways.[62] First, they rejected official repopulation programs. This was particularly clear with the refugees in Honduras. Statistics showed that upward of 95 percent of refugees refused to sign on to government-sponsored repatriation projects, and interviews revealed a continued distrust of officials. "If we return to the government-controlled areas that [officials] proposed, do you know what will happen?" a man at the Colomoncagua refugee camp asked. "In a couple of months, all our projects will be destroyed by sabotage and harassment. We don't want to throw out nine years of work like that."[63] In a similar vein, refugees repudiated the Tripartite Commission process; because it was *tri*partite, it could not adequately represent refugee interests. Rather than submit to these official programs and plans, displaced campesinos developed their own organizations, including CRIPDES, CNR, and PADECOMSM in El Salvador and the various Comités de

Repoblación in the refugee camps. Through these organizations campesinos designed their own return and repopulation projects. In so doing they challenged Salvadoran government's authority over their individual bodies and their collective political body.

Second, grassroots repopulation entailed establishing what might be called "segregated communities."[64] Rather than join settlement projects organized and operated by government or Catholic Church officials, grassroots repopulators returned to their lugares de origen. To be sure, not everyone who rebuilt the community at San José Las Flores or joined the retorno to Meanguera was a native of those particular towns. Yet the designation "places of origin" was intentional. It distinguished grassroots sites from "other" sites. At the same time it included an underlying moral argument: if government depopulation policies had intended to remove campesinos from their places of origin, then campesinos intended to return to those very same places. Likewise, in response to the disarticulation of communities through state-sponsored violence and terror, campesinos cultivated and brought to the forefront their unity and collectivity. This was particularly evident in the retornos from Honduras when, rather than returning in groups of one hundred as government officials demanded, refugees insisted on returning en masse—thousands at a time. The mass repopulations of rural villages, then, stood as a direct challenge to government counterinsurgency efforts.

An important aspect of the segregated communities was a certain degree of autonomy from the state. Repopulated communities resisted the armed forces' efforts to organize them into civil patrols, for example, and refugees returning from Honduras integrated such resistance into their repatriation platforms. Many communities also refused to accept funding from government ministries in the rebuilding of their villages due to concerns regarding the possible "strings" attached. Yet autonomy did not mean isolation. Indeed, the repopulated communities refused to be isolated. In addition to continuing to develop their own regional and national organizations, they also launched commercial and social collaborations with other sectors and continuously negotiated agreements with military and government officials regarding travel, transport of food and clothing to communities, security, and other issues. Thousands of refugees had returned to El Salvador, moreover, without official documentation; their continued demands before Salvadoran authorities offer a particularly symbolic example of how these communities refused to be isolated.

A third way in which the repopulation movement challenged the Salvadoran regime was by establishing and promoting alternative social, political, and economic structures. This was not a new trend; for decades campesinos had established and participated in myriad organizations and movements to secure their livelihoods, as well as rights and recognition. What was new, however, was the openness with which repopulators pursued these efforts. No longer were directivas or cooperatives underground operations; they were fully public, intentionally high profile.

In fact, these alternative structures—and the repopulated communities in general—had an international profile. The return of more than twenty thousand refugees to Salvadoran territory between 1986 and 1990 heightened world awareness of the repopulation movement. This, combined with the work of organizations representing the repopulations, introduced new resources into the rural countryside, including international attention, moral and physical accompaniment, and material and financial aid. With their international allies and solidarity networks, campesinos constructed another alternative, a sort of transnational space, which presented yet another challenge to the Salvadoran regime.

Through the construction of a transnational space and the promotion of autonomous structures, repopulated communities represented an alternative conception of the nation-state. Rather than simply professing liberty and equality for all, repopulators sought to make such ideals a reality. Contrary to what their detractors claimed, however, they did not profess socialism or communism. Instead they pursued a participatory social democracy—a democracy committed to the collective good. The repopulation movement intended to build such a system from the ground up. In the words of a refugee at Colomoncagua on the eve of retorno, "We are returning to El Salvador even though the war continues because we want to forge [impulsar] democracy from inside."[65]

Finally, the repopulation movement challenged the Salvadoran regime and altered the national landscape by impelling the peace process. Here it is important to recall that the apogee of the repopulation movement was between 1986 and 1990—before FMLN and government forces began earnest negotiations. In light of this, northern campesinos argue that they were leaders in the transition to a new El Salvador. From many sites of refuge, both within and beyond El Salvador's borders, they posed political and moral challenges to the Salvadoran regime and worked to raise international awareness about the realities and consequences of civil war. The repopulation movement, moreover, did what the FMLN had been unable to do for years: break open the Salvadoran regime and force those in power to respond to popular demands. Among their many pressure points, repopulators demanded that the Salvadoran government commit in earnest to a negotiated settlement to the war. According to Norberto, such a large civilian presence in the north meant that "the government was not going to soften . . . which compelled negotiations." In the words of Alejandro, a founding member of the first Comité de Ropoblación at Mesa Grande, "The people's return . . . was a grain of sand of contribution to the peace process. . . . They saw those who achieved it, they saw the solidarity, they saw that the people were returning home and that they wanted peace and they didn't want war. There was, by example, a clear manifestation, and this was a first step in starting the process."[66]

Conclusion

Campesinos,
Collective Organization, and
Social Change

In March 2009, Salvadorans went to the polls to elect a new president. The winner: Mauricio Funes of the FMLN. Although FMLN candidates had consistently won local and departmental elections since its transformation into a political party with the end of the war in 1992, these elections were historic in that they marked the first time the FMLN had won the presidency. For seventeen years of peacetime, that office had been the exclusive domain of the Alianza Republicana Nacional (National Republican Alliance, ARENA), a conservative party with ties to the traditional elite as well as the wartime military and death squads. For many, the ouster of ARENA symbolized much more than simple electoral defeat. "I really can't tell you what this is like," exclaimed Roberto Lovato in the wake of the elections, "when you're talking about ending not just the ARENA party's rule, but you're talking about 130 years of oligarchy and military dictatorship."[1]

Funes promises change. "The time has come for the excluded," he announced upon his victory. "The opportunity has arrived for genuine democrats, for men and women who believe in social justice and solidarity."[2] Many campesinos in El Salvador's northern repopulated communities want to believe such promises; they want to believe that change is on the way. Yet they remain skeptical. They are unsure how "the Right" will respond in both the short and long terms. There simply is no precedent that allows them to believe that a smooth transfer of power to "the opposition" can or will occur or that

Funes will be allowed to remain in office for his full term. Indeed, just as Funes took office in El Salvador, the military in neighboring Honduras staged a coup d'état against its own constitutionally elected president, Manuel Zelaya. To many this appeared to be a cruel foreshadowing of what might come at home.

Further explanation of campesino skepticism can be found in the popular saying *la lucha sigue* (the struggle continues). From this perspective, the January 1992 Peace Accords between the Salvadoran government and the FMLN insurgent forces simply marked the end of *la guerra abierta* (open war). As one phase of the war ended, another began. In this new phase, combatants on both sides demobilized, the FMLN competed in elections as a political party, and bombs no longer fell on rural communities. Yet conditions throughout the country remain in many ways as precarious as they were in 1950, 1960, and 1970; violence and corruption continue to top national headlines, and extreme poverty still reigns for the majority of the population. Old patterns combine with new forces—violence of street gangs, privatization of water and health care, foreign mining interests and the Central American Free Trade Agreement, to name just a few—to perpetuate insecurity.

In light of the ongoing struggle, the "past" of the Salvadoran civil conflict may be too present yet to fully unpack. Nonetheless, that is precisely what I begin to do in this study. More specifically, I uncover one of the hidden versions of late-twentieth-century Salvadoran history—that of campesinos on the figurative and literal margins of the nation. As previously noted, studies of this period have emphasized the role of Salvadoran and Honduran officials, the FMLN opposition forces, and international actors, including the United States and the UN. Such studies approach campesinos as problems to solve, crises to resolve; either they are threats to established orders or they are victims of war in need of succor. In other words, governments, observers, and analysts have displaced campesinos from Salvadoran national history. This study seeks to re-place them in the story not as violent rebels or passive victims but as complex human agents and protagonists of history.

My focus for re-placement is, perhaps ironically, the displaced—more specifically, campesinos from El Salvador's northern tierra olvidada who, due to combinations of force and choice, abandoned their homes for much or all of the country's civil war. Rather than frame their experiences in terms of loss and detachment, however, I highlight their associations and engagements at the local, national, and international levels. Toward this end I examine what I call "mobile communities." These two words carry multiple, relevant meanings. By "community," I do not refer to simple assemblages of people—peasants in this case. Rather, community here entails a communal ethos. That is, people cultivate a sense of belonging; they are active members with a solidary commitment to one another and the group as a whole. That these communities are mobile signifies not only their physical mobility through geographic space. It also means that they are not fixed or static; their boundaries, meanings, and actions are constantly shifting, ever evolving. These communities are mobile as well in that they are actively, politically mobilized. In short I approach both community and mobility as resources that can enable and empower. In this Salvadoran case, communal ethos and mobility become new weapons of both war and peace.

The mobile communities examined here critiqued and challenged the "Salvadoran order of things."[3] They began by turning their isolation in the tierra olvidada to their advantage. As chapter 1 detailed, the north found relative freedom from many pressures common in other regions of the country during the mid-twentieth century. This allowed northerners to develop unique paths, including the formation of extended spaces of livelihood. They also established and participated in a variety of organizations to help them strive for and attain both concrete, material objectives (e.g., new roads) and more ethereal or nonmaterial goals (e.g., the right to organize and the opening of the authoritarian regime).

By the late 1960s and through the 1980s, the Salvadoran government and military struggled to control these organized communities. They applied counterinsurgency tactics not only to armed insurgents but also to civilians. To divide and conquer communities, they engaged the UCS, ORDEN, and other orejas (spies). To remove especially troublesome communities from the picture, they used scorched earth operations, forced relocations, and massacres. Organized communities in the north responded to such tactics through both physical mobility and political mobilization. They developed the guinda system and established refuge sites both within and beyond national borders. In those refuge sites they elaborated communal governance structures, including the PPLs and the refugee camp committees. They also established alliances with groups that Salvadoran officials deemed threats: the FMLN and progressive international solidarity workers and networks. Alliances with the FMLN were particularly important during the guindas and in the refuge sites in northern zones under FMLN control. Alliances with los internacionales were similarly important for those whose guindas took them across the border into Honduras. Just as alliances with progressive Catholics in the late 1960s and 1970s often changed power dynamics in rural villages, so too did refugee–international alliances contribute to a shift in power dynamics on the battlefield in El Salvador. International accompaniment, both during exile and in the subsequent processes of repatriation and repopulation, proffered campesino refugees new resources, which they activated in their struggles against the old (repression, exclusion, authoritarianism) and in favor of the new (equality, justice, democracy, peace). International scrutiny exhorted the Salvadoran government (and the FMLN for that matter) to play by different rules; no longer did depopulation policies, forced recruitment campaigns, and human rights violations go unnoticed.

This series of actions on the part of campesinos reveals that state-sponsored violence neither weakened beyond repair nor destroyed communities. On the contrary it prompted campesinos to forge an even deeper communal ethos. The insistence on collectivity—both en guinda and at refuge sites—offered a potent moral critique of the regime's actions and the traditional order of things. Indeed, one of the more striking aspects of this history is the campesinos' emphasis on collectivity and, more specifically, the horizontal relations within their ever-shifting mobile communities. They highlighted how the organizations they established, both within and beyond their home villages, had strong foundations in the concepts of equality and justice. Members of directivas and other committees, for example, were elected rather than appointed. In a similar vein, the workshops of the refugee camps gained staff and apprentices through a lottery cycle, which made the workshops accessible to all rather than a select few. Likewise, all refugees had the opportunity to attend school, receive health care, and vote in elections for (and serve as) representatives. Campesinos described their personal involvement with these and other grassroots organizations in much the same way: *me organizé, me involucré,* and *me integré.* Although each of these phrases carried a distinct meaning— "I organized myself," "I involved myself," "I integrated myself"—all of them implied an individual voluntarily choosing to become part of a larger whole.

Campesinos emphasized horizontal relations not only within their own organizations but also within the broader struggle against the Salvadoran regime. Interestingly, people often referred to this larger whole as *un organismo,* which in the Spanish language has a dual definition of "organization" and "organism." Campesinos came to see themselves as part of a sort of living organism, a body in which each part contributed to the survival and development of the whole. Such a perspective allowed campesinos to underscore their own worth and value as campesinos, as humans, as citizens. It also enabled them to present their own actions as contributions to the greater good. By providing education, health care, public works, and other services, their organizations helped to fill gaps caused by state neglect and thus set a precedent for positive change nationwide.

As they highlighted their own work and contributions, campesinos distinguished themselves from the FMLN. And here it is important to emphasize an insight afforded by the long historical view adopted by this study: those who ultimately abandoned their homes during the civil war had previous experience with collective organization, alliance building, negotiation, and protest. The campesino movement was not, then, *a creation of* outside forces that spurred the "unblocking" (*desbloqueo*) of campesino consciousness; nor was it *the result of* religious or political "conversion," as Cabarrús and others have posited. This study follows the campesinos themselves in highlighting their autonomy—most specifically from the FMLN. To be sure, coercion was a reality within the FMLN zones of control. Yet even in northern Morazán, where the ERP apparently maintained much tighter control than the FPL or the RN did in Cabañas or Chalatenango, campesinos maintained "a substantial degree of autonomy."[4] Campesinos underscored this autonomy by describing themselves as but one part of a broader coalition of social, political, and military organizations that together comprised la lucha popular. Thus, even as they understood and perhaps rallied behind the FMLN's armed endeavors, campesinos emphasized their own choice of peaceful means. Both were important, necessary contributions to the struggle for change.

It is also relevant to note that mobile campesino communities understood "revolution" in ways that were significantly different from those of the FMLN. Interviews and documents reveal that, although campesinos espoused substantial and even radical changes to El Salvador's national structures, they did not necessarily demand a new state system. They certainly favored a change of regime, an end to authoritarianism. They did not, however, promote the installation of communist or socialist systems. Indeed, they emphasized that El Salvador's system was, at its core, good; the people in charge of the system, in contrast, were bad. Their belief in the inherent quality of the system led them to seek recognition through state mechanisms: they applied for personería jurídica for their leagues and cooperatives, voted in elections, and demanded national documents, for example. Within their own organizations, moreover, they emulated an ideal; rather than the "facade democracy" (*democracia de fachada*) of the reigning government, theirs was a true "participatory democracy."

Although campesinos emphasized horizontal relations within the popular movement and their own organizations, it is important to keep in mind that Salvadoran communities, like the rural Mexican and Peruvian communities examined by Florencia Mallon, "were themselves political creations whose solidarity and unity were precariously articulated through processes of communal hegemony."[5] The chapters here offer some insights into how such processes played out within Salvadoran mobile communities during flight. Chapter 2, for instance, revealed the importance of discipline (*disciplina*) to the campesinos' guindas through the northern highlands. Although those en guinda did not directly identify a person or group of people imposing order, they clearly described complying with values and codes of conduct—the new moral economy so unique to the guinda experience. Subsequent chapters illustrated how both discipline and special codes of conduct continued beyond the guindas as well: the Batallón Pacho's "stern talks" with those who misbehaved at Mesa Grande, the public denunciations of good-for-nothings (*haraganes*), the work of the refugees' public relations and communications committees, the existence of prisons in the refugee camps, recollections of peer-imposed repatriation, and rumors of murder. Although these examples only begin to explain the inner workings of the mobile communities' own hegemonic processes, they serve as a reminder that Salvadoran campesinos were complex and layered actors rather than flat and fastened.

Even as it recognizes the existence of such layers, this study documents and emphasizes campesino solidarity and collectivity. In so doing it approaches mobile communities from a social movements perspective. As Jeffrey Rubin noted, a "central characteristic" of any social movement is its apparent flatness. That is, social movements "are about essentializing—claiming fixed, shared, and enduring identities that may differ significantly from people's daily experiences and beliefs."[6] This study reveals how northern Salvadoran campesinos created such an identity. Various chapters examined how, through formats such as popular education and Christian reflection on the Bible, they came to "read reality" with one voice and to "write history" in the same hand. Other chapters illustrated how they "staged" themselves in various ways and particularly for international audiences. In short, essentializing was a crucial tool with which mobile communities challenged the Salvadoran state.

At the core of the campesino challenge was the issue of sovereignty. As the Salvadoran state strove for control—often "performing" its power through military violence—campesinos transformed their individual and political bodies into weapons. They retained as much control as possible over these bodies. They moved them (or didn't move them) to make political statements, and they maintained physical and political attachments to and engagement with their patria. Perhaps the clearest example of this challenge was the campesinos' "conquest" of the rural north during the repopulation movement. Through the physical occupation of Salvadoran space, they also recuperated political rights.

In postwar interviews, campesinos explained that they had attained recognition from the state *de hecho y no de derecho*, a phrase that may be translated as "by deed or direct action, not by given or written rights" (or, even more roughly, "actions speak louder than words"). From this perspective the Salvadoran authorities did not voluntarily accede to campesino demands for recognition as citizens and civilians. "The government didn't see us in legal terms," explained Santiago. "They have never seen what we do in a good light. . . . They never take us into account." Mobile communities, therefore, had to rely on "our own inspiration, our own desires to do things well."[7] Rosa concurred, declaring, "We have achieved everything with concrete actions—not because our rights have been assigned to us. . . . We didn't achieve legality but by forcing the issue."[8]

In "forcing the issue," Salvadoran campesinos shared much in common with social movements around the world. They also shared the "essentializing" tendency. What sets this case apart from others, however, is the campesinos' utilization of mobility and displacement as resources. As evidenced by the guinda system and their actions in exile, they transformed even extreme, forced movement into methods of resistance. That these mobile communities crossed international borders only brings this into sharper relief. Campesinos integrated new allies—los internacionales—into their defense systems, as well as into their more contentious actions before Honduran, UN, and Salvadoran authorities; in so doing they blurred the boundaries between the local, national, and global spheres. As they moved between and among these spheres, they transformed movement from a strategy for economic and social survival to a method of *political* empowerment. They also challenged state-centric conceptions of sovereignty.

Case studies from other world regions suggest that just as "the peasantry" is only "hypothetically isolated," so too are "the displaced" only hypothetically displaced.[9] Displaced people and refugees from Guatemala, Palestine, and Peru established organizations in their host and/or home communities to serve their needs and promote their interests. Refugees from Eritrea, Mozambique, and other countries on the African continent organized and executed what the UNHCR continues to refer to as "spontaneous repatriations." Displaced people in Colombia united to form "peace communities." In Australia, people imprisoned in "refugee detention centers" sewed their mouths closed and set themselves on fire. In Germany, asylum seekers established a center where refugees receive free access to the Internet. All these actions suggest that the displaced are political beings or, to use Bariagaber's term, "considered decision-makers."[10] Scholars and other analysts must work to better understand this. And as we do we must also recognize that the displaced are people with histories.

Notes

Introduction

1. Cartoon by Roberto Williams (Rowi), published in *Diario La Prensa*, 5 February 1982. See chapter 4 for a reproduction of this cartoon along with additional commentary.

2. United Nations High Commissioner for Refugees (hereafter UNHCR) 1982b.

3. I prefer the Spanish term "campesino" over the usual English translation, "peasant." Following Salvadoran usage, "campesino" refers to a poor rural dweller whose livelihood depends primarily on agricultural activities. The term, which literally means "of the *campo*," or "countryside," incorporates a wide range of agriculturalists from smallholders to those who rent land from others (for cash or kind) to day laborers and permanent employees on medium or large properties.

4. UNHCR 1982a.

5. I borrow the phrase "national order of things" from Malkki 1995b.

6. Scholars have only recently begun to unpack the great irony of this; at the top of the refugee aid regime's hierarchy is the UNHCR, which was created by national governments in the wake of World War II and "purposefully designed to safeguard [UN member states'] sovereignty while modestly coordinating their new-found but highly defensive desire to protect refugees" (Barnett 2001, 251). For a critique in the Central American context, see Loescher 1988.

7. Countless studies exclude campesinos, present them in passing, or consider them solely as victims. Among the most egregious are Armstrong and Shenk 1982; Gettleman, Lacefield, Menashe, and Mermelstein 1987; Martínez Peñate 1997; Montgomery 1995; and Chepe 1999. A recent study that offers wonderful insights into campesino communities and agency but does so solely in relation to the FMLN is Wood 2003. Two early studies that explored campesino autonomous agency—Cabarrús 1983 and Pearce 1986—positively require codas.

8. Cagan and Cagan 1991, 13. On repatriation and repopulation in the Salvadoran context, consider Compher and Morgan 1991; Edwards and Tovar Siebentritt 1991; Macdonald and Gatehouse 1995; Thompson 1995; and Weiss Fagen and Eldridge 1991.

9. Lauria-Santiago and Binford 2004b, 2.

10. In addition to Mallon 1995; Rubin 1997; and Thurner 1997; consider Boyer 2003; Joseph and Nugent 1994; and Purnell 1999.

11. See Gould 1990, 1998; Forster 2001; Grandin 2000; and Warren 1998.

12. Valladares Lanza and Peacock 1998.

13. In this context it is relevant to note that the Universidad Nacional de El Salvador (National University of El Salvador) initiated its first history program in 2002.

Chapter 1. Remapping the *Tierra Olvidada*

1. Crown Representative Peinado, quoted in Browning 1971, 136.

2. "Los Indios," *Diario Oficial*, 23 August 1855, quoted in Browning 1971, 299.

3. Paige 1997, 123.

4. Martín-Baró 1973, 487, 484, respectively.

5. *Prensa Gráfica*, 23 November 1965.

6. World Bank 1979, 6–7.

7. Particularly influential "systems studies" include Browning 1971; Lindo-Fuentes 1990; Montes 1979; McClintock 1998; Montgomery 1995; and Stanley 1996. On the events of 1932, see in particular Anderson 1971.

8. Browning 1971, 163.

9. Pérez Brignoli 1995, 247.

10. Browning 1971, esp. chaps. 4b, 6a.

11. Ibid., 208.

12. Data for this paragraph are drawn from Salvadoran government sources as well as Browning 1971, esp. 232–34; Lindo-Fuentes 1990, esp. 73–78; Williams 1986, esp. 20–24; and Pearce 1986, 49.

13. Bracamonte and Spencer 1995, 5.

14. "Agitadores extranjeros manipulan a refugiados," *Diario de Hoy*, 14 August 1988, 3.

15. On Mexico, see also the work of Boyer (2003); Tutino (1986), whose first chapter offers a fine overview of the development of agrarian studies historiography; and Joseph and Nugent (1994). Many authors in this field drew inspiration from the anthropological work of James C. Scott (1976, 1990), as well as the field now known as subaltern studies.

16. See in particular Chomsky and Lauria-Santiago 1998; Gould 1990; Grandin 2000; and Warren 1998.

17. Consider especially Ching and Tilley 1998; Ching 1998; Gould and Lauria-Santiago 2008; Henríquez Consalvi and Gould 2003; Lindo-Fuentes, Ching, and Lara Martínez 2007; and Pérez Brignoli 1995.

18. On the war period, see in particular the works of Binford (1996, 1997, 1999, 2004) and Hammond (1993, 1998, 1999). On the popular movement more broadly, see especially Baloyra 1982. The works of Cabarrús (1983, 1985), Kincaid (1987), Brockett (1998, 2005), Wood (2003), and Viterna (2003) examine opportunity structures,

grievances, and moral factors that prompted campesinos to engage in radical political activism, including armed insurgency. It is important to note that many of these studies examine campesino actions and mobilizations in relation to the FMLN rather than as acts in their own right.

19. Mbembe 2000, 268.

20. See Lauria-Santiago 1999a, 1999b; and Browning 1971 for arguments regarding smallholders producing indigo and coffee for export markets. Gilly 1998 offers an in-depth discussion of a similar process in Chiapas, Mexico.

21. The term *finca* generally refers to a large coffee estate, while *hacienda* refers to a large landholding dedicated to grains, cotton, sugar, or cattle ranching. One hectare is equivalent to 2.47 acres.

22. It must be noted that legal titles were often rather ambiguous; holding title to a property did not always translate into legal ownership.

23. The national average was 62 percent according to El Salvador–Ministerio de Economía 1954.

24. Browning clearly mapped the trend of larger, "fuzzier" tracts in the north (1971, 191).

25. Stepputat and Sørensen 2001, 773, 778. See also de la Cadena 2000 and Smith 1991.

26. Stepputat and Sørensen 2001, 773.

27. World Bank 1979, 8.

28. Sermeño Lima 1999; El Salvador–Ministerio de Economía 1965, 1974.

29. Industry expanded from 9.5 to 19.2 percent of the gross domestic product between 1942 and 1971 (Griffith and Gates 2004, 73).

30. The following overview of the pull of Honduras for northern Salvadorans draws especially from interviews conducted in the border region (my own and those of Carlos Lara Martínez [transcripts at AGN]), as well as Morales Molina 1973 and Proyecto de Desarrollo Rural del Sur de Lempira 1999. Durham (1979) and Anderson (1981) also discuss cross-border relations, though to a more limited extent.

31. By 1985 the governments had turned over their case to the International Court of Justice in The Hague. I return to the border delineation issue in later chapters.

32. There were exceptions to this pattern, however, as in 1944 when national-level protests helped to force General Maximiliano Hernández Martínez out of the presidency.

33. See Kincaid 1987; and Cabarrús 1983, 1985, for example.

34. For more on Martínez's efforts and reactions to them, consider Ching 2004, 54; Ching and Tilley 1998; Díaz 1986; and Lara Martínez 2004. The National Social Defense Board became the Mejoramiento Social in December 1942 and, eight years later, the Instituto de Colonización Rural. Other organizations were established to work on rural issues, including the Administración de Bienestar Campesino around 1967 and the Instituto Salvadoreño de la Transformación Agraria in June 1975.

35. Lara Martínez 2004, 89.

36. Article 145 declared that "those economic associations that tend to increase

general wealth through better utilization of natural and human resources, and that promote a fair distribution of the benefits and goods resulting from their activities, will be encouraged and protected" (El Salvador 1950, 48–49).

37. Jackson 1980, esp. 142–43, 158.

38. For more on these cooperatives, see especially Díaz 1986, 21–23; Jackson 1980; Pelupessy 1998, 42; and Montes 1980, 209.

39. The following overview of the UCS draws especially from Jackson 1980 and Montes 1980. Additional information is from Pearce 1986, 94–97; Montgomery 1995, 106; and McClintock 1985, 156.

40. Montes 1980, 272–73. Cabarrús 1983 and Gould and Lauria-Santiago 2008 also note the material benefits that came with UCS membership.

41. Montes 1980, 272.

42. Ibid., 209.

43. Cabarrús 1983, 202.

44. Although the Salvadoran government allowed the UCS to hold *personería jurídica* (legal status) as a campesino organization, official concerns about rural protest were obvious in government insistence on particular terminologies; campesino organizations were to be called community associations rather than unions.

45. Montes 1980, 211.

46. Ibid., 272.

47. Gould and Lauria-Santiago 2008, 263. These authors, as well as Kincaid (1987), note this shift in particular reference to the western countryside.

48. Montes 1980, 211.

49. See in particular Díaz 1986 and Jackson 1980. Browning (1971) maps the haciendas involved in the state land reform program since 1932.

50. On these efforts in the area of El Mozote, see Binford 1996, 79–81.

51. Servicio Jesuita para el Desarrollo "Pedro Arrupe" (hereafter SJDPA) 1994, 28. This collection of oral history interviews, edited by the Salvadoran Jesuit Development Service, appeared in the wake of the Peace Accords.

52. Keune 1996, 7.

53. Ibid.

54. Another man explained that he and the others who had initiated local efforts "gained the affection and will of the people, since it was about helping each other" (SJDPA 1994, 7, 24).

55. I borrow the concept of "pleasure in agency" from Wood 2003.

56. SJDPA 1994, 22–23.

57. Pearce 1986, 146–47. Hammond (1998) describes similar collective agricultural ventures in northern Morazán.

58. See Díaz 1986, 22–23.

59. Keune 1996, 12.

60. Rosa, interview by author, 24 February 2003, Chalatenango, El Salvador. Indignation has received some attention within discussions of resource mobilization. On the Salvadoran context in particular, consider Kincaid 1987 and Wood 2003.

61. Rosa, interview by author.

62. Ascoli 1995, 30.

63. Pearce 1986, 100.

64. Ibid, 141.

65. Ascoli 1995, 25, 33, 30, respectively.

66. Although the definitive histories of FECCAS and the UTC have yet to be written, several studies have broken important ground. On FECCAS, see in particular Cabarrús 1983 and Alas 2003. On the UTC, see Ascoli 1995 and Pearce 1986.

67. Cabarrús 1983.

68. José described this situation, and his subsequent departure from ORDEN, in Studemeister 1986, 6.

69. Cabarrús (1983, 1985) aptly illustrates this for the communities of Aguilares. Political scientists have also theorized on this for the Salvadoran case. See especially Wood 2003 and Brockett 1998.

70. There were certainly other influences at play as well, including the dominance of large landowners in a particular area or the presence of more conservative parish priests.

71. The overview of liberation theology and the Salvadoran Popular Church draws from Pearce 1986; Sobrino 1988; Montgomery 1995; Peterson 1997; Hammond 1998; Binford 2004; and a number of works by Phillip Berryman.

72. Peterson 1997, 50; Pearce 1986, 111.

73. Pearce 1986, 112.

74. Keune 1996, 7.

75. Pearce 1986, 120.

76. Ibid, 118.

77. Rosa, interview by author.

78. SJDPA 1994, 29.

79. These centers began as rural development projects promoted by the Catholic Archdiocese of El Salvador before the birth of liberation theology in light of Vatican II. With time, the centers integrated many of the ideals of liberation theology into their programs.

80. Such training centers and sites included Santa Ana; San Lucas and Centro Reina de la Paz in El Castaño (also known as El Castaño), both in San Miguel city; Centro Los Naranjos in Jiquilisco, Usulután; Seminary San José de la Montaña in the city of San Salvador; and Chalatenango.

81. Peterson 1997, 57.

82. Montgomery 1995, 87. It is relevant to note that according to Binford 2004 the majority of those from Morazán who attended the El Castaño training center in San Miguel were from the middle sectors of the campesino population.

83. Santiago, interview by author, 25 February 2003, Chalatenango, El Salvador.

84. Binford 2004, 112. My interviews, as well as those conducted by Carlos Lara Martínez and Jenny Pearce, revealed similar stories of transformation.

85. I borrow this terminology from Binford 2004. In earlier works Feierman (1990) and Mallon (1995) refer to grassroots leaders like these as "peasant intellectuals."

86. Binford 2004, 117.

87. SJDPA 1994, 29.

88. See in particular Brockett 2005; Montgomery 1995; Lungo Uclés 1991, 1995; and Zamora 1991.

89. Member parties of the UNO included the Partido Demócrata Cristiano (Christian Democrat Party, PDC), the Movimiento Nacional Revolucionario (National Revolutionary Movement, MNR), and the Unión Democrática Nacionalista (Nationalist Democratic Union, UDN).

90. María, interview by author, 2 April 2003, Cabañas, El Salvador.

91. By 1975, members of FECCAS and the UTC already had begun to work together toward similar ends. This "revolutionary alliance" propelled the FTC onto the national stage as the "largest and most combative campesino movement in the history of El Salvador" (FTC 1979, 36; Ascoli 1995, 40).

92. FTC 1979.

93. FTC 1982, 7. Land occupations occurred in the departments of Chalatenango, Cabañas, San Vicente, Santa Ana, San Salvador, La Paz, and Usulután.

94. Pearce 1986, 175.

95. During the occupation, representatives from FECCAS, the UTC, and a variety of other civil society organizations established the Bloque Popular Revolucionario (Popular Revolutionary Bloc, BPR), which would subsequently draw hundreds of thousands of people into the streets for protest actions.

96. Binford 2004, 122.

97. In addition to the ERP and the FPL, the smaller politico-military organizations that united to form the FMLN in October 1980 were the Resistencia Nacional (National Resistance, RN), the Partido Revolucionario de los Trabajadores (Worker's Revolutionary Party, PRTC), and the PCS. For details on these groups, consult in particular McClintock 1998 and Montgomery 1995.

98. This and the following firsthand accounts are quoted from Cabarrús 1983, 135, 170.

99. Cáceres Prendes 1989, 125.

100. FTC 1979, 51–52, 61.

Chapter 2. Organizing Flight

1. In colloquial Salvadoran Spanish, *la guinda* is a noun perhaps best translated as "the flight"; *guindear* is the related verb, as in "to run or flee"; and *en guinda* means "on a guinda" or "in the process of fleeing." Such utilizations of the term are quite different from what occurs elsewhere in the Spanish-speaking world, yet the links are obvious. In the Caribbean, for example, *la guinda* refers literally to a heavily forested, vertical terrain that is difficult or impossible to access while *las guindas* refers more figuratively to a remote or impossible place. According to the Real Academia Española, *echar guinda* is a colloquial expression used in reference to the difficulty or futility of a particular effort. Thus, while Salvadorans did not invent a new word, they certainly

penned a new and unique definition particular to the experiences of Salvadoran campesinos. I am indebted to Francisco Scarano for discussions about the etymology of this term.

2. Malkki 1990, 33.

3. Malkki (1992) offers a cogent critique of this traditional approach. See also Sørensen and Stepputat 2001 and Hansen and Stepputat 2005.

4. Lungo Uclés 1995, 157.

5. This is the FMLN's "six-point platform of principles" (quoted in McClintock 1998, 57).

6. On this nationwide mobilization, see Lungo Uclés 1987 and Baloyra 1982, esp. chaps. 4–6.

7. United Nations Commission on the Truth for El Salvador (hereafter UN Truth Commission) 1993, 20.

8. LeoGrande 1998, 50.

9. Socorro Jurídico 1981, esp. 36–39; UN Truth Commission 1993, 43–44. To calculate the campesino percentage of the dead, I drew from charts 2 and 3 of the Socorro Jurídico report and used only the numbers of dead with known professions.

10. UN Truth Commission 1993, 126.

11. This estimate includes both refugees (displaced outside of El Salvador) and internally displaced persons (displaced within El Salvador's borders).

12. UNHCR 1982b.

13. Universidad Centroamericana José Simeón Cañas (hereafter UCA) 1985, 35. Hundreds of thousands more made their way to places around the world, including Canada, Bolivia, Australia, and Sweden.

14. Socorro Jurídico 1981, 215; UCA 1985, 39.

15. Socorro Jurídico 1981, 251.

16. Ibid. See also UCA 1985.

17. CONADES, "Investigación socio-económica a nivel de grupo familiar desplazado, informe de resultados," report, August 1982, AW.

18. Binford 1999, 11.

19. Hammond 1999, 84.

20. Keune 1996, 195.

21. Binford 2004, 123. By 1980 in Usulután many campesino activists no longer slept at home due to similar patterns of violence (Wood 2003, 104).

22. Many campesino families did not have access to farmland in the immediate vicinity of their homes, so men and young boys often had to travel significant distances to tend to their crops. The majority of the campesinos I interviewed, moreover, had long relied on multiple and dispersed small plots for subsistence. In these instances males often worked a full day in one field and then spent the night there either in a rough hut constructed for such a purpose or with extended family in a nearby town. The next day they moved on to another plot, worked it, and slept there. In this fashion they moved between their multiple fields and were often away from their homes for long periods of time.

23. Instituto de Estudios Políticos para América Latina y Africa (hereafter IEPALA) 1984, 2–3.

24. Keune 1996, 19.

25. IEPALA 1984, 3.

26. Keune 1996, 39–40. Interviews I conducted in the area of Portillo del Norte between 2000 and 2003 corroborated this pattern.

27. Carpio, Payeras, and Wheelock 1983, 22.

28. Keune 1996, 59.

29. SJDPA 1994, 55.

30. As Stepputat notes for the Guatemalan case, the terminology "scorched earth" ascribes an indiscriminate nature to such campaigns, one that "obscures [their] differentiated character: some villages and areas were targeted, others were not." He argues, instead, that the aim of such counterinsurgency programs was "to establish an interconnected system of 'proper places,' from where the environment could be observed and gradually brought under control" (1999, 62–63).

31. Cagan and Cagan 1991, 18.

32. Gómez, Meyers, Vasquez, and Williams 1999, 55.

33. SJDPA 1994, 43.

34. Cagan and Cagan 1991, 18.

35. Keune 1996, 28–29.

36. SJDPA 1994, 54.

37. Wood 2003, 94–95. Her reference was to the CEB movement, which was inspired by liberation theology.

38. UCA 1985, 101–7.

39. Binford (1996) notes that many relatively well-to-do campesinos chose not to leave the area around El Mozote, Morazán, in the days prior to the 1981 massacre despite warnings of the impending military sweep. Comparatively wealthy, they had the most to lose by abandoning their homes and so chose to stay and protect their investments.

40. Estimates of the civilian population remaining in northern Morazán during the 1980s, for example, range between ten and twenty thousand. It is worth nothing that those from northern comunidades organizadas who remained at home often received special attention from my interviewees; Chalatecos, for example, frequently referred to the Arcatao 5, five people who remained in the environs of Arcatao for the duration of the war.

41. Keune 1996, 185–86. The description of preparations for subsequent departures draws especially from Esther and Rosa, interviews by author, 21 February 2003 and 24 February 2003, respectively, Chalatenango, El Salvador.

42. The following discussion on tatús draws especially from conversations with campesinos in the areas of Arcatao, Chalatenango, and Cinquera, Cabañas. Between 2000 and 2003 I had several opportunities to see tatús in both regions. Because conversations with my guides were not recorded, in the pages that follow I rely for quotes on Keune 1996, 54, 59, 100, 130–38.

43. Tatús could also be excavated horizontally into the side of a hill or ravine. In such cases the body of the tatú would have a "zigzag" shape to provide protection against bullets and flying shrapnel in case the entrance were discovered. In areas where the earth was *pelado* (bald or bare), tatús were especially important given the lack of trees and other natural cover.

44. In testimonies and interviews collected during the civil war, campesinos pointed to specific battalions as responsible for attacks, disappearances, killings, and other such incidents. Aid workers, journalists, and observers appeared to take the campesinos' identification of perpetrators at face value; nowhere in the written historical record did I find any explanation of how campesinos were able to identify and distinguish the various battalions. Although campesinos pointed to experience, it is possible that their connections to FMLN combatants aided in these identification processes. It is also possible that those who were not active foot soldiers learned details well after the specific incidents through the work of forensic anthropologists and the Truth Commission.

45. These were highly mobile counterinsurgency battalions trained and equipped in the early 1980s with assistance from the United States. Numerous studies, including those conducted by the Truth Commission on El Salvador, have linked them to some of the most egregious human rights violations of the war.

46. Studemeister 1986, 8.

47. Keune 1996, 167.

48. Many used this anthill analogy in interviews and conversations. It was also common to liken campesinos en guinda to a herd of cattle. Many used words and phrases such as *gentillos* and *un gran puñado*, both signifying a great yet indefinite number of people.

49. Keune 1996, 134. This was corroborated in interviews with Esther and Rosa. The shift in guinda size is also visible in photographs from the period.

50. Military assistance from the United States increased from 25 million dollars in 1980 to 500 to 600 million annually in the mid-1980s. During the same period the number of Salvadoran troops nearly doubled (from 17,000 in 1980 to 40,000 in 1984), and the air force took on new importance as its fleet of airplanes more than doubled (to 38) and its fleet of helicopters more than quintupled (to 32). Binford 1999, 12; Lungo Uclés 1991, 64.

51. Binford describes this as a shift from "a war of position (large units defending territory) to a war of movement (small-scale guerrilla warfare, hit-and-run operations, sabotage) expanded to previously untouched areas" (1999, 15).

52. Keune 1996, 167.

53. Esther and Rosa, interviews by author.

54. Studemeister 1986, 9.

55. Keune 1996, 62. My understanding of the guinda norms is especially indebted to my interviews and conversations with Esther, Rosa, Santiago, René, Luis, Chepe, Reynaldo, and María.

56. Studemeister 1986, 9.

57. Keune 1996, 179.

58. Ibid., 180.

59. Ibid., 179.

60. Mallon 1995, 11.

61. Interviews in Chalatenango and Cabañas revealed similar patterns of tensions between neighboring villages, with the accompanying label of "oreja." Wood (2003, 2004) notes similar tensions between northern and southern villages in the Tenancingo region.

62. Keune 1996, 37.

63. Ibid., 51–52.

64. Roseberry 1994, 361.

65. On this process of essentializing in a Mexican context, see Rubin 2004.

66. Keune 1996, 179. My interviews revealed multiple variations on this same theme.

67. Thompson 1971. In applying Thompson's concept I benefited from numerous discussions with Steve Stern, as well as from the works of Scott (1976), Desan (1989), and Edelman (2005).

68. Keune 1996, 179.

69. Ibid., 176. These incidents clearly devastated parents and had both immediate and long-term impacts. In testimonies and interviews collected during the 1980s, campesinos described what happened as a type of torture—for the child, understandably, but also for the parent. As recently as 2003, inhabitants of rural communities described mothers who *andaba loca* (were crazy) and fathers who were *mal de cabeza* (wrong in the head) as a result of losing a child in this way. Rather than ostracizing these parents, the community tended to understand and support them or, in some cases, simply tolerate them as being different. Many campesinos rationalized alcoholism and other social ills in a similar vein. In short, during the war and to this day, those who lost sons or daughters to accidental suffocation received great empathy and respect, with both the absence of the children and the afflictions of the parents serving as a constant reminder that "to save a ton of people" they had made the ultimate sacrifice.

70. Studemeister 1986, 9.

71. Keune 1996, 64–65.

72. Ibid., 77.

73. Ibid., 136.

74. Ibid., 182. Every campesino had at least one story about what happened when people were *indisciplinados* (undisciplined) while en guinda. Sebastián S. referred to the woman who refused to hide or to take off her white shirt as "indisciplinada" and claimed that the government's attack on their location was "because of her lack of discipline."

75. The following discussion on discipline and leadership draws especially from my interviews with Esther and Rosa.

76. Studemeister 1986, 10.

77. Keune 1996, 97.

78. Ibid., 135.

79. Ibid., 181.

80. Macdonald and Gatehouse 1995, 122.

81. Keune 1996, 51.

82. Wood 2003.

83. Such sentiments usually did not arise in the interviews I conducted, which is to be expected given the fact that the people I spoke with tended to be past and present members of comunidades organizadas; they had continued their organizational activities at refuge points both within El Salvador and across the border in Honduras. As I discuss in later chapters, members of these communities had established a common, accepted historical narrative; although alternatives to this narrative no doubt exist, campesinos ran risks in exposing them. Furthermore, the passage of time may have led campesinos to recollect the positive aspects more readily.

84. Keune 1996, 176.

85. Ibid., 112.

86. UCA 1985, 103.

87. Binford 1999, 15.

88. International representatives passed this information along to their constituencies. For two examples, consider Lawyers Committee for International Human Rights (hereafter LCIHR) 1985 and Pastor Ridruejo 1987. The report of the Truth Commission (UN Truth Commission 1993) also noted forced recruitment as part of the violence attributable to the FMLN.

89. Keune 1996, 158.

90. On the milicias civiles, see Harnecker 1993, esp. 163–75. It is also worth noting here that military service is required of all male Salvadorans. Therefore, most men had some level of training. In addition the historical record reveals that some career soldiers chose to desert their posts with the government. It is likely that some of these deserters—whether they became FMLN combatants or not—provided information to campesinos. For the story of one government soldier who joined the FMLN, see Mena Sandoval 1990.

91. Ventura 1983, 103. Some campesinos described a sort of ladder of involvement with regard to security measures in particular. "It was a sort of scale," Ovidio D. explained. "For example, from the organized civilian population [*masas*], one moved on to become a militant member [*miliciano*], from *miliciano* to guerrilla, from guerrilla to special forces—that is, the pure guerrilla soldiers: how to attack the enemy, how to defend the masas" (Keune 1996, 157). Several of the campesinos interviewed by Pearce (1986) and Wood (2003) noted similar kinds of scales, as did FPL political commissioner "Valentín" (Harnecker 1993, 173).

92. For details about the medical relations between civilians and the FMLN combatants, I am especially indebted to interviews and conversations with Esther, Élida, Reynaldo, Rosa, and Norma. Marc Rosenthal of the U.S.–El Salvador Sister Cities network also provided important insights. Among the published accounts consider Clements 1984 and Metzi 1988.

93. Keune 1996, 158.

94. Studemeister 1986, 24.

95. Studemeister 1986; Ventura 1983; Carpio, Payeras, and Wheelock 1983, 24–26.

96. Studemeister 1986, 11. Guardado continued to insist on the autonomy of the directivas and the PPLs in postwar interviews. For insights into the PPLs from the FMLN perspective, see FMLN 1982.

97. Ventura 1983, 100. Although Orlando R. refers only to FMLN milicias, it is likely they pertained more specifically to the RN.

98. Binford 1999, 28–29.

99. "Cabañas," interview by Carlos B. Lara Martínez, 9 February 2002, transcript, Archivo General de la Nación (hereafter AGN).

100. Keune 1996, 37.

101. Ibid.

102. Ibid., 97.

103. My informal conversations with José, Alejandro, and Ábel were particularly enlightening on this subject.

104. Some even sought ways to make amends in peacetime. Felipe T., for example, explained, "After the war, I spoke with the man from whom we took several cows—a rich man but also *consciente*—and I explained why we did it. And he says: 'I am *consciente*, I have seen what you all ate but I give it with pleasure'" (Keune 1996, 98).

105. On the CPRs, see especially Falla 1998 and Cabanas 1999. More recent academic studies that provide additional contextual information on the CPRs include Manz 2004; Sanford 2003; and Stølen 2007. In a similar vein, Gould 1990 highlights how Nicaraguans in the rural Chinandega area developed their own revolutionary ideas and practices prior to allying themselves with the Frente Sandinista.

106. According to one member of the FMLN, it was a strategic decision on behalf of the insurgents to establish camps in precisely the regions where campesinos had organized and mobilized in earlier eras (see Studemeister 1986, 26). Ventura refers to these grassroots governments as "the incipient form that alternative power takes on in the Salvadoran struggle" (1983, 61). Álvarez designates them "selfgovernments," and Lungo Uclés notes that they represented "a new legality" (for both, see Lungo Uclés 1991, 42).

107. Álvarez, quoted in Lungo Uclés 1991, 42.

108. This terminology runs throughout writings about the PPLs whether by the displaced and refugees, academics, politico-military activists, or others. I return to this subject in later chapters.

Chapter 3. Internationalizing *La Guinda*

1. Guardado's story can be found in Camarda 1987, 45–47.

2. The exact number of campesinos killed by the Salvadoran armed forces in this incident has never been verified. The Truth Commission cited a minimum of three hundred, but investigations carried out by Hondurans immediately after the incident

placed the number at more than six hundred (UN Truth Commission 1993, 121). See also "Iglesia hondureña denuncia matanza de 600 salvadoreños," *La Tribuna*, 24 June 1980. "Human carnage" (*carnicería humana*) is quoted from Torres Calderón, "La Masacre del Sumpul traumatiza la frontera," reprinted in *Sumpul* 1980.

3. UN Truth Commission 1993, 126. Using data obtained from the Human Rights Commission of Segundo Montes, Binford (1996, 102) concluded that between 1980 and 1982, a minimum of twenty massacres occurred in the northern sectors of Morazán alone, accounting for nearly two thousand victims.

4. The Salvadoran defense minister General José Guillermo García initially denied that anything took place at Sumpul. One year later he admitted that a few civilians had died in a clash between government and insurgent forces but claimed that the numbers had been exaggerated by the international press. In a similar vein, it took several months for Salvadoran president José Napoleón Duarte to publicly recognize that anything out of the ordinary had occurred on the banks of the Sumpul River. He, too, indicated that the international press had blown the situation out of proportion. Only around three hundred people had died, he said, and they were all "communist guerrillas." UN Truth Commission 1993, 121–25.

5. Father M. and Marta, interview by author, 17 July 2003, Copán, Honduras.

6. I use the term "regime" intentionally. Although it is beyond the purview of this study to examine in detail the politics of humanitarian aid, my approach has been influenced by scholars in the field of refugee studies. Consider especially the work of Barnett (2001), Loescher (1998), Loescher and Monahan (1990), and Hyndman (2000).

7. Wright 1994, 8.

8. Camarda 1987, 63.

9. The precise number of refugees is impossible to ascertain; many immigrants never received official refugee status in their host countries. Most statistics include only those registered with the UNHCR. The estimates included here draw from a variety of governmental and nongovernmental sources, including reports by Central American governments to the Conferencia Internacional sobre los Refugiados de Centroamérica (International Conference on Central American Refugees, hereafter CIREFCA), UN documents, and dispatches from AW and Amnesty International.

10. Within the very light historiography of these diasporas, Costa Rica has received the most attention (consider Hayden 2003 and Quizar 1998). Other studies address the Central American refugee crisis more broadly, often from immigration policy and international law perspectives.

11. Descriptions of this back-and-forth travel appear in my own interviews, as well as interviews conducted by Lara Martínez (2004), Keune (1996), and SJDPA (1994).

12. Camarda 1987, 47.

13. Suyapa, interview by Carlos B. Lara Martínez, 9 February 2002, transcript, AGN.

14. Even a decade after the war it was impossible to distinguish the borderline between the two countries, as I discovered for myself on several trails in the La Cañada mountain range. Although hundreds of footpaths crisscross the border, the

three official crossings into Honduras continue to be El Poy, Chalatenango; La Galera, Morazán; and El Amatillo, La Unión.

15. Due to the background noise at this point in the recording of Luis's interview, it is not clear whether he said "Nosotros no teníamos una maña vivida por donde forjar los límites" or "Nosotros no teníamos una manía vivida por donde forjar los límites." *Maña* generally signifies a skill or craft, but it is also used in reference to an evil habit. *Manía*, like the English word *mania*, can refer to a rage, craze, or simply a peculiarity in behavior. My translation, therefore, is quite loose, allowing for both a general statement and a more critical commentary on government behaviors. Luis and María, interview by author, 2 April 2003, Cabañas, El Salvador.

16. Honduras–Grupo de Expertos, "Antecedentes, análisis del problema, conclusiones, recomendaciones: Refugiados en Honduras," report, ca. 1988, private collection (emphasis mine).

17. Leo Valladares Lanza, comments to CIREFCA, 24–26 November 1988, Instituto Interamericano de Derechos Humanos (hereafter IIDH), San José, Costa Rica.

18. Honduras–Grupo de Expertos, "Antecedentes."

19. Callejas Bonilla 1982, 88.

20. Honduras–Grupo de Expertos, "Antecedentes."

21. Interestingly, Honduran officials turned a blind eye to the Nicaraguan Contras, who operated relatively unhindered within the northeastern refugee camps. Among the myriad studies of U.S. involvement in Central America, consider especially LaFeber 1993 and LeoGrande 1998. On Honduras in particular, see Lapper and Painter 1985.

22. Notes from a meeting of the Comisión Nacional de Refugiados (hereafter CONARE), 9 May 1984, private collection, quoted in Valladares Lanza 1989.

23. Francisco Merino in *Tiempo Nacional*, quoted in A. C. Zoller, "Summary of Report of International Delegation to Central America," 1981, papers of David Holiday, Americas Watch El Salvador, San Salvador, p. 36.

24. Such accusations can be found throughout government documents from the period, with notes from CONARE meetings carrying particularly heavy charges.

25. These stories were published in *Tiempo Nacional* (ca. September 1985), *Prensa Gráfica* (10 November 1985), and *Tiempo Nacional* (4 November 1989), respectively.

26. "Acuerdo No. X," draft accord between Honduras and UNHCR, ca. 1985, private collection.

27. These numbers represent the higher population levels and are based on official UNHCR documentation. Thousands more continued to reside in the border towns throughout the 1980s. These campesinos were not officially recognized as refugees; they did not receive UN assistance, nor were they included in official statistics.

28. Buenos Aires was the only exception to this trend. That unique case is discussed later in more detail.

29. I found interviews and Honduran government documents especially enlightening on these various efforts, along with several reports from international visitors to the camps.

30. Manuel, interview by Carlos B. Lara Martínez, 9 February 2002, transcript, AGN.

31. Esther, interview by author, 21 February 2003, Chalatenango, El Salvador.

32. Members of the FMLN leadership who offered important details on this subject include Walter, José Luis, Facundo, Gustavo, and Lupe. It will be fascinating to reassess the FMLN's relations with the campesinos en guinda if and when the organization's documentation becomes available to researchers.

33. García Carranza 1985, 73.

34. Esther, interview by author.

35. Zoller, "Summary of Report," 13–15, 32–33.

36. Ibid., 5.

37. Although the numbers of troops stationed at each camp varied over time and according to regional events, it was not unusual for several dozen to be present at any given time. To cite just one example, a June 1981 report noted an increase in military personnel in the zone of Colomoncagua to thirty-two soldiers and a lieutenant along with additional posts on the edge of the nearby disputed bolsones (Funes de Torres 1984, 158).

38. Recounted in Funes de Torres 1984, 159–60.

39. "Mesa Grande: Rescate cultural," a collection of writings of Salvadoran refugees at Mesa Grande (1982–84), compiled by Gisela Ursula Heinrich, 1999, private collection.

40. One version of "El guanaco encampamentado" (The "Encamped" Guanaco) is included in "Mesa Grande: Rescate cultural." A version performed by a refugee conjunto is included in "Documentacion Mesa Grande," collection of interviews with and songs by Salvadoran refugees at the Mesa Grande camp, Honduras, compiled by Gisela Ursula Heinrich, private collection. A truly representative translation of this song is difficult given its use of Central American slang. In addition to its use in Central America as a slang term for a Salvadoran, *guanaco* has other meanings that are worth noting here. The guanaco is a wild, undomesticated animal similar in appearance to the llama and alpaca. *Guanaco* also refers to a simple, ignorant person from a rural background. In addition to its use as a slang term for a Honduran, *catracho* also refers to a regional food comprised of fried tortillas, beans, and cheese.

41. John Hammond (1998) has referred to the refugee camps in Honduras and the prisons within El Salvador as "protected spaces." Although it may seem oxymoronic to refer to these closed refugee camps as such, they did allow Salvadoran campesinos to remain in one place for long periods of time, which, in turn, offered a sense of stability that was simply impossible in northern El Salvador at the time. In addition, campesino refugees discovered a new kind of security in the international attention and support they received at the camps, a topic later addressed in more detail.

42. Compher and Morgan 1991, 40.

43. Colonel Abrahám García Turcios, interview by author, 30 May 2003, Tegucigalpa, Honduras.

44. Volunteer personnel of international agencies, "Salvadoreños refugiados en

Honduras," report, March 1984, file 2591, Centro de Documentación de Honduras (hereafter CEDOH), Tegucigalpa.

45. García Turcios, interview by author.

46. Working for local large landowners proved to be a double-edged sword for Salvadorans. Although it provided refugees with much-needed cash, it also subjected them to extreme exploitation by the landowners, a practice that Honduran parish and aid workers denounced on more than one occasion. On 22 May 1981, for instance, the Honduran paper *El Tiempo* carried the denunciation "The hacienda owners mercilessly exploit the Salvadoran refugees in Guarita and La Virtud, whom they pay only $.75 daily for they work they do."

47. SJDPA 1994, 74.

48. Cagan and Cagan 1991, 52.

49. This overview of construction work is culled particularly from SJDPA 1994; Compher and Morgan 1991; and Comunidad de Santa Marta, "Sistematización de la educación popular," draft manuscript, 2002, private collection.

50. Compher and Morgan 1991, 47; Cagan and Cagan 1991, 51–52.

51. Santa Marta, "Sistematización." Documents suggest that refugees elsewhere established similar family-based distribution systems.

52. SJDPA 1994, 77. The workshop had been established by late 1981 in either the San Antonio or Colomoncagua refugee camp; the original source attribution is unclear.

53. Particularly useful for this overview of the refugees' health work were interviews and documents from international voluntary aid agencies. It is notable that while aid workers and international visitors repeatedly painted almost grotesque pictures of human suffering and bodily injury—massive flesh injuries infested with flies, miscarriages, and muteness and convulsions induced by post-traumatic stress disorder—the refugees did not. It was far more common, in fact, for them to detail Salvadoran military attacks on their hometowns and the hardships associated with the guindas.

54. García Turcios, interview by author.

55. Santiago, interview by author, 25 February 2003, Chalatenango, El Salvador. In this interview, Santiago described the Secretaría de Conflictos in his Salvadoran community. Mediation in the refugee camps followed a similar pattern.

56. Information for this overview of women's roles in the refugee camps draws especially from my interviews, as well as from Vásquez, Ibañez, and Murguialday 1996 and Vásquez 2000.

57. "Suyapa," interview by Carlos B. Lara Martínez.

58. Vásquez 2000, 93. It is worth noting that discrimination against women in El Salvador prompted the formation of numerous women's organizations in the late 1980s and early 1990s. Among them is the Asociación de Mujeres por la Dignidad y la Vida (National Association of Women for Dignity and Life, also known as Las Dignas). Many campesinas who spent time in the refugee camps became involved with Las Dignas and other local and regional women's organizations upon their return to El Salvador.

59. Rosa, interview by author.

60. "Mesa Grande: Rescate cultural."

61. Salvadoran Refugees at Mesa Grande, "Refugiados salvadoreños en luto," communiqué to international solidarity groups, 9 July 1988, file 2671, CEDOH.

62. Information about these transfers draws especially from interviews with María and Rosa, as well as from "Oficio No. 413-S-85—URGENTE," Arnulfo Pineda López to Gen. Walter López Reyes, 4 September 1985, private collection; and Leo Valladares Lanza, notes from meeting between Honduras, UNHCR, and Latin American ambassadors to Honduras, 17 February 1984, private collection.

63. Interviews were the principal source for information about the relations between refugees and insurgents. I have chosen not to identify specific individuals here, even in pseudonym, because of the continued sensitivity of this topic.

64. I am indebted to Florencia Mallon for bringing the power of rumors to my attention. Also instructive were White 2000 and Turner 2005.

Chapter 4. The Politics of Exile

1. This reconstruction draws from interviews with García Turcios and others; Transcripciones Radio Venceremos, 4 December 1987; Page, "Situation Alert," 15 December 1987, file 2671, CEDOH; and Cagan and Cagan 1991.

2. "Acuerdo No. X," draft accord between Honduras and UNHCR, ca. 1985, private collection.

3. Norberto, interview by author, 22 February 2003, Chalatenango, El Salvador.

4. Dilling 1984, 132.

5. Interviews with Albert Depienne, Adán, and Roberto all corroborate this fact.

6. Dilling 1984, 212.

7. Honduras–Departamento de Censos y Estadísticas, "Población refugiada existente en Honduras por nacionalidad y campamento en la década de los años 80," table, ca. 1990, private collection. Interestingly, this document includes in its tally neither Salvadorans at Buenos Aires camp nor Haitians and other non-camp-based refugee groups.

8. Inter-Church Committee for Refugees (Canada), "Report and Recommendations to the United Nations High Commissioner for Refugees Regarding the Protection of Refugees and the Coordination of Material Assistance by the UNHCR in Honduras, September 1982," file 2671, CEDOH, 12, 23; Dilling 1984, 61. Although a great distance separated UN and aid agency personnel, the UN was even more distant from the Salvadoran refugees. Dilling noted that many visitors to the camps stayed with the refugees. "The UNHCR representatives ought to try this sometime," she quipped. "They might learn from it" (128).

9. This strategy was noted by several of my interviewees, as well as in Dilling 1984, 60–61, 116.

10. An especially strained relationship existed between agency coordinators and field staff. The majority of field staff were Honduran nationals who endured the

dangers and inconveniences of life in the refugee camps: crude shelters, overcrowding, insufficient water and food, inadequate medical attention and defective communications systems, intolerable heat, military harassment, and so on. For their efforts they received meager salaries and little—if any—job or physical security. In contrast nearly all agency coordinators were internationals who received high salaries and worked out of comfortable offices in the Honduran capital of Tegucigalpa. Field staff considered these *capitaleros* too far removed from the realities of life as a refugee.

11. It is relevant to note that World Vision, today an international Christian humanitarian organization, was founded in the United States in 1951. According to World Vision's 2009 financial statements, approximately one-third of its funding comes from government agencies, including the U.S. Agency for International Development. Caritas also developed in the early 1950s and is today an international organization based at Vatican City. I use the name here specifically to refer to Honduran affiliates of Caritas, many of whom were influenced by liberation theology. The Honduran nongovernmental organization CEDEN was founded by evangelical Christians in the wake of the 1969 Hundred-Hour War with El Salvador. It first offered assistance to displaced populations and "abandoned" regions along the border and further expanded its operations in the wake of Hurricane Fifi (1974), which devastated already poverty-stricken border areas.

12. Zoller, "Summary of Report," 59. Unfortunately, attempts to obtain copies of World Vision documentation from the 1980s were unsuccessful; thus, I rely on secondhand sources for the World Vision perspective despite the obvious questions this raises.

13. Ibid., 57–59.

14. Reprinted in CEDOH 1982, 3.

15. Zoller, "Summary of Report," 60.

16. Nidia, interview by author, 8 July 2003, Tegucigalpa, Honduras. Other CEDEN affiliates offered similar versions of this assessment. Note that Nidia's definition is not quite correct; the official name is Directorio de Investigación Nacional (National Directorate of Investigations). For those on the left, "DIN" was another way of saying the "secret police."

17. World Vision's detractors argued that the organization's staff provided intelligence to the U.S. and Honduran militaries about "subversive activities" going on in the refugee camps, leading to the detention of multiple voluntary agency personnel and refugees. An AW report concluded that "World Vision appears more and more as the Trojan Horse of the U.S. and of the ultra-conservative Honduran classes" (Zoller, "Summary of Report," 60). Dilling also noted that World Vision was "an aid organization that I have heard people complaining about." She described being warned not to let World Vision know that she was "with the Catholics." In light of such warnings, her first encounter with an agency worker left her with the sense that she "had had a brush with the military" (1984, 31–32).

18. Funes de Torres (1984, 160) reported that the resignation occurred in February 1982.

19. David and Manuel, interview by author, 15 May 2003, Tegucigalpa, Honduras.

20. Honduras–Secretaría de Gobernación y Justicia, "Agenda revisada: Negociaciones delegación de Honduras-ACNUR [Alto Comisionado de las Naciones Unidas para los Refugiados] en Ginebra, 7–10 de enero de 1985," private collection.

21. Quoted from Honduras–Comisión Especial, "Algunas consideraciones sobre el problema de los refugiados en Honduras," report prepared for National Security Council, 25 July 1984, private collection; and Leo Valladares Lanza, comments to CIREFCA, 24–26 November 1988, private collection.

22. Valladares Lanza, comments to CIREFCA. Available Honduran government documents illustrate that between about 1984 and 1986, high-level Honduran officials attempted to restructure the national refugee commission, CONARE, in an effort to more effectively address their concerns. Despite the obvious assessment and planning that occurred, CONARE continued to operate according to its original structure and mandate.

23. Valladares Lanza, comments to CIREFCA. See also Honduras–Grupo de Expertos, "Antecedentes."

24. Honduras–Grupo de Expertos, "Antecedentes." This statement appeared in the context of the proposal to relocate Salvadoran refugees to the Honduran province of Olancho. If relocation were to happen, officials said, more problems would result because the UNHCR and its supporting agencies "will attempt to maintain control . . . and thus impede the involvement of Honduran authorities in the command, administration, and supervision of these camps."

25. Honduras–Grupo de Expertos, "Antecedentes."

26. Honduras–Secretaría de Relaciones Exteriores, "Recomendaciones sobre el documento presentado por las Fuerzas Armadas titulado Plan General para la Supervisión y Control de los Refugiados," memo to National Security Council, 2 July 1985, private collection.

27. "Una grave acusación," *La Prensa*, 13 September 1985.

28. *La Prensa*, 5 February 1982.

29. International Council of Voluntary Agencies (hereafter ICVA), "Mission to Honduras 1988," Center for Democracy in America records, Wisconsin Historical Society (hereafter CDA records, WHS), Madison.

30. Refugees' assessments were cited in Inter-Church Committee for Refugees, "Report and Recommendations," 5 (emphasis in original).

31. Ibid., 23n26.

32. The Central American records at UNHCR headquarters reveal a distinct pattern. Representatives of the high commissioner's office regularly responded in writing to Europeans, North Americans, and other international inquiries. In contrast, I found not one example of a written response to the dozens of inquiries sent by individual refugees and camp committees.

33. Salvadoran Refugees at Colomoncagua, public denunciation, 16 April 1988, and "Comunicado 3," July 1988, both in file 2671, CEDOH; Salvadoran Refugees in Honduras, *INFORESAL* 1, newsletter, October 1986, 17, AW; "La reubicación de los refugiados salvadoreños," in CEDOH 1985.

34. Salvadoran Refugees in Honduras–Comité de Coordinación, communiqué, March 1988, CDA records, WHS.

35. LCIHR 1985, 3.

36. Terry 2002, 97.

37. "Comunicado 3," July 1988.

38. HON/HCR/0486, Cable, UNHCR-Tegucigalpa to UNHCR-Geneva, 29 June 1988, ACNUR files, Centro de Paz, Centro de Documentación e Investigación Histórica (hereafter CEPAZ), San Salvador, El Salvador.

39. Hansen and Stepputat 2005, 12.

40. In the wake of similar campaigns, Caritas, World Vision, and the Mennonite Central Committee also either threatened or carried out reductions in operations or withdrawals from the aid regime.

41. "Comunicado 3," July 1988.

42. HON/HCR/0462, cable, UNHCR-Tegucigalpa to UNHCR-Geneva, 22 June 1988, ACNUR files, CEPAZ.

43. The quote is from HON/HCR/0465, cable, UNHCR-Tegucigalpa to UNHCR-Geneva, 23 June 1988, ACNUR files, CEPAZ.

44. Edelman 1999, 41, 28.

45. Father M. and Marta, interview by author, 17 July 2003, Copán, Honduras. Such "hesitation" was also noted in UCA 1985.

46. Salvadoran refugees at San Antonio–Junta Directiva, public denunciation, 12 April 1988, file 2671, CEDOH; transcripts, testimony from Salvadoran refugees at La Virtud, Honduras, collected by U.S. congressman Ronald V. Dellums, November 1981, file 2602, CEDOH.

47. Salvadoran refugees at San Antonio–Junta Directiva, public denunciation, 12 April 1988.

48. UNHCR and voluntary agency statistics indicate that the number of adult males in the refugee camps was significantly lower than that of women. This led the directors of at least one survey of the refugee population to identify women rather than men as heads of household (UCA 1985).

49. "Mesa Grande: Rescate cultural."

50. Salvadoran refugees at San Antonio–Junta Directiva, public denunciation, 26 January 1988, file 2671, CEDOH.

51. Salvadoran refugees at San Antonio–Junta Directiva, public denunciation, 24 March 1988, file 2671, CEDOH.

52. For example, see *El Tiempo*, 5 September 1985, reprinted in CEDOH 1982, 30; and Salvadoran refugees at San Antonio–Junta Directiva, public denunciation, 12 April 1988.

53. Salvadoran refugees at San Antonio to UNHCR-Geneva, 28 November 1983, file 2591, CEDOH.

54. Camarda 1987, 70–71.

55. Dilling 1984, 200–201, 203, 260.

56. SJDPA 1994, 76.

57. Salvadoran refugees at Colomoncagua to international solidarity, 27 November 1983, file 2591, CEDOH.

58. "Mesa Grande: Rescate cultural."

59. See "Chalatenango," "Los 4 compañeros a Potonico," "Compañero Chepe," and "Los héroes de octubre," all in "Mesa Grande: Rescate cultural."

60. See "Los Poderes Populares," in "Mesa Grande: Rescate cultural."

61. "Mesa Grande: Rescate cultural."

62. Salvadoran Refugees in Honduras–Comité de Coordinación, communiqué, March 1988, CDA records, WHS. Levanchy was then associate director for the Latin American region. I found no evidence that he ever presented the refugees with a copy of the advertisement.

63. Dilling 1984, 255.

64. Open letter, 7 December 1983, file 2591, CEDOH.

65. Ibid.; letter to international solidarity, ca. 7 December 1983, file 2591, CEDOH.

66. *El Periódico*, newsletter, February 1984, file 2591, CEDOH.

67. Agamben 1998.

68. I borrow these phrases from Turner 2005.

Chapter 5. Salvadorans to the Soul

1. Manuel, interview by Carlos B. Lara Martínez, 9 February 2002, transcript, AGN.

2. Even a cursory look at the solidarity archives of the WHS reveals the patterns of accumulation of both national organizations such as the Committee in Solidarity with the People of El Salvador (CISPES) and local organizations such as the Madison-based Community Action on Latin America. The personal archives of scholars and solidarity workers such as Beth and Steve Cagan hold a similar wealth of refugee-produced news journals, posters, drawings, embroideries, letters, audio and video recordings, photographs, and more.

3. "Historia de El Salvador," in "Mesa Grande: Rescate cultural." In this context the Spanish term *valor* carries multiple meanings, not only worth, importance, or significance but also the virtue, courage, and strength to overcome challenges.

4. "Mesa Grande," in "Mesa Grande: Rescate cultural." "Compañero" signifies more than the simple English translation "companion" suggests. Soldiers of the FMLN referred to their brothers in arms as *compañeros*. In a similar vein, Salvadoran campesinos in exile used *compañero* to refer to their compatriots and trusted international aid and solidarity workers who dedicated themselves to the campesino rights struggle and the broader fight for a new and just El Salvador. The Pipil were indigenous inhabitants of western El Salvador during pre-Columbian times.

5. Poetry excerpts are from "Madre salvadoreña," "Río Sumpul," and "El imagen de El Salvador," all in "Mesa Grande: Rescate cultural." The drawings of refugee children depict much the same violence. It is worth noting that the last selection mixed

the verbs *estar* and *ser*. Although both signify "to be," the former indicates a temporary state of being and the latter a more permanent state. This terminology is discussed in more detail later in this chapter.

6. "Mesa Grande: Rescate cultural." The Salvadoran term *choco* does not translate easily into English, for it compounds various different words and meanings. In several Latin American countries, including Chile and Guatemala, *choco* may be used in reference to a person who is blind or missing some body part. Hondurans use the term to refer to someone or something that is twisted or crooked. It is worth considering, too, the similarities between *choco* and the word *chueco*, which Salvadorans and Hondurans, among others, use to describe something that is poorly made, defective, or useless. There are also similarities with the verb *chocar*, which means "to bother or annoy" or "to crash." I am grateful to Florencia Mallon for conversations about the layers of meaning in this and other "Salvadoranisms."

7. "Ay madrecita," in "Mesa Grande: Rescate cultural." *Madrecita* is a term of endearment for *madre* (mother). References to napalm, white phosphorous, and other chemical weapons are scattered throughout the refugees' own documentation, as well as the reports of human rights agencies. Research on this topic has long been dangerous; numerous people investigating the use of chemical weapons in El Salvador have been murdered, including the president of the independent Salvadoran Human Rights Commission, Marianela García. See also White 1987.

8. These examples were among the most frequently cited by campesinos. I draw them from my interviews, documentation produced by refugees, and the materials of various U.S.-based solidarity organizations.

9. A monthly calendar, for example, reported that four men dressed as women had entered Mesa Grande; the four were presumably members of the Salvadoran security forces. See Salvadoran refugees at Mesa Grande, "Informe sobre el mes de febrero–julio de 1983," report, July 1983, file 2591, CEDOH.

10. Such language is used throughout refugee writings. These specific examples are drawn from "El 6 de agosto" and "Mujeres guerrilleras," both in "Mesa Grande: Rescate cultural."

11. "Poema al guerrillero," in "Mesa Grande: Rescate cultural."

12. "Una voz en mi ranchito," in "Mesa Grande: Rescate cultural."

13. Salvadoran Refugees at Colomoncagua–Comunicación Social, *Comunidad en desarrollo* 5, 16 February 1990, Cagan papers.

14. Salvadoran Refugees at Colomoncagua–Comunicación Social, "La Patria en lucha," n.d., Cagan papers.

15. *Taconazo* comes from the word *tacón*, meaning "heel." In this context, "taconazo" refers to a great kick or scoring shot.

16. "El Taconazo," "La consigna del FMLN," and "La mecha encendida" all appear in "Mesa Grande: Rescate cultural."

17. The latter phrase (*de valor por nuestro pueblo*) is especially intriguing given that the word *valor* carries multiple meanings, including "value," "courage," strength," and "audacity." Likewise, the phrase *responsables de valor* may refer either to those who are

responsible for advocating valor among community members or to the responsables in the community who are the strongest and most courageous.

18. "Pero, como eres un pájaro valiente," in "Mesa Grande: Rescate cultural."

19. After returning to El Salvador, however, many adults considered the children born in the refugee camps in Honduras to have dual citizenship despite the fact that none of them had Honduran papers attesting to this fact.

20. Salvadorans who lived as refugees in Panama named their camp Ciudad Romero after the archbishop.

21. Compare this with Peteet 2005, which describes Palestinian refugees in Lebanon.

22. "La Constitución de la República de El Salvador es como una prostituta porque todos la violan." In Spanish the plural subject "they" is generally gendered male while the noun "constitution" is gendered female. It becomes quite easy, therefore, to make such a statement work both literally and figuratively.

23. Especially informative on this topic were interviews with Esther and Marta.

24. These quotes are drawn from "El 6 de agosto," "El silencio de los campesinos," and "Refugiados," all in "Mesa Grande: Rescate cultural"; and Camarda 1987, 35.

25. Salvadoran refugees at Mesa Grande and Colomoncagua, "Manual para instructores populares," 1982, private collection.

26. "La mecha encendida," in "Mesa Grande: Rescate cultural."

27. Steve Cagan, personal communication, 20 August 2006. Cagan was in the Colomoncagua camp at the time of this incident.

28. Salvadoran refugees at Colomoncagua, calendar, December 1983, file 2671, CEDOH.

29. Funes de Torres 1984, 158.

30. See, for example, Salvadoran refugees at Mesa Grande, "Informe sobre el mes de febrero–julio de 1983." International agency reports often reiterated the refugees' reports, as Human Rights Watch did in 1981 (Zoller, "Summary of Report," 37–38).

31. English translation of a petition released by Colomoncagua refugees on 27 June 1982, reprinted in Inter-Church Committee for Refugees, "Report and Recommendations," 26. I was unable to locate the original Spanish-language document; it would be interesting to clarify the terminology that the refugees utilized to refer to Honduras. Did they really refer to Honduras as their "homeland"? Might their terminology carry another meaning, perhaps akin to "hostland"?

32. See Elvir Sierra 2002 for the Honduran perspective on the "long diplomatic process" toward the Lima Treaty. The Salvadoran perspective can be gleaned from news coverage from the period, as well as annual reports of the Ministerio de Relaciones Exteriores.

33. Funes de Torres 1984, 158. Additional commentary along these lines can be found in refugee documents and the reports of international delegations.

34. English translation of a petition by Salvadoran refugees at Mesa Grande to High Commissioner Poul Hartling, 15 September 1982, box 10, folder 19, CDA records, WHS.

35. These specific events were reported in numerous sources by refugees and the UNHCR.

36. Honduras–Secretaría de Relaciones Exteriores, aide memoire, 20 January 1984, private collection. During 1984 and 1985 the topic of relocation dominated the documents from Honduran government sources and the UNHCR.

37. Salvadoran refugees at Colomoncagua to international solidarity, 27 November 1983, file 2591, CEDOH.

38. Salvadoran refugees at Mesa Grande to international solidarity, 8 November 1983, file 2591, CEDOH.

39. Salvadoran refugees at Colomoncagua to international solidarity, ca. late 1983–early 1984, file 2591, CEDOH.

40. LeoGrande 1998, 395. The U.S. Congress had restricted the number of U.S. military personnel allowed in El Salvador; as a result thousands of Salvadoran troops received training both in the United States and at the U.S. Army School of the Americas, located in Panama at the time. In part to cut costs, the U.S. military suggested training Salvadorans in Honduras. Although the Honduran high command continued to consider El Salvador as its traditional enemy, the threat of a civil war spillover from El Salvador prompted government officials to authorize the establishment of the CREM without consulting Congress. A fury of debates ensued; many argued, in fact, that the establishment of the CREM violated the Honduran Constitution. For more on the CREM and the Washington–Honduras nexus at the time, see Schulz and Schulz 1994 and LaFeber 1993.

41. Salvadoran refugees at Colomoncagua to international solidarity, 27 November 1983, file 2591, CEDOH.

42. Salvadoran refugees at Colomoncagua to international solidarity, ca. 7 December 1983, file 2591, CEDOH. A sudden change of leadership in the Honduran government in March 1984 prompted a shift in refugee-related policies, as well as a reassessment of relations with the United States. When Washington refused to meet the new government's demands, Honduras began denying Salvadoran CREM trainees entry into the country. In June 1985 the CREM closed.

43. Salvadoran Refugees in Honduras, "Objetivo yanqui: Despoblar la frontera," *Patria Nueva* 3, no. 5 (1988), Cagan papers.

44. Salvadoran Refugees at Colomoncagua–Comité de Madres Gloria Nohemy Blanco, Mother's Committee magazine, no. 10 (September–October 1989), Cagan papers.

45. In this, the Salvadorans were full and active members of a "transnational advocacy network" described in Keck and Sikkink 1998.

46. "Refugiados (Repaso sobre un proyecto de las clases del 2°. nivel)," in "Mesa Grande: Rescate cultural."

47. Interviews with former refugees and aid workers were most helpful in understanding the talleres. I am also grateful for conversations with Steve and Beth Cagan and Marc Rosenthal.

48. "Poema dedicado a todos los refugiados," in "Mesa Grande: Rescate cultural."

49. Salvadoran refugees at Mesa Grande and Colomoncagua, "Manual para instructores populares."

50. Haraganes often fell into this dependency category. The same kinds of charges resurfaced years later in the repopulated northern villages of El Salvador. They were particularly strong against the last communities to return to El Salvador.

51. Cagan and Cagan (1991) describe one such overhaul at the Colomoncagua refugee camp during the later 1980s.

52. Salvadoran refugees at Mesa Grande and Colomoncagua, "Manual para instructores populares."

53. "Refugiados," in "Mesa Grande: Rescate cultural."

Chapter 6. (Re)Writing National History from Exile

1. Salvadoran refugees in Honduras to Elisa Valle Martínez, 25 July 1987, file 2671, CEDOH.

2. UNHCR and Honduras, "Memorandum of Understanding," 3 June 1987, private collection.

3. Salvadoran refugees in Honduras to international humanitarian aid agencies, 5 August 1987, file 2671, CEDOH.

4. Rosa, interview by author, 24 February 2003, Chalatenango, El Salvador.

5. Keune 1996, 118–21.

6. Ibid., 123. A few campesinos reported that education simply did not happen during the guindas of the early 1980s. Many more indicated that, although schooling did happen during the period, it was erratic, with classes sometimes stalling for months on end.

7. I found no evidence of an education system—popular or official—in the Buenos Aires camp. It is likely that no system was ever established in the camp, perhaps due to the fact that refugees tended to stay there for shorter periods of time. Documents from the period also indicate that the Honduran government imposed fewer restrictions on the Buenos Aires camp given that its inhabitants were aligned more with the Salvadoran government than the insurgents. This relative freedom suggests that attendance at a local school might have been a possibility for Buenos Aires refugees.

8. These statistics are culled from Cáritas-Santa Rosa de Copán (Honduras), "Proyecto de capacitación de instructores refugiados salvadoreños," grant proposal, 30 October 1988, file JG/N CP, IIDH; Cagan and Cagan 1991; Hammond 1998; and McElhinny 2004.

9. Equipo Maíz 2000, 13, 12. One of the great pillars of the popular education movement in Latin America, Paulo Freire, argued that "radicalization, nourished by a critical spirit, is always creative. Radicalization criticizes and thereby liberates. Radicalization involves increased commitment to the position one has chosen, and thus ever greater engagement in the effort to transform concrete, objective reality" (1997, 19).

10. "Eso es verdad," in "Mesa Grande: Rescate cultural."

11. Equipo Maíz 2000, 13.

12. Salvadoran refugees at Mesa Grande and Colomoncagua, "Manual para instructores populares." The following discussion draws especially from the first section of this manual, titled "¿Cuáles son los temas de nuestra alfabetización?"

13. Salvadoran refugees at Mesa Grande and Colomoncagua, "Manual para instructores populares."

14. Hammond 1998, 82. As Hammond notes, this phraseology has a much more basic sound in the Spanish language: "La casa de María era quemada."

15. Ibid.

16. Salvadoran refugees at Mesa Grande and Colomoncagua, "Manual para instructores populares." It is worth noting that the refugees' system closely paralleled popular education efforts that took place among the mobile communities in the FMLN-controlled zones of northern El Salvador. According to an FMLN description of literacy efforts, "The students utilize the resources and the reality of their environment: machetes, shovels, arms, birds, rivers, mountains. . . . Then they learn the letter "a" for *arma* [weapon], "b" for boot, "c" for comrade, etc., thus discovering the meaning of the word and its implications before they try to write it" (FMLN 1982, 17).

17. On "the word," see especially chapter 3 in Freire 1997.

18. Salvadoran refugees at Mesa Grande and Colomoncagua, "Manual para instructores populares."

19. I found such concerns reported in UNHCR, Honduran, and voluntary aid agency documents, as well as the refugees' own writings. The quotes are from Salvadoran refugees in Honduras to international humanitarian aid agencies, 5 August 1987, and to Jean-Pierre Hocké, 26 July 1987, both in file 2671, CEDOH.

20. Salvadoran refugees in Honduras to international humanitarian aid agencies, 5 August 1987.

21. "Soy instructor," in "Mesa Grande: Rescate cultural."

22. Salvadoran refugees at Mesa Grande and Colomoncagua, "Manual para instructores populares."

23. On this "national order of things," see Malkki 1995b.

24. Paige 1997, 108.

25. Jenny Pearce opined that official revenge was "grotesque" (1986, 85). The information about burials comes from Stanley 1996, 42. The exact number of civilians killed during the Matanza, of course, will never be known. Estimates range anywhere from four thousand to more than fifty thousand. Thirty thousand has been the most commonly used figure.

26. Commander V. Brodeur, quoted in Pérez Brignoli 1995, 245.

27. Paige 1997, 123–24.

28. Ibid., 103; Pérez Brignoli 1995, 236. Scholarly explanations range from liberal economics to political infighting, from ethnic divisions to outsider influences, and combinations of these and other factors. For a traditional version of events, consult Anderson 1971. Recent revisionist accounts reveal that neither the PCS nor outside influences were as prevalent as previously assumed. See especially Ching 1998; Ching and Tilley 1998; and Henríquez Consalvi and Gould 2003.

29. It is interesting that the refugees did not distinguish, as scholars continue to do, between the various geographical regions of El Salvador. The principal sites for the 1932 uprising were in the western and central regions of the country; these zones were the areas of least rebel activity in the 1970s and 1980s. The northern departments, which saw little activity during the early 1930s, were among the most conflicted during the civil war. This variation did not seem to matter to the refugees, nor did the racial and ethnic overtones of the 1932 incident. Rather they represented the uprising as a nationwide event spurred by peasants tired of being exploited by the oligarchy.

30. FTC 1979, 39–40. It is worth recognizing here that such displays of violence can be traced back to the period of Spanish conquest and colonization of the region, and observers have noted similar theatricalities throughout the history of the Latin American region.

31. "Historia de Farabundo," in "Mesa Grande: Rescate cultural." *Historia* may be translated as either "history" or "story."

32. As with any conflict, this war was not as simple as these labels contend. There was, in fact, a multitude of contributing factors to the outbreak of hostilities, including long-standing tensions over the delineation of the border between El Salvador and Honduras (traceable back to the early years of independence), regional strains due to the uneven economic development resulting from the Central American Common Market, and heavy migration of Salvadoran campesinos to Honduras. Additional factors could be found in the growing economic, social, and political frictions within each country, particularly with regard to agrarian issues. For more discussion on these issues, consult Carías and Slutzky 1971; Anderson 1981; and Kapuściński 1992.

33. General Fidel Sánchez Hernández, quoted in Ministerio de Relaciones Exteriores de El Salvador 1970, 44, 90.

34. Transcription of presidential speech to the Salvadoran public, 14 July 1969, quoted in Ministerio de Relaciones Exteriores de El Salvador 1970, 30–31.

35. Morales Molina 1973, 49–50. Such glowing reports of Salvadorans were often set in stark contrast to rather lowly estimations of Hondurans. Not only were they lazy and slow, this same colonel argued, but they were also backward: "In a backward country that 'the train left behind' like that of our neighbors, people still behave as they did in the middle of the last century" (ibid., 76). Moreover, Hondurans were not even savvy enough to appreciate all that Salvadoran immigrants accomplished on their behalf: "A primitive pueblo by nature, [Honduras] tenaciously resists understanding that its prosperity and progress are due to immigrants—especially to the great number of Salvadorans" (ibid., 51).

36. Ministerio de Relaciones Exteriores de El Salvador 1970, 72.

37. Guerrero sent the formal complaint by telegram on 24 June 1969. It is reprinted in Ministerio de Relaciones Exteriores de El Salvador 1969, 72.

38. General Sánchez Hérnandez, quoted in Ministerio de Relaciones Exteriores de El Salvador 1970, 44. It is interesting to note that the Salvadoran government was quick to point out that its military had caused no harm or damage to Honduran campesinos

or property. Honduran sources, of course, differ on this account. Compare, for example, Blaise and Zuniga 1972.

39. See transcription of presidential speech to the Salvadoran public, 14 July 1969, quoted in Ministerio de Relaciones Exteriores de El Salvador 1970, 30–31, 44–45.

40. For the following discussion, unless otherwise noted, I draw from my own interviews with Salvadoran campesinos. Alejandro, Esther, Luis, and Rosa offered particularly eloquent analyses. It is interesting to note that, in a curious turn of fate, many of the campesino families from Honduras in 1969 ultimately recrossed the border a decade later when seeking refuge from the Salvadoran civil war. Although the younger generations did not directly experience the Hundred-Hour War, the war lore of parents, grandparents, uncles, and aunts made up part of their family history and memory. It is relevant to note, too, that while living in Honduras, campesinos did not often directly address the subject of the Hundred-Hour War. At the time, of course, they relied on the Honduran government for their physical spaces of refuge; explicitly calling up the history of conflict between the two countries might have had considerable negative consequences for their refugee status. Despite the dearth of materials written by Salvadoran campesinos about 1969, however, it is clear that the war served as a backdrop to their experiences of the 1970s and 1980s.

41. Esther, interview by author, 21 February 2003, Chalatenango, El Salvador.

42. Santiago, interview by author, 25 February 2003, Chalatenango, El Salvador.

43. Ministerio de Relaciones Exteriores de El Salvador 1970, 30–31.

44. Alejandro, interview by author, 27 July 2003, Chalatenango, El Salvador.

45. Luis and María, interview by author, 2 April 2003, Copán, Honduras.

46. Rosa, interview by author.

47. Norberto, interview by author, 22 February 2003, Chalatenango, El Salvador.

48. Pedro, interview by author, 18 November 2002, Chalatenango, El Salvador.

49. See Salvadoran Refugees in Honduras, *INFORESAL* 1, October 1986, AW; and Dilling 1984, 90.

50. Transcription of presidential address, ca. 18 July 1969, quoted in Ministerio de Relaciones Exteriores de El Salvador 1970, 90–91.

51. FTC 1979, 7–8.

52. "Imagen de El Salvador," in "Mesa Grande: Rescate cultural."

53. "Historia de El Salvador," in "Mesa Grande: Rescate cultural."

54. These phrases appear in numerous refugee writings, as well as in FTC 1979, 26.

55. Such phrases can be found in numerous refugee writings, including "La bota de Magaña" and "Pueblo sin cabeza," both in "Mesa Grande: Rescate cultural."

56. "Pueblo sin cabeza," in "Mesa Grande: Rescate cultural." The Spanish-language term *mandracado* poses some difficulty for translation into English, as it appears to be a concoction peculiar to Salvadoran campesinos. It is likely that *mandar* (to order, to send) is the primary base, with the latter half of the word possibly deriving from one or more of the following: *draconiano* (draconian), *dragado* (to clean the sea with mines), or *drogado* (drugged). This last option is perhaps most likely if we consider that misspellings speckled the peasants' written work and they regularly referred to the "drugged" and "crazy" nature of the Salvadoran troops trained by U.S. forces.

57. "Insurección," in "Mesa Grande: Rescate cultural."

58. "Pueblo sin cabeza," in "Mesa Grande: Rescate cultural." Commentary on U.S. military involvement can be found in many other songs and poems in this collection, including "Chalatenango," "Ronald Reagan," and "Cloromiro el divertido." Oral interviews from the 1980s and the postwar period are also replete with such references.

59. A more recent example of Salvadoran campesino perceptions of the United States appeared during my field research period. At that time El Salvador was in the process of exchanging its own currency for the U.S. dollar; in both formal interviews and informal conversations, former refugees repeatedly commented on this shift as yet another piece of the bigger puzzle of U.S. intervention in Salvadoran affairs. They also pointed out that their old currency, *el colón*, was named after the first conquistador, Christopher Columbus.

60. Salvadoran refugees at Mesa Grande and Colomoncagua, "Manual para instructores populares." "La Segunda Independencia" appeared on Inti-Illimani's album *¡Viva Chile!* originally released in 1973. I am grateful to Florencia Mallon for helping me to identify this connection. Salvadoran refugees performed other selections from the nueva canción and folk/protest genres, including songs by Víctor Jara and Pete Seeger.

61. Such sources never mentioned Martí's disillusion with Sandino's ideology nor their ultimate split.

62. Jesús Rojas was the alias of Antonio Cardenal, who was a member of the political commission of the FPL and served as commander in chief of the FMLN army in Chalatenango.

63. The memorial portrays Rojas as a brave and dedicated soldier; his image is framed by the red FMLN flag and two quotes: "Luchar por los pobres significa sacrificio, pero hay que hacerlo" (To fight for the poor signifies sacrifice, but it must be done) and "Compañero Jesús Rojas. . . . ¡Hasta la victoria siempre!!" (Companion Jesús Rojas. . . . Always unto victory!). For examples of more general commentary on Nicaragua, consider "La Paloma (de Ana María)" and "Poema de las madres," both in "Mesa Grande: Rescate cultural."

64. See "La resquiña," in "Mesa Grande: Rescate cultural."

65. Ibid. In a similar vein, in nearly all the interviews I conducted during 2002 and 2003, former refugees drew parallels between the Salvadoran civil war, the Vietnam War, and the George W. Bush administration's invasion of Iraq.

66. Dilling 1984, 77–78.

67. Ibid., 63.

68. "Navidad campesina," in "Mesa Grande: Rescate cultural."

Chapter 7. ¡Retorno!

1. Salvadoran refugees at Mesa Grande, "Proyecto de retorno," platform for first mass return, January 1987, CDA records, WHS.

2. UNHCR–El Salvador (Rodríguez-Casasbuenas/Beliard) to UNHCR–Geneva, cable, 19 February 1987, 610.HON.SAL, records of the Central Registry, Fonds 11, Series 2, UNHCR.

3. Noted in UNHCR records, as well as in Central American Refugee Center 1989.

4. Schrading 1991, 56; Male (49 years old), interview by Carlos B. Lara Martínez, 18 November 2002, transcript, AGN; Alejandro, interview by author, 27 July 2003, Chalatenango, El Salvador.

5. SAL/HCR/048, UNHCR–El Salvador (Rodríguez-Casabuenas/Mendiluci) to UNHCR-Geneva (Lavanchy), cable, 10 October 1987, 610.HON.SAL, records of the Central Registry, Fonds 11, Series 2, UNHCR.

6. Thompson 1995, 150.

7. McElhinny 2004, 148.

8. Thompson 1995, 122.

9. The UNHCR promoted the CIREFCA conference in the context of the Central American regional peace talks and in light of the 1987 Esquipulas II accord. Representatives of Belize, Costa Rica, El Salvador, Guatemala, Honduras, Mexico, and Nicaragua attended the inaugural meeting in May 1989 along with some representatives of NGOs.

10. Redmond 1995; Valladares Lanza 1989, 32.

11. Salvadoran Refugees in Honduras, *INFORESAL* 1, October 1986, AW.

12. Salvadoran refugees in Honduras to the High Commissioner for Refugees, 29 April 1986, AW. The UNHCR documents record multiple instances of the apprehension of repatriates. Representatives also note that such information, "which is known at camps," influenced resistance to repatriation. UNHCR–Costa Rica to UNHCR-Geneva, cable, 6 August 1986, 610.HON.SAL, records of the Central Registry, Fonds 11, Series 2, UNHCR.

13. All quotes are from HON/HCR/0378, UNHCR-Honduras to UNHCR-Geneva, cable, 26 May 1988, ACNUR records, CEPAZ. Various other cables reported similar issues.

14. For a scathing review of the elections, see Chomsky and Herman 1988. LeoGrande (1998, 246–53) noted that the CIA provided more than 5 million dollars in covert aid to boost the Christian Democrat Party between 1982 and 1984 and the U.S. Agency for International Development an additional million. The Department of State paid the 10.5-million-dollar bill for the U.S.-organized election.

15. The Tenancingo repopulation project has received significant attention from analysts. Consider Central American Refugee Center 1989; Edwards and Tovar Siebentritt 1991; and, more recently, Wood 2003, 2004.

16. Interview with CRIPDES founder, quoted in Thompson 1995, 124.

17. The organization also had initiated projects to relocate displaced persons from urban slums to unclaimed lands in the eastern provinces. See especially Central American Refugee Center 1989, 65; and Thompson 1995, 124.

18. I borrow this term from Schrading 1991.

19. Ibid., 49.

20. Ibid., 20.

21. Ibid., 43.

22. "Refugiados," in "Mesa Grande: Rescate cultural."

23. Tobías, interview by author, 9 March 2000, Chalatenango, El Salvador.

24. Alejandro, interview by author, 27 July 2003, Chalatenango, El Salvador.

25. "Troubling information," report of a voluntary aid worker, ca. August 1986, and "Repatriación de refugiados de Mesa Grande," memoir of voluntary aid worker in Honduras, 20 April 1987, both in CDA records, WHS.

26. Joseph Eldridge, report, 9 October 1987, AW.

27. Gustavo, interview by author, 21 January 2003, San Salvador, El Salvador.

28. Walter, interview by author, 5 February 2003, San Salvador, El Salvador.

29. Schrading 1991, 71.

30. Eldridge report, 9 October 1987.

31. HON/HCR/0449, UNHCR-Honduras to UNHCR-Geneva, cable, 19 June 1988, CEPAZ.

32. Interviews with former refugees in Cabañas.

33. Cagan and Cagan 1991 offers an eyewitness overview of this.

34. Eldridge report, 9 October 1987.

35. Other organizations included, among others, the Fundación Salvadoreña para la Reconstrucción y el Desarrollo (Salvadoran Foundation for Reconstruction and Development, REDES); Comité de Reconstrucción y Desarrollo Económico-Social de las Comunidades de Suchitoto, Cuscatlán (Committee for Reconstruction and Socioeconomic Development in the Communities of Suchitoto, Cuscatlán, CRCC); and the Asociación de Desarrollo Económico y Social (Economic and Social Development Association, ADES) of Santa Marta, Cabañas.

36. Julio Guardado to María, 16 July 1988, CDA records, WHS.

37. Alejandro, interview by author.

38. Going Home Campaign, "Bulletin 2," 10 May 1988, CDA records, WHS.

39. SAL/HCR/0147, UNHCR–El Salvador to UNHCR-Geneva, cable, 2 July 1988, CEPAZ.

40. UNHCR report, February 1985, quoted in Weiss Fagen and Eldridge 1991, 137.

41. "F.A. revela plan comunista para manipular repatriados," *Diario de Hoy*, 14 August 1988, 10.

42. "Denuncian pretensión FMLN de manipular a refugiados," *Diario de Hoy*, 31 August 1989, 3, 36.

43. Salvadoran refugees at Colomoncagua (with Patronato para el Desarrollo Comunal en El Salvador, PADECOES), "Carta abierta al Ing. Francisco Merino," *Diario El Mundo*, 26 September 1989, 12.

44. Billard 1987, 34.

45. Salvadoran Refugees at Mesa Grande–Comité de Repoblación to President Duarte, 4 April 1987, AW.

46. Eldridge report, 9 October 1987.

47. English translation of public announcement, Salvadoran refugees at Mesa Grande, platform for fourth mass return, 12 August 1989, CDA records, WHS.

48. Going Home Campaign, "Questions and Answers about the Mesa Grande Repatriation/Repopulation to El Salvador," 23 August 1982, CDA records, WHS.

49. Central American Refugee Center 1989, 106.

50. To determine this figure, I took the average of percentages reported in UNHCR–El Salvador to UNHCR-Geneva, cable, 20 September 1987, 610.HON.SAL, Records of the Central Registry, Fonds 11, Series 2, UNHCR; Lamb 1987; and Central American Refugee Center 1989, 93.

51. "F.A. revela plan comunista," 10.

52. "Proyecto de retorno," platform for first mass return, January 1987, CDA records, WHS.

53. Going Home Campaign, "Proposed Work Plan," 15 June 1987, CDA records, WHS (emphasis in original).

54. Male (forty-nine years old), interview by Carlos B. Lara Martínez, 18 November 2002, transcript, AGN.

55. The UNHCR was also cognizant of these risks. In several instances Geneva headquarters staff highlighted refugees' statements regarding the arrest and detention of repatriates and requested confirmation from field officers. Reports and requests for additional information followed.

56. Salvadoran refugees at Mesa Grande–Comité Nacional de Repoblación, "Gobierno y ACNUR obstaculizan proceso de repatriación," *El Mundo*, 25 October 1989, 27.

57. Diaconía, "Informe sobre el segundo retorno en comunidad de refugiados de Mesa Grande, República de Honduras," August 1988, file JG/CO Ci, IIDH.

58. For more on this return, see Cagan and Cagan 1991, 123–29.

59. Schrading 1991, 66.

60. See Clifcorn 1990.

61. Cagan and Cagan 1991, 133.

62. Scott 1990.

63. Cagan and Cagan 1991, 143. For more details about government coercion and corruption in the handling of repopulation programs and aid, see Central American Refugee Center 1989; Edwards and Tovar Siebentritt 1991; and Elisabeth Wood's work on Tenancingo (2003, 2004).

64. I borrow this term from Stepputat 1999.

65. Clifcorn 1990.

66. Alejandro, interview by author.

Conclusion

1. Roberto Lovato, interview by Amy Goodman, *Democracy Now*, 16 March 2009; audio and transcript of the interview available at http://www.democracynow.org/2009/3/16/fmln_candidate_mauricio_funes_wins_el (accessed 8 March 2010).

2. "Journalist Mauricio Funes Wins El Salvador Presidency," *Guardian*, 16 March 2009.

3. This is, of course, a play on Liisa Malkki's "national order of things" (1995b).

4. Binford 1999, 29. Binford points out, as well, that the levels of autonomy grew as the 1980s progressed.

5. Mallon 1995, 312.
6. Rubin 2004, 125.
7. Santiago, interview by author, 25 February 2003, Chalatenango, El Salvador.
8. Rosa, interview by author, 24 February 2003, Chalatenango, El Salvador.
9. I borrow the phrase "hypothetically isolated" from Nugent 1998, 15.
10. Bariagaber 2001.

References

Archives and Private Collections

Anonymous, Central America records (private collection)
Archivo General de la Nación, San Salvador, El Salvador (AGN)
Beth Cagan and Steve Cagan, El Salvador records (Cagan Papers)
Centro de Documentación de Honduras, Tegucigalpa, Honduras (CEDOH)
Centro de Paz, Centro de Documentación e Investigación Histórica, San Salvador, El Salvador (CEPAZ)
David Holiday, Americas Watch–El Salvador records (AW)
Instituto Interamericano de Derechos Humanos, San José, Costa Rica (IIDH)
United Nations High Commissioner for Refugees, Geneva, Switzerland (UNHCR)
Wisconsin Historical Society, Center for Democracy in America records, Madison (WHS)

Published Sources

Agamben, Giorgio. 1998. *Homo Sacer: Sovereign Power and Bare Life.* Translated by Daniel Heller-Roazen. Stanford: Stanford University Press.

Alas, José Inocencio. 2003. *Iglesia, tierra y lucha campesina: Suchitoto, El Salvador, 1968–1977.* San Salvador: Algier's Impresores.

Anderson, Thomas. 1971. *Matanza: El Salvador's Communist Revolt of 1932.* Lincoln: University of Nebraska Press.

———. 1981. *The War of the Dispossessed: Honduras and El Salvador, 1969.* Lincoln: University of Nebraska Press.

Armstrong, Robert, and Janet Shenk. 1982. *El Salvador: The Face of Revolution.* Boston: South End Press.

Ascoli, Juan Fernando. 1995. *Tiempo de guerra y tiempo de paz: Organización y lucha de las comunidades del nor-oriente del Chalatenango (1974–1994).* San Salvador: Equipo Maíz.

Baloyra, Enrique. 1982. *El Salvador in Transition*. Chapel Hill: University of North Carolina Press.

Bariagaber, Assefaw. 2001. "The Refugee Experience: Understanding the Dynamics of Refugee Repatriation in Eritrea." *Journal of Third World Studies* 18, no. 2: 47–70.

Barnett, Michael. 2001. "Humanitarianism with a Sovereign Face: UNHCR in the Global Undertow." *International Migration Review* 35, no. 1: 244–77.

Berryman, Phillip. 1984. *The Religious Roots of Rebellion: Christians in Central American Revolutions*. Maryknoll, N.Y.: Orbis Books.

———. 1986. "El Salvador: From Evangelization to Insurrection." In *Religion and Political Conflict in Latin America*, edited by Daniel H. Levine, 58–78. Chapel Hill: University of North Carolina Press.

———. 1987. *Liberation Theology: Essential Facts about the Revolutionary Movement in Latin America—and Beyond*. Philadelphia: Temple University Press.

———. 1994. *Stubborn Hope: Religion, Politics, and Revolution in Central America*. Maryknoll, N.Y.: Orbis Books.

Billard, Annick. 1987. "Large-Scale Return to El Salvador Unprecedented Operation." *Refugees* 47:34.

Binford, Leigh. 1996. *The El Mozote Massacre: Anthropology and Human Rights*. Tucson: University of Arizona Press.

———. 1997. "Grassroots Development in Conflict Zones of Northeastern El Salvador." *Latin American Perspectives* 24, no. 2: 56–79.

———. 1999. "Hegemony in the Interior of the Salvadoran Revolution: The ERP in Northern Morazán." *Journal of Latin American Anthropology* 4, no. 1: 2–45.

———. 2004. "Peasants, Catechists, Revolutionaries: Organic Intellectuals in the Salvadoran Revolution, 1980–1992." In *Landscapes of Struggle: Politics, Society, and Community in El Salvador*, edited by Aldo Lauria-Santiago and Leigh Binford, 105–25. Pittsburgh: University of Pittsburgh Press.

Blaise, Michel, and Melba Zuniga. 1972. *Estudio del contexto socioeconómico de los 5 departamentos de la frontera con El Salvador*. Tegucigalpa: Consejo Superior de Planificación Económica.

Boyer, Christopher R. 2003. *Becoming Campesinos: Politics, Identity, and Agrarian Struggle in Postrevolutionary Michoacán, 1920–1935*. Stanford: Stanford University Press.

Bracamonte, José Angel Moroni, and David E. Spencer. 1995. *Strategy and Tactics of the Salvadoran FMLN Guerrillas: Last Battle of the Cold War, Blueprint for Future Conflicts*. Westport, Conn.: Praeger.

Brockett, Charles D. 1998. *Land, Power, and Poverty: Agrarian Transformation and Political Conflict in Central America*. Boulder, Colo.: Westview Press.

———. 2005. *Political Movements and Violence in Central America*. Cambridge: Cambridge University Press.

Browning, David. 1971. *El Salvador: Landscape and Society*. Oxford: Clarendon Press.

Cabanas, Andrés. 1999. *Los sueños perseguidos: Memoria de las Comunidades de Población en Resistencia de la Sierra*. Guatemala City: Magna Terra Editores.

Cabarrús, Carlos Rafael. 1983. *Génesis de una revolución: Análisis del surgimiento y desarrollo de la organización campesina en El Salvador.* Ediciones de la Casa Chata, no. 16. Mexico, D.F.: Centro de Investigaciones y Estudios Superiores en Antropología Social.

———. 1985. "El Salvador: De movimiento campesino a revolución popular." In *Historia política de los campesinos latinoamericanos,* vol. 2, edited by Pablo González Casanova, 77–115. Mexico, D.F.: Siglo Veintiuno Editores.

Cáceres Prendes, Jorge. 1989. "Political Radicalization and Popular Pastoral Practices in El Salvador, 1969–1985." In *The Progressive Church in Latin America,* edited by Scott Mainwaring and Alexander Wilde, 103–48. Notre Dame, Ind.: Notre Dame University Press.

Cagan, Beth, and Steve Cagan. 1991. *This Promised Land, El Salvador.* New Brunswick, N.J.: Rutgers University Press.

Callejas Bonilla, Policarpo. 1982. "Aspectos jurídicos del tratamiento a los migrantes refugiados en América." *Revista de Derecho* 13:78–89.

Camarda, Renato. 1987. *Traslado forzado: Refugiados salvadoreños en Honduras.* Tegucigalpa: Centro de Documentación de Honduras.

Carías, Marco Virgilio, and Daniel Slutzky. 1971. *La guerra inutil: Análisis socioeconómico del conflicto entre Honduras y El Salvador.* San José, Costa Rica: Editorial Universitaria Centroamericana.

Carpio, Salvador Cayetano, Mario Payeras, and Jaime Wheelock. 1983. *Listen, Compañero: Conversations with Central American Revolutionary Leaders, El Salvador, Guatemala, Nicaragua.* Berkeley: Center for the Study of the Americas (CENSA).

Central American Refugee Center. 1989. *The Repopulation of Rural El Salvador.* Washington, D.C.: Central American Refugee Center.

Centro de Documentación de Honduras (CEDOH). 1982. *Los refugiados en Honduras.* Tegucigalpa: Centro de Documentación de Honduras.

———. 1985. *Honduras, historias no contadas.* Tegucigalpa: Centro de Documentación de Honduras.

Chepe. 1999. *La Metamorfosis del pulgarcito: Transición política y proceso de paz en El Salvador.* Barcelona: Icaria/Antrazyt-Facultad Latinoamericana de Ciencias Sociales (FLACSO).

Ching, Erik. 1997. "From Clientelism to Militarism: The State, Politics, and Authoritarianism in El Salvador, 1840–1940." PhD diss., University of California, Santa Barbara.

———. 1998. "In Search of the Party: The Communist Party, the Comintern, and the Peasant Rebellion of 1932 in El Salvador." *The Americas* 55, no. 2: 204–39.

———. 2004. "Patronage and Politics under General Maximiliano Hernández Martínez, 1931–1939." In *Landscapes of Struggle: Politics, Society, and Community in El Salvador,* edited by Aldo Lauria-Santiago and Leigh Binford, 50–70. Pittsburgh: University of Pittsburgh Press.

Ching, Erik, and Virginia Tilley. 1998. "Indians, the Military, and the Rebellion of 1932 in El Salvador." *Journal of Latin American Studies* 30:121–56.

Chomsky, Aviva, and Aldo Lauria-Santiago, eds. 1998. *Identity and Struggle at the Margins of the Nation-State: The Laboring Peoples of Central America and the Hispanic Caribbean*. Durham, N.C.: Duke University Press.

Chomsky, Noam, and Edward Herman. 1988. *Manufacturing Consent: The Political Economy of the Mass Media*. New York: Pantheon.

Clements, Charles. 1984. *Witness to War: An American Doctor in El Salvador*. Toronto: Bantam Books.

Clifcorn, John. 1990. "Masivo retorno de salvadoreños." *Noticias Aliadas* (Peru) 27, no. 7: 3.

Compher, Vic, and Betsy Morgan. 1991. *Going Home: Building Peace in El Salvador, the Story of Repatriation*. New York: Apex Press.

de la Cadena, Marisol. 2000. *Indigenous Mestizos*. Durham, N.C.: Duke University Press.

Desan, Suzanne. 1989. "Crowds, Community, and Ritual in the Work of E. P. Thompson and Natalie Davis." In *The New Cultural History*, edited by Lynn Hunt, 47–71. Berkeley: University of California Press.

Díaz, Salvador A. 1986. "History of the Agricultural Cooperative Movement in El Salvador." Master's thesis, West Virginia University, Morgantown.

Dilling, Yvonne. 1984. *In Search of Refuge*. Scottsdale, Pa.: Herald Press.

Durham, William. 1979. *Scarcity and Survival in Central America: Ecological Origins of the Soccer War*. Stanford, Calif.: Stanford University Press.

Edelman, Marc. 1999. *Peasants against Globalization: Rural Social Movements in Costa Rica*. Stanford, Calif.: Stanford University Press.

———. 2005. "Bringing the Moral Economy Back in . . . to the Study of 21st-Century Transnational Peasant Movements." *American Anthropologist* 107, no. 3: 331–45.

Edwards, Beatrice, and Gretta Tovar Siebentritt. 1991. *Places of Origin: The Repopulation of Rural El Salvador*. Boulder, Colo.: Lynne Rienner.

El Salvador. 1950. *Constitución política*. San Salvador: Imprenta Nacional.

El Salvador–Ministerio de Economía. 1954. *Primer censo agropecuario, 1950*. San Salvador: Dirección General de Estadística y Censos.

———. 1965. *Tercer censo nacional de población, 1961*. San Salvador: Dirección General de Estadística y Censos.

El Salvador–Ministerio de Relaciones Exteriores. 1969. *Informe labores ministerio de relaciones exteriores de El Salvador, 1968–1969*. San Salvador: Ministerio de Relaciones Exteriores.

———. 1970. *Informe labores ministerio de relaciones exteriores de El Salvador, 1969–1970*. San Salvador: Ministerio de Relaciones Exteriores.

Elvir Sierra, César. 2002. *El Salvador–Estados Unidos–Honduras: La gran conspiración del gobierno salvadoreño para la guerra de 1969*. Tegucigalpa: Litografía López.

Equipo Maíz. 2000. *Harina para mi costal: Una experiencia de educación popular en El Salvador*. San Salvador: Equipo Maíz.

Falla, Ricardo. 1998. *The Story of a Great Love: Life with the Guatemalan "Communities of Population in Resistance."* Translated by Minor Sinclair. Washington, D.C.: Ecumenical Program on Central America and the Caribbean (EPICA).

Federación de Trabajadores del Campo (FTC). 1979. *Perspectiva histórica del movimiento campesino revolucionario en El Salvador.* San Salvador: Ediciones Enero 32. Communiqué originally released in April 1977.

———. 1982. *Los trabajadores del campo y la reforma agraria en El Salvador.* San Salvador: Federación de Trabajadores del Campo.

Feierman, Steven. 1990. *Peasant Intellectuals: Anthropology and History in Tanzania.* Madison: University of Wisconsin Press.

Forster, Cindy. 2001. *The Time of Freedom: Campesino Workers in Guatemala's October Revolution.* Pittsburgh: University of Pittsburgh Press.

Freire, Paulo. 1997. *Pedagogy of the Oppressed.* Translated by Myra Bergman Ramos. New York: Continuum.

Frente Farabundo Martí para Liberación Nacional (FMLN). 1982. *Local Popular Power and the Advance of the Liberation Struggle in El Salvador.* Managua: Documentation Centre of Radio Farabundo Martí.

Funes de Torres, Lucila. 1984. *Los derechos humanos en Honduras.* Tegucigalpa: Centro de Documentación de Honduras (CEDOH).

García Carranza, Carlos Antonio. 1985. "La problemática de los refugiados y la protección de la población civil en los conflictos armados." Bachelor's thesis, Universidad Nacional Autónoma de Honduras, Tegucigalpa.

Gettleman, Marvin E., Patrick Lacefield, Louis Menashe, and David Mermelstein, eds. 1987. *El Salvador: Central America in the New Cold War.* Rev. ed. New York: Grove Press.

Gilly, Adolfo. 1998. "Chiapas and the Rebellion of the Enchanted World." In *Rural Revolt in Mexico: U.S. Intervention and the Domain of Subaltern Politics*, edited by Daniel Nugent, 261–333. Durham, N.C.: Duke University Press.

Gould, Jeffrey L. 1990. *To Lead as Equals: Rural Protest and Political Consciousness in Chinandega, Nicaragua, 1912–1979.* Chapel Hill: University of North Carolina Press.

———. 1998. *To Die in This Way: Nicaraguan Indians and the Myth of Mestizaje, 1880–1965.* Durham, N.C.: Duke University Press.

Gould, Jeffrey, and Aldo Lauria-Santiago. 2008. *To Rise in Darkness: Revolution, Repression, and Memory in El Salvador, 1920–1932.* Durham, N.C.: Duke University Press.

Gómez, Ileana, Carmen Meyers, Manuel A. Vásquez, and Philip Williams. 1999. "Religious and Social Participation in War-Torn Areas of El Salvador." *Journal of Interamerican Studies and World Affairs* 41, no. 4: 53–71.

Grandin, Greg. 2000. *The Blood of Guatemala: A History of Race and Nation.* Durham, N.C.: Duke University Press.

Griffith, Kati, and Leslie Gates. 2004. "Colonels and Industrial Workers in El Salvador, 1944–1972: Seeking Societal Support through Gendered Labor Reforms." In *Landscapes of Struggle: Politics, Society, and Community in El Salvador*, edited by Aldo Lauria-Santiago and Leigh Binford, 71–84. Pittsburgh: University of Pittsburgh Press.

Hammond, John. 1993. "War-Uprooting and the Political Mobilization of Central American Refugees." *Journal of Refugee Studies* 6:105–22.

———. 1998. *Fighting to Learn: Popular Education and Guerrilla War in El Salvador.* New Brunswick, N.J.: Rutgers University Press.

———. 1999. "Popular Education as Community Organizing in El Salvador." *Latin American Perspectives* 26, no. 4: 69–95.

Hansen, Thomas Blom, and Finn Stepputat, eds. 2005. *Sovereign Bodies: Citizens, Migrants, and States in the Postcolonial World.* Princeton, N.J.: Princeton University Press.

Harnecker, Marta. 1993. *Con la mirada en alto: Historia de las FPL Farabundo Martí a través de sus dirigentes.* San Salvador: UCA Editores.

Hayden, Bridget A. 2003. *Salvadorans in Costa Rica: Displaced Lives.* Tucson: University of Arizona Press.

Henríquez Consalvi, Carlos, and Jeffrey Gould, directors. 2003. *1932, Cicatriz de la memoria.* Documentary. San Salvador, El Salvador: Museo de la Palabra y la Imagen and First Run/Icarus Films.

Hyndman, Jennifer. 2000. *Managing Displacement: Refugees and the Politics of Humanitarianism.* Minneapolis: University of Minnesota Press.

Instituto de Estudios Políticos para América Latina y Africa (IEPALA). 1984. *Salvadoreños refugiados en Honduras.* Madrid: IEPALA Editores.

Jackson, Donald R. 1980. "The Communal Cooperative Experience: An Example from El Salvador." PhD diss., University of Wisconsin–Madison.

Joseph, Gilbert, and Daniel Nugent, eds. 1994. *Everyday Forms of State Formation: Revolution and Negotiation of Rule in Modern Mexico.* Durham, N.C.: Duke University Press.

Kapuściński, Ryszard. 1992. *The Soccer War.* New York: Vintage Books.

Keck, Margaret E., and Kathryn Sikkink. 1998. *Activists beyond Borders: Advocacy Networks in International Politics.* Ithaca, N.Y.: Cornell University Press.

Keune, Lou. 1996. *Sobrevivimos la guerra: La historia de los pobladores de Arcatao y de San José Las Flores.* San Salvador: Adelina Editores.

Kincaid, A. Douglas. 1987. "Peasants into Rebels: Community and Class in Rural El Salvador." *Comparative Studies in Society and History* 29, no. 3: 466–94.

LaFeber, Walter. 1993. *Inevitable Revolutions: The United States in Central America.* 2nd ed. New York: W. W. Norton.

Lamb, Sidni. 1987. "El Salvador, próxima parada: El hogar." *Refugees* 32:20–21.

Lapper, Richard, and James Painter. 1985. *Honduras: State for Sale.* London: Latin America Bureau.

Lara Martínez, Carlos B. 2004. "The Formation of a Rural Community: Joya de Cerén, 1954–1995." In *Landscapes of Struggle: Politics, Society, and Community in El Salvador,* edited by Aldo Lauria-Santiago and Leigh Binford, 85–100. Pittsburgh: University of Pittsburgh Press.

Lauria-Santiago, Aldo. 1999a. *An Agrarian Republic: Commercial Agriculture and the Politics of Peasant Communities in El Salvador, 1823–1914.* Pittsburgh: University of Pittsburgh Press.

———. 1999b. "Land, Community, and Revolt in Late-Nineteenth-Century Indian Izalco, El Salvador." *Hispanic American Historical Review* 79, no. 3: 495–534.

Lauria-Santiago, Aldo, and Leigh Binford, eds. 2004a. *Landscapes of Struggle: Politics, Society, and Community in El Salvador.* Pittsburgh: University of Pittsburgh Press.

———. 2004b. "Local History, Politics, and the State in El Salvador." In *Landscapes of Struggle: Politics, Society, and Community in El Salvador,* edited by Aldo Lauria-Santiago and Leigh Binford, 1–11. Pittsburgh: University of Pittsburgh Press.

Lawyers Committee for International Human Rights (LCIHR). 1985. *Honduras: A Crisis on the Border, a Report on Salvadoran Refugees in Honduras.* New York: Lawyers Committee for International Human Rights.

LeoGrande, William M. 1998. *Our Own Backyard: The United States in Central America, 1977–1992.* Chapel Hill: University of North Carolina Press.

Lindo-Fuentes, Hector. 1990. *Weak Foundations: The Economy of El Salvador in the Nineteenth Century, 1821–1898.* Berkeley: University of California Press.

Lindo-Fuentes, Hector, Erik Ching, and Rafael Lara Martínez. 2007. *Remembering a Massacre in El Salvador: The Insurrection of 1932, Roque Dalton, and the Politics of Historical Memory.* Albuquerque: University of New Mexico Press.

Lischer, Sarah Kenyon. 2000. *Refugee Involvement in Political Violence: Quantitative Evidence from 1987–1998.* New Issues in Refugee Research, Working Paper no. 26. Geneva: UNHCR.

———. 2005. *Dangerous Sanctuaries: Refugee Camps, Civil War, and the Dilemmas of Humanitarian Aid.* Ithaca, N.Y.: Cornell University Press.

Loescher, Gil. 1988. "Humanitarianism and Politics in Central America." *Political Science Quarterly* 103, no. 2: 295–320.

Loescher, Gil, and Laila Monahan, eds. 1990. *Refugees and International Relations.* Oxford: Clarendon Press.

López Contreras, Carlos. 1984. *Las negociaciones de paz: Mi punto de vista.* Tegucigalpa: Imprenta Lithopress.

———. 1987. *Informe de labores.* Tegucigalpa: Secretaría de Estado en el Despacho de Relaciones Exteriores.

Lungo Uclés, Mario. 1987. *La lucha de las masas en El Salvador.* San Salvador: UCA Editores.

———. 1991. *El Salvador en los años 80: Contrainsurgencia y revolución.* Havana: Casa de las Américas.

———. 1995. "Building and Alternative: The Formation of a Popular Project." In *The New Politics of Survival: Grassroots Movements in Central America,* edited by Minor Sinclair, 152–79. Washington, D.C.: Ecumenical Program in Latin America and the Caribbean (EPICA) /Monthly Review Press.

Macdonald, Mandy, and Mike Gatehouse. 1995. *In the Mountains of Morazán: Portrait of a Returned Refugee Community in El Salvador.* London: Latin American Bureau.

Malkki, Liisa. 1990. "Context and Consciousness: Local Conditions for the Production of Historical and National Thought among Hutu Refugees in Tanzania." In *Nationalist Ideologies and the Production of National Cultures,* edited by Richard G. Fox, 32–62. Washington, D.C.: American Anthropological Association.

———. 1992. "National Geographic: The Rooting of Peoples and the Territorialization of National Identity among Scholars and Refugees." *Cultural Anthropology* 7, no. 1: 24–44.

———. 1995a. *Purity and Exile: Violence, Memory, and National Cosmology among Hutu Refugees in Tanzania.* Chicago: University of Chicago Press.

———. 1995b. "Refugees and Exile: From 'Refugee Studies' to the National Order of Things." *Annual Review of Anthropology* 24:495–523.

———. 1996. "Speechless Emissaries: Refugees, Humanitarianism, and Dehistoricization." *Cultural Anthropology* 11, no. 3: 377–404.

Mallon, Florencia E. 1995. *Peasant and Nation: The Making of Postcolonial Mexico and Peru.* Berkeley: University of California Press.

Manwaring, Max, and Court Prisk, eds. 1988. *El Salvador at War: An Oral History of Conflict from the 1979 Insurrection to the Present.* Washington, D.C.: National Defense University Press.

Manz, Beatriz. 1988a. *Refugees of a Hidden War: The Aftermath of Counterinsurgency in Guatemala.* Albany: State University of New York Press.

———. 1988b. *Repatriation and Reintegration: An Arduous Process in Guatemala.* Washington, D.C.: Hemispheric Migration Project Center for Immigration Policy and Refugee Assistance, Georgetown University.

———. 1988c. "The Transformation of La Esperanza, an Ixcán Village." In *Harvest of Violence: The Maya Indians and the Guatemalan Crisis*, edited by Robert Carmack, 70–89. Norman: University of Oklahoma Press.

———. 2004. *Paradise in Ashes: A Guatemalan Journey of Courage, Terror, and Hope.* Berkeley: University of California Press.

Martín-Baró, Ignacio. 1973. "Psicología del campesino salvadoreño." *Estudios Centroamericanos* 297–98:476–95.

Martínez Peñate, Oscar. 1997. *El Salvador: Del conflicto armado a la negociación, 1979–1989.* San Salvador: Editorial Nuevo Enfoque.

Massey, Doreen. 1999. "Imagining Globalization: Power-Geometries of Time-Space." In *Global Futures: Migration, Environment, and Globalization*, edited by Avtar Brah, Mary Hickman, and Máirtín Mac au Ghaill, 27–45. London: Macmillan.

Mbembe, Achille. 2000. "At the Edge of the World: Boundaries, Territoriality, and Sovereignty in Africa." *Public Culture* 12, no. 1: 259–84.

McClintock, Cynthia. 1998. *Revolutionary Movements in Latin America: El Salvador's FMLN and Peru's Shining Path.* Washington, D.C.: U.S. Institute of Peace Press.

McClintock, Michael. 1985. *The American Connection: State Terror and Popular Resistance in El Salvador.* London: Zed Books.

McElhinny, Vincent J. 2004. "Between Clientelism and Radical Democracy: The Case of Ciudad Segundo Montes." In *Landscapes of Struggle: Politics, Society, and Community in El Salvador*, edited by Aldo Lauria-Santiago and Leigh Binford, 147–65. Pittsburgh: University of Pittsburgh Press.

McIlwaine, Cathy. 1998. "Contesting Civil Society: Reflections from El Salvador." *Third World Quarterly* 19, no. 4: 651–73.

Mena Sandoval, Francisco Emilio. 1990. *Del ejército nacional al ejército guerrillero*. San Salvador: Ediciones Arcoiris.

Menjívar, Rafael. 1962. *Formas de tenencia de la tierra y algunos otros aspectos de la actividad agropecuaria*. Régimen de Tenencia de la Tierra y Condiciones de Trabajo Agrícola de El Salvador, monograph no. 1. San Salvador: University of El Salvador.

Metzi, Francisco. 1988. *Por los caminos de Chalatenango: Con la salud en la mochila*. San Salvador: UCA Editores.

Meyer, David, and Sam Marullo. 1992. "Grassroots Mobilization and International Politics: Peace Protest and the End of the Cold War." *Research in Social Movements, Conflict, and Change* 14:99–140.

Montes, Segundo. 1979. *El compadrazgo: Una estructura de poder en El Salvador*. San Salvador: UCA Editores.

———. 1980. *El agro salvadoreño (1973–1980)*. San Salvador: UCA Editores.

———. 1988. *La resistencia no violenta ante los regimenes salvadoreños que han utilizado el terror institucionalizado en el período 1972–1987*. San Salvador: UCA Editores.

Montgomery, Tommie Sue. 1995. *Revolution in El Salvador: From Civil Strife to Civil Peace*. 2nd ed. Boulder, Colo.: Westview Press.

Morales Molina, Manuel. 1973. *El Salvador: Un pueblo que se rebela*. San Salvador: Tipografía Central.

North, Lisa. 1981. *Bitter Grounds: Roots of Revolt in El Salvador*. Toronto: Between the Lines.

Nugent, Daniel. 1998. "Introduction: Reasons to Be Cheerful." In *Rural Revolt in Mexico: U.S. Intervention and the Domain of Subaltern Politics*, edited by Daniel Nugent, 1–22. Durham, N.C.: Duke University Press.

Nyers, Peter Gregory Andrew. 2002. "Body Politics in Motion: Refugees and States of/ in Emergency." PhD diss., York University.

Paige, Jeffery M. 1997. *Coffee and Power: Revolution and the Rise of Democracy in Central America*. Cambridge, Mass.: Harvard University Press.

Pastor Ridruejo, Jose Antonio. 1987. *Question of the Violation of Human Rights and Fundamental Freedoms in Any Part of the World, with Particular Reference to Colonial and Other Dependent Countries and Territories: Final Report on the Situation of Human Rights in El Salvador*. Submitted to the United Nations Commission on Human Rights. New York: United Nations.

Pearce, Jenny. 1986. *Promised Land: Peasant Rebellion in Chalatenango, El Salvador*. London: Latin America Bureau.

Pelupessy, Wim. 1991. "Agrarian Reform in El Salvador." In *A Decade of War: El Salvador Confronts the Future*, edited by Anjali Sundaram and George Gelber, 38–57. New York: Monthly Review Press.

———. 1998. *Políticas agrarias en El Salvador, 1960–1990*. San José, Costa Rica: Editorial Universitaria Centroamericana.

Perales, Ious. 1986. *Chalatenango: Un viaje por la guerrilla salvadoreña*. Madrid: Editorial Revolución.

Pérez Brignoli, Héctor. 1995. "Indians, Communists, and Peasants: The 1932 Rebellion in El Salvador." In *Coffee, Society, and Power in Latin America*, edited by William Roseberry, Lowell Gudmundson, and Mario Samper Kutschbach, 232–61. Baltimore: Johns Hopkins University Press.

Pérez del Castillo, Gonzalo, and Marika Fahlen. 1985. *CIREFCA: An Opportunity and Challenge for Inter-agency Cooperation—Joint UNDP/UNHCR Review.* Geneva: United Nations.

Peteet, Julie M. 1995. "Transforming Trust: Dispossession and Empowerment among Palestinian Refugees." In *Mistrusting Refugees*, edited by E. Valentine Daniel and John Chr. Knudsen, 168–86. Berkeley: University of California Press.

———. 2000. "Refugees, Resistance, and Identity." In *Globalizations and Social Movements: Culture, Power, and the Transnational Public Sphere*, edited by John A. Guidry, Michael D. Kennedy, and Mayer N. Zald, 183–209. Ann Arbor: University of Michigan Press.

———. 2005. *Landscape of Hope and Despair: Palestinian Refugee Camps.* Philadelphia: University of Pennsylvania Press.

Peterson, Anna L. 1997. *Martyrdom and the Politics of Religion: Progressive Catholicism in El Salvador's Civil War.* Albany: State University of New York Press.

Peterson, Brandt Gustav. 2005. "Unsettled Remains: Race, Trauma, and Nationalism in Millennial El Salvador." PhD diss., University of Texas, Austin.

Ponceele, Rogelio, and María López Vigil. 1987. *Muerte y vida en Morazán: Testimonio de un sacerdote.* San Salvador: UCA Editores.

Portes, Alejandro. 1997. *Globalization from Below: The Rise of Transnational Communities.* Working Paper no. 98–08. Princeton, N.J.: Center for Migration and Development, Princeton University.

Proyecto de Desarrollo Rural del Sur de Lempira. 1999. *El comercio no controlado entre Honduras y El Salvador.* Tegucigalpa: Editoral Guaymuras.

Purnell, Jennie. 1999. *Popular Movements and State Formation in Revolutionary Mexico: The Agraristas and Cristeros of Michoacán.* Durham, N.C.: Duke University Press.

Quizar, Robin Ormes. 1998. *My Turn to Weep: Salvadoran Refugee Women in Costa Rica.* Westport, Conn.: Bergin and Garvey.

Redmond, Ron. 1995. "The Human Side of CIREFCA." *Refugees* 99, no. 1: 15–21.

Roseberry, William. 1994. "Hegemony and the Language of Contention." In *Everyday Forms of State Formation: Revolution and the Negotiation of Rule in Modern Mexico*, edited by Gilbert M. Joseph and Daniel Nugent, 356–66. Durham, N.C.: Duke University Press.

Rubin, Jeffrey W. 1997. *Decentering the Regime: Ethnicity, Radicalism, and Democracy in Juchitán, Mexico.* Durham, N.C.: Duke University Press.

———. 2004. "Meanings and Mobilizations: A Cultural Politics Approach to Social Movements and States." *Latin American Research Review* 39, no. 3: 106–42.

Sanford, Victoria. 2003. *Buried Secrets: Truth and Human Rights in Guatemala.* New York: Palgrave Macmillan.

Schirmer, Jennifer. 1993. "The Seeking of Truth and the Gendering of Consciousness: The Comadres of El Salvador and the CONAVIGUA Widows of Guatemala." In

Viva: Women and Popular Protest in Latin America, edited by Sarah A. Radcliffe and Sallie Westwood, 30–64. London: Routledge.

Schrading, Roger. 1991. *El Movimiento de repoblación en El Salvador*. San José: Instituto Interamericano de Derechos Humanos.

Schulz, Donald E., and Deborah Sundloff Schulz. 1994. *The United States, Honduras, and the Crisis in Central America*. Boulder, Colo.: Westview Press.

Scott, James C. 1976. *The Moral Economy of the Peasant: Rebellion and Subsistence in Southeast Asia*. New Haven, Conn.: Yale University Press.

———. 1990. *Domination and the Arts of Resistance: Hidden Transcripts*. New Haven, Conn.: Yale University Press.

Seligson, Mitchell. 1995. "Thirty Years of Transformation in the Agrarian Structure of El Salvador." *Latin American Research Review* 30, no. 3: 43–74.

Sermeño Lima, José Arnoldo. 1999. *Medición e interpretación histórica de los movimientos internos de la población de El Salvador*. Colección Aportes, no. 6. San Salvador: Facultad Latinoamericana de Ciencias Sociales.

Servicio Jesuita para el Desarrollo "Pedro Arrupe" (SJDPA). 1994. *Tiempo de recordar y tiempo de contar: Testimonios de comunidades repatriadas y reubicadas de El Salvador*. San Salvador: SJDPA.

Siddiq, Muhammad. 1995. "On Ropes of Memory: Narrating the Palestinian Refugees." In *Mistrusting Refugees*, edited by E. Valentine Daniel and John Chr. Knudsen, 87–101. Berkeley: University of California Press.

Sieder, Rachel. 2001. "War, Peace, and Memory Politics in Central America." In *The Politics of Memory: Transitional Justice in Democratizing Societies*, edited by Alexandra Barahona de Brito, Carmen González-Enríquez, and Paloma Aguilar, 161–89. Oxford: Oxford University Press.

Silber, Irina Carlota. 2000. "A Spectral Reconciliation: Rebuilding Post-war El Salvador." PhD diss., New York University.

Simon, Laurence, and James Stephens. 1981. *El Salvador Land Reform, 1980–1981: Impact Audit*. Boston: Oxfam America.

Slater, David. 1998. "Rethinking the Spatialities of Social Movements: Questions of (B)Orders, Culture, and Politics in Global Times." In *Cultures of Politics/Politics of Cultures: Re-visioning Latin American Social Movements*, edited by Sonia E. Alvarez, Evelina Dagnino, and Arturo Escobar, 380–403. Boulder, Colo.: Westview Press.

———. 2008. "Power and Social Movements in the Other Occident: Latin America in an International Context." In *Latin American Social Movements in the Twenty-first Century: Resistance, Power, and Democracy*, edited by Richard Stahler-Sholk, Harry E. Vanden, and Glen David Kuecker, 21–38. Lanham, Md.: Rowman and Littlefield.

Smith, Gavin. 1991. *Livelihood and Resistance: Peasants and the Politics of Land in Peru*. Berkeley: University of California Press.

Smith, Jackie, Charles Chatfield, and Ron Pagnucco, eds. 1997. *Transnational Social Movements and Global Politics: Solidarity beyond the State*. Syracuse, N.Y.: Syracuse University Press.

Smith, Jackie, and Hank Johnston, eds. 2002. *Globalization and Resistance: Transnational Dimensions of Social Movements*. Lanham, Md.: Rowman and Littlefield.

Sobrino, Jon. 1988. *Spirituality of Liberation: Toward Political Holiness*. Translated by Robert R. Barr. Maryknoll, N.Y.: Orbis Books.

Socorro Jurídico. 1981. *El Salvador: Del genocidio de la junta militar a la esperanza de la lucha insurreccional*. San Salvador: Socorro Jurídico, Arzobispado de San Salvador.

Soguk, Nevzat. 1999. *States and Strangers: Refugees and Displacements of Statecraft*. Minneapolis: University of Minnesota Press.

Sørensen, Ninna Nyberg, and Finn Stepputat. 2001. "Narrations of Authority and Mobility." *Identities* 8, no. 3: 313–42.

Stanley, William. 1996. *The Protection Racket State: Elite Politics, Military Extortion, and Civil War in El Salvador*. Philadelphia: Temple University Press.

Starn, Orin. 1992. "'I Dreamed of Foxes and Hawks': Reflections on Peasant Protest, New Social Movements, and the Rondas." In *The Making of Social Movements in Latin America: Identity, Strategy, and Democracy*, edited by Arturo Escobar and Sonia Alvarez, 89–111. Boulder, Colo.: Westview.

———. 1998. "Villagers at Arms: War and Counterrevolution in the Central-South Andes." In *Shining and Other Paths: War and Society in Peru, 1980–1995*, edited by Steve J. Stern, 224–57. Durham, N.C.: Duke University Press.

———. 1999. *Nightwatch: The Politics of Protest in the Andes*. Durham, N.C.: Duke University Press.

Stedman, Stephen John, and Fred Tanner, eds. 2003. *Refugee Manipulation: War, Politics, and the Abuse of Human Suffering*. Washington, D.C.: Brookings Institution Press.

Stepputat, Finn. 1999. "Politics of Displacement in Guatemala." *Journal of Historical Sociology* 12, no. 1: 54–80.

———. 2004. "Marching for Progress: Rituals of Citizenship, State, and Belonging in a High Andes District." *Bulletin of Latin American Research* 23, no. 2: 244–59.

Stepputat, Finn, and Ninna Nyberg Sørensen. 2001. "The Rise and Fall of 'Internally Displaced People' in the Central Peruvian Andes." *Development and Change* 32: 769–91.

Stølen, Kristi Anne. 2007. *Guatemalans in the Aftermath of Violence: The Refugees' Return*. Philadelphia: University of Pennsylvania Press.

Studemeister, Margarita, ed. 1986. *The New El Salvador: Interviews from the Zones of Popular Control*. San Francisco: Solidarity Educational Publications.

Sumpul: Una masacre contra refugiados salvadoreños. 1980. San Francisco: Casa El Salvador "Farabundo Martí."

Terry, Fiona. 2002. *Condemned to Repeat? The Paradox of Humanitarian Action*. Ithaca, N.Y.: Cornell University Press.

Thompson, E. P. 1971. "The Moral Economy of the English Crowd in the Eighteenth Century." *Past and Present* 50:76–136.

Thompson, Martha. 1995. "Repopulated Communities in El Salvador." In *The New Politics of Survival: Grassroots Movements in Central America*, edited by Minor

Sinclair, 108–51. Washington, D.C.: Ecumenical Program on Central America and the Caribbean (EPICA)/Monthly Review Press.

Thurner, Mark. 1997. *From Two Nations to One Divided: Contradictions of Post-colonial Nation-Making in Andean Peru.* Durham, N.C.: Duke University Press.

Tilley, Virginia Q. 1997. "Indigenous People and the State: Ethnic Meta-conflict in El Salvador." PhD diss., University of Wisconsin–Madison.

———. 2005. *Seeing Indians: A Study of Race, Nation, and Power in El Salvador.* Albuquerque: University of New Mexico Press.

Turner, Simon. 2005. "Suspended Spaces: Contesting Sovereignties in a Refugee Camp." In *Sovereign Bodies: Citizens, Migrants, and States in the Postcolonial World,* edited by Thomas Blom Hansen and Finn Stepputat, 312–32. Princeton, N.J.: Princeton University Press.

Turner, Victor. 1969. *The Ritual Process.* Chicago: Aldine.

Tutino, John. 1986. *From Insurrection to Revolution in Mexico: Social Bases of Agrarian Violence, 1750–1940.* Princeton, N.J.: Princeton University Press.

United Nations Commission on the Truth for El Salvador. 1993. *From Madness to Hope: The 12-Year War in El Salvador.* San Salvador and New York: United Nations.

United Nations High Commissioner for Refugees (UNHCR). 1982a. "Gracias al grupo de emergencia." *Refugiados,* July–August, pp. 9–10.

———. 1982b. "Refugiados en Centroamérica y Panamá." *Refugiados,* April, p. 14.

Universidad Centroamericana José Simeón Cañas (UCA). 1985. *El Salvador, 1985: Desplazados y refugiados salvadoreños.* San Salvador: Instituto de Investigaciones de la Universidad Centroamericana de El Salvador José Simeón Cañas.

———. 1986. *El Salvador 1986: En busca de soluciones para los desplazados.* San Salvador: Instituto de Investigaciones e Instituto de Derechos Humanos de la Universidad Centroamericana de El Salvador José Simeón Cañas.

Valladares Lanza, Leo. 1989. "Organizing the Homeward Movement." *Refugees* 62 (March): 31–32.

Valladares Lanza, Leo, and Susan Peacock. 1998. *In Search of Hidden Truths: An Interim Report on Declassification by the National Commissioner for Human Rights in Honduras.* Tegucigalpa: Comisionado Nacional de los Derechos Humanos.

Vásquez, Norma. 2000. *Las mujeres refugiadas y retornadas: Las habilidades adquiridas en el exilio y su aplicación a los tiempos de paz.* San Salvador: Las Dignas.

Vásquez, Norma, Cristina Ibañez, and Clara Murguialday. 1996. *Mujeres-montaña: Vivencias de guerrilleras y colaboradoras del FMLN.* San Salvador: Las Dignas.

Ventura, José. 1983. *El poder popular en El Salvador.* Mexico, D.F.: Mex Sur.

Viterna, Jocelyn S. 2003. "When Women Wage War: Explaining the Personal and Political Outcomes of Women's Guerrilla Participation in the Emerging Democracy of El Salvador." PhD diss., Indiana University.

Warren, Kay B. 1998. *Indigenous Movements and Their Critics: Pan-Mayan Activism in Guatemala.* Princeton, N.J.: Princeton University Press.

Weiss Fagen, Patricia, and Joseph T. Eldridge. 1991. "El Salvador: Mobilized and Poor." In *Repatriation under Conflict in Central America,* edited by Mary Ann Larkin,

Frederick Cuny, and Barry Stein, 116–86. Washington, D.C.: Center for Immigration Policy and Refugee Assistance.

Wheaton, Philip. 1980. *Agrarian Reform in El Salvador: A Program of Rural Pacification*. Washington, D.C.: Ecumenical Program on Central America and the Caribbean (EPICA).

White, Alastair. 1973. *El Salvador*. London: Ernest Benn.

White, Luise. 2000. *Speaking with Vampires: Rumor and History in Colonial Africa*. Berkeley: University of California Press.

White, Richard Alan. 1987. "The Use of Napalm, White Phosphorus, and Other Antipersonnel Weapons: Reprisals against the Civilian Population." In *Intervention on Trial: The New York War Crimes Tribunal on Central America and the Caribbean*, edited by Paul Ramshaw and Tom Steers, 17–23. New York: Praeger.

Williams, Robert G. 1986. *Export Agriculture and the Crisis in Central America*. Chapel Hill: University of North Carolina Press.

Wood, Elisabeth Jean. 2003. *Insurgent Collective Action and Civil War in El Salvador*. Cambridge: Cambridge University Press.

———. 2004. "Civil War and Reconstruction: The Repopulation of Tenancingo." In *Landscapes of Struggle: Politics, Society, and Community in El Salvador*, edited by Aldo Lauria-Santiago and Leigh Binford, 126–46. Pittsburgh: University of Pittsburgh Press.

World Bank. 1979. *El Salvador: Demographic Issues and Prospects*. Washington, D.C.: Latin America and the Caribbean Regional Office, World Bank.

Wright, Scott. 1994. *Promised Land: Death and Life in El Salvador*. Maryknoll, N.Y.: Orbis Books.

Zamora, Rubén. 1991. "The Popular Movement." In *A Decade of War: El Salvador Confronts the Future*, edited by Anjali Sundaram and George Gelber, 182–95. London and New York: Catholic Institute for International Relations/Monthly Review Press.

Zolberg, Aristide, Astri Suhrke, and Sergio Aguayo. 1989. *Escape from Violence: Conflict and the Refugee Crisis in the Developing World*. New York: Oxford University Press.

Index

Note: Page numbers in italics indicate an illustration.

El Salvador (*continued*)
17, 183–84, 255n32; liberal ideas and, 7; liberation of, 49, 66, 81, 142, 145–46, 153–54, 160, 161, 165, 166, 219; peace in, 5, 10, 11, 116, 161, 194, 195, 196, 209, 222; postwar period in, 11, 222; solidarity groups in, 205–6, 217–18; UNHCR in, 209, 215; urbanization and, 26–27; U.S. aid to, 64, 157, 158

El Salvador, armed forces of, 5, 12, 16, 19, 48, 56, 57, 67, 78, 80, 83, 89, 95, 141, 146, 180–81, 196, 215, 221, 223, 226; actions of, 46, 48, 154, 155–56, 177, 194, 196, 244n53; collaboration with Honduran armed forces, 85, 93, 111, 113, 156, 157, 158, 181, *182*; coup d'état, 53, 175; government and, 30, 45, 49, 53, 177, 221; relations with campesinos/refugees, 62–63, 67, 129, 143, 144, 145, 147, 155, 156–57, 160, 163, 191, 250n9; repatriation/repopulation and, 198, 208, 212–13, 215, 217–18; service in, 17, 60, 239n90; U.S. assistance to, 64, 146, 157–58, 185–86, 237n50, 252n40, 256n56. *See also* death squads; El Salvador, government of; scorched earth; *and specific forces*

El Salvador, government of: "agrarian crisis" and, 31–35; campesino demands and, 30, 32, 5–36, 39, 46, 48, 53, 60, 80, 141, 146, 153, 155, 172; campesino support for, 106, 212; FMLN and, 194, 196, 210, 219, 222; fomentation of rural organization (orthodox), 30, 32–36, 55; as illegitimate, 141, 143–47, 185–86, 225; international attention and, 83, 224; officials displaced from north, 81, 148; reactions to rural organizing (progressive), 16, 18, 29, 37, 46, 56, 178, 223; refugees and, 4, 8, 14, 99, 116, 134, 152–53, 191–92, 199, 204, 207–10, 214–16; shift in tactics, 64; United States and, 64, 146, 178, 184–86; violence of, 16, 29, 46–49, 53–54, 83, 143–44, 147, 167, 175. *See also* border (El Salvador–Honduras); elections; El Salvador, armed forces of; Hundred-Hour War

Equipo Maíz, 168

ERP (Ejército Revolucionario Popular), 47,
49, 67, 77, 92, 106, 200–201, 225, 234.
See also FMLN

FECCAS (Federación Cristiana de Campesinos Salvadoreños), 31, 39, 40, 44, 45, 46, 48, 52, 55, 57, 234n91, 234n95

Flores Auceda, 89

FMLN (Frente Farabundo Martí para Liberación Nacional), 16, 18, 19, 30, 41, 45, 47, 49, 51–55, 62, 67, 71, 73, 89, 94, 106, 153, 156, 163, 186–87, *187*, 194, 196, 198, 210, 212, 216, 219, 221–22, 224, 234n97, 237n51, 239nn90–91, 240n106, 241n4, 249n4, 257nn62–63; campesinos' negative perceptions of, 60, 73–74, 239n88; Final Offensive and, 216; relations with campesinos/refugees, 14, 41, 55, 64, 73, 74, 75–79, 81, 92–94, 110–11, 132–35, 141–42, 145–48, 186, 223–25 passim, 237n44; manipulation of campesinos/refugees, 4, 5, 13, 18, 52, 57, 80, 89, 99, 121–22, *122*, 125, 129, 132, 192, 200–201, 208–9, 216; zones of control, 55, 73, 74, 76, 81, 89, 92, 133, 147–48, 151, 201, 210, 223, 225, 254n16. *See also* ERP; FPL; PCS; PPL; RN

food: aid to refugee camps, 84, 98, 99, 101, 126, 130, 138, 208, 215; FMLN and, 74, 75; *guindas* and, 52, 64, 65, 69, 70, 71, 79, 92, 94; as political tool, 107, 126, 130, 131, 208, 215; PPLs and, 148; in prewar period, 20, 33, 46, 138, 174; refugee camps and, 96, 98, 99, *100, 101*, 102, *103*, 105, 135, 162, 245–46n10; *retornos*/repopulations and, 215, 218

Forster, Cindy, 6

FPL (Fuerzas Populares de Liberación), 47, 49, 58, 67, 76, 77, 92, 106, 201, 225, 234n97, 257n62. *See also* FMLN

Freire, Paulo, 253n9

FTC (Federación de Trabajadores del Campo), 45–46, 49, 234n91

Funes, Mauricio, 221–22

gangs, 11, 222

García, José Guillermo, 241n4

García, Marianela, 250n7

Ilobasco, 46
indigenous peoples (El Salvador), 15, 16, 19,
    142, 183, 249n4; La Matanza and, 176;
    land use, 25
INSAFOCOOP (Instituto Salvadoreño para
    el Fomento de Cooperativas), 33. *See also*
    cooperatives
Inter-American Commission on Human
    Rights, 179
internacionales: definition and use of term, 116.
    See also alliances (campesino/refugee)
International Court of Justice, 8, 87, 231n31
Intibucá, *2*, *86*, 112
Inti-Illimani, 186, 257n60
Iraq, 12, 257n65
ISTA (Instituto Salvadoreño de Transforma-
    ción Agraria), 34. *See also* land use and
    tenancy

Jara, Victor, 257n60
Joya de Cerén, 32, 55

labor and migration, 3, 25, 26, 27, 28, 30, 39,
    46, 56, 88
La Cabaña, 45, 47, 48
La Cañada, 73
La Cuchinama, 210
La Hacienda, 82, 86
La Libertad: agricultural reform and, 32; dis-
    placement and, 55; land use and tenancy
    in, *21–24*; mobilization in, 46
la lucha: campesinos and, 45, 55, 80, 81, 167;
    definition and use of term, 30; postwar
    period and, 10, 222; refugees and, 85,
    109, 141, 145, 146, 153–64, 166, 177, 195,
    199, 220, 222, 224, 225; repression and,
    48; Salvadoran government and, 31
land use and tenancy, 16–17, 21, 231n22; in
    north vs. export regions, 20–27; reforms
    regarding, 31–35
La Paz, 29, 33, 46, 87, 210, 234n93
Las Aradas, 82–83, 86, *182*. *See also* massacres:
    Sumpul River (1980)
Las Vueltas, 46, 204
La Unión, 33, 241–42n14
La Virtud (refugee camp), 85, *86*, 90, 95, 101,
    104, 106, 116, 131, 132, 150, 157, 168, 171,
    188, 244n46

Lempa River, 114, 150, 181, 188
Lempira, *2*, 29, *86*, 87, *197*
Levanchy, Phillipe, 134, 135, 249n62
Lima, Leila, 124, 207–8
Lima Treaty, 29, 156, 181, 182
Los Hernández, 85
Los Patios, 156
Los Valles, 57
Lovato, Roberto, 221
low-intensity warfare, 64
Lutheran World Federation, 206

Mapulaca, 85
Marcala, 130
Mallon, Florencia, 6, 18, 225
Martí, Farabundo, 145, 175, 177, 186
Martín-Baró, Ignacio, 15
Martínez, Maximiliano Hernández. *See*
    Hernández Martínez, Maximiliano
Martínez de Pauveti, Elisa Valle, 165–66
Masferrer, Alberto, 176
massacres, 4, 48, 83, 129, 147, 150, 154, 167, 181,
    194, 223, 241n3; El Mozote (1981), 150,
    236n39; La Matanza (1932), 14, 15, 16, 19,
    29, 30, 31, 33, 35, 36, 49, 145, 174, 178,
    179, 184, 185, 196, 255n29; Sumpul River
    (1980), 82–84, 86, 119, 150, 181–82, *182*,
    240–41n2, 241n4
Meanguera/San Francisco Gotera, 55, 56, 205,
    216, 218
Memorandum of Understanding, 112–14, 123,
    165, 166, 172–73
Mennonite Central Committee, 117, 248n40
Merino, Francisco, 208, 209
Mesa Grande (refugee camp), *86*, 90, 106,
    116, 150, *151*, 156, 160, 204–6, 250n9;
    FMLN and, 134–35, 146; forced reloca-
    tion to, 117, 131, 157, 158; internal ten-
    sions and control mechanisms, 106, 108,
    109, 226; popular education in, 162–63,
    170; as prison, *96*, 139, 142, 148; repatri-
    ation from, 135, 191–92, 194, 195, 198–
    201, 204–10, 212–15, 220. *See also* Ba-
    tallón Pacho; education; health; moral
    economy; refugee camps; relocation (of
    refugees); repatriation (official); *retorno*
    (grassroots)
Mexico, 6, 18, 27, 54, 80, 85, 258n9

migration and labor, 3, 25, 26, 27, 28, 30, 39, 46, 56, 88

MNR (Movimiento Nacional Revolucionario), 234n89

mobile communities, 6, 13, 64, 66, 68, 75, 76, 77, 79, 81, 85, 91, 92, 93, 95, 111, 147, 163, 217, 222–27, 254n16

model villages, 212

Montes, Segundo, 33

moral economy: on *guindas*, 52–53, 64–80, 226; in refugee camps, 108–11, 195

Morazán, 2, 241–42n14; *bolsones* and, 29, 87; campesino mobilization in, 36, 40–41, 44, 47, 55, 67, 77, 233n82; FMLN and, 67, 74, 77, 106, 201, 225; Hundred-Hour War and, 180; isolation of, 12, 16, 17; land use and tenancy in, 20–25; outmigration from, 27; refugees from, 99, 106, 155, 205–6, 216; repopulations in, 198, 201; violence in and *guindas* from, 55, 57–62, 66, 72–73, 105–6, 236nn40, 241n3. *See also* El Mozote; *tierra olvidada*

MSF (Médecins Sans Frontières), 84, 102, 117, 125–26, 128. *See also* aid regime

mutual aid, 35–38, 42, 44, 52, 138, 167, 178, 180. *See also* cooperatives; *directiva comunal*

Nahuizalco, 25

National Council of Churches, 206

National Guard, 48, 50, 53, 82–83, 104, 156, 175, 177

"national order of things," 4, 51, 174, 189, 223, 224

National Plan, 212

National Social Defense Board, 31, 231n34

NGOs (nongovernmental organizations), 4, 8, 83, 116, 128, 168, 206, 246n11, 258n9. *See also* aid regime; alliances (campesino/refugee); *and specific organizations*

Nicaragua, 6, 80, 258n9, 240n105; Contras and, 242n2; FMLN and, 89; refugees from, 88, 90, 98; Salvadoran refugees in, 85; solidarity with Salvadorans, 146, 186–87, 189

Normandía, 210

Nueva Trinidad, *197*, 205

OAS (Organization of American States), 29, 32, 160, 178

Ochoa Pérez, Sigifredo, 59, 198

Ocotepeque, *2*, 29, *86*, 87

Olanchito, 157–58. *See also* relocation (of refugees)

Operation Phoenix, 59, 197

ORDEN (Organización Democrática Nacionalista), 30, 40, 55, 78, 80, 82, 96, 130, 223

oreja, 66, 223, 238n61

organización: definition and use of term, 55, 77

Osorio, Oscar, 31, 36

PADECOMSM (Patronato de Desarrollo de las Comunidades de Morazán y San Miguel), 206, 217

Panama, 252n40; Salvadoran refugees in, 85, 251n20

Panamerican Union, 32

PCN (Partido de Conciliación Nacional), 35, 45

PCS (Partido Comunista de El Salvador), 16, 234n97, 254n28

PDC (Partido Demócrata Cristiano), 35, 196, 234n89

peace process: Central American, 209–10, 258n9; refugees and, 210, 219–20; Salvadoran, 5, 10, 14, 84, 94, 194, 196, 209, 210, 219, 222

Perquín, 155

Peru, 6, 18, 26, 225, 227

Picacho mountain, 155

Popayan, 210

popular movement, 10, 11, 18, 45, 52, 55, 48, 49, 73, 76, 97, 106, 146, 148, 160, 225, 234n95; *frentes de masa* and, 45, 78, 239n91; occupation of National Cathedral and, 47, 206

Portillo del Norte, 36–37, 43, 57

PPL (Poder Popular Local), 76, 78, 81, 111, 147–48, 151, 186, 223

Project 1,000, 212

PRTC (Partido Revolucionario de los Trabajadores), 234n97

Puerto Castilla, 157–58, 185, 252n40, 252n42

Quipur, 181

Radio Venceremos, 89, 146
Reagan, Ronald, 12, 185
Red Cross, 93, 146
refugee camps, 3, 5, 54, 74, *86*, 90, 91, 107, *147*,
168, 170; agricultural production in, 102,
103, 105; aid regime and, 13, 84–85, 95, 98,
101–2, 114, 116, 117, 121–22, *122*; alcohol
abuse in, 107; arrival to, 92, 94, 95, 155–
56; black market and, 107; as civilizing
force, 5; as "closed," 90, 91, 95, 130, 162,
195; communications about, 94, 116–17;
conditions in, 94, 98, 118, 130, 136, 142,
198, 201, 208, 245–46n10; coordination
between, 105; demographics of, 130, 134,
248n48; departure from, 152, 195–96, 212;
dependency and, 4, 102, 162, 173, 253n50;
as extensions of El Salvador, 148–53; "extraterritoriality" of, 120–22; gender roles
in, 107–8, 109, 161–62; international attention and accompaniment in, 95, 124,
132, 136, 139, 168, 206, 245n8; "layered
sovereignty" of, 136; military incursions
and harassment in, 93, *96*, 113, 114, 116,
118, 120, 123, 129, 130, 131, 132, 136, 144,
182, 208; organized nature of, 98–99, 157,
162, 164, 168; as prisons, *96*, 96–*97*, 139;
as "protected spaces," 97–98, 139, 162,
243n41; refugee control over, 13, 149, 158;
religious proselytism in, 119; restrictions
in, 90–91, 94, 95, 102, 108, 113–14, 120,
122, 129, 138, 152, 156, 214, 243n37,
247n24; security in, 103–4, 116; as strategic sites, 85; "subversives" and, 3–4, 89,
99, 121–22, *122*, 246; *talleres* in, 98, 102,
107, 109, 136, 160–64, *161*; use as military bases, 135, 157. *See also* alliances
(campesino/refugee); education; health;
moral economy; refugees; *and specific
camps*
"refugeeness," 6
refugees, 3, 54, 85, 116; as citizen refugees,
138, 141, 164, 166, 175; as committed
to El Salvador, 98, 102, 109, 116, 135–
36, 140–42, 141, 148–53, 163, 166, 190,
210; historical narratives of, 174–89;

self-governance of, 7, 95, 98–105, *105*, 128,
146–47, *147*, *211*; staging (of identities),
128–37, 139, 158–59, 208; support for popular movement, 97, 153–64, 166, 195, 199,
220, 224, 225; tensions among, 106–11,
124, 226, 253n50; unofficial, 3; use of
international law, 7, 117, 123, 131–32, 144,
199, 212. *See also* alliances (campesino/
refugee); refugee camps
relocation (of refugees): to Honduran interior, 116, 125, 130, 131, 135, 137, 149, 152,
153, 157–58, *161*, 173, 170, 200, 247n24,
252n36; to Mesa Grande, 116–17, 131,
157; to third country, 85, 109; as U.S.
strategy, 157, *159*
repatriation (official): as "durable solution" to
refugee crisis, 194; as forced, 126, *161*,
200, *210*; as political act, 196; programs
for, 194–95, 200, 209, 210, 212, 217, 218;
refugee resistance to, 194–95, 258n12;
suspension of, 216; voluntary, 120, 190–
92, 194. *See also* repopulation; *retorno*
(grassroots)
repopulation, 5, *187*, 193, 196, *197*, 198, 217,
221; Catholic Church, 196, *197*; collaboration with refugees, 204–5; contribution to peace process, 219–20; as demilitarized zones, 191, 196, 218; FMLN
and, 201, 209; grassroots movement
and, 14, 193–94, 198, 218; harassment
of, 204, 213, 214; international solidarity and, 219, 223; organization of, 196–
97; as resistance, 198, 217–19, 226; as
segregated communities, 218. *See also*
CNR; CRIPDES; repatriation (official);
retorno (grassroots); rights; Tenancingo
retorno (grassroots), 190–220 passim;
CIREFCA and, 193; as conquest, 217;
as contribution to peace, 162–63, 219;
fears of, 205–6; FMLN and, 200–201,
209–19; forge democracy, 219; as goal,
142, 149, 152, 165; international solidarity and, 116, *127*, 197, 206, 219,
223; as invasions, 216–17; to *lugares de
origen*, 192, 197, 210, 212, 217, 218; vs.
official repatriation programs, 199, 212–
13, 218; official response to, 208, 210,

Critical Human Rights